A HISTORY OF MODERN AMERICAN CRIMINAL JUSTICE

A HISTORY OF MODERN AMERICAN CRIMINAL JUSTICE

JOSEPH F. SPILLANE
University of Florida

DAVID B. WOLCOTT
Educational Testing Service

Los Angeles | London | New Delhi
Singapore | Washington DC

Los Angeles | London | New Delhi
Singapore | Washington DC

FOR INFORMATION:

SAGE Publications, Inc.
2455 Teller Road
Thousand Oaks, California 91320
E-mail: order@sagepub.com

SAGE Publications Ltd.
1 Oliver's Yard
55 City Road
London EC1Y 1SP
United Kingdom

SAGE Publications India Pvt. Ltd.
B 1/I 1 Mohan Cooperative Industrial Area
Mathura Road, New Delhi 110 044
India

SAGE Publications Asia-Pacific Pte. Ltd.
3 Church Street
#10-04 Samsung Hub
Singapore 049483

Acquisitions Editor: Jerry Westby
Publishing Associate: MaryAnn Vail
Production Editor: Eric Garner
Copy Editor: Michelle Ponce
Typesetter: C&M Digitals (P) Ltd.
Proofreader: Laura Webb
Indexer: Rick Hurd
Cover Designer: Gail Buschman
Marketing Manager: Terra Schultz
Permissions Editor: Karen Ehrmann

Printed in the United States of America

Library of Congress Cataloging-in-Publication Data

Spillane, Joseph F.

A history of modern American criminal justice / Joseph F. Spillane, David B. Wolcott.

p. cm.
Includes bibliographical references and index.

ISBN 978-1-4129-8133-0
(cloth)—ISBN 978-1-4129-8134-7 (pbk.)

1. Criminal justice, Administration of—United States—History. 2. Criminal procedure—United States—History. 3. Punishment—United States—History. 4. Crime—United States—History. 5. Crime—Government policy—United States. 6. Criminal justice, Administration of—United States--Case studies. I. Wolcott, David B. II. Title.

HV9950.S667 2013
364.97309—dc23 2012039559

This book is printed on acid-free paper.

SFI label applies to text stock

12 13 14 15 16 10 9 8 7 6 5 4 3 2 1

Brief Contents

Detailed Contents

Preface

This textbook emerged out of our own experience as scholars and teachers. We are both scholars of modern criminal justice history, writing books and articles in fields such as corrections, juvenile justice, policing, and drug control. We are both teachers of this history as well. Over the years, we have offered courses on crime and punishment in American history, delinquency and juvenile justice, drugs and crime, violence in American history, and general surveys of criminal justice history. We often discussed with one another just what an ideal textbook would look like and finally determined to try our hand at producing such a thing.

This is, first of all, a history of modern criminal justice. As professional historians, we appreciate as much as anyone the value of history across all time and places but concluded that the most valuable textbook for both history and criminal justice students should focus on the evolution of our modern system. Toward that end, we have remained conscious of the need to make this text relevant to students of contemporary criminal justice. Students should learn that history is not interesting trivia and antiquarian curiosities but a mechanism by which they may place the present system of criminal justice into a stream of time and, in so doing, obtain a valuable perspective on why change occurs.

In organizing this text, we chose to take a thematic approach to criminal justice history, rather than a strictly chronological approach. In part, we have been influenced by most basic introductory courses on criminal justice, which provide students with a sequential introduction to the various components of the system. By taking a similar approach, we hope to give students a perspective on history that is complementary to the ways in which they see contemporary criminal justice issues. Of course, a broadly chronological focus is still built into the text, as the overlapping stories move forward in time, chapter by chapter.

In the writing and publication of this text, we have incurred a great many debts. First and foremost, we are grateful to Jerry Westby for encouraging the development of a proposal, for seeing the value in what we were aiming to do, and for offering a great deal of patient counsel as we slowly worked our way through the process. We could not have asked for a more generous editor. The authors share a common graduate advisor, Steven Schlossman, whose own work on the history of criminal justice inspired our own, and whose commitment to excellence in scholarship has, we hope, made at least a faint imprint on this text. We are deeply appreciative of our many students, graduate and undergraduate, with whom we have been able to explore these issues in the classroom—and without whose thoughtful comments, questions, and insights, the idea of the book might never have been born. Colleagues at the University of Florida and Educational Testing Service have been a source of support. And, of course, our families have patiently allowed us to carve out the necessary time to see this project through to completion. The most special note of thanks, therefore, goes to Jennifer, Maggie, Lily, and to Elizabeth and Eleanor.

We would also like to thank the reviewers of this first edition, who offered many useful comments and suggestions on different parts of the text: Gad Bensinger (Loyola University Chicago); Ashley Blackburn (University of North Texas); George Eichenberg (Tarleton State University); Nicole Hendrix (Radford University); Peter Johnstone (University of North Texas); Eric Rise (University of Delaware); Larry Salinger (Arkansas State University); Quanda Stevenson (Athens State University and the University of Alabama); and Mike Witkowski (University of Detroit Mercy).

A Note on the Cover: The cover illustration is a photograph of the "Bridge of Sighs," that connected the Allegheny County Courthouse in Pittsburgh, Pennsylvania with the old Allegheny County Jail. Constructed in the 1880s, the arched bridge was used to walk many thousands of prisoners from jail to court, and back again. Still in use, the bridge is a reminder of the constant flow of people through the elements of the criminal justice system. The juxtaposition with a modern skyscraper also highlights the connections between past and present in that system.

1

Introduction

Criminal justice in the United States has a rich and important history. Some people might ask, however, why they should invest time and energy in reading and writing that history. That question is merely a more specific version of one asked many years ago by the well-known historian Marc Bloch (1953): "were the nearly universal fascination of history its only justification—if it were, in short, only a pleasant pastime, like bridge or fishing—would it be worth all the trouble we take to write it? To write it, I mean, with integrity, with truth, with the utmost possible penetration into its hidden causes, and, hence, with difficulty?" (p. 8) We believe that the answer to Bloch's question comes with an understanding of history as a living thing. By this we mean, first of all, that history is an ongoing project, subject to new interpretations and new evidence. A constant supply of new evidence and new source materials continually becomes available to historians. Sometimes these new sources challenge old interpretations, sometimes they suggest an entirely new story. Moreover, historians are constantly asking new questions of the existing evidence and making new connections that had not previously been made. What we know about the past, quite frankly, depends a great deal on what we go out looking for. Historians of prisons, for example, are today far more attentive to issues of gender and the ways in which men's and women's experiences might have differed from one another in the past.

It is a good example of the way in which scholarship on contemporary issues led historians to look anew at old evidence and why this text tries to bring together all of the latest developments in the historical study of the criminal justice system.

When we say that history is a living thing, we also mean that history—or the understandings of history that we carry around with us—influences the way we define and understand the present. Students, policymakers, and criminal justice practitioners are nearly always making historical observations when they talk about the present—even if they do not realize it. Consider, for example, that any description of crime or criminal justice today that involves relative statements like *more*, *less*, *new*, *unprecedented*, or *traditional*, is a statement about the present that can only be understood in relation to the past. Given that the use of history is nearly inevitable, we believe that every effort should be made to ensure that we really understand that history. Long after some of this text's details may fade from memory, we hope that students will retain a habit of thinking explicitly about history.

❖ VENTURING INTO THE PAST: MURPHY'S MONOPLANE

Novelist L. P. Hartley (2011) once wrote that "the past is a foreign country: they do things differently there," (p. 17) by which he meant to express the profound sense of strangeness and dissimilarity between past and present. Like a foreign country, we have trouble navigating the past, speaking the language, or having a clear sense of what is happening around us. Part of the challenge for historians of criminal justice is to make sure the past does not become too strange—for if it does, then the past is severed from the present, and it loses relevance. And once that happens, we stop looking for the rich complexity we take for granted in the present and reduce the past to simple expressions of how strange and odd things once were. That would be a great tragedy, for we cannot escape our past—our modern criminal justice system cannot be understood apart from its historical antecedents.

Historians, therefore, need to make the past familiar enough to navigate. On the other hand, if the past becomes too familiar, we risk imposing our present day worldview on historical actors who may or may not have looked at the world in those same terms. When that happens, the past loses all sense of difference, and historical actors simply become older versions of our selves. And this, too, would lead history into irrelevance, for one can simply study the present if history is largely the same thing.

We can illustrate the dilemma for students of history with a single photograph.

Source: Courtesy of the Library of Congress, LC-DIG-ggbain-16436.

The photo to the right was taken around 1913, by a newspaper photographer for the Bain News Service. The historical aspects of the photograph are not hard to discern. It shows Charles M. Murphy, a New York City police officer, posing in an early monoplane, built no more than a decade after the Wright brothers had made the world's first powered human flight.

If we search a bit for some familiarity, however, we quickly locate an interesting point of commonality with present-day criminal justice. Murphy (known as "Mile-A-Minute Murphy" for having been the first bicyclist ever to ride for one mile in less than one minute) was posing in his airplane as part of his campaign to persuade the New York Police Department (NYPD) to adopt this new technology in the service of catching criminals. "Why, of course," said Murphy to some assembled reporters, "the aeroplane is bound to suggest itself to the police as a means of apprehending criminals" (*New York Times*, 1914). And, indeed, the NYPD, some years later, did in fact become the first city police department with an air unit (though not until Murphy had retired from the force). This aspect of Murphy's monoplane transports us from the unfamiliar (an old-Wright brothers-era flying machine) to something readily comprehensible—the use of the latest in technology by law enforcement in the service of crime control.

As familiar as that sounds, however, some strangeness remains about Mile-A-Minute Murphy's crusade for policing by air. To begin with, Murphy (along with other commentators of the time) was convinced that air-based policing would be necessary to combat what he was certain would be a wave of air-based criminality. "Crooks," Murphy announced, would soon be able to take flying machines anywhere they wanted, swoop down, and fly away with big hauls of stolen goods. "There isn't any doubt in my mind that New York City before very long is going to hear of a big robbery in an aeroplane, made possible simply because the men who do that sort of work are of the cleverest and know how to make sure of the very latest inventions. . . Maybe a flying machine will never be employed in just that manner, but I believe firmly that they will be used when they are more common" (*New York Times*, 1914). Of course, Murphy's vision of an airplane-aided wave of burglaries and robberies never materialized, a useful reminder that though the past can be made more familiar, it is never simply a mirror of modern thoughts and ideas.

This textbook, then, attempts to navigate what Wineburg (2001) has called the "tension that underlies every encounter with the past: the tension between the familiar and the strange, between feelings of proximity and feelings of distance in relation to the people we seek to understand" (p. 5). Toward that end, we advance here three key concepts that inform this book's approach to criminal justice history.

Concept #1: Focus on the Process of Change, Not Just Difference

As Murphy's rickety old monoplane makes clear, differences between past and present are easy to spot. We argue in this text, however, that the history of criminal justice should not be reduced to a chronicle of difference, for that reduces history to simple curiosity—interesting for its own sake but not otherwise relevant to the present day. Rather, history is about a process of perpetual change, which forces a consideration of just how and why change takes place. It is this search for the *why* that constitutes historical analysis.

To understand the processes of change (or the related question of why in other cases things stay the same rather than changing), historians need to consider questions of *historical causality*. By this, we mean general ways of explaining how new outcomes emerge. When Charles Murphy and others predicted that criminals would soon be using airplanes to rob and steal, they were probably analogizing air transportation to the changes that police had already begun observing from the automobile. If changes to transportation technology like the automobile had allowed criminals new means to find victims and escape detection, why wouldn't the airplane? That the analogy did not hold up forces the historian to consider what sorts of things might have had a more meaningful influence on the behavior of urban criminals.

One thing quickly becomes clear in studying the history of modern criminal justice in the United States: there are many different ways of explaining change and continuity. Some studies emphasize factors that are *internal* to the criminal justice system, while other studies focus on the influence of *external* forces. Likewise, some historians highlight the role of cultural and intellectual changes, while others are more likely to concentrate on the influence of structural and economic factors.

A brief example shows the challenge of locating historical causality. In the 1970s, criminal justice researcher Alfred Blumstein and his colleagues began to investigate the use of imprisonment in the United States. They observed that the rates of imprisonment had remained fairly level over the previous five decades. This notable continuity in criminal justice practice led Blumstein to develop what he called the "stability of punishment" hypothesis. Blumstein argued that society attempted to impose a relatively constant level of punishment, creating a kind of homeostatic system that would self-adjust, using prison more freely in moments of lower crime and less freely when crime went up (Blumstein & Cohen, 1973). Ironically, no sooner had Blumstein and colleagues begun to develop the stability of punishment argument, than imprisonment rates began to increase, reaching historically unprecedented levels and ushering in an age of mass incarceration (see Chapter 9). While Blumstein himself acknowledged this "radical departure" from a "prior stable pattern," there remained the question of how to explain this dramatic change (Blumstein & Beck, 1999). Did it invalidate the previous notion of a homeostatic system, or had wholly new circumstances arisen that disrupted the formerly stable system? A vast array of studies have subsequently attempted to explain mass incarceration, offering causal factors that include rising crime rates, racism, economic and structural changes, cultural moralism and popular anxiety over crime, and the influence of law and order politics. Probably the most accurate assessment comes from Michael Tonry (2001): "No single factor, or several, can possibly explain why countries' punishment policies and practices differ or why they change over time" (p. 526). Throughout this text, we argue for this complex understanding of historical causality in which multiple factors come together to produce change. Even when we know what happened—such as the fact that imprisonment rates were relatively stable, then they rose dramatically—hindsight is not exactly 20-20 if we cannot understand the causes at work.

Concept #2: History Does Not Move in One Direction

For much of modern history, observers of criminal justice were convinced that all of the changes they observed were part of an overall trend toward a modern, humane, and rational approach to governing society. To the extent that they believed that this movement was inevitable, they joined the ranks of those who believed in some form of *historical determinism*—in other words, that history moved in a particular and mostly inevitable direction. From the determinist perspective, the struggles and strains of individual historical actors largely took place within a framework—whether structural, economic, political, and so on—that dictated directions and outcomes. Related to this idea is the notion that the past unfolds in a generally linear direction in which present-day conditions are the inevitable result. The past simply becomes a series of steps towards the present.

The converse of historical determinism is *historical contingency*, by which we mean that the directions of history are not wholly predictable but are subject to variations in individual choices, in peculiar arrangements of circumstance, and even to some extent, to chance itself. Throughout this text, we endeavor to strike a reasonable balance between the predictable directions of determinism and the indeterminacy of historical contingency. That balance, we argue, properly acknowledges that individuals and groups have the ability to shape and reshape the criminal justice system at various moments in history, but the ability to change criminal justice practices are bounded, to some extent, by social and economic circumstances and the influence of current procedures.

The result is a history of criminal justice that does not move in any single or predictable direction and, in fact, changes directions at various points in time. This contingent history is, in some ways, a kind of liberating force for those of us living in the present. After all, if what has been true in the past need not be true in the future, it follows that we may embrace a commitment to change and reform in criminal justice. On the other hand, historical contingency is also a cautionary tale. It reminds us that history is by no means a story of universal progress (even if we could, in fact, agree on what constituted progress in the first place) or predictable cycles. Many times in the past, changes in criminal justice have produced dark and disturbing consequences. The great harms of Jim Crow justice, for example, were not rooted in some inevitable force of history—rather, a rapidly ascendant white majority imposed Jim Crow justice upon the South in the years following the Civil War. Throughout this text, readers will observe that promising reforms meet unexpected reversals, and practical policy changes break apart on the rocks of corruption or politics. In this sense, history offers lessons both inspiring and humbling for the present day.

Concept #3: Examine Rhetoric and Reality, Ideas and Practice

Few aspects of criminal justice are easier for the historian to access and reconstruct than ideas. Ideas are reproduced in all sorts of ways—books, articles, magazines, administrative documents, public speeches, and media reports can all convey a clear sense of what the criminal justice system was supposed to be doing, what it was intended to do, or what it was understood to be doing. But there are serious problems that can arise when historians place too much emphasis on ideas. One such problem is an obsessive focus on what we call the pioneer stories of criminal justice—the moments of inspiration and creation when new ideas are hatched. While there is nothing wrong with tracking these moments, it tends to obscure the long history between the hatching of an idea and actual criminal justice practice. Historians of technology, for example, remind us that there is a complex process between the idea of, for example, using radio waves to communicate and the social practices that resulted in millions of people in the 1920s listening to commercial radio station broadcasts on radio sets they purchased. These practices were the result, not simply of an idea, but of economics, politics, and policymaking. This holds true for criminal justice as well. Documenting the birth of an idea, like the juvenile court, does not tell us anything about the ways in which the court would be accepted and implemented in actual practice. In the case of Murphy's monoplane, his idea of applying aircraft to police work would not take off (so to speak) until years after he first made the case for crime control in the sky and, even then, not in the ways that he had originally imaged.

There are other hazards for historians who dwell too much on new ideas or dominant rhetoric. Such a focus might cause us to miss the *diversity* of practices at any one moment in time. Juvenile courts, for example, might well have been born from a common idea, but actual practice varied considerably from location to location. This variance suggests yet another problem for historians: the *divergence* of criminal justice practices from criminal justice ideas. At numerous points in the history of modern criminal justice, reformers have made the case that certain new kinds of criminal justice policies would have certain effects, and it is hard not to be attracted by these very public claims. Returning to the example of juvenile justice, we know that reformers made the case that the juvenile court would transform the manner in which young boys and girls would be processed by the justice system—and many historians, whether they are critical or supportive of the juvenile court, have accepted that idea uncritically. But, when we look at how young people were actually handled by the justice system, a more complicated picture emerges, in which we often see far more continuity in practice. Indeed, as one of us has explored in some detail (Wolcott, 2005), the most important figures in the justice system, from the point of view of the young person, remained the police, not the juvenile courts. Throughout this book, readers find numerous instances where criminal justice in practice diverged from stated intentions.

At this juncture, readers may well ask just what room is left for ideas themselves. Do they even matter? We argue in this text that they do matter—not as a guide to practice, per se, but as one mechanism by which practice is guided and shaped. Ideas have a way of helping to frame the world of politics and perception and of shaping the ways in which actors internal and external to the criminal justice system understood what they were doing. Ideas like progress, barbarism, professionalism, deviance, and many others have a way of influencing action. David Garland (2001) has examined this phenomenon and argues that ideas are not merely a starting point by which we judge practice but that they exist in relationship to practice, both guiding and guided by events. In this way, Garland observed, "sometimes 'talk' is action." We agree, and this text takes seriously the power of ideas to influence the criminal justice system, even as we take care not to confuse ideas with reality.

❖ ORGANIZATION OF THIS BOOK

In telling the story of modern criminal justice in the United States, this text presents a series of thematic chapters, which simultaneously move the narrative forward chronologically. Consequently, the earliest thematic chapters focus on the early twentieth century and nineteenth century antecedents, while the later chapters in the text move the story forward into the middle of the twentieth century and finally to the most recent historical experience.

Chapter 2 examines the emergence of modern policing in the first three decades of the twentieth century. Police agencies attempted to manage disparate and often conflicting goals. These same tensions are at the heart of Chapter 3, which looks at the changing face of the courts as the lynchpins of the criminal justice system. During the Progressive Era, the criminal courts assumed many of their modern forms, becoming larger, more elaborate, and more bureaucratic. Just how to use that capacity, however, became an issue of central concern, and this chapter highlights the struggle between demands for crime control and social reform.

Chapter 4 provides an overview of Progressive Era developments in the punishment of criminal offenders. Inspired by the hope of bettering society, progressive reformers developed systems of probation and parole and laid out ambitious plans for managing the offender behind bars—though, in the end, actual practice often fell well short of ambition. Crime control took a distinctive turn in the South, as Chapter 5 demonstrates. The region's distinctive political and economic structures—including powerful localism, undemocratic one-party rule, and racist systems of labor control—helped create a repressive system of criminal justice.

Chapter 6 examines the growth of research, from the early surveys of the 1920s, through the development of sophisticated systems analysis, program evaluations, and field studies. This chapter demonstrates the interconnected nature of criminal justice professionalism as well. Chapter 7 considers two legacies of twentieth-century liberalism—often contradictory to one another—for the criminal justice system. One, the pursuit of a therapeutic approach to the criminal offender, promoted aggressive state intervention by promising to solve the underlying causes of crime. The other, a commitment to due process rights for criminal defendants, attacked discretionary state action as a threat to individual freedom and liberty.

Chapter 8 tracks the expansion of the national government's crime control capacities, from the 1930s through the end of the twentieth century. During these decades, the Federal Bureau of Investigation (FBI) became the nearest thing to a national police force. Federal prisons helped shape a national conversation about punishment, federal narcotics enforcement defined the war on drugs, and federal criminal law helped set the national crime-fighting agenda. Chapter 9 explores the rise of "law and order" politics in the 1960s and places the phenomenon of mass incarceration into historical context. The tough-on-crime decades that ended the twentieth century brought with them changes in criminal justice practice that, for better or worse, define our system today.

Chapter 10 concludes this review of modern criminal justice history by considering the processes by which the United States became embedded in global systems of criminal justice. Far from being a very recent phenomenon, transnational connections and relationships in criminal justice have a long and important history. Still, the pace of globalization has picked up over the past century, placing the United States at the center of international efforts to control organized crime, terrorism, and illicit trades.

Each chapter offers a comprehensive overview of the broad trends and major issues within a particular area of criminal justice history. Readers will observe that individual chapters conclude with a rather extensive list of references to other scholarly work. By now, we hope to have persuaded readers that the writing of criminal justice history is an active and ongoing process, and these detailed reference lists are intended to be the most comprehensive and up-to-date reporting of that work. Of course, the best in scholarship includes older work as well, and readers will find in each chapter's references a useful guide to important classic works of criminal justice history. By listing references by chapter, rather than together at the very end of the text, we hope to give readers interested in particular subjects a helpful roadmap to further reading.

Within each chapter, two special features are included to facilitate the process of thinking about both history and criminal justice—and their connection. "Case Studies in Criminal Justice" introduces readers to some of the specific individuals whose lives and work embody the themes of each particular chapter. The case studies move beyond the broad strokes of generalization to reveal the complex experience of real people making history through their own lives. Each chapter also includes a "What's the Evidence?" feature, designed to highlight different kinds of historical sources. These explorations are intended to introduce readers to the practical challenges involved in researching and writing history and to serve as a guide to students interested in exploring historical sources on their own. The writing of history belongs to everyone, and we hope to have inspired our readers to join with us in appreciating the value the past holds.

❖ REFERENCES

Bloch, M. (1953). *The historian's craft*. New York, NY: Vintage Books.

Blumstein, A., & Beck, A. J. (1999). Population growth in U.S. prisons, 1980-1996. *Crime and Justice 26*: 17-61.

Blumstein, A., & Cohen, J. (1973). A theory of the stability of punishment. *Journal of Criminal Law and Criminology 64*: 198-207.

Garland, D. (2001). *The culture of control: Crime and social order in contemporary society*. Chicago, IL: University of Chicago Press.

Hartley, L. P. (2011). The go-between. New York, NY: New York Review of Books.

Tonry, M. (2001). Symbol, substance, and severity in western penal policies. *Punishment & Society 3*: 517-536.

Sees Police Flying After Air Burglars. (1914, August 11). *New York Times*, 13.

Wineburg, S. S. (2001). *Historical thinking and other unnatural acts: Charting the future of teaching the past*. Philadelphia, PA: Temple University Press.

Wolcott, D. B. (2005). *Cops and kids: Policing juvenile delinquency in urban America, 1890-1940*. Columbus: Ohio State University Press.

2

The Challenge of Policing, 1830s–1920s

Why start a book about the history of modern criminal justice by focusing on police? Police were not the first criminal justice institutions created in the United States; courts, jails, and prisons preceded them. Police have become, however, the iconic symbol of the justice system, the rock stars of the law. They are on the front lines of the modern criminal justice system. They are the most visible justice agency in most Americans' everyday lives and the institutions through which people first encounter the criminal justice system.

The functions of police began to change dramatically between roughly 1900 and 1930 as police began to assume their modern roles. Early twentieth-century police understood their primary function as maintaining public order. This involved many diverse tasks. In the course of a day, an early twentieth-century police officer might have needed to deal with stray dogs and livestock, help a lost child get home, enforce saloon closing laws, kick a vagrant out of town, chat with local merchants, and maybe—just maybe—make an arrest. Between 1890 and 1930, however, one function became more prominent than all the others: controlling crime.

At the same time, how to maintain public order and to control crime remained open questions among both the police and the public. In some cases social reformers sought to use the police to eliminate vice and to improve society. In other cases, prominent police administrators sought to improve police operations and achieve greater efficiency. In still other cases, good government reformers sought to separate policing from politics and make law enforcement operate more like a business. While many interested parties agreed that professionalization and crime control were desirable goals, few agreed on what these goals might look like or how to achieve them.

❖ POLICE IN THE NINETEENTH-CENTURY UNITED STATES

When were police created in America? It depends on what is meant by *police*. Some sort of law enforcement agencies existed since the founding of European settlements in North America, but institutions recognizable as modern police emerged only in the middle of the nineteenth century and even then featured tremendous variation in their function and nature.

Urban upheavals led directly to the creation of modern police, particularly in the large seaports on the east coast (the story in the South, discussed in Chapter 5, is quite different). Between the 1830s and the 1870s, eastern cities in the United States faced unprecedented amounts of riot and mob violence. These conflicts resulted from a myriad of sources: ethnic tensions resulting from Irish and German migration to the United States, religious disputes between Protestants and Roman Catholics, racial hostilities against free blacks and abolitionists, vigorous political competition, moral outrage against brothels, and ultimately the Civil War. Existing police mechanisms were inadequate to deal with this violence. Moreover, while riots themselves were comparatively rare, they highlighted the inability of existing constables and night watchmen to handle more typical disruptions. As a result, city after city experimented with creating new police organizations to quell violence and maintain order (Wadman & Allison, 2004; Walker, 1977).

In Boston, for example, a series of riots in the 1830s accelerated the evolution of the police system. Beginning in 1801, the mayor of Boston had had the additional title of "superintendent of police." In this capacity, the mayor was responsible for inspecting public works projects and monitoring government departments. When the city of Boston was incorporated in 1822, the mayor, Josiah Quincy, established a new police position, "marshal of the city." This new officer set a precedent for police assuming catchall duties of maintaining public safety. Among other functions, the marshal was responsible for licensing dogs, preventing poaching of animals in Boston Common, and coordinating firefighting. The duty of crime control, however, remained with the small night watch, hard pressed to deal with a growing city. In 1838, Boston Mayor Samuel A. Eliot used a wave of major riots—notably the burning of the Charlestown Convent in 1834, the attack on abolitionist William Lloyd Garrison in 1835, and the Broad Street Riot in 1837 between volunteer firemen and an Irish funeral procession—to convince the city to hire full-time police officers within the marshal's office. Even so, the police remained separate from the night watch and both groups had limited authority; the two were only merged in 1854 (Lane, 1967; Wadman & Allison, 2004).

Philadelphia and New York, likewise, gradually established full-time police forces in the first half of the nineteenth century. In Philadelphia, a night watch established in 1797 coexisted with a small group of police officers created in 1833 to patrol the streets during the day until the two agencies were consolidated into the Philadelphia Police Department in 1854. Likewise in New York City, political conflicts delayed the creation of a consolidated police department under the control of the city government until 1845. Even then, the New York City police remained a political football. Democratic Mayor Fernando Wood, elected in 1854, used assignments in the Municipal Police to consolidate his power. In 1857, Republican reformers in the state legislature transferred law enforcement to a state-controlled Metropolitan Police Department. Following confrontations between the Municipal and Metropolitan police, an appeals court ruled in favor of the state, abolished the city-controlled Municipal Police, and placed the New York City police fully under state authority. In 1870, political fortunes shifted again, and the state allowed control of the police to revert to the city government and local bosses (Miller, 1999; Wadman & Allison, 2004; Walker, 1977).

All of these urban police forces were modeled on the London Metropolitan Police established in 1829 by Sir Robert Peel. The London Metropolitan Police was the first force to combine the functions of constables and night watches with a daytime patrol and to place them under a central command modeled loosely on the military. Police in the United States, however, differed from the London police in significant ways. While the London police were an arm of the national government, police in the United States were local institutions, authorized by state or municipal governments and often tightly integrated in city and neighborhood politics. The republican tradition of local self-government in the United States fostered public resistance to creating police and limited the authority that they could exercise. The legitimacy of the London police derived from the law, and they went out of their way to operate as consciously neutral arbiters. The legitimacy of American police, by contrast, derived from their communities, so individual police officers in the United States had to generate authority from their personal interactions with citizens (Miller, 1999; Monkkonen, 1981b; Walker, 1977).

Outside of large cities, in areas where official systems of law enforcement were perceived to be weak, the popular role in law enforcement remained greater, and community members took the law into their own hands (Dale, 2011). Vigilantism was particularly common in the mid-nineteenth-century West, where vigilantes often maintained that they were expressing the will of the community. The San Francisco Vigilance Committee, for example, was organized in 1856 by local business leaders in response to what they perceived to be law enforcement corruption generated by political rivals. They organized an armed force of at least 6,000 people, tried and hanged four men accused of crime, and drove 28 others out of the city (Walker, 1977; Walker, 1998). Western communities, however, gradually developed regularized police systems as they became more settled. Some brand-new frontier towns briefly hired gunfighters such as "Wild Bill" Hickok and Bat Masterson as sheriffs, but more typically towns established small police forces to maintain order. By the end of the nineteenth century, larger western cities such as Denver, Dallas, and Los Angeles maintained police departments that had more in common with Boston, Philadelphia, and New York than with the Wild West. At the same time, less developed areas of the nineteenth-century West received some law enforcement services from federal agencies such as the U.S. Marshals and state agencies such as the Texas Rangers (Wadman & Allison, 2004).

So what defined a modern police department in the United States? The key element was a centralized organizational structure that consolidated constables and night watches into an around-the-clock patrol system. Yet it is difficult to demonstrate when this happened because the transition to centralized administrations was often drawn out over decades. The historian Eric Monkkonen (1981b) has argued that the adoption of uniforms constituted the key transition because these symbolically demonstrated the presence of political authority in daily life. The spread of uniformed police from the largest cities to smaller ones also represented the growth and spread of an expectation that municipal governments provide social services to their residents. In this case, the service provided was general protection by officers on patrol. Nineteenth-century police could not do much more than their predecessors to control riots, but they did act as street-level agents of government. Moreover, rather than simply react to problems as their predecessors had, they were designed to proactively discourage crime.

❖ THE WORK OF POLICE AT THE TURN OF THE TWENTIETH CENTURY

What did police do in the late nineteenth and early twentieth centuries? The legal scholar James Q. Wilson (1968) has argued that the job of police patrolmen is defined more by maintaining public order than by enforcing the law. This was very much the case in the late 1800s and early 1900s. Rather than adopting what Wilson would characterize as a legalistic style focused on making arrests, turn-of-the-twentieth-century police leaned heavily toward a watchman style, in which they sought to maintain order primarily through personal discretion, or toward a service style, in which they provided general assistance to their communities.

Who were the police at the turn of the twentieth century? Broadly speaking, they tended to be white working-class men with limited training. Of course there were exceptions. Political ties between Republican mayors and African American communities led northern cities to hire a small number of black officers in the nineteenth century. Chicago, for example, hired its first black policeman in 1872 and employed 23 black policemen by 1894. Philadelphia hired 35 African American officers in 1884. Other cities tended to be slower. Detroit hired its first African American policeman in 1883 but still had no more than a handful in its ranks in 1918. New York did not hire an African American officer until 1905. African Americans actually constituted a greater proportion of police officers in southern cities such as New Orleans during the Reconstruction period of the 1870s than they did in the North, but they were gradually removed from policing at the turn of the twentieth century as racial segregation became more overt in the South (Dulaney, 1996; Reed, 1992; Walker, 1977). In terms of occupation, police recruits were most often drawn from skilled and semiskilled blue-collar work. In Detroit, between 1880 and 1918, more than 86% of police recruits were previously employed in working-class jobs. Most typically, police officers had performed skilled work such as carpentry or semiskilled work such as transporting goods or driving motor coaches (Reed, 1992). Immigrants and children of immigrants were also disproportionately represented on police forces. Policing offered relatively high pay compared with other working-class occupations with minimal educational requirements. In addition, because patronage politics influenced appointments, members of ethnic groups that exercised political influence in late nineteenth-century cities had access to jobs. As a result, the Irish were overrepresented among police officers in cities such as Boston, New York, and Chicago, and Germans were overrepresented in Cleveland, Cincinnati, and St. Louis. Finally, police had almost no formal training for their jobs. Most cities published rulebooks, but most new officers learned their jobs by conducting patrols accompanied by a more experienced officer (Walker, 1977).

The work of turn-of-the-century police officers typically involved walking beats and responding to local neighborhood issues. Patrolmen accumulated a myriad of duties loosely related to keeping the peace. They checked doors and windows at night, reported on dead animals and unlighted street lamps, dealt with runaway horses and livestock loose on city streets, operated ambulances, sheltered the homeless, found lost children, and monitored youths loitering on the streets. As historian Christopher Thale (2007) put it, "Patrolmen were instructed, of course, to nab felons, but even more important they were also expected to deal with window breakers and apple stealers" (p. 185). (See also Fogelson, 1977; Haller, 1976; Monkkonen, 1981b; Walker, 1977).

Our clearest view of the day-to-day work of a late nineteenth-century police officer comes from a diary kept in 1895 by one patrolman, Stillman S. Wakeman, who lived and worked in the South Roxbury section of Boston. Wakeman's diary indicates that he was very much rooted in his neighborhood, and much of his work was based on the demands of neighborhood residents. These residents were particularly concerned about private property. Wakeman spent a good bit of his time investigating break-ins and petty larceny, although he had limited success in recovering stolen goods. Wakeman also investigated complaints from storekeepers and residents about boys breaking windows, sneaking into homes, and setting fires. In cases like these, Wakeman demonstrated extensive discretion, sometime bringing charges but more often just reprimanding those responsible. In these low-level disputes, Wakeman acted as roving magistrate. Patrolmen like him offered local residents a forum to resolve grievances and conflicts. As with police officers elsewhere, Wakeman also conducted a wide range of duties not directly connected to law enforcement. These included distributing permits, regulating dogs, and reporting faulty street and sidewalk conditions. According to historian Alexander von Hoffman (1992), patrolmen like Wakeman were particularly attuned to the demands of middle- and working-class residents of their communities because they lived and worked in the same neighborhoods over extended periods of time.

Other studies, however, have cast doubt on whether this idyllic neighborhood-oriented policing was typical. While the New York City Police Department (NYPD) initially had a loose rule that patrolmen should live in the precinct where they worked, this rule was abolished in 1857. By 1887, only 41% of patrolmen lived in the precinct where they worked, and by 1928, only 3% did. The growth of businesses drove residences out of some neighborhoods, while rising housing costs prevented police officers from being able to afford to live in others. Plus, corruption investigations consciously sought to transfer officers out of home precincts where they were too familiar. The NYPD bureaucracy reassigned officers fairly often, so between the 1880s and the 1920s, only about one third of officers served in the same precincts as they had four years earlier. Their shift schedules and beats patrolled tended to be irregular as well (Thale, 2004). As a result, turn-of-twentieth-century patrolmen who were deeply embedded in the lives of their neighborhoods may have been more the exception than the rule in big cities.

This photograph from about 1911 of a police officer directing traffic in New York City illustrates both the older and newer functions of police. On one hand, they continued to interact closely with members of the community; on the other hand, they also assumed new modern responsibilities such at traffic control.

Source: Courtesy of the Library of Congress, LC-USZ62-123183.

Regardless, the day-to-day work of police was highly decentralized and informal. Patrolmen still had to maintain relationships with people in their precincts. They chatted with shopkeepers in their stores, mothers out with their children, and older people on the streets. Patrolmen benefitted not only in terms of knowledge to do their jobs but also small gratuities that people provided. Offering a free meal, a drink, or a place to get inside out of the weather helped businesses and residents reinforce a symbiotic relationship with the police protecting them (Thale, 2007). Police officers also used informal means to discipline young people. Cops broke up disorderly gatherings when they had to, but they also went out of their way to make sure that boys—particularly those between roughly ages 10 and 16 who were likely to be out on their own—avoided real trouble. In the 1890s, Chicago beat officer Edward J. Talbot supervised vagrant boys and street children, even intervening on their behalf in court and providing them with Thanksgiving meals. In return, boys often alerted him to low-level crimes in their neighborhood. The Detroit police also systematically made sure that young offenders whom they arrested went to court far less often than adults. Sometimes though, they had a little fun with kids. In 1907, after two boys ages 13 and 11 had been arrested for vagrancy for performing music outside of saloons, the lieutenant in charge insisted they play their mandolin and violin for the collected officers. After the boys performed, the cops let them go with a warning (Wolcott, 2005; see also Haller, 1976; Thale, 2007).

When police made arrests in the late nineteenth and early twentieth centuries, they were overwhelmingly for violations of public order such as drunkenness, vagrancy, and disorderly conduct. Arrests of course do not represent the complete work of police, but they do offer some reflection of where police priorities lie. In city after city, police on their own initiative arrested a lot of people for minor offenses (Monkkonen, 1981a; Monkkonen, 1981b; Watts, 1981; Watts, 1983). When arrests have been studied in more detail, other patterns become apparent. Those arrested tend to be relatively young, disproportionately foreign-born or African American, disproportionately drawn from working-class occupations, and overwhelmingly male (Friedman and Percival, 1981; Wolcott, 2005).

This approach had a limited impact on crime. Police might be better understood as regulating crime rather than preventing it or solving it after it took place. In some cities, police helped professional pickpockets define territories and regulate themselves. If a prominent person lost something of value, police could work with criminals to ensure its recovery (and sometimes to ensure that a percentage of the proceeds reached intermediaries and police themselves). In other cities, police worked to keep known criminals out of their towns and used arrests on suspicion to discourage potential offenders. When crimes against property or persons did occur, police had little capacity to investigate them beyond asking for information from witnesses or informants. If businesses intended to protect their property, they relied on privately hired police. Most cities granted these so-called special officers the same authority as regular municipal officers even though they were accountable to private employers rather than the public. Corporations and, in some cases, municipal governments, came to consider national organizations such as the Pinkerton Detective Agency in the late nineteenth century and the William J. Burns Detective Agency in the early twentieth century the most reliable sources of security and investigation. Moreover, estimates suggest that more men in Detroit served as "additional patrolmen"—guards and watchmen for private businesses—than as regular police (Reed, 1992; Walker, 1977).

❖ PROBLEMS OF CORRUPTION AND VIOLENCE

In the late nineteenth and early twentieth centuries, urban police remained intimately linked to the politics of their cities and reflected the sensibilities of their times. These conditions contributed to widespread corruption and police violence.

By the 1890s, many U.S. cities were dominated by political machines. These were loosely affiliated ward organizations that achieved and maintained power by getting out voters to support their candidates. It did not matter if they were Democrats, as with New York City's Tammany Hall, or Republicans, as in Philadelphia and Cincinnati. The machines controlled appointments to municipal jobs, most especially the police. For most patrolmen, job performance was less important for getting appointments, gaining desirable postings, and achieving promotion than was maintaining favor with their ward leaders and local machines (Fogelson, 1977).

Political interests also shaped how police approached particular problems. Because organized vices such as gambling, prostitution, and saloons provided services urban residents wanted, they were generally tolerated or supported by machine politicians. In Chicago, many of the people who ran illegal enterprises had ties to political leaders. As a result, police licensed vice rather than suppressing it. Police allowed gambling operations, brothels, and unlicensed saloons to operate under implicit conditions and within defined territories. Often these districts were widely known: Chicago's Levee, New York City's Tenderloin, San Francisco's Barbary Coast. Vice entrepreneurs gave police regular pay offs, maintained orderly operations, and steered clear of middle-class neighborhoods. In exchange, police allowed them to operate in peace. In cities like Oakland or Chicago, newspaper attention or public outrage occasionally prompted police to make arrests for gambling or other vices, but when attention died down, business resumed as usual (Fogelson, 1977; Friedman and Percival, 1981; Lindberg, 1998).

Under these circumstances, many nineteenth-century urban police departments struggled to generate legitimate authority. Unlike the London police, who derived their authority from the law, police departments in the United States had to derive their authority from their actions on the streets. The effort to establish authority contributed to violence by police (Johnson, 2003; Miller, 1999).

On the most basic level, police officers often had to use violence to make arrests. If patrolmen arrested drunks or vagrants while walking their beats, they needed to subdue recalcitrant prisoners and transport them to stationhouses. Violence proved to be one answer. More generally, the localism of policing and politics often undermined public respect for police officers. In response, some police officers used force to generate respect. Moreover, police officers sometimes believed that they themselves should punish offenders. Nineteenth-century courts, like police, were highly politicized and ineffective, so some police units developed a culture in which they regarded the use of violence to administer punishment as legitimate (Haller, 1976; Walker, 1977). Historian Marilynn Johnson (2003) found 270 cases of police brutality documented in the *New York Times* between 1865 and 1894. The majority of these involved clubbing, in which uniformed officers bludgeoned unarmed suspects or civilians with batons or nightsticks. Often these incidents arose over minor issues, such as persons ignoring orders to move along. Police were particularly likely to use violence to deal with young men who refused to cooperate with them, in that way asserting their own masculine authority. Of course New York City is unique because of its large scale and the sizeable amount of research that has been done about it, but these very qualities also help make New York City a useful proxy for understanding policing in other cities as well.

The NYPD's Alexander "Clubber" Williams gained widespread notoriety for his use of violence to enforce his version of the law. He famously quipped, "there is more law in the end of a nightstick than in a decision of the Supreme Court" (Johnson, 2003, p. 41). Williams' rough approach to law enforcement often gained the support of merchants and business owners in districts where he worked but also generated public protest. In 1879 Williams was the target of two major investigations for assault, and by 1887 he had more than 350 formal complaints lodged against him. Williams also made himself a lightning rod for criticism by openly insulting labor unionists, Irish immigrants, and Jews in the press. Williams gave voice to police attitudes that led them to use violence disproportionately against immigrants and ethnic minorities.

By the early twentieth century, violence had become fairly pervasive in some big city police departments. On three occasions between 1900 and 1905, NYPD officers joined white crowds in attacking African Americans, Jews, and groups of immigrants. In August of 1900, police officers participated in the violence as white mobs attacked African Americans in the Tenderloin district on the near West Side in response to the killing of a patrolman. In 1902, the New York police failed to provide adequate protection of a Jewish funeral procession on the lower East Side which found itself in a confrontation with Irish workers; the police sought to restore order by using their clubs to disperse the funeral marchers. Finally, in the summer of 1905, police engaged in a series of low-level confrontations with African Americans already angry over violent police tactics. Each incident highlighted the way in which police—largely aligned with white working-class communities—sought to defend neighborhoods against the perceived challenges of migrations by African Americans and other new groups. At the same time, the press tended to blame lax police discipline and financial corruption for the upheavals (Johnson, 2003). The nexus of ethnic tension, politics, indiscipline, and corruption helped spawn a movement to transform police in the early 1900s.

❖ POLICE REFORM—EXTERNAL AND INTERNAL

By the early twentieth century, widespread efforts to reform police emerged, intertwined with the broader progressive movements of the day. Reformers drew on a nexus of ideas that included belief that social problems such as inequality contributed to disorder and a sense that people's collective efforts—particularly organized by experts and the government—could achieve social change (McGerr, 2003). The main steps in reforming police were to separate police from their political and local groundings and to achieve greater efficiency. In the 1890s, advocates of police reform emerged largely from moral reform concerns with urban corruption and vice and were very much outsiders to the police. After 1900, however, and particularly after 1910, police themselves—or at least police administrators—also increasingly concerned themselves with reform. Unlike moral reformers, the thrust of their changes focused on improving police operations. Many reform advocates compared police to the military, but in reality, the model they most commonly adopted was that of big business. By the 1910s, the leading police reformers drew on a strand of progressivism primarily concerned with achieving good government. Thus, they sought to make police more corporate and efficient (Walker, 1977).

The Lexow Committee investigation of the NYPD in 1894 and 1895 exemplifies the initial pattern in which attempts at reform came from the outside. In 1892, the Reverend Charles Parkhurst, minister of the Madison Square Presbyterian Church, president of the Society for the Prevention of Crime, and moral reform activist, delivered a series of sermons condemning corruption in the NYPD. When Republicans gained control of the New York state legislature, they capitalized on the furor generated by Parkhurst's sermons to authorize a commission to investigate the Democratic Party-controlled NYPD. On March 9, 1894, a committee chaired by Republican Senator Clarence Lexow opened hearings in New York City to pursue Parkhurst's charges. Initially intended to simply conduct a few weeks of hearings and issue a report, the Lexow Committee expanded its mandate to continue its inquiry throughout the year. Not only did it call police officers to testify, it also heard from a wide gamut of people who interacted with the police including gamblers, saloon keepers, prostitutes, and con men. The witnesses painted a picture of police protecting organized vice in exchange for payoffs, rigging elections to aid the Democratic Party, and buying and selling jobs and promotions. The hearings also highlighted police violence, especially when the committee subpoenaed over 100 police officers, all of whom had been convicted of assaults in the previous three years. Exhibiting this so-called "clubber's brigade" allowed the Lexow Committee to link police brutality with corruption and to blame their rough justice on administrative failures. The Lexow investigation helped force the retirement of Alexander "Clubber" Williams in 1895 and led to the removal of several other officers (Fogelson, 1977; Johnson, 2003; Walker 1977).

Beyond these personnel shifts, only limited change resulted from the Lexow Committee investigation. On the one hand, it did lead the NYPD to be reorganized under the leadership of a bipartisan board of commissioners, two Democrats and two Republicans. It also inspired similar investigations of police departments in Kansas City, Baltimore, Chicago, Los Angeles, and San Francisco before the end of the nineteenth century (Fogelson, 1977). On the other hand, little improvement actually resulted. In 1895, former state legislator and future president of the United States Theodore Roosevelt was appointed to the New York City Board of Police Commissioners and immediately sought to transform the NYPD. He aimed to enforce the law fully, eliminate police corruption, and improve the training and performance of patrolmen. He soon found, however, that the power of liquor and vice interests made it very difficult to regulate alcohol as the law outlined or to prevent payoffs to individual officers. Moreover, Roosevelt's support for aggressive law enforcement promoted the use of violence. Under Roosevelt, the Board of Commissioners rescinded a police ban on the use of clubs. They also issued standard firearms to officers and mandated training in their use but did not provide training in what circumstances to use them, creating conditions the contributed to a series of highly publicized police shootings in the 1890s. After two years in the job, Roosevelt resigned from the Board of Commissioners, citing his frustration at achieving fundamental change under the bipartisan commission, and the NYPD reverted back to a single-commissioner system in 1901 (Johnson, 2003; Walker, 1977).

Nor did investigations prompt corporations and cities to abandon their reliance on private police. In the early twentieth century, railroad companies routinely employed their own police officers to maintain security on trains that moved from jurisdiction to jurisdiction. Cities hired additional private patrolmen during moments of disorder such as strikes, weather emergencies, and large gatherings (Reed, 1992). And cities often brought in private detective agencies to conduct investigations that exceeded the reach of their own police. After a bomb destroyed the *Los Angeles Times* Building on October 1, 1910, killing 21 people, the city of Los Angeles contracted with the William J. Burns National Detective Agency to solve the case. The Burns agency conducted a cross-country inquiry in a way that the Los Angeles Police Department (LAPD) of the time would not have been able to do. The investigation focused on a series of earlier bombings that resembled the *Times* attack and a network of labor activists who had targeted the notoriously anti-union newspaper. When the Burns agency concluded that John J. McNamara and James McNamara, two brothers associated with the leadership of an ironworkers' union, were responsible for the *Times* bombing, it engineered their kidnapping from Indiana and returned them to Los Angeles to stand trial (Blum, 2008; Shapiro, 1977).

After the turn of the twentieth century, police departments in the United States self-consciously sought to become more effective and to operate in ways that paralleled businesses. The International Association of Chiefs of Police (IACP), under the leadership of District of Columbia police superintendent Richard Sylvester, helped drive this change. In 1893, the IACP started out as a loose-knit association, the National Chiefs of Police Union, but Sylvester's assumption of its presidency helped transform it into a prominent advocate of police professionalization. Sylvester's leadership of the IACP between 1901 and 1914 established a precedent that its annual conventions would become a forum for promoting new approaches to crime prevention, efficiency, and reform (Carte & Carte, 1975; Walker, 1977).

Reformers generally agreed that they needed to upgrade police personnel by raising the standards for recruits. Around the turn of the century, most big-city police departments tightened height, weight, and age requirements so that recruits would be young and fit and insisted they could read and write English. In many cases, they placed new employees under civil service rules, requiring recruits to take exams for hiring and promotion and in turn insulating hiring decisions from political pressures. One 1915 survey found that 122 of the 204 largest police departments in the United States had adopted civil service (Fogelson, 1977; Walker, 1977). The goal of these reforms was to improve both the physical and mental capacities of officers. As early police reformer Leonhard F. Fuld (1909) put it, "It is certainly true that the police officer must possess physical powers rather than intellectual powers, that he must first act rather than think, but a moment's reflection will convince anyone that he must think as well as act" (p. 152). Efforts to improve police personnel, however, achieved only modest gains. Surveys and investigations undertaken in the 1920s continued to find limited educational attainments and poor scores on intelligence tests among police officers. Departments still struggled to attract high-quality applicants and to weed out low-quality ones, especially at a time when cities were growing and urban police departments were expanding their ranks (Fogelson, 1977). Reed's (1992) study of the Detroit police department between 1880 and 1918 found that turnover rates among police officers and length of service were not particularly related to police professionalization efforts. Police reformers also expressed qualms that civil service tended to disassociate hiring and promotion from the actual work of police. Raymond Fosdick (1920/1972) argued that, "in trying to nullify the effects of incompetence and favoritism, we nullify capacity and intelligence too" (p. 271). Likewise, New York City police commissioner Arthur Woods (1918) suggested that, "In forces where promotion is made according to civil service systems . . . a man attains promotion without any reference to the qualities of his day-to-day work" (p. 96–97).

Initiating training also represented a key element of police reform. The Cincinnati police department established an elaborate training program in 1886, but no other police force followed its example. After the turn of the century, a smattering of other initiatives began. Cleveland, for example, started an informal program in 1903 in which precinct captains taught short classes on local laws. Detroit opened a police school for new recruits in 1911, offering instruction on practical matters such as how to interact with citizens and under what circumstances to use firearms. New York City under commissioner Arthur Woods reorganized its Police Training School in 1914 to provide instruction for new recruits and continuing education for experienced officers. But for the most part, formal police training did not become common until the 1920s (Reed, 1992; Wadman & Allison, 2004; Walker, 1977).

August Vollmer, elected town marshal of Berkeley, California, in 1905 and later appointed its police chief, exemplified progressive police reform. In 1908, he established the Berkeley Police School, a prototype for other police in-service training programs. There, Vollmer, police officials from nearby Oakland, and professors from the University of California offered off duty officers instruction on the theory and practice of policing. By the late 1910s, Vollmer began to recruit college students to serve in his department in order to improve the quality of patrolmen. These so-called "college cops" elevated the educational level of Berkeley's police department and spread Vollmer's approach as they moved to other departments. Early in his tenure, Vollmer also instituted several reforms to modernize his department, putting officers on bicycles to improve their mobility, creating an alarm system to communicate with officers on the beat, and improving police recordkeeping. Vollmer later began to incorporate more scientific methods of crime investigation such as using forensic labs and fingerprinting. By the 1920s, Berkeley's police adopted further technological aides such as polygraph testing and radios in police cars. Operating in a relatively small university town offered Vollmer unique advantages: modest crime rates, a well-educated population, and a supportive local government. In ways that would not have been possible in bigger cities, Vollmer could legitimately encourage his officers to get to know everyone on their beats and be alert to prevent crime. Vollmer's Berkeley operated as something of a laboratory for progressive policing, experimenting with new ideas that could be refined and transferred elsewhere (Carte & Carte, 1975; Liss & Schlossman, 1984; Walker, 1977).

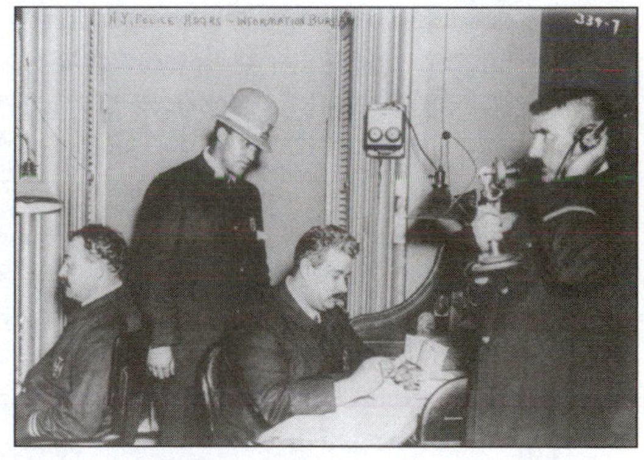

This photograph from about 1908 shows the NYPD's Information Bureau. The introduction of technologies such as telephones gave the public new means to contact the police and provided the police with new means of communicating and responding to calls.

Source: Courtesy of the Library of Congress, LC-USZ62-50070.

Case Studies in Criminal Justice: James Couzens, Detroit Police Commissioner

Some progressive police reformers such as James Couzens in Detroit sought to apply the lessons of business directly to policing. Often coming from corporate backgrounds or believing that corporations were more efficient than governments, they sought to implement similar approaches within police departments.

Born in 1872, Couzens made his fortune in industry before pursuing a career in public service. He oversaw day-to-day operations for the Ford Motor Company during the height of its innovation between 1902 and 1914. In particular, he helped implement innovations such as automated assembly lines, profit-sharing plans, and minimum wage policies. After he left Ford, Couzens served as Detroit's police commissioner between 1916 and 1918, as mayor between 1919 and 1922, and as a U.S. senator from 1922 to 1936 (Barnard, 1958; Lacey, 1986; Wolcott, 2005).

As police commissioner, Couzens brought approaches similar to those he had used in his former position to policing. As Couzens' associate Parker Sercombe wrote in the annual report of the Detroit Police Department for 1917, "there is no more reason why police departments or other public bureaus should run their business in a haphazard manner . . . than there is for Standard Oil or the Steel Corporation to run their affairs without a well organized statistical plan" (Detroit Police Department, 1917, p. 239). Couzens also adapted ideas articulated by industrial management expert Frederick W. Taylor in *Principles of Scientific Management* (1911). In accord with the Taylorist notion of dividing jobs into their component parts, the Detroit police greatly increased specialization among officers, expanding branches to include an auto recovery bureau, a criminal identification bureau, a traffic regulation squad, and a vice squad. Under Couzens, the Detroit police also introduced a merit system to give patrolmen financial rewards if they reduced crime and maintained order on their beats. Finally, the Detroit police established a statistical division to collect data on officers' work and compare them against specific performance metrics in the hopes of achieving better long-term results (Wolcott, 2005).

This business-like model also dovetailed with a social service model. Under Couzens, the Detroit police sought to engage in what he called "child-friendly policing." Couzens claimed that he intended to replace police regulation of public behavior with education that would help prevent crime and disorder. To this end he proposed the creation of a junior police force where children could help officers with routine tasks, sent his officers into public schools, used patrolmen as school crossing guards, and sponsored boy scout troops (Detroit Police Department, 1917; Wolcott, 2005).

In his relatively brief term as police commissioner, Couzens sought to make fundamental changes in how police operated and, at least in the short-term, he succeeded. The problem in Detroit and elsewhere, however, was that these sorts of top-down reforms implemented by administrators rarely outlasted the efforts of individual reformers.

❖ CRIME PREVENTION AND SOCIAL IMPROVEMENT

In many cases, administrative reforms co-existed with police reforms intended to improve society more generally. Those police leaders who embraced social reform saw it as intertwined with crime control. At the same time, they saw crime prevention as having broader social benefits.

As chief of the Cleveland police between 1903 and 1909, Frederick J. Kohler launched a series of reforms aimed at helping adult offenders. Unlike most other progressive police administrators of his time, Kohler had worked his way up through the ranks of patrolmen and implemented little in the way of administrative reform. But he was sympathetic to the thousands of working people caught up by the police for minor charges each year. In 1905, Kohler established a "sunrise court." In it, people arrested overnight exchanged an admission of guilt for release at an early hour that let them get to work on time. Beginning in 1908, Kohler initiated a "golden rule policy" that police officers were to handle minor offenses such as drunkenness or disorderly conduct with a reprimand rather than an arrest. Kohler (1908) explained to the delegates at the IACP that,

> I know, and you know men who have erred thus in youth, and yet later have become good citizens. . . Now, I finally concluded that it was our duty not to help these unfortunates on their downward course, but to save them. It seemed to me it was up to the police to learn to know the difference between a thief, a mischievous man or boy. And why not? Of all men, who is so able to judge whether an arrest is necessary as a policeman if given the opportunity? Who knows the neighborhood? Who is first on the scene? . . . I determined to have my policemen use their best human instincts. I proposed that my men should exercise that discretion that judges did not always exercise (p. 31).

Kohler in effect diverted offenders from the criminal justice system and decriminalized minor offenses by formalizing the discretion of his officers. Kohler's policies did not last past his administration, but they did offer an example of how relaxing traditional police policies could help achieve social reform.

In other cases, toughening standards of law enforcement was expected to improve public order. Efforts to combat vice offer an example. In the early twentieth century, progressive campaigns to improve urban society and eliminate social conditions thought to lead to crime targeted prostitution, gambling, and narcotics. These campaigns were rooted both in the public reaction against the open vice districts that flourished in many cities and in more diffuse concerns that changing urban societies were contributing to moral degradation. The movement of young women into cities and into the labor force dovetailed with popular—and probably vastly exaggerated—concerns that young women were being captured and sold into prostitution in a form of white slavery. In this context, police who had earlier tolerated vice operations—and often profited from them—faced increasing pressure to suppress them. In Cleveland, the police under Kohler took the lead repressing organized vice by stationing officers outside of known brothels in order to identify and embarrass customers and actively enforcing liquor laws in order to repress illegal saloons (Walker, 1977).

More typically, the police found themselves responding to antivice campaigns undertaken by private organizations. In Chicago, church and business groups sought to eliminate vice from local neighborhoods. In October 1909, the evangelist Gypsy Smith led a protest march through Chicago's Levee district to highlight conditions there. In 1911, the Chicago Vice Commission, appointed by the mayor at the behest of church organizations, issued a report detailing the extent and nature of prostitution in the city. Also in 1911, Chicago business and church leaders organized a Committee of Fifteen, which hired investigators and monitored vice conditions on an ongoing basis. This pressure led to police action. In 1912, prosecutions by the state attorney's office and frequent raids by the police closed most operations in the Levee, but in so doing unintentionally encouraged drinking, gambling, and prostitution to spread elsewhere in the city. Furthermore, after his election as mayor in 1915, William H. Thompson sought to remove the leaders of the police vice squad and allowed a return to unofficial toleration of vice. Public pressure to do something persisted, but it also ran up against countervailing pressure from the close relationship among police, politicians, and illegal enterprise (Haller, 1971; Lindberg, 1998).

These conditions frustrated antivice activists. As Louise deKoven Bowen, head of the Juvenile Protective Agency, an activist group that sent investigators to saloons and dance halls looking for evidence that they served alcohol to children, complained in 1920, "the Juvenile Protective Association is obliged to depend largely upon the help of the police in its work for children; it believes that it has a right to expect that when it reports to the police department violations of law that endanger childhood, the police will take immediate action. Yet in hundreds of instances during the past year where the welfare of children was involved, the service rendered by the police has been inadequate or entirely negligible" (Wolcott, 2005, p. 110).

Despite their problems with police, social reformers also sought to use police departments as vehicles for change. Antivice campaigners, concerned that modern commercial entertainments such as amusement parks, dance halls, and movie theaters presented moral hazards to young women and girls, urged police departments to hire female officers. These new policewomen were to conduct preventive work, protecting women and girls from harm. In 1905, the city of Portland, Oregon, authorized Lola Baldwin to serve as a police operative for the duration of that city's World's Fair. In 1910, social welfare advocates such as the Woman's Christian Temperance Union pressured the LAPD to hire social worker Alice Stebbins Wells to serve as a full-time policewoman. By 1917, at least 30 U.S. cities had hired policewomen. In many cases, moral reform groups paid part of policewomen's salaries and employed them as joint appointments together with police departments. Policewomen did not serve as conventional patrolmen. Instead, they engaged in a form of crime prevention defined by moral concerns. The LAPD, for example, administratively divided its policewomen into two branches. One, the City Mothers' Bureau, functioned very much like a social work agency, encouraging parents to come to them with their daughters' problems. The other, the Juvenile Bureau, conducted preventive investigations more typical of policewomen elsewhere. Juvenile Bureau officers—women as well as some men—patrolled places where young people congregated. They focused on preventing young women and girls having fun from becoming involved with drinking, drugs, or promiscuity (Schulz, 1995; Appier, 1998). Progressive Era advocates of policewomen embraced an ideology that gender differences gave female officers a unique ability to protect young women and girls from the risks of modern urban life (Appier, 1998). The LAPD's Wells (1913) argued, "The woman officer is an emphasis upon the prevention spirit of police work" (p. 401).

This highly gendered model of preventive policing became less visible in the late 1910s and 1920s. The historian Janis Appier (1998) argues that it was undermined by politics within police departments, increasing public concern about serious crime, and the emergence of male professionals asserting new approaches to crime prevention. It seems equally plausible to suggest, however, that thinking about crime prevention shifted from an exclusive focus on girls to one that concentrated more on boys. Males committed far more crimes than females, so it was only logical that overwhelmingly male police forces came to focus on boys and young men as targets for crime prevention. In New York City, reform-minded police commissioner Arthur Woods argued that boys' search for play and excitement in modern cities often led them to trouble. As a means of crime prevention, his NYPD sought to redirect them. Beginning in 1914, the NYPD closed some roads to be designated "play streets" and initiated a junior police force in which boys and girls under age 15 were assigned minor duties assisting the police such as cleaning streets and reporting petty offenses (Johnson, 2003; Wolcott, 2005; Woods, 1918).

Like Woods, August Vollmer in Berkeley also saw crime prevention and social reform as intertwined with administrative reform of police. Already established as the leading police reformer of his time, in the late 1910s Vollmer devoted increasing attention to the causes of crime. Borrowing ideas from the emerging field of child psychology, Vollmer became increasingly convinced that "predelinquent" traits in children and youth could be identified and treated. And the police were positioned best to do so. In 1919, he argued before the IACP that police officers should act like social workers. "No single individual in the community has more opportunities to do good, solid, constructive social service than the intelligent, sympathetic, and trained policeman," he argued. "By close cooperation with schools and public welfare agencies, he will soon learn who the potential delinquents and dependents are, and can do much to assist in preventing them from becoming social failures" (Vollmer, 1919, p. 35–36). In a manner consistent with his approach to administrative reform, Vollmer proposed that police officers build relationships with schools and teachers, systematically track children who could become problems, and turn to experts for analysis and guidance on resolving problems. Vollmer worked with psychiatrists and educators in the Berkeley community and formed a voluntary coordinating council to link the antidelinquency efforts of police, schools, recreation bureaus, and social welfare agencies. The Berkeley police also established a Crime Prevention Division under the leadership of a psychiatric social worker, Elizabeth

Lossing, to spearhead its work with young potential offenders (Carte & Carte, 1975; Liss and Schlossman, 1984; Wolcott, 2005).

While reformers such as Vollmer viewed police social service work as complementing administrative efficiency and crime control, other police leaders believed that these goals were at odds with one another. These leaders expressed two basic concerns. First, some asserted that police needed to be tough in order to control crime. In 1908, Frank Cassada, chief of the Elmira, New York police, told the IACP that, " . . . every police chief ought to make every man take his hat off and respect the law. When we arrest a man we are too lenient." Contrary to Frederick Kohler, he proposed that police should, "Put the iron rule on them—not the golden rule. Knock their blocks off" (Walker, 1977, p. 104). Second, others worried that adding social service work ran counter to the administrative goal of narrowing the function of police. Even though the purpose of work like intervening with boys and controlling narcotics was to prevent crime, the work itself added to the roster of police duties. Moreover, the historian Robert Fogelson (1977) argues that early twentieth-century police found it difficult to shed some of their nineteenth-century functions such as cleaning streets, inspecting tenements, and supervising elections, and in fact lacked clear criteria for determining the appropriate work of police.

Long-term analyses of police departments' operations, however, indicate that real changes did take place and that their timing was roughly consistent with campaigns for reform. Police succeeded in narrowing their functions. The historian Eric Monkkonen (1981b) uses the provision of overnight accommodations for homeless people and tramps and the recovery of lost children as two proxies for the more general social service functions of police. In an era of a highly mobile labor force where many men walked from town to town in search of work, providing lodging for them was a big responsibility that fell to the police. Police reformers, however, sought to shed this duty. In New York City, for example, Theodore Roosevelt led the fight to close police lodgings in 1896. Data from 23 cities indicate that rates of police lodging dropped steadily between 1860 and 1920, with the sharpest drop coming in the 1890s. Data on returns of lost children—also a common problem in late nineteenth century cities—also reflect the changing functions of police. Parents' requests that police find their missing offspring increased noticeably in the first 10 years after cities established uniformed police forces, but then dropped steadily in ensuing years. Both of these changes seem to reflect changes in police priorities and policies. Likewise, overall arrest rates per 1,000 residents also declined in these same 23 cities. This change may seem counterintuitive; after all, if police were dropping their catchall social service functions, they might spend more time making arrests. The large majority of arrests in this era, however, were for minor offenses such as disorderly conduct, vagrancy, and drunkenness. Police reduced these arrests for violations of public order, but increased arrests for more serious crimes. Historians such as Monkkonen (1981a, 1981b) and Eugene Watts (1981, 1983) disagree somewhat over the precise timing and nature of these shifts, but the overall pattern seems clear. Police departments altered their priorities and narrowed their functions sometime around the beginning of the twentieth century. They moved from making generalized efforts to maintain public order among poor, disestablished, and transient urban residents to more targeted efforts to control criminal offenses.

What's the Evidence?: Annual Reports of Police Departments

The annual reports of municipal police departments provide some of the most systematic evidence about police activities in the late nineteenth and early twentieth centuries. Most cities published annual reports in most years. But according to the historian who has used them most systematically, Eric Monkkonen (1979), they appeared in a wide array of different formats and do not necessarily remain consistent even for a single city.

Very occasionally, some annual reports provide surprisingly detailed information. The 1917 annual report of the Detroit Police Department, for example, offers a shockingly thorough 340-page discourse on the ideology and practice of a single department at the height of progressive reform, and the annual reports of the New York Police Department from the 1930s offer honor roll descriptions of all officers awarded medals or killed in the line of duty. More typically, however, annual reports offer boilerplate descriptions of what police bureaus did in a given year—often using the same language year after year—and statistics on their accomplishments.

The greatest value of most annual reports lies in the numbers they contain. Annual reports quantify as many police activities as they can, from arrests to expenses to the number of Boy Scout troops sponsored and everything in between. They may not report these numbers consistently from year to year and certainly not consistently from city to city. Nonetheless, quantitative analysis of annual report data can generate insight into both police behaviors and the social conditions that police dealt with.

Police annual reports are relatively easy to access. The Library of Congress houses the largest collection of police annual reports, and university research libraries often hold police annual reports from several cities. Individual cities' annual reports can usually often be found in those cities' libraries, typically in the local history section. In addition, Monkkonen's dataset derived from annual reports, *Police Departments, Arrests and Crimes in the United States, 1860–1920*, is held by the Inter-University Consortium on Political and Social Research and can be accessed on-line at http://dx.doi.org/10.3886/ICPSR07708.v2

❖ CAMPAIGNS FOR CRIME CONTROL

For many police agencies in the first third of the twentieth century, a move toward increasingly tough crime control coexisted with reform movements. This shift reinforces the notion that police moved from a priority of maintaining public order to a priority of fighting crime. Despite some innovations, however, methods of crime fighting remained fairly primitive and often violent. Nonetheless, a trend toward overtly defining policing in terms of crime control that began with the reform movements of the 1900s and 1910s accelerated in the 1920s.

In New York City, Theodore Roosevelt's successors as police commissioner sought to maintain his get-tough approach to crime but did so in a police department with limited tools other than the personal authority of officers. As a result, the police use of violence became a pervasive issue in New York City in the 1900s and 1910s. Theodore Bingham, who served as police commissioner from 1906 to 1909, encouraged officers to use nightsticks against disorderly persons and suspected criminals. The NYPD's rough approach, however, generated controversy and increased public opposition. Socialists and labor unions organized rallies to protest police brutality, and ordinary citizens complained in the newspapers of police repression. In one resulting controversy, William J. Gaynor, a federal district judge adopted the cause of his 17-year-old milk deliveryman who had been the victim of police harassment. The resulting public outcry mobilized sentiment against police violence and propelled Gaynor into the mayor's office in 1910. As mayor, Gaynor prioritized civil liberties and sought to stop police brutality. He instituted a new general order that police commanders hear all assault complaints against patrolmen and forward them to headquarters. Gaynor also ordered the police to back off aggressive vice control tactics of previous administrations. These reforms placed patrolmen in a difficult position. Critics complained that the new policies invited crime and that police officers, given no alternatives to the violent tactics now denied to them, tended to back off confrontations. Gaynor's successor, the reformer John Purroy Mitchell, and Mitchell's police commissioner, Arthur Woods, publicly reversed Gaynor's position and promoted rough tactics. Mitchell told the *New York Times* in 1914, "I hope the police will use their clubs on every gunman on whom they can lay their hands." Despite these public proclamations, the training programs that Woods instituted may have actually reduced police brutality. By teaching patrolmen rules for making arrests and using firearms, the NYPD under Woods sought to give officers a better sense of circumstances in which they should and should not use violence (Johnson, 2003, p. 108).

Prohibition accelerated police efforts to get tough on crime. The ratification of the Eighteenth Amendment in 1919 banning alcohol fostered a sharp expansion of illegal enterprise in the forms of bootlegging, gambling, and racketeering. Police administrations typically responded by stepping up enforcement. During the brief period from 1921 to 1923 when New York had a strong enforcement law, the courts were flooded with prohibition cases. Moreover the NYPD often used extreme violence in raiding speakeasies and other sources of illegal alcohol. Several scandals resulted from police brutality on liquor raids. Equally problematic were the increased possibilities for corruption that prohibition created. For decades, alcohol purveyors who skirted the edges of liquor regulations had paid police officers to ignore their operations, but under Prohibition, when all nightclubs, saloons, and speakeasies were illegal, this issue expanded many times over. Most troublesome, Prohibition fostered the growth of open gang warfare between criminal enterprises fighting for control of the alcohol trade. Police tended to respond in one of three ways, sometimes a combination of all three within a single police department. First, they went about their normal business, sometimes raiding speakeasies and sometimes accepting bribes to look the other way. Second, and probably least often, they sought to enforce the law as professionally as they could. In Chicago between 1925 and 1927, Mayor William Dever and police commissioner Morgan Collins promised to uphold the alcohol laws. In spite of the pervasive illegal enterprise in their city, they instituted a crackdown on speakeasies and alcohol production. These periods of vigorous enforcement tended to be short-lived; Dever lost the 1927 mayoral election and Chicago reverted to more wide-open ways. Third, many police departments responded to the increase in illegal enterprise and the perception that crime was on the rise with violence of their own. In the late 1920s, the NYPD instituted mass arrests of suspected offenders in and around speakeasies and organized several strong-arm units with explicit instructions to patrol known criminal gathering spots and rough up gangsters (Johnson, 2003; Lindberg, 1998).

As a result of these conditions, police use of firearms was far more pervasive than it is today. Well-armed gangsters resorting to gunplay to defend their businesses contributed to this situation. So too did the pervasiveness of armed robbery in the early twentieth century. Police felt that they had no choice but to fight back. Chicago police killed 76 robbers between 1900 and 1920 (Adler, 2006) and, according to historian Roger Lane (1997) shot to death dozens of people each year in the 1920s in efforts to fight crime. These conditions also applied to smaller cities. According to the *Pittsburgh Post-Gazette* (1929, Dec. 4) the Pittsburgh police ordered patrolmen and detectives "to shoot to kill any bandit they surprise in the perpetuation of a crime, or while fleeing from the scene of a crime." Any officer who did so would be publicly commended.

State and Federal Policing

The state and federal governments also became increasingly involved in crime control in the first third of the twentieth century. Law enforcement had been an overwhelmingly local responsibility, but as more problems crossed jurisdictional boundaries, the state and federal governments stepped in and created their own police agencies. Other states had state law enforcement officers before, but the Pennsylvania State Constabulary—established in 1905—represented the first large-scale, centrally administered state police agency. It had a broad mandate to deal with rural crime. In the wake of the anthracite coal strike of 1902 that created a national crisis, however, the main job of the Pennsylvania State Constabulary came to be dealing with labor strife. Assigned to barracks spread across the state, it offered a military-style response to problems beyond the scope of local police. The Pennsylvania police became a model for similar agencies organized in New York in 1917, Michigan, Colorado, and West Virginia in 1919, and elsewhere in the 1920s (Walker, 1977; Ray, 1995).

The federal government also established the Bureau of Investigation—the agency that would become the Federal Bureau of Investigation—in 1908. As with state police, this was not the first federal police agency. The U.S. Marshals service existed since 1789 to apprehend and transport fugitives, the Secret Service was created in 1865 to fight counterfeiting (and in 1901 assumed the duty of presidential protection), and various agents of the Treasury Department had enforced tax and alcohol regulations. But in 1908, President Theodore Roosevelt created the Bureau of Investigation within the Department of Justice to function as an independent detective agency for the federal government. In its early years, the Bureau of Investigation had little to do because very few offenses crossed state lines and fell under federal jurisdiction. Congress's 1910 passage of the Mann Act, or the White Slave Traffic Act, however, created one clear function for the Bureau. In the context of the Progressive Era panic about prostitution and white slavery, this law made it illegal to "transport . . . any woman or girl" across state lines "for the purpose of prostitution or debauchery, or for any other immoral purpose." Under the new law, the Bureau of Investigation found itself with the main responsibility for policing any sort of sexuality that involved interstate transit. Enforcement, not surprisingly, turned out to be highly discretionary and, in some cases, discriminatory. Most famously, the African American heavyweight boxing champion Jack Johnson—the target of much white anger both for his success in the ring and for his flouting of racial standards—was arrested under the Mann Act in 1917 for conducting an ongoing affair with a white woman with whom he travelled (Friedman, 1993; Langum, 1994; Walker 1977).

The federal government gradually expanded its law enforcement functions in the 1910s and 1920s. The 1914 passage of the Harrison Narcotics Act—which restricted physicians and pharmacists from dealing in cocaine and narcotics—brought the federal government into an arena which had been the province of state and local governments. The Act required Treasury Department agents to become increasingly involved in regulating drug distribution. A 1915 magazine article spoke of a new "AntiDrug War" and observed: "foes of the drug evil are welcoming the arrival of a new howitzer battery, so to speak" (Spillane, 2004, p. 18). Federal agents, in these early years, focused on supporting local law enforcement efforts, controlling drug smuggling, and pressuring physicians who were deemed to be overprescribing narcotics (or prescribing to known drug addicts). Annual convictions under the Harrison Act, which numbered only about 100 in 1915, rose to over 5,000 a decade later (Spillane, 2004).

The First World War and its aftermath contributed to a further expansion of federal law enforcement. Following the entry of the United States into the war in April 1917, Congress passed the Espionage Act in

June outlawing any speech or political activity encouraging resistance to the military draft or to U.S. military operations. Under this law and a series of succeeding acts—including the Sedition Act passed in May, 1918 outlawing criticism of the United States government—federal agents arrested and tried over 1,000 radicals, socialists, labor unionists, and war resisters. These included 4-time Socialist Party presidential candidate Eugene V. Debs, who was convicted under the Sedition Act and incarcerated in federal prison until 1923.

This crackdown on radicalism accelerated after the war. In late April and early May, 1919, bombs were discovered in the mail sent to prominent politicians and figures in the financial world; almost all were found or failed to reached their targets due to insufficient postage. On June 2, bombing attacks succeeded in New York and Washington, including one at the home of U.S. Attorney General A. Mitchell Palmer. Anonymous radicals claimed credit for the attacks and promised more. In response, the Justice Department stepped up its efforts to control socialists and activists. Beginning in November, 1919, the Radical Division of the Bureau of Investigation—headed by a young administrator named J. Edgar Hoover—rounded up foreign-born radicals and deported over 500 by the end of the year. The Justice Department overreached, however, when it targeted organizations that included significant shares of U.S. citizens in a January, 1920 crackdown (known after their architect as the Palmer Raids). In this case, at least 4,000 radicals were taken to detention centers and their organizations' offices searched. Abuse of suspects helped turn the opinion of the public and of government officials against this second round of raids. Eventually pressure from Congress forced most detainees to be released and Palmer to resign (Powers, 1986; Gage, 2009). In these instances, the sudden concentration of law enforcement power in the hands of the federal government exceeded both public support and its administrative abilities.

Two other instances illustrate the continued limitations of federal law enforcement, even as it tried to get tough on crime in the 1920s. First, on September 16, 1920, a bomb exploded outside the offices of the J. P. Morgan and Company financial firm in New York City, killing 38 people and damaging surrounding buildings. The NYPD, the Bureau of Investigation, and the Burns Detective Agency all scrambled to solve the crime, seeking to link it to the 1919 attacks and sending investigators to Europe to explore connections to foreign communists and anarchists. In the end, each law enforcement agency undercut the others and none succeeded in finding the bomber (Gage, 2009). Second, efforts to enforce Prohibition devolved into failure. Under the National

Prohibition Enforcement Act (also known as the Volstead Act) the federal government created the Bureau of Prohibition within the Treasury Department to enforce alcohol regulation and placed federal prosecutor Mabel Walker Willebrandt in charge. Appointing a woman with ties to the temperance movement to lead enforcement efforts and allocating over 1,500 agents to the cause made for good politics. These gestures, however, proved insufficient to meet the challenge. The biggest problem facing the Bureau of Prohibition was dealing with individual stills and small-scale breweries, and Congress never allocated enough officers for the job. Furthermore, the agency was underfunded and its officers were ill paid and poorly qualified for the job. Federal agents also struggled to work out lines of authority with local police and to penetrate relationships local police had with criminals and bootleggers. By the mid-1920s, the Bureau of Prohibition became a model of ineffective law enforcement (Potter, 1998). Although the federal government put on a show of getting tough on crime in the 1920s, it did not make a commitment to creating administrative structures necessary to do so.

Challenges to Local Policing

At the local level, police departments struggled to deal with changes in the populations that they policed in the late 1910s and 1920s. The slow migration of African Americans from rural areas in the South into urban areas and the North accelerated markedly beginning around 1916. The First World War created new demands for labor even as white workers were being drawn into the military, so employers opened positions to African Americans. As black migrants moved into cities, many white residents feared that they would compete with them for jobs, housing, space, and recreation. These conditions aggravated racial tensions and contributed to a series of race riots in East St. Louis in 1917, in Washington and in Chicago in 1919, and in Tulsa in 1921. Each riot followed a similar pattern. Whites assaulted blacks in response to a report of some violation of a racial boundary, blacks retaliated, and large-scale confrontations ensued in which whites attacked predominately black neighborhoods. In Chicago, when a 17-year-old African American crossed a line between white and black areas on a beach, whites assaulted him and he drowned. When police failed to arrest the white perpetrators, blacks attacked whites in retaliation. Whites responded with large-scale violence over six days in which 38 people were killed and over

500 injured. In these riots, police tended to take sides. In Chicago, over two-thirds of the people arrested were African American, yet so were three-quarters of those injured, suggesting that police apprehended black perpetrators but did little to protect black victims. Subsequent investigations of these riots tended to blame the slow and ineffective responses of police for allowing riots to continue for days (Walker, 1977; Wadman & Allison, 2004).

Several police departments—Detroit and Philadelphia prominent among them—that had embraced reform in the 1910s shifted to emphasizing tougher and more arbitrary crime control in the 1920s. This pattern suggests that trends toward professionalization were not linear stories of progress, and that reforms experienced unexpected reversals. The Detroit Police Department mounted a "general drive" to battle a perceived increase in crime in the early 1920s, putting every available officer (including clerical workers) on night duty. It also launched a campaign against men carrying concealed weapons in which officers shot 31 suspects in just the last three months of 1920, killing nine (Detroit Police Department 1921). The Philadelphia police, like those in Detroit, underwent a burst of reform in the 1910s. Between 1911 and 1915, a new city administration had established formal police training, implemented an efficient platoon system, and emphasized nonpartisan public service. Beginning in 1924, however, another Philadelphia police administration under the leadership of former Brigadier General Smedley Butler abolished training and formal procedures for determining promotion. He also encouraged crime control through arbitrary spasms of enforcement. Upon taking office, he ordered the police to eliminate vice in Philadelphia within 48 hours. Butler also organized a squad of officers with sawed-off shotguns to rush to scenes of armed robberies, reasoning that an effective approach to bandits was to "shoot a few of them and make arrests afterward" (Walker, 1977, p. 67).

Racial divisions also contributed to rough police justice in the 1920s. Investigations of race riots tended to be curiously mute on police-community relations. The Chicago Commission on Race Relations' report, *The Negro in Chicago* (1922), for example, offers a detailed sociological analysis of the city's African American community in the midst of the Great Migration, but devotes its discussion of policing to specific riot control techniques. Likewise, the IACP annual meetings and the major works on police administration such as the Detroit Police Department's 1917 annual report and Fosdick's *American Police Systems* (1920/1972) have almost nothing to say about race (Walker,

1977). Yet the issue of race was almost unavoidable in these years. As southern migrants moved into the cities of the North, the African American population of Detroit increased from approximately 5,000 in 1910 to 120,000 in 1930; the African American population of Chicago increased from approximately 44,000 in 1910 to 224,000 in 1930. According to one investigation of the Mayor's Interracial Committee (1926), arrest rates (per 1,000 people) in 1925 were more than two and a half times higher for African Americans than for whites. While this investigation—like most others of the time—foregrounded the assumption that African Americans committed more crimes than whites, it also cited anecdotal evidence that African Americans were more likely to be arrested and provided detailed examples of police harassment. In the 18 months from January 1925 through June 1926, a time when African Americans comprised less than 8% of Detroit's population, the Detroit police killed 25 African Americans and 24 whites.

Urban police of the 1920s were probably no more racially discriminatory than was the population as a whole, but their structures and practices embodied the racial dispositions of their time. The Detroit police coped with the massive growth of the city after the early twentieth-century establishment of the automobile industry with a massive expansion of the department. The Detroit Police Department opted not to hire African Americans—it employed only 14 black officers in 1925 out of 3,000 officers—but instead recruited from the white migrants also moving into the city from the South. The Ku Klux Klan—active nationwide in the 1910s and 1920s—had also established a presence in the Detroit Police Department. As a result, the police generally supported the racial status quo. This became a public controversy when in 1925, an African American physician, Dr. Ossian Sweet, purchased a house in a previously all-white neighborhood. Sweet requested police protection when white neighbors expressed anger, but the police did little to prevent a mob from gathering outside of Sweet's home soon after he and his family moved in. Someone inside the house fired guns into the crowd, killing one person and wounding another. At that point, the police burst into Sweet's home and arrested him for murder, along with family members and friends there with him. After one highly publicized trial ended in a mistrial, Sweet was eventually acquitted (Boyle, 2004). The episode emphasizes that racial discrimination did not solely involve disproportionate arrests or police violence; it also involved police support for existing arrangements and failure to provide equal protection.

The Dynamics of Reform

When police reform was effective in the 1920s, it tended to focus on crime control and administrative improvements. As often as not, pressure for change still came from outside of police departments, from business people and professionals concerned about social reform and about their cities being safe places to conduct trade. In Chicago, historian Mark Haller (1971) has argued, reformers had their greatest success when they accepted entrenched relationships between police, communities, political factions, and often, illegal enterprise. Antivice campaigns like that of the Committee of Fifteen tended to have limited impacts because they failed to break the connections between various interests. By contrast, reformers who aimed to improve police operations had somewhat more success. The Chicago Crime Commission, formed in 1919, sought to increase punishments and deter crimes against persons and property, goals the police generally shared. In particular, the Chicago Crime Commission and police department worked together to increase the size of the city's police force by 1,000 men in the 1920s. In 1929, a second organization comprised mainly of business leaders and academic scholars—the Citizen's Police Committee—formed with the goal of improving day-to-day operations of the Chicago police. This organization worked closely with the police commissioner to improve training, manage records better, and streamline administration.

In the period between roughly 1900 and 1930, police agencies pursued several disparate goals that did not necessarily mix well. The primary goal of maintaining public order was a given, and in the first three decades of the twentieth century, public order was increasingly defined in terms of crime control. The notion of professionalization suggested that police could do it all. They could effectively interact with their communities, operate as efficient business-like bureaucrats, provide social welfare for at-risk populations, investigate offenses effectively, and apprehend criminals. The reality was more complicated. The goals of administrative efficiency and social welfare reform, for example, often contradicted each other, suggesting police should simultaneously do less and do more. A focus on greater efficiency and social service sometimes helped investigate and prevent crime; but sometimes the immediate goal of responding to crimes or the visceral satisfaction of dealing roughly with criminals trumped these more professional approaches to law enforcement. And often the realities of policing a rapidly changing and urbanizing society—particularly racial and ethnic tensions and opportunities for corruption—complicated efforts to improve the quality of policing. The many goals of policing in this period—maintaining public order, controlling crime, achieving social reform, operating efficiently—did not correlate especially well. Neither, however, were these goals mutually exclusive. Police did achieve reform and professionalization in the early twentieth century, but they did so through often-unacknowledged trade-offs between the different outcomes they sought to achieve.

❖ REFERENCES

Adler, J. S. (2006). *First in violence, deepest in dirt: Homicide in Chicago, 1875-1920.* Cambridge, MA: Harvard University Press.

Appier, J. (1998). *Policing women: The sexual politics of law enforcement and the LAPD.* Philadelphia, PA: Temple University Press.

Barnard, H. (1958). *Independent man: The life of Senator James Couzens.* New York, NY: Scribner.

Boyle, K. (2004). *Arc of justice: A saga of race, civil rights, and murder in the jazz age.* New York, NY: Henry Holt.

Blum, H. (2008). *American lightning: Terror, mystery, the birth of Hollywood, and the crime of the century.* New York, NY: Crown.

Carte, G. E., & Carte, E. H. (1975). *Police reform in the United States: The era of August Vollmer, 1905-1932.* Berkeley: University of California Press.

Chicago Commission on Race Relations. (1922). *The negro in Chicago: A study in race relations and a race riot.* Chicago, IL: University of Chicago Press.

Dale, E. (2011). *Criminal justice in the United States, 1789-1939.* New York, NY: Cambridge University Press.

Detroit Police Department. (1917). *Story of the Detroit Police Department, 1916–17.* n.p.

Detroit Police Department. (1921). *Annual Report for the Year Ending December 31, 1920.* n.p.

Dulaney, W. M. (1996). *Black police in America.* Bloomington: Indiana University Press.

Fosdick, R. S. (1920/1972). *American police systems* (reprint). Montclair, NJ: Patterson Smith.

Fogelson, R. M. (1977). *Big-City police.* Cambridge, MA: Harvard University Press.

Friedman, L. M. (1993). *Crime and punishment in American history.* New York, NY: BasicBooks.

Friedman, L. M., & Percival, R. V. (1981). *The roots of justice: Crime and punishment in Alameda County, California, 1870–1910.* Chapel Hill: University of North Carolina Press.

Fuld, L. F. (1909). *Police administration.* New York, NY: G.P. Putnam's Sons.

Gage, B. (2009). *The day Wall Street exploded: A story of America in its first age of terror.* Oxford: Oxford University Press.

Haller, M. H. (1971). Civic reformers and police leadership: Chicago, 1905–1935. In H. Hahn (Ed.), *Police in urban society* (pp. 39-56). Beverly Hills, CA: Sage Publications.

Haller, M. H. (1976). Historical roots of police behavior: Chicago, 1890–1925. *Law and Society Review, 10*, 303-323.

Johnson, M. S. (2003). *Street justice: A history of police violence in New York City*. Boston, MA: Beacon Press.

Kohler, F. J. (1908, 1971). Arrests of first offenders. In *Proceedings of the Annual Conventions of the International Association of Chiefs of Police, 1906–1912* (Vol. 2). Presented at the International Association of Chiefs of Police, 15th Annual Session, Detroit, Michigan, June 2 to 5, 1908. Reprint, New York, NY: Arno Press and the *New York Times*.

Lacey, R. (1986). *Ford: The men and the machine*. Boston, MA: Little, Brown.

Lane, R. (1967). *Policing the city: Boston, 1822-1885*. Cambridge, MA: Harvard University Press.

Lane, R. (1997). *Murder in America: A history*. Columbus: Ohio State University Press.

Langum, D. J. (1994). *Crossing over the line: Legislating morality and the Mann Act*. Chicago, IL: University of Chicago Press.

Lindberg, R. (1998). *To Serve and collect: Chicago politics and police corruption from the Lager Beer Riot to the Summerdale Scandal*. Carbondale and Edwardsville: Southern Illinois University Press.

Liss, J., & Schlossman, S. L. (1984). The contours of crime prevention in August Vollmer's Berkeley. *Research in Law, Deviance, and Social Control, 16*, 79–107.

Mayor's Interracial Committee. (1926). *The Negro in Detroit*. Detroit, MI: Detroit Bureau of Governmental Research.

McGerr, M. E. (2003). *A fierce discontent: The rise and fall of the Progressive movement in America, 1870–1920*. New York, NY: Free Press.

Miller, W. R. (1999). *Cops and bobbies: Police authority in New York and London, 1830-1870* (2nd ed.). Columbus: Ohio State University Press.

Monkkonen, E. H. (1979). Municipal reports as an indicator source: The nineteenth-century police. *Historical Methods, 12*, 57–65.

Monkkonen, E. H. (1981a). A disorderly people? Urban order in the nineteenth and twentieth centuries. *Journal of American History, 68*, 539–559.

Monkkonen, E. H. (1981b). *Police in urban America, 1860-1920*. Cambridge, MA: Cambridge University Press.

Potter, C. B. (1998). *War on crime: Bandits, g-men, and the politics of mass culture*. New Brunswick, NJ: Rutgers University Press.

Powers, R. G. (1986). *Secrecy and power: The life of J. Edgar Hoover*. New York, NY: Free Press.

Ray, G. W. (1995). From cossack to trooper: Manliness, police reform, and the state. *Journal of Social History, 28*, 565–586.

Reed, R. (1992). *Regulating the regulators: Ideology and practice in the policing of Detroit, 1880–1920*. (Doctoral dissertation). The University of Michigan.

Schulz, D. M. (1995). *From social worker to crimefighter: Women in United States municipal policing*. Westport, CT: Praeger.

Shapiro, H. (1977). The McNamara case: A crisis of the progressive era. *Southern California Quarterly, 59*, 271–287.

Shoot to Kill Order is Given Police of City. (1929, December 4). *Pittsburgh Post-Gazette*.

Spillane, J. F. (2004). The road to the Harrison Narcotics Act: Drugs and their control, 1875-1918. In J. Erlen, & J. F. Spillane (Ed.), *Federal drug control: The evolution of policy and practice* (pp. 1–24). New York, NY: The Haworth Press.

Taylor, F. W. (1911). *The principles of scientific management*. New York, NY: Harper.

Thale, C. (2004). Assigned to patrol: Neighborhoods, police, and changing deployment practices in New York City before 1930. *Journal of Social History, 37*, 1037–1064.

Thale, C. (2007). The informal world of police patrol: New York City in the early twentieth century. *Journal of Urban History, 33*, 183–216.

Vollmer, A. (1919, 1971). The policeman as a social worker. Presented at the International Association of Chiefs of Police, Proceedings 26th Convention, New Orleans, Louisiana, April 14, 15, and 16, 1919. Reprint New York, N.Y: Arno Press and the *New York Times*.

von Hoffman, A. W. (1992). An officer of the neighborhood: A Boston patrolman on the beat in 1895. *Journal of Social History, 26*, 309–330.

Wadman, R. C., & Allison, W. T. (2004). *To protect and serve: A history of police in America*. Upper Saddle River, NJ: Pearson/Prentice Hall.

Walker, S. (1977). *A critical history of police reform: The emergence of professionalism*. Lexington, MA: Lexington Books.

Walker, S. (1998). *Popular justice: A history of American criminal justice* (2nd ed.). New York, NY: Oxford University Press.

Watts, E. J. (1981). Police priorities in twentieth-century St. Louis. *Journal of Social History, 14*, 649–673.

Watts, E. J. (1983). Police response to crime and disorder in twentieth-century St. Louis. *Journal of American History, 70*, 340–348.

Wells, A. S. (1913). Women on the police force. *American City, 8*, 401.

Wilson, J. Q. (1968). *Varieties of police behavior: The management of law and order in eight communities*. Cambridge, MA: Harvard University Press.

Wolcott, D. B. (2005). *Cops and kids: Policing juvenile delinquency in urban America, 1890–1940*. Columbus: Ohio State University Press.

Woods, A. (1918). *Crime prevention*. Princeton, NJ: Princeton University Press.

3

Progressivism and the Courts, 1890s–1920s

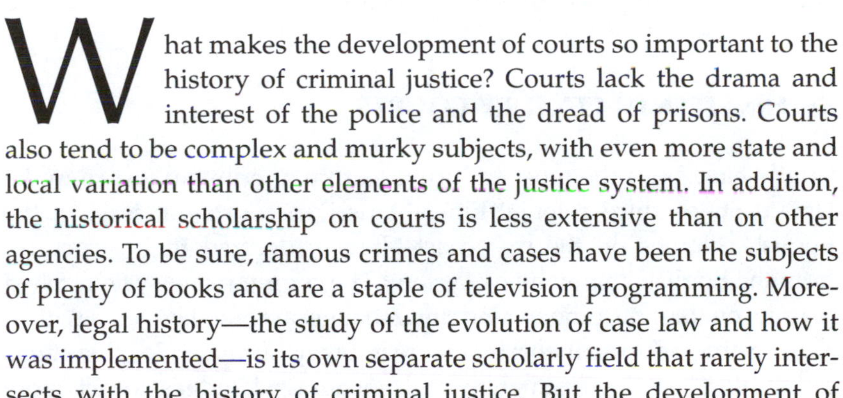

What makes the development of courts so important to the history of criminal justice? Courts lack the drama and interest of the police and the dread of prisons. Courts also tend to be complex and murky subjects, with even more state and local variation than other elements of the justice system. In addition, the historical scholarship on courts is less extensive than on other agencies. To be sure, famous crimes and cases have been the subjects of plenty of books and are a staple of television programming. Moreover, legal history—the study of the evolution of case law and how it was implemented—is its own separate scholarly field that rarely intersects with the history of criminal justice. But the development of courts as institutions—and in particular the role of courts in criminal justice —has been comparatively neglected.

Courts, however, represent the lynchpin of the justice system. They are the institutions where decisions are most explicitly and most publicly made. Furthermore, as with police, courts experienced a profound transformation between the 1890s and the 1920s, a period that historians often call the Progressive Era. More so than any other criminal justice agency, courts assumed their modern forms in the early twentieth century. This chapter analyzes the changes in courts as institutions. In the nineteenth century, courts tended to be casual organizations staffed part-time. They represented the authority of the law but were highly informal in their practices. In the last decades of the nineteenth century, however, courts became more extensive, more bureaucratic, and more professional. By the twentieth century, new concepts that courts could not only dispense justice but also achieve social reform had a profound impact. Juvenile courts—first created at the turn of the twentieth century—manifested these new ideas most obviously, but criminal courts reflected them as well.

Of course this pattern of development was highly uneven, varying from place to place and court to court. A punitive impulse also shaped the functioning of courts and at times held sway over enthusiasm for reform. This chapter, however, tends to focus on innovative courts that were in the vanguard of change. These courts were probably exceptions to the general practices, but they were important exceptions because their models and ideals gradually diffused to courts elsewhere, encouraging a slow process of change nationwide. Even as overt support for reform declined in the wake of World War One and increased concern about crime, many elements that had represented innovations in the early years of the twentieth century gradually became standard procedures by the 1920s.

❖ NINETEENTH-CENTURY COURTS

Courts have been the most enduring feature of criminal justice in the United States since colonial times. American courts—at least in the English colonies on the east coast—largely derived their structures from the English common law system. The common law system relied mainly on oral testimony and interchange among lawyers, with a judge acting as a mediator; by contrast, other European legal systems relied more on documentation and encouraged judges to act more inquisitorially. The English common law relied on juries more often than judges to make decisions about guilt or innocence. By the nineteenth century, courts in the United States typically operated at the county level of government. Like the police, they had a wide range of functions, potentially dealing with criminal cases (prosecutions by the state) and civil cases (disputes between private parties) as well as other functions like tax collecting. Depending on state and local law, judges could be either appointed by governors or elected by citizens (Friedman, 1993; Walker, 1998).

As cities grew in the nineteenth century, they developed ad hoc solutions to the resulting greater demands on courts. They evolved a minor judiciary centered on local elected officials such as aldermen. In 1854, Philadelphia had over 50 aldermen, each of whom operated their own low-level court. These courts received cases not from police—who barely existed in the first half of the nineteenth century—but from city residents who brought forward cases both civil and criminal, ranging in the words of historian Allen Steinberg (1989) "from marriage to murder" (p. 17). Ordinary people took their concerns and disputes to aldermen and for a fee the aldermen dispensed justice. This arrangement allowed people to mobilize the power of the law to pursue their own interests, to ensure that their private conflicts as well as their public complaints that they had been victims of crime would be addressed in court. Constables attached to each alderman served summons and warrants to make sure the opposing parties appeared as well. The ensuing hearings often became popular spectator events, as audiences streamed into offices and courtrooms to witness the confrontations. Alderman had the authority to hand out basic dispositions, particularly in civil cases and minor criminal complaints. If the alderman determined that further action was necessary, the case would be returned to the more official courts of record. This system of private prosecutions initiated the majority of criminal cases in Philadelphia County (Steinberg, 1989).

In the latter half of the nineteenth century, the increased importance of other players in the justice system reduced private prosecutions. In Philadelphia, the police established relationships with the aldermen after the 1850 consolidation of the force. This tended to bring a new flow of cases into the aldermen's courts and reduce the need for private prosecutions. In addition, court systems became more formalized. Philadelphia abolished the office of alderman and its fee-for-service approach to justice in 1874 in favor of new magistrate courts to hear low-level cases. Finally, public prosecutors—often known as district attorneys and generally elected by voters—assumed greater importance. At least nominally responsible for pursuing criminal cases, prosecutors' offices gradually evolved into major drivers in the justice system, embodying the sense that crimes were offenses against the state rather than against individuals (Friedman & Percival, 1981; Steinberg, 1989; Walker, 1998).

❖ THE CRIMINAL JUSTICE WEDDING CAKE

By the end of nineteenth century, court systems assumed a pyramidal hierarchy. This hierarchy contributed to a criminal justice system that can be imagined as a wedding cake with multiple layers. The bottom layer was the justice courts or police courts (also sometimes called magistrates, justices of the peace, or a variety of other names) that handled the most basic civil and criminal cases. The middle layer consisted of more formal criminal courts, handling felonies and the more serious cases and following more thorough procedures. In Alameda County (Oakland), California—one of the very few historical court systems studied intensively and hence a focal point in this chapter—the Superior Court represented the main criminal court, hearing all felony cases. And the top layer consisted of the appeals courts that resolved ongoing disputes. In California, the Supreme Court heard all appeals coming out of county-level Superior Courts (Friedman & Percival, 1981; Friedman, 1993).

The bottom layer of the justice system dealt with the large majority of criminal cases. In Alameda County, between 1872 and 1910, after people were arrested (most often for misdemeanors offenses like drunkenness or disorderly conduct), they would typically be held in jail until they appeared before a magistrate or judge of the police court. Over 90% of people arrested for misdemeanors were prosecuted (Friedman & Percival, 1981, p. 113–117). In late-nineteenth-century Chicago, justices of the peace similarly decided low-level cases including misdemeanors with a fine less than $200, assaults, and violations of local ordinances. These justice courts, derisively called "justice shops," continued to charge fees for each service they provided. If the justice found evidence of a more serious crime, the case would be bound over to the grand jury of the Cook County Criminal Court. In reality, however, the vast majority of criminal cases—96% in 1890—were decided in justice courts (Willrich, 2003). The processing of misdemeanors in magistrates' courts tended to be quick and dirty. In Oakland in 1880 and 1881, nearly all defendants prosecuted in magistrates' courts had their cases heard on the day of arrest or on the following one. Trials, particularly for minor offenses, could last just moments. Charges would be read, pleas entered, a few words exchanged, and verdicts rendered. Typically people convicted of misdemeanors had the choice of paying a fine or spending a few days in jail; most ended up serving time because they had no money to pay (Friedman & Percival, 1981).

Procedures in the middle layer, felony cases in the criminal courts, were more elaborate. In turn-of-the-twentieth-century Alameda County, cases typically began with victims or witnesses or police filing complaints with magistrates. If the accused was not already in custody, the magistrate could issue an arrest warrant and then conduct a preliminary arraignment, informing the accused of the charges against them and of his or her right to an attorney. During the preliminary stages, however, accused individuals were on their own to find legal representation; the state would only pay for a defense attorney if the case reached a trial. Next, the same judge or magistrate who conducted the arraignment would conduct a preliminary examination to determine if the case should go forward for trial. This stage offered a variety of means by which defendants could avoid felony prosecution—outright dismissals, court discharges, reduction of charges to misdemeanor—but as often as not the case proceeded. If so, the magistrate would bind over the case to the Superior Court. At trial, if defendants could not afford an attorney, the court would appoint one. At this time, however, counties and states did not maintain public defenders. Instead, courts appointed counsel from local criminal defense attorneys (Friedman & Percival, 1981).

Actual trial procedures in Superior Court closely paralleled those today, although the due process protections were far less extensive. Defendants entered pleas, sometimes bargaining for lesser sentences, sometimes accepting guilt in hopes of easy treatment, sometimes declaring themselves not guilty. In this last instance—about 43% in Alameda County between 1880 and 1910, more often with more serious charges—the case went to a jury trial. And there, after prosecutors and defense attorneys presented their cases and the judge issued instructions, a jury of 12 men would render a verdict of guilt or innocence. Or they would sometimes fail to reach a verdict, in which case the prosecutor decided whether to try again. As is still true today, the process offered numerous points where a case could be stalled and defendants could find themselves free. At the same time, the odds were stacked against the poor and ill-prepared men who made up the bulk of defendants and could not pay for bail or private legal representation. For them, the chances of being found guilty increased significantly (Friedman & Percival, 1981).

Defense attorneys, judges, and prosecutors together formed the core of what would today be called courtroom work groups that allowed a more streamlined processing of cases. These structural changes seem to have contributed to a gradual decline in trials by jury in the late nineteenth century and permitted a certain amount of plea bargaining. Because it is based on personal agreements, plea bargaining is difficult to detect in historical records, but in Alameda County between 1880 and 1910 it is evident in the fact that 14% of defendants changed their pleas from not guilty to guilty. In many cases, defendants would plead guilty to a lesser offense in exchange for a lighter sentence. Just as one example, in 1880, Albert McKenzie was charged with embezzling $52.50 from his employer, a felony. After he, his attorney, and the district attorney all appeared in court, he changed his plea to guilty of embezzling less than $50, a misdemeanor. The court accepted the plea, and issued a light sentence. In the interest of a conviction, all parties—defense attorney, prosecutor, judge—accepted the convenient fiction that McKenzie had stolen an amount below the threshold that would make the crime a felony (Friedman, 1993; Friedman & Percival, 1981).

Most trials remained fairly obscure, but sometimes the criminal justice wedding cake was decorated with spectacular trials that generated enormous public attention. These trials taught the public how the legal system worked. Sometimes the offense was especially lurid; sometimes the victim or suspect was well known or capable of capturing public imagination; sometimes these cases highlighted issues percolating in the culture of the time. The 1893 murder trial of Lizzie Borden became the most famous trial in U.S. history until the contemporary media age because it exemplified all of these factors. On August 4, 1892, Andrew Borden, a prominent banker in Fall River, Massachusetts, and his wife were both found murdered in their home by multiple blows with an axe. Suspicion immediately fell upon the Borden's adult daughter Lizzie, who was apparently at home with them at the time of the killings. The unique violence of the case and Andrew Borden's local stature generated a good deal of attention, but the fact that the only real suspect was a 32-year-old unmarried woman active in social reform movements attracted national press coverage. At a time when gender standards were changing sharply, Lizzie Borden's lawyers successfully played upon ingrained ideas that a woman—especially a middle-class white woman—was not capable of such a crime. In the end, they won their client an acquittal. Trials like Borden's often became less about the evidence than about the theater of the event. Whichever side could construct a more convincing narrative—one that drew on the conventional moral ideas of the time—tended to win (Friedman, 1993, p. 252–254; Nickerson, 1999).

Appeals represented the top layer of the wedding cake structure of the court system. If defendants lost, they had to right to appeal to a higher court. Alameda County Superior Court cases were appealed to the Supreme Court of California. State prosecutors, by contrast, could not appeal a not guilty verdict; they could only appeal narrow procedural rulings. Appeals were quite rare, roughly three per year from Alameda County between 1880 and 1910, although more frequent the more serious the conviction and the sentence. One reason appeals were rare is that retaining an attorney to mount an appeal was expensive, and few convicts had the resources to do so. Another reason was that grounds for appeal were fairly narrow. Appellants had to convince the

Supreme Court that a mistake had been made in the criminal conviction, most often that evidence had been improperly admitted or excluded or that the trial judge's instructions to the jury had been in error. Appellants also rarely succeeded. When the Supreme Court finally heard their cases, only about one in four defendants won. Even then victory did not mean that the defendant went free, although the odds were improved greatly. In about two-thirds of cases, the Supreme Court ordered a new trial, and the prosecutor decided whether to pursue the case again. The appeals process, at least in turn-of-the-century California, offered a narrow opening through which a few defendants escaped and a few mistakes were corrected, but as a whole it very rarely overturned the decisions made in criminal courts (Friedman & Percival, 1981).

❖ CHANGES IN THE COURTS

Courts, like police, experienced a gradual process of reform and professionalization in the late nineteenth and early twentieth centuries. Explicit efforts to reform the courts emerged from Progressive Era endeavors to consolidate and professionalize city government. In Chicago, the fee-based system of justices of the peace faced increasing criticism in the late nineteenth and early twentieth centuries. Many Chicago lawyers criticized the existence of fees as a source of corruption. To some extent, this represented the efforts of elite attorneys seeking to establish professional standards for their occupation by marginalizing the newcomers who often occupied the local courts, but it also represented real concern that low-income Chicagoans did not have the same access to justice as did the more affluent. Reformers also criticized the justice of the peace system as favoring litigants with political influence. Finally, reformers argued that the decentralized nature of the justices of the peace invited abuses, as litigants sometimes went to the justices of the peace most likely to grant them a favorable outcome. As an alternative, a committee of leading Chicago reformers—political leaders, judges, attorneys, business people—drafted a new law to replace the justices of the peace with a more centralized judicial system. This plan introduced a more professional bureaucratic structure to the judiciary and was ultimately passed in 1905 (Willrich, 2003).

Efforts to reform the court system were also rooted in a larger intellectual debate over the nature of crime. The basic question was whether criminal offenders were free agents who made choices for themselves, or whether they were products of their social conditions. U.S. criminal law had been rooted in the notion that individuals were rational actors who decided between right and wrong. This assumption, however, faced a series of challenges in the late nineteenth and early twentieth centuries (Willrich, 2003). Biological or hereditary theories of crime, ideas that criminal behaviors resulted in part from physical or innate differences, first challenged the rational-actor model in the late nineteenth century. Richard L. Dugdale's 1877 best-selling study, *"The Jukes": A Study in Crime, Pauperism, Disease, and Heredity*, introduced American readers to an inbred rural clan of over 1,200 offenders and provided a popular image for the nascent eugenics movement. By the 1890s, the work of Italian criminologist Cesare Lombroso inspired a new intellectual discipline in the United States of "criminal anthropology." These thinkers argued that a criminal class existed, physically and psychologically different from other people. For many of these thinkers, bad heredity led to mental weakness and moral failings (Rafter, 1997).

Ideas that factors in the social environment contributed to crime also challenged assumptions of individual responsibility. By the turn of the twentieth century, charity activists, social workers, and some criminologists routinely cited drunkenness, parental neglect, poor education, poor housing, and child labor as sources of crime, particularly among young offenders. This line of argument suggested that society, more so than individuals, was responsible for crime. As University of Chicago sociologist Albion Small told the Chicago Congregational Club in 1900, "We are making or maintaining the conditions that will predispose people to be better or worse. . . . Our cities are vast machines for producing conditions favorable to crime" (quoted in Willrich 2003, p. 85). This focus on social responsibility implied that reformers could address the problems of crime by intervening in social conditions that produced it or by providing individual treatment—rather than punishment—to offenders.

❖ THE EMERGENCE OF JUVENILE JUSTICE

Juvenile courts exemplify efforts by activists to remake the court system to protect the youngest, most vulnerable offenders and to use the courts to implement social reforms. Juvenile courts also exemplify the professionalization of court personnel. Established first in Cook County, Illinois (Chicago) in 1899, and in most other cites by 1910, juvenile courts were conceived as helping, rather than punitive, institutions. For their advocates, juvenile courts offered, at minimum, a solution to a pressing problem in criminal justice and, for their most ardent supporters, a panacea for many of the ills of urban life. They also represent a bridge that helps connect nineteenth-century courts with new types of courts that emerged in the early twentieth-century Progressive Era.

Separate criminal justice institutions for young offenders existed long before juvenile courts. These were established based on a loose assumption that children were somehow different from adults, less responsible for their actions and more amenable to reform. In the midst of rapid urban growth in the early nineteenth century, reformers concerned about poverty among working-class youth and dissatisfied with existing poorhouses sought to create new institutions to address these problems. The New York Society for the Prevention of Pauperism renamed itself the Society for the Reformation of Juvenile Delinquents, obtained a charter from the state of New York, and in 1825 opened the New York House of Refuge. This was the first reform school for young offenders. Reformers elsewhere followed a similar process and opened the Boston House of Reformation in 1826 and the Philadelphia House of Refuge in 1828. These institutions took in children—typically between ages 10 and 16, mostly boys but some girls held separately—not only for criminal offenses but also for poverty, vagrancy, or other conditions that were thought to lead to crime. Refuge managers sought to rehabilitate their inmates through a strictly scheduled regimen of prayer, work, and schooling. They ultimately released their charges to apprenticeships. All this was intended simultaneously to establish the authority of the refuge as a substitute parent and to prepare the inmates to earn a living on their own (Bernard, 1992; Mennel, 1973).

Separate protective legal procedures for children were based on the doctrine of *parens patrie*, a rule allowing the state to intervene on behalf of children if authorities determine them to be at risk. *Parens patrie* was incorporated in U.S. case law through the Pennsylvania Supreme Court case *Ex Parte Crouse* in 1838. After Mary Ann Crouse was institutionalized in the Philadelphia House of Refuge as a potential pauper, her father sued to have her released on the grounds of habeas corpus, that she was being held without being convicted of a crime. The Pennsylvania Supreme Court, however, ruled against Crouse, arguing that inmates were being taught morality and religion, being trained to earn their own livelihood, and in essence being helped rather than punished. The case established a legal precedent that juvenile justice institutions did not need to follow strict rules of due process because they operated for the benefit of young people (Bernard, 1992; Schlossman, 1977).

Over the course of the nineteenth century, institutions for juvenile offenders became more common. They tended to develop along several different tracks. At one extreme were congregate reform schools, in which large numbers of inmates—usually boys—were housed together in one facility and taught manual trades. By the second half of the century, states more often than charitable organizations operated reform schools. They also occasionally operated reform schools for girls; the first, the Massachusetts State Industrial School for Girls at Lancaster opened in 1856. The tendency to call these institutions "industrial schools" highlighted their orientation toward teaching young offenders manual trades. At the other extreme, charitable agencies created new, purely noninstitutional mechanisms to help children they viewed as being at risk—not necessarily ones who had committed crimes but those who were growing up in poverty. They would recruit urban children, transport them out of the cities, and place them in apprenticeships with rural families, expecting the experience to separate them from the corruption of cities and teach them job skills and the value of hard work. The most famous of these "placing out" agencies, the New York Children's Aid Society, founded in 1849, relocated over 90,000 young people by 1890. Between these two extremes were hybrid institutions, such as reform schools built as small cottages to emulate a family and agencies that combined temporary institutionalization with placements in apprenticeships (Gish, 1999; Mennel, 1973; Schlossman, 1977; Schlossman, 1998; Schneider, 1992).

These institutions, however, did not cleanly segregate young offenders from the criminal justice system. In the late nineteenth century, children were still treated much the same way as adults under criminal law. They were subject to the same criminal codes, tried in criminal courts, and detained prior to hearings and sentences in police lock-ups together with adults. After sentencing, young offenders could find themselves in reform schools or other juvenile institutions, but they could also find themselves in adult prisons or jails. The number of reform schools grew in the second half of the nineteenth century, but still in 1890 fewer than 60 operated nationwide. And while roughly 9,000 boys ages 16 and under were institutionalized in reform schools in 1890, at least 2,000 were in state prisons and county jails, and many more awaited trial in local jails and police lock-ups (Wolcott, 2005, p. 16–18). Chicago social reformer Timothy Hurley (1907) opined that "Before the bar of a criminal court there was no difference, from the viewpoint of the law, between the adult and the infant." In his view, jails and prisons where young people mixed with adults were "so many hatcheries for criminals" (p. 9–11).

The case of Charley Miller, a.k.a. "Kansas Charley," brought national attention to the treatment of young offenders. Miller, a teenage veteran of "placing out" agencies, travelled the country as a stowaway on train freight cars. In 1890 in Wyoming, at age 15, he shot to death two other young men travelling with him. He was arrested and, after a three-day trial, convicted and sentenced to hang. The decision to execute a boy so young, however, elicited widespread public sympathy, letter-writing campaigns from social reform organizations requesting clemency, and questions about the placement agencies that dealt with him when he was younger. Despite the controversy, the state of Wyoming proceeded with his execution in 1892, when Miller was still only 17 (Brumberg, 2003).

By the 1890s, social reformers became increasingly worried about young people in criminal courts and jails. One solution was diverting juvenile offenders to other institutions. In 1893, for example, the Chicago Woman's Club marshaled the concerns of sociologists and corrections officials to convince the Chicago Board of Education to assume responsibility for boys under age 17 committed to the city's jail. The Board of Education opened a separate facility—named the John Worthy School in 1897—to teach both truants and youths accused of crime. Eventually it also offered juvenile detention facilities apart from the city jail (Platt, 1977). Furthermore, police and judges in the 1890s used their own discretion to informally divert young offenders away from criminal courts and corrections facilities. The Detroit police, for example, disposed of a significantly larger percentage of juvenile arrests prior to court hearings than they did adult arrests. And when kids' cases did go to court, these cases were less likely than adults to result in jail sentences and often led to placement in institutions for juveniles (Wolcott, 2005).

Informal diversion, however, did not satisfy social reformers, who sought greater authority for the professional and the expert. In Chicago, a diverse network of social reformers sprang up in the 1890s around the idea that separate courts should be created for juveniles. The Chicago Woman's Club brought together both society matrons and younger female activists to advocate for this cause. These women worked alongside Catholic and Protestant charities and lawyers from the Chicago Bar Association. These disparate groups shared certain common beliefs. They discounted the hereditary theories common at the time that biological factors drove delinquency. Instead they saw the sources of delinquency in factors in the social environment, especially poverty, unemployment, bad housing, and inattentive parenting. They also embraced the social scientific disciplines emerging in their day and believed that through careful observation and analysis, the particular factors contributing to delinquency could be identified and solutions developed. Finally, they believed deeply in the ability of the government to solve social problems, thinking that governments had both the responsibility and the ability to address issues like delinquency (Getis, 2000; Tanenhaus, 2004).

❖ EARLY JUVENILE COURTS

The first law establishing a separate juvenile court—covering Cook County (Chicago), Illinois—passed the Illinois General Assembly in spring 1899 and went into effect on July 1. Reformers elsewhere developed parallel ideas or latched onto the model of the Cook County Juvenile Court, and almost every state adopted some sort of provision for a juvenile court by 1920. The Cook County Juvenile Court, however, was the seminal institution, most closely studied by sociologists at the time and by historians since. As defined in the original law, the Cook County Juvenile Court had jurisdiction over children under age 16 who had violated city or state laws (delinquents) or who were destitute, homeless, abandoned, or without parental care (dependents). Also under the court's jurisdiction were status offenses, behaviors somewhere between delinquency and dependency such as truancy or incorrigibility that were mainly defined by the status of being a juvenile. As the law was originally written, any person could petition the court about a child, and the court would send a probation officer to investigate. With this information, a judge would decide the case, choosing among a number of options, including putting children under the supervision of probation officers, placing children in other homes, or sentencing children to reformatories or industrial schools. At all stages, the official procedure was relatively informal. Because the juvenile court defined itself as helping, rather than punishing, children, it did not adhere to strict constitutional provisions for due process (Getis, 2000; Tanenhaus, 2004).

What made juvenile courts different from other courts? Most obviously, once they were established, they diverted the vast majority of young offenders from criminal courts (Zimring, 2002). But historian Steven Schlossman (1977, p. 58–62) points to four more subtle elements. First, juvenile courts introduced preventive and diagnostic functions into court hearings. Juvenile courts sought explicitly to understand and to treat the sources of children's delinquency and dependency. Second, juvenile courts created wholly separate detention facilities for children and youth. Third, many juvenile courts had the authority to hold adults responsible for contributing to children's misbehavior. And fourth, juvenile courts dramatically expanded the use of probation; probation officers represented juvenile courts' main tools for treating delinquency. While some scholars (Platt, 1977; Sheldon & Osbourne, 1989) have critiqued juvenile courts as mechanisms of control that invented new categories of delinquency and expanded the reach of criminal justice, others (Getis, 2000; Tanenhaus, 2004) have suggested that the emergence of juvenile courts might better be understood in terms of building the mechanisms of a modern government or state. Like other state-building processes taking place during the Progressive Era, the development of juvenile courts drew in particular on faith in new social sciences to diagnose social problems and in government to provide means of addressing them. It also, as we shall see later, drew on particular assumptions about gender roles common at this time.

It is tempting to assume that juvenile courts emerged fully developed, but, as historian David Tanenhaus (2004) emphasizes, they were very much works in progress in their early years. The new courts needed to balance their ideals with the practical limitations they faced. The first key element they had to address was finding the right judge. Although not part of the conscious design of juvenile courts, the leading early juvenile court judges—men like Richard Tuthill in Chicago and Ben B. Lindsey in Denver—emphasized a very personal, almost avuncular, approach to disciplining young offenders. Tuthill, for example, would quiz the boys before him as well as the police officers or citizens who brought them in not only about the alleged offense but also about the suspect's home and family life. Tuthill, like many early juvenile court advocates, embraced the notion that crime and delinquency resulted mainly from the social environment rather than innate depravity or personal choice. When asked about "born criminals," Tuthill rejected the notion. He declared, "Stuff! There are no born criminals. If I believed that, I should lose my faith in God. Society makes criminals; environment and education make criminals, but they are not born so" (*Chicago Tribune*, 1899). Likewise, Ben Lindsey, who also began operating a juvenile court in Denver in 1899, exemplified friendly intervention in children's lives. He declared that juvenile courts "would take care of these children in adolescence, when character is plastic and can be molded as clay in the potter's hands" (Lindsey 1904, p. 31). Like Tuthill, Lindsey presented his methods as eschewing formal courtroom confrontations in favor of offering young offenders personal guidance. Lindsey explained that, "I delight in knowing all of these boys, and becoming to a certain extent, very companionable with them. It has not been in the court room that I have learned most, but around my table in

Judge Ben B. Lindsey meets with boys in his chambers sometime between 1910 and 1915. The environment more closely resembles a family dinner table than a court hearing.

Source: Courtesy of the Library of Congress, LC-USZ62-127585.

chambers, or in long walks in the city with some of the boys" (Lindsey 1905, p. 352).

In many cases private efforts—largely by women's organizations—supplemented the work of juvenile courts. These groups frequently initiated services with the expectation that local governments would eventually assume responsibility for them. For example, the Chicago Woman's Club spun off a separate organization, the Juvenile Court Committee (JCC), to help the court operate. It paid the salaries of 15 probation officers, operated a detention home, and transported children to and from court in an aging omnibus. A lack of probation officers represented a major hurdle for early juvenile courts. Although probation was central to juvenile court design, the initial laws in Illinois and elsewhere did not provide for paid probation officers. As a result, courts had to rely on volunteers or privately funded workers who faced enormous caseloads. Only in 1905 did Illinois change its laws to pay probation officers, and only gradually did governments assume this function. In 1907, the JCC still paid seven probation officers while the county paid 23. The Chicago Police Department also assigned men to probation work. By 1911, private agencies had ceased to fund probation work, while Cook County supported 30 male and three female probation officers, and the police department tasked 30 officers with probation work (Getis, 2000; Mennel, 1973; Tanenhaus, 2004). Other key elements of juvenile court work also emerged as add-ons to the original model. Seeking to handle enormous caseloads in the early years of the Cook County Juvenile Court, Judge Julian Mack developed a complaint system in which police and probation officers investigated and screened cases, bringing to court only those cases that seemed to truly warrant its attention. By the 1920s, police probation officers resolved over 85% of complaints they investigated on their own; only a small minority of suspected juvenile offenders ever reached juvenile court (Tanenhaus, 2004; Wolcott, 2005).

In some cases, early juvenile courts had to fight for their political survival. On the one hand, court challenges reinforced the core principle of *parens patrie*. The Pennsylvania Supreme Court found in *Commonwealth* v. *Fisher* (1905)—a habeas corpus challenge to the detention of 14-year-old Frank Fisher in the Pennsylvania House of Refuge for larceny—that the juvenile court had the authority to institutionalize young offenders. Moreover, the Pennsylvania Supreme Court ruled that the good intentions and treatment functions of juvenile courts outweighed the need for formal due process (Bernard, 1992; Schlossman, 1977). On the other hand, juvenile courts still met resistance in practice. The Michigan Supreme Court ruled that state's initial 1905 juvenile court law to be an unconstitutional delegation of judicial powers before it eventually accepted a scaled-back version in 1907 (Wolcott, 2005). The groundbreaking Cook County Juvenile Court faced a series of political challenges in the 1910s. The fact that the juvenile court increased the power of the state over children and families created the basis for more outlandish charges that the court sold children into slavery and led to a series of highly charged investigations in 1911 and 1912. Later, in 1917, political opponents on the Cook County Board of Commissioners convinced a Superior Court judge to issue an injunction to halt the payment of all juvenile court employees' salaries. The court only survived through the efforts of Chicago philanthropists and the legal community to ensure that employees would be paid until the injunction was overturned (Tanenhaus, 2004).

The work of juvenile courts was divided between dependency cases and delinquency cases. The dependency cases involved children of all ages, both boys and girls. Through these cases, juvenile courts administered social welfare services, either providing guidance for families or in some cases removing children from homes in order to care for them in institutions (Tanenhaus, 2004). The delinquency cases focused largely on teenage boys, often of immigrant backgrounds, accused of minor crimes or status offenses. Again, Chicago is a representative example. In the first 10 years of the Cook County Juvenile Court's operation, between 1899 and 1909, approximately 80% of its delinquency cases involved boys. Of these boys, over 93% were between ages 10 and 16. In the ethnic melting pot of turn-of-the-century Chicago, roughly 17% were characterized as "white" (native-born) and 4% as "colored" (African American), but the large majority were listed as foreign-born or children of foreign-born parents, most often German, Irish, or Polish. Roughly 50% appeared in court for stealing (see Figure 3.1); they were accused of offenses like stealing from trains, stealing junk, or shoplifting, typically crimes of opportunity in which they grabbed what was available. The remaining boys were charged with offenses such as incorrigibility, disorderly conduct, and malicious mischief (Breckinridge & Abbott

Figure 3.1 Delinquent Boys Brought to the Cook County Juvenile Court, 1899 to 1909, by Offense

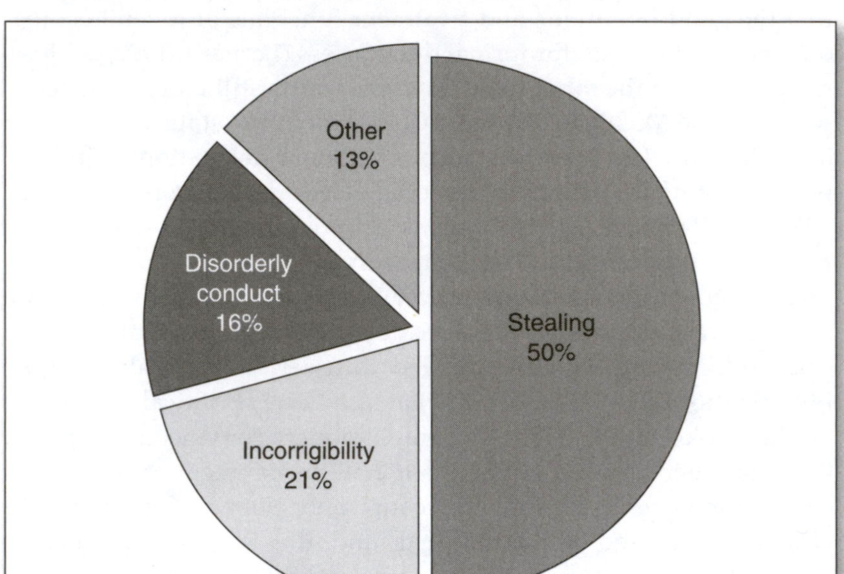

Source: Breckinridge & Abbott , 1912/1970, p. 28.

1912/1970). The Chicago court, however, did not always assert its jurisdiction over young offenders. It tacitly allowed the Illinois State's Attorney to prosecute a small number of the most serious cases—those involving violent crimes or crimes committed while on probation—in criminal courts. This process of passive transfer insulated the juvenile court from political criticism that it was soft on crime (Tanenhaus, 2000; Tanenhaus, 2004).

For boys whose cases were heard in juvenile courts in the early twentieth century, the most likely outcome was probation. In Chicago from 1899 to 1909, the juvenile court placed 59% of defendants on probation; it committed roughly 21% of defendants to institutions, dismissed about 17% of cases, and resolved the remaining 3% of cases in other fashions (see Figure 3.2; Breckinridge & Abbott 1912/1970, p. 40). Similar patterns characterized other cities, such as Milwaukee. There, probation represented approximately 66% of dispositions between 1908 and 1914, despite caseloads for individual probation officers ranging from 100 to 300. A closer look at court cases in Milwaukee—made possible by case files and transcripts—reveals that many decisions about dispositions were based on judges' perceptions of underlying causes of delinquency and what occurred in court rooms, not so much on actual offenses. Sometimes children's visible displays of contrition and servility won them probation or dismissal. In other cases, parents' assertions of their rights to discipline their children themselves earned judges' ire and landed their children in institutions. Historian Steven Schlossman (1977) argued that, despite its positive rhetoric, the Milwaukee court relied mainly on intimidation, threats, and short-term detention to correct young offenders. Race could further complicate dispositions for young offenders. In Chicago, many private institutions and families that took in probationers refused to accept African Americans. As a result, the juvenile court found itself committing black boys—both delinquent and dependent—to the state reform school sooner and for lesser issues than it would children of other ethnicities (Tanenhaus, 2004).

Figure 3.2 Disposition of Boys' Cases Brought to the Cook County Juvenile Court, 1899 to 1909

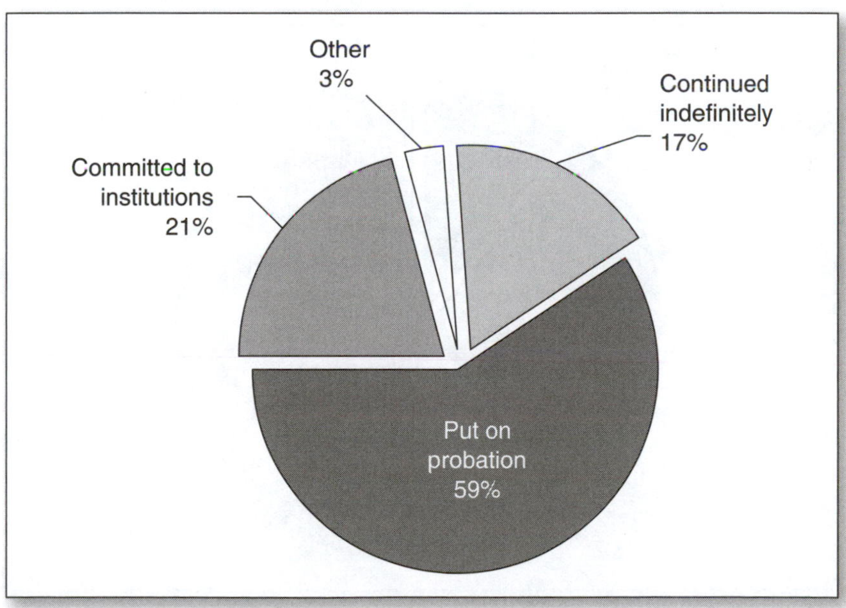

Source: Breckinridge & Abbott 1912/1970, p. 40.

Gender also determined the ways that juvenile courts treated young offenders. In contrast to their approaches to boys, Progressive Era social reformers and juvenile courts concerned themselves deeply with precocious sexuality among teenage girls (Alexander, 1995; Knupfer, 2001; Myers, 2006; Odem, 1995; Schlossman & Wallach, 1978). Of the girls brought before the Cook County Juvenile Court between 1899 and 1909, 43% were charged with incorrigibility (see Figure 3.3). For girls in this context, incorrigibility meant behaviors associated with sexuality: staying away from home, going to "tough" dances, associating with "vicious" persons or a "rough crowd of boys," or remaining out all night. Another 31% were charged with immorality, which meant that official had found girls in houses of prostitution or "low" rooming houses used for sexual liaisons (Breckinridge & Abbott, 1912/1970, p. 35–38). Likewise, in 1920, the Los Angeles County Juvenile Court charged 81% of girls brought before the court with moral or sexual offenses (Odem, 1995, p. 136).

Figure 3.3 Delinquent Girls Brought to Cook County Juvenile Court, 1899 to 1909, by Offense

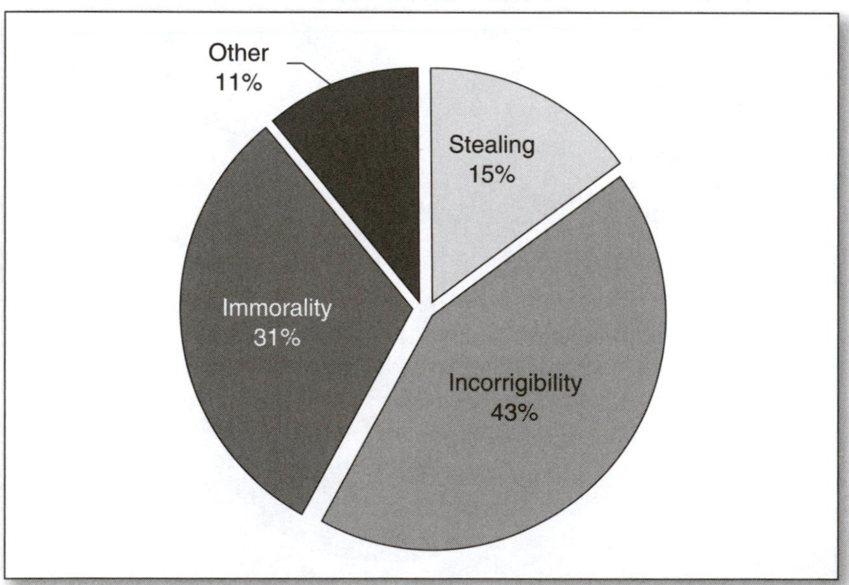

Source: Breckinridge & Abbott, 1912/1970, p. 36.

This pattern emerged from the confluence of new concerns about adolescent female sexuality and new efforts by female social reformers to regulate it. In the eyes of social activists, the greater autonomy for girls and young women that the growth of cities provided also created new risks. In this context, female social reformers acknowledged girls' sexual agency but also sought to provide institutional structures that would protect them from potentially harmful consequences—through legal coercion if necessary. Doing so also established a professional niche for the female reformers themselves. Juvenile courts appointed college-educated women, often with backgrounds in social service work, to serve as probation officers with female delinquents. In addition, women reformers also came to decide girls' cases. The Cook County Juvenile Court appointed lawyer and children's advocate Mary M. Bartelme to serve as a referee in girls' cases in 1913. She won a seat on the bench as a circuit court judge in 1923 and became presiding judge over the juvenile court in 1927. Similarly, in 1915, the Los Angeles County Juvenile Court appointed Orfa Jean Shontz, a lawyer and former probation officer, to be a referee with full authority to decide girls' cases. In 1920, it chose social worker Miriam Van Waters to succeed her (Freedman, 1996; Odem, 1995).

These social reformers sought to apply what historians have characterized as "maternalism" or "maternal justice" to female juvenile offenders (Freedman, 1996; Knupfer, 2001; Odem, 1995). In parallel to the efforts of male judges with boys, they too sought to get at the roots of girls' misbehavior through personal interviews and intensive investigations of home lives. In contrast to juvenile courts' reliance on probation to deal with boys, however, juvenile courts were much more likely to commit girls to institutions. From 1899 to 1909, the Cook County Juvenile Court institutionalized over 52% of girls brought before the court; it placed 38% of the girls on probation and only dismissed 10% of cases (see Figure 3.4; Breckinridge and Abbott, 1912/ 1970, p. 39–43). Likewise the Los Angeles County Juvenile Court removed 47% of girls from their homes in 1920 (Odem, 1995, p. 146). As the social investigators Sophonisba P. Breckinridge and Edith Abbott (1912/1970) explained at the time, "The girl is not brought into court until her environment has proved too dangerous to be rendered safe by the services of a probation officer. She is in peril which threatens the ruin of her whole life, and the situation demands immediate action; her only hope of rescue seems to lie in prompt removal from her old surroundings and associates" (p. 41).

The juvenile courts, however, were sometimes used as tools of parents seeking leverage over their daughters. In 1920 Los Angeles, parents

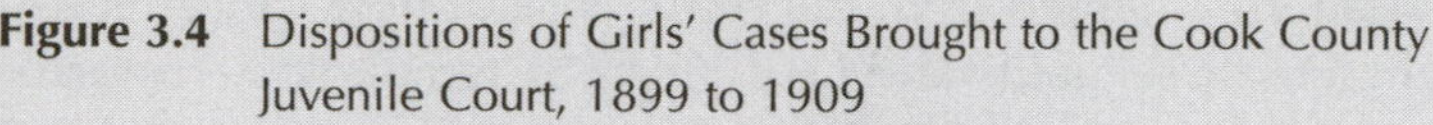

Figure 3.4 Dispositions of Girls' Cases Brought to the Cook County Juvenile Court, 1899 to 1909

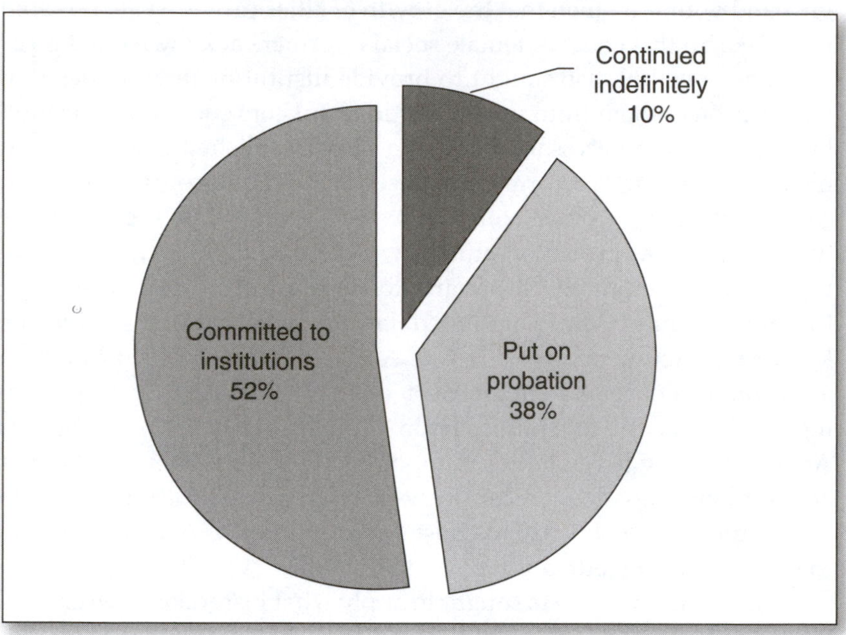

Source: Breckinridge & Abbott, 1912/1970, p. 40.

initiated 47% of girls' cases (this pattern seems to be much less common in boys' cases). They did so as means of resolving family disputes. Young women would want to stay out with friends, keep money they earned, or date young men of their choosing, but sometimes families resisted—particularly more traditional immigrant families or families headed by single mothers. Sometimes these conflicts escalated so far that it made sense for families to involve public officials. In some cases, the juvenile courts provided exactly what parents wanted, giving girls a stern talking-to and even occasionally placing girls in institutions if parents wanted to remove them from negative influences. In other cases, though, juvenile courts went farther than parents desired, committing girls to institutions regardless of parental wishes and placing them with foster families upon their release (Odem, 1995). Pleasing parents was not a priority for Progressive Era juvenile courts. Instead they were quite willing to utilize legal coercion to act in what they perceived to be the best interests of the child.

Case Studies in Criminal Justice: Julia Lathrop, Child Welfare Advocate

Julia C. Lathrop exemplified the female reformers who helped create the first juvenile courts. Born in 1858, she was among the first generation of college-educated women in the United States, graduating from Vassar in 1880. After working in her father's law firm, she moved to Chicago in 1890 to join Jane Addams's Hull House Social Settlement. Social settlement houses like Hull House were institutions established in turn-of-the-twentieth-century cities to provide social services, education, and recreation to the largely immigrant communities surrounding them. They became hubs for social reform and attracted a generation of the best and brightest activists, women and men like Lathrop.

As a result of Lathrop's research conducted at Hull House, Illinois governor John Peter Altgeld appointed her to the State Board of Charities, where Lathrop was again the first woman. In this capacity, she visited every jail, almshouse, and asylum in Illinois and also travelled to Europe to report on jail conditions there. In so doing, Lathrop became part of a larger transatlantic community intent on solving the problems of crime and poverty. Also, unlike an earlier generation of female activists who saw social reform as a philanthropic extension of women's domestic roles, Lathrop made social work her fulltime and lifelong career.

In the 1890s, Lathrop helped drive the campaign to create a separate court for juveniles. Together with Lucy Flower of the Chicago Women's Club, she convinced Judge John Hurd and the Chicago Bar Association to advocate for a juvenile court bill in the Illinois legislature and in 1898 organized a conference to build support for the bill. Following the 1899 passage of the law and the establishment of the Cook County Juvenile Court, Lathrop became the first president of the JCC, a private organization that helped the juvenile court function by maintaining a detention home for children, operating a bus to move detainees back and forth to juvenile court, and paying probation officers. Eventually, the court itself took over these activities. The JCC's work illustrates another key characteristic of Progressive Era reforms: beginning programs in the private sector but encouraging the government to eventually assume responsibility for them.

Lathrop herself maintained a carefully measured tone in her public pronouncements, even while arguing vigorously on behalf of reform. To a degree, this may have resulted from the constraints on women of her time.

(Continued)

(Continued)

It may also have resulted from an effort to present juvenile courts as a natural evolutionary reform, even if they were in fact quite radical. Consider, for example, how she presented her case in the following excerpt from a 1905 article.

"It will be seen that the Chicago method [of operating a juvenile court] is hardly a 'system' so far as its mechanism is concerned. It is rather a series of contrivances which have grown up to meet the situation as necessity demanded. In practice it works well in many ways. The public has confidence in the value of the probation officers, and in the committee, and contributes the money for salaries and for the home. There is no political complication, or interference in the appointment of officers, and certainly the personnel of the staff shows a very high order of ability and unselfish devotion. Yet it may be fairly suggested that the work of the court lacks the coordination and power that it might have were the responsibility less distributed. The city, the county, and the volunteer society are all working amicably and disinterestedly, but with some loss of effectiveness. In my own opinion it is clear that a juvenile court, like other courts of record, should be maintained by public funds. Freedom from political interference should be secured by the application of a merit law to govern appointment of officers, or rather to secure suitable persons to nominate the judge; and above all by the demands of an active public interest. There would still be need of the aid of private societies and individuals in caring for individual cases, and in supplementing the work of the paid staff of probation officers. Such taking over by the public of work begun by private effort has a good precedent in the introduction of the kindergarten in the public schools" (Lathrop, 1905, p. 346).

Lathrop shifted her work to a larger stage when, in 1912, she was appointed to be the first head of the United States Children's Bureau. While in this position she took on national issues such as child labor, she also remained an advocate of juvenile courts, sponsoring investigations by Sophonisba Breckinridge and Edith Abbott (1912) and by Evelina Belden (1920). Even as enthusiasm for juvenile courts faded in the 1920s, Lathrop remained one of their foremost supporters, speaking on their behalf at the 1924 conference commemorating their 25th anniversary. Although women could not vote in Illinois or national elections for most of Lathrop's career, she and women like her exercised tremendous political influence, effecting legal changes, doing the work necessary to allow institutions to function, and promoting reform.

❖ PROGRESSIVE ERA COURT REFORM

Criminal courts gradually became more professional during the first two decades of the twentieth century. Two parallel concerns drove this trend. First, court reformers advocated greater administrative efficiency and more formal adherence to the law. Second, court reformers also moved in parallel to the juvenile courts and saw the legal system as an instrument to enact social reform as well as carrying out justice.

At the national level, courts began to pay somewhat greater attention to due process rights for defendants. The U.S. Supreme Court began to define the boundaries of acceptable criminal court practices with its ruling in *Weeks v. United States* (1914). Fremont Weeks was convicted in federal court for running an illegal lottery through the mail based on evidence obtained in searches of his home, first by a police officer, then by a U.S. marshal, neither of whom had search warrants. The Supreme Court, however, overturned the conviction on the grounds that the evidence violated the Fourth Amendment protection against illegal search and seizure. On the one hand, this ruling established an important precedent in that it established the exclusionary rule, barring evidence obtained illegally from a criminal trial. On the other hand, this ruling also illustrated the persistent limitations on due process at this time in that it only applied to the very few criminal trials in federal court (Roth, 2005, p. 204).

Due process protections also expanded incrementally with the establishment of the first public defenders' offices to provide legal representation for the poor. Los Angeles created the first public defenders' office in 1914, and a private legal defense association emerged in New York City in 1917. Public defenders' offices, however, also represent the limitations of due process protections. They were slow to catch on and only became widespread in the 1960s (Walker, 1998, p. 141–142).

At the local level, cities and counties moved toward court reform. Via the Municipal Court Act of 1905, Chicago replaced its justices of the peace system with a more coordinated system of courts. The Chicago Municipal Court went into operation in 1906 with former prosecutor Harry Olson as its chief justice. Unlike the earlier arrangement, the Chicago Municipal Court was highly centralized and bureaucratic. It divided the city into five districts that each had at least one civil and one criminal court. Rather than pay its judges and staff through fees, each official received a fixed salary and was subject to civil service rules. Rather than allowing litigants to choose the venues for hearings, the Municipal Court acted as a clearinghouse, determining in which court each case should be heard. In addition to a large civil caseload, the Municipal Court had jurisdiction over misdemeanors and conducted preliminary hearings in felony cases before binding them over to the Cook County Criminal Court for grand jury hearings and trials. The rapidly growing caseload in the early twentieth century forced the court to hire a staff numbered at 332 people in 1915. Institutions like the Municipal Court reflected a new commitment to more professional management of the legal system (Willrich, 2003).

Institutions like the Chicago Municipal Court also grew out of new legal arguments for a more sociological approach to jurisprudence. Beginning in the late nineteenth century, progressive legal scholars increasingly rejected a model of the law as a set of unvarying rules in favor of a model of the law more concerned with social justice. Most notably, Roscoe Pound—a law professor at the University of Chicago and later the dean of the Harvard Law School—demonstrated that many of the purportedly timeless doctrines of law that tied the hands of late-nineteenth-century courts were in fact recent inventions. Rejecting the notion of courts hamstrung by theoretical abstractions disconnected from reality, Pound instead advocated a model of "sociological jurisprudence" or "socialized law." This approach saw the law as a means of balancing competing social interests. Pound regarded institutions like the Municipal Court of Chicago as instruments to bring order to the chaos of competing rights in a modern city (Willrich, 2003). In a fashion similar to the assumptions behind juvenile courts, this notion of socialized law viewed the law as a means of generating social reform and improving society.

These lines of argument helped justify modes of discipline based on individual treatment rather than uniform punishments. On a national scale, many states adopted indeterminate sentencing and parole in the early twentieth century. State legislatures increasingly mandated broad sentencing ranges for particular offenses, gave judges discretion to determine minimum and maximum terms, and authorized parole boards to decide when a convict should be released. In this way, corrections officials could provide individualized treatment and discipline appropriate to a particular offender. The concept of indeterminate sentences was not new. Widespread executive pardons of convicted offenders had created de facto indeterminate sentences in the nineteenth century, and reform schools for juveniles and reformatories for young men had long made flexible release part of their practice. In the early twentieth century, however, states gradually made indeterminate sentencing part of official policy for adult criminal offenders. Moreover, new laws placed decision-making authority in the hands of judges and parole boards that were designed to apply professional expertise to individual cases. It is important to note, however, that these measures were not adopted overnight or without controversy. Pennsylvania adopted indeterminate sentencing for adult felons in 1909, curtailed it in 1917 in the face of criticism, and revived it in 1923 only to face repeal campaigns in 1928 and 1935. But by the 1930s, most states had adopted some form of indeterminate sentencing and parole (Walker, 1998).

At a local level, legal administrators also sought to put socialized law into practice. The Chicago Municipal Court established specialized courts to deal with particular kinds of criminal cases and get at their sources. It created a Domestic Relations Court, for example, in 1911, to adjudicate violations of a state law that made it a crime for a husband to desert or to fail to support his family. At a time of tremendous concern that poverty led to crime, the cases in this court sought to hold wage-earning men responsible for the financial well-being of their families. The Municipal Court also created a Morals Court in 1913 to specialize in cases of vice and prostitution. This court sought to deal with widespread public concerns about sexual enterprise by abandoning the practice of fining prostitutes (which forced them to return to their trade to make money to pay their fines). Instead, it explicitly criminalized the selling of sex, allowing the court to place convicted prostitutes on probation and offer them social services and various forms of treatment. Finally the Municipal Court created a Boys' Court in 1914 to function as a hybrid of a juvenile court and a criminal court for a somewhat older population, young men from ages 17 to 21. While youths entered the court through the same arrest procedures as adult offenders, judges reduced charges against first-time offenders and assigned probationers to work with social service agencies. In all of these instances, the new courts designed their procedures and treatments to try to resolve the factors that they understood to contribute heavily to crime (Willrich, 2003).

Other agencies also sought to use the criminal law to deal with social issues. In the 1920s, the Committee of Fourteen, a New York City antivice organization, sought to change state law to address the problem of prostitution. Since 1905, the Committee of Fourteen had used investigators to target for arrest women who sold sexual services. Beginning in the late 1910s, however, the Committee increasingly sought to target prostitutes' male clients. A revised vagrancy law making it illegal for men to purchase sexual services would, they believed, improve public morality and cut off the demand for prostitutes. This episode, however, also illustrates the limits of using criminal law to enact social reform. Although the Committee convinced representatives to introduce their proposal into the New York state legislature in three separate sessions in the 1920s, the bill never reached the assembly floor for debate or a vote. Instead, opponents successfully built alliances among police, judges, and legal professionals by arguing that a bill expanding the reach of the criminal law would undermine existing means of controlling prostitution (Mackey, 2005).

❖ ROOTING OUT CRIME

The same trends that contributed to legal reform—increased concern with social conditions, greater faith in new professional disciplines, the concept of social responsibility for crime—also contributed to the increased institutional importance of eugenics in the early twentieth century. Most notably, beginning in 1906, Henry H. Goddard, director of the Vineland Laboratory at the New Jersey Training School for Feebleminded Boys and Girls, used intelligence tests to correlate what was termed "feeblemindedness" in inmates with criminal histories. In so doing, he put the tools of social scientific research to work to help identify potential offenders. In a series of studies published in the early 1910s, Goddard sought to demonstrate and popularize the notions that criminal offenders were born without certain moral and mental faculties, and that if people lacking these attributes could be identified, their offenses could be prevented. In parallel with sociological approaches to the law, these studies implied that criminals lacked full responsibility for their actions, that society shared some responsibility for preventing their offenses (Rafter, 1997). In response, some states sought to institutionalize potential offenders. More dramatically, others passed sterilization laws to prevent them from reproducing. Indiana made sterilization official policy in 1907, endorsing the work of Dr. Harry Sharp at the Indiana Reformatory, who began performing vasectomies on 236 young men beginning in 1899. Likewise, in 1909, California permitted the "asexualization" of prisoners if they gave "evidence while . . . in a . . . prison in this state that he is a moral or sexual pervert" (Friedman, 1993, p. 335–338; Rafter, 1997, p. 152–153).

State and local prisons, reformatories, jails, and courts also established criminological clinics in the 1910s and 1920s to get at medical or psychological causes of crime. These often had a eugenicist orientation. The Municipal Court of Chicago, for example, added to its array of specialized agencies in 1914 by opening a Psychopathic Laboratory under the leadership of Dr. William J. Hickson. A former student of

Goddard, Hickson used memory tests to determine if defendants referred to his laboratory by the court were suffering from mental defects. Judges were encouraged to look for possible "defectives" among the people who came before them. The socialized branches of the Municipal Court—the Boys' Court, the Domestic Relations Court, and the Morals Court—generated the majority of cases that reached the Psychopathic Laboratory, while the criminal courts sent relatively few. These investigations had real consequences; under a 1915 law, over 1,000 persons per year who the Psychopathic Clinic examined were committed to state institutions for the insane or feebleminded. This sort of eugenic practice is often thought of as contrary to the environmentalist approach of Progressive Era social and judicial reform, but in fact they had a great deal in common. Both sought to get at the root causes of crime and to use expert analysis and state intervention to dig them out (Willrich, 2003).

What's the Evidence?: Court Records

Court records provide valuable—but not necessarily user-friendly—resources for the study of criminal justice history. Most often courts operate at the county level, so county governments tend to retain control of the records. Historical court records are rarely digitized or published; to see them, a researcher usually needs to go in person to wherever the records are held. In some cases, the counties maintain modern archival facilities that are open and inviting to the public. In other cases, historic court records might be found in the basements of old county court houses. George Fisher (2006) describes descending into the cellar of the Alameda County (CA) courthouse to use the records analyzed by Friedman and Percival (1981). Also, records are likely incomplete. The Cook County Circuit Court Archives in Chicago holds Municipal Court of Chicago Criminal Records used by Willrich (2003) on microfilm, but only selected cases from a limited number of years have been preserved.

Once court records have been located, the information they contain can be highly variable. Sometimes court dockets simply record the outcome of criminal proceedings. These can be helpful for reconstructing the patterns of a court's business but leave out much of the detail and context of the proceedings. By contrast, the richest mines of historical material tend to come from case files, collections of information tracking individual cases.

(Continued)

(Continued)

Case files provide individual-level information on alleged offenders, the offenses, and the processing of cases by the courts. They might include arrest records, formal statements of complaints, documentation on the suspect, requests for detention, records of dispositions, and other resources. From these records, researchers can reconstruct individual cases or paint broader pictures of patterns within the justice system. Historians can also use court case records to study patterns of behavior that otherwise might seem lost to history. George Chauncey (1994), for example, used the case files of the Manhattan District Attorney housed at the New York City Municipal Archives to reconstruct patterns of gay male sociability in early twentieth-century New York City, while Stephen Robertson (2005) used these same records to analyze the history of sexual offenses against children.

Juvenile court records have an additional layer of complication. Because juvenile proceedings are usually confidential, their records tend to be closed to the public. Only a few juvenile courts have ever granted scholars access to their files. Steven Schlossman (2005) relates the story of how, in the early 1970s, he traveled from state to state searching for accessible court records. Finally, the chief probation officer of the Milwaukee Juvenile Court invited him into his office, grilled him for two hours on the history of juvenile justice, and, after he was convinced that Schlossman was a legitimate scholar, invited him into the basement to peruse the records. Even then, Schlossman had to obtain official permission from the court to systematically analyze the files. Tanenhaus (2004) relates that in the 1990s, when procedures had become more formal, he too had to obtain permission from the presiding judge of the Cook County Juvenile Court to access its records. Other historians under other circumstances, however, have tried and failed to gain access to these same sources (Knupfer, 2001).

❖ RETREAT FROM REFORM

During the 1920s, the pace of criminal court reform slowed considerably. Enthusiasm for social reform and flexible sentencing faced increasing challenges from renewed support for deterrence and punishment. Prosecutor Robert E. Crowe exemplified this new position when in 1920, during his campaign for State's Attorney for Cook County, he proclaimed "Swift, implacable justice is the only remedy that will cure Chicago of its malady of crime" (quoted in Willrich, 2003, p. 282).

The wedding cake model persisted in the 1920s. Crime commission surveys in both Chicago and New York found that roughly half of all cases were decided in preliminary hearings. Other crime surveys found that, when cases reached the criminal courts, jury trials continued to decline, replaced by either plea bargains or a new innovation, bench trials decided solely by judges (Friedman, 1993, p. 386–393). And spectacular crime continued to decorate the cake, reflecting larger cultural concerns of the time. In March 1927, for example, Ruth Snyder and her lover, Judd Gray, murdered her husband, Albert, in their suburban home outside of New York City. They tried to make the crime look like a robbery, but when suspicion fell on Ruth Snyder, she quickly confessed, then tried to blame Gray. Gray then also confessed, but presented Snyder as the architect of the plot. The crime became a newspaper sensation, reported nationwide in breathless detail not only by tabloids but also by the more staid *New York Times*. The ensuing media coverage—intertwined with debates over the changing roles of modern women in the 1920s—portrayed Snyder both as an example of a woman gone wrong and as not a woman at all, as something cold and lacking human sympathy. Both narratives, oddly, provided support for her execution, and she and Gray were put to death in the electric chair at New York's Sing Sing prison in January 1928 (Ramey, 2004).

In the 1920s, courts increasingly focused on administrative efficiency rather than addressing the social and environmental sources of crime. One measure of this was the declining influence of eugenics. On a national level, geneticists expressed growing skepticism about eugenics and funding agencies increasingly rejected grant applications to pursue research in eugenics. On a local level, the Municipal Court of Chicago again provides a barometer. In Chicago, the Juvenile Protective Association (JPA)—a wide-ranging social reform agency that had evolved from the Juvenile Court Committee in 1909—tacitly withdrew its support for Hickson's Psychopathic Laboratory. Harry Olson, the chief justice of Municipal Court, continued to endorse the Psychopathic Laboratory, but the Laboratory became increasingly marginal to the court system. Chicago shifted control over it to the Department of Public Health in 1925, and when Hickson resigned in 1929, the city appointed a successor who did not share his enthusiasm for eugenics (Willrich, 2003).

The movement toward more organized courts expanded in the 1920s, stressing efficiency over social reform and often taking the Municipal Court of Chicago as a model. States, spurred by business leaders and prominent attorneys, created judicial councils to help coordinate state court systems and assign judges to jurisdictions with the largest caseloads. At the federal level, former president and current chief justice of the Supreme Court, William Howard Taft led a movement to more systematically manage the federal courts. This type of administrative reform reflected the general advocacy of business-like efficiency common in the politics of the 1920s (Willrich, 2003, p. 284-286).

In the aftermath of World War One, labor strife, incidents of anarchist terrorism, racial conflict, and increased urban crime and violence all undercut support for approaches to the law that emphasized the social responsibility for crime. Furthermore, the beginning of Prohibition in 1920 fostered violence between criminal syndicates, and efforts to enforce Prohibition tended to exacerbate the conflicts. In Chicago, attempts by Mayor William Dever's administration to crack down on alcohol coincided with the most brutal phase of Chicago's beer wars in which at least 115 men were killed in gangland violence between 1924 and 1926. For most Chicagoans, of course, gangland violence did not represent an everyday reality. The Municipal Court received a dramatically increased number of cases in the 1920s, but the vast majority were misdemeanors such as disorderly conduct and pickpocketing and new infractions such as automobile violations. In this atmosphere, however, civic organizations such as the Chicago Crime Commission were able to make a convincing argument that courts should get tough on crime. Using the courts as instruments of social reform lost public support in favor of using the courts to impose just desserts (Willrich, 2003, p. 286–296).

The juvenile courts also began to drift away from a social reform model as early as the 1910s as they introduced psychiatric approaches to delinquency. Again, Chicago led the way. Concerned about the problem of recidivism among young offenders, philanthropist Ethel Sturges Dummer gathered a group of leading child welfare activists to find a solution. They concluded that the Cook County Juvenile Court needed a psychiatric arm to deal with specific individual problems. Bankrolled by Dummer, in 1909 they established the Juvenile Psychopathic Institute as an adjunct to the juvenile court and hired as its director Dr. William Healy, a Harvard-trained physician and neurologist with ties to the Chicago legal community. Under Healy, the Psychopathic Institute sought to get at the root causes of delinquent behavior. Healy's 1915 textbook on diagnosis, *The Individual Delinquent*, emphasized the multiple and interacting causes of delinquency and the need for individualized treatment plans. In contrast to the eugenicists of his time, Healy minimized hereditary elements and instead favored a therapeutic approach. In 1916, soon after the publication of *The Individual Delinquent*, Healy left Chicago to go to the Judge Baker Foundation in Boston, an arm of that city's juvenile court. From there he continued to develop follow-up studies tracking repeat offenders in the 1920s and exercised tremendous influence over the juvenile court movement. While psychopathic clinics never became common—they tended to be attached only to juvenile courts in the biggest cities—they did have the effect of undermining the fundamentally environmental premise of juvenile courts. They suggested that, rather than seeking to change the social environment in which children grew up, the best results could be achieved by focusing on individual offenders. Moreover, by the 1920s, the individualized approach of Healy and his followers increasingly highlighted the inability of many courts and reform schools to give young offenders adequate care (Getis, 2000; Mennel, 1973; Tanenhaus, 2004).

Questions of criminal responsibility became widely debated public issues with the 1924 trial of Nathan F. Leopold Jr. and Richard A. Loeb. On May 21, 1924, Leopold (age 19) and Loeb (age 18) kidnapped and murdered 14-year-old Bobby Franks in Chicago. After a relatively brief investigation, Leopold and Loeb were arrested and they freely confessed. Their case became a public sensation because of who they were—affluent, Jewish, well educated, homosexual—and because of their seeming indifference to the crime, having apparently committed it for the thrill of it. No one doubted the outcome of their trial—they pleaded guilty—but the case nonetheless raised larger questions of the degree to which they were responsible for their actions. Their legal team—led by Clarence Darrow, the most prominent defense attorney of his day—waived a jury trial and argued in a bench trial before a single judge that Leopold and Loeb should be sentenced to life in prison rather than to death. Darrow premised their case both on Leopold and Loeb's youth and on new psychiatric approaches to understanding crime. Defense witnesses included William Healy and other leading figures in modern psychiatric criminology, who suggested that Leopold and Loeb were not fully responsible for their actions. In the end, the judge sentenced them to prison, not the death penalty, resting his decision more on their youth than on the psychiatric arguments (Geis & Bienen, 1998).

The Leopold and Loeb decision, however, fostered a hostile public outcry, generating criticism of the notion that criminals were not fully responsible for their actions (Tanenhaus, 2004; Willrich, 2003). The decision also prompted some legal experts who had been sympathetic to notions of social responsibility to rethink their positions. In symposium on the case in the *Journal of the American Institute of Criminal Law and Criminology*, Dean John Henry Wigmore of the Northwestern University School of Law, an earlier supporter of court reform and psychiatric clinics, rejected psychiatric arguments as tending to "undermine the whole penal law." He wrote that deterrence should be the centerpiece of the criminal law. "The fear of being overtaken by the law's penalties is, next to morality, what keeps most of us from being offenders." Moreover, a lax penalty in the Leopold and Loeb case would undermine deterrence in other cases. Wigmore argued, "Would the remission of the extreme penalty for murder in the Loeb-Leopold case lessen the restraints on the outside class of potential homiciders? The answer is yes, emphatically" (Wigmore, 1924, p. 401–403).

❖ THE SLOW FADE OF JUVENILE JUSTICE

In the 1920s, the optimism that had characterized the early years of juvenile courts also faded. Activists in the child welfare and court reform movements developed an increasing sense that juvenile courts did not represent a magic bullet to cure social ills. As the first generation of advocates moved toward retirement, a new generation of workers in the child welfare field encountered persistent problems. A 1920 U.S. Children's Bureau report by investigator Evelina Belden highlighted the limited reach of juvenile courts and made clear that, in practice, juvenile courts did not live up to their initial promises. Although almost all states had passed juvenile court laws, many courts still detained children in adult jails, less than half offered probation services, and only 7% had psychiatric services. In addition, studies by Healy and others discovered that, even when juvenile courts did operate as intended, they still had high recidivism rates. By 1924, many of the speeches at a conference commemorating the 25th anniversary of the Cook County Juvenile Court—later published as *The Child, the Clinic, and the Court* (1925)—highlighted not the court's accomplishments but disenchantment. They tended to emphasize the court's bureaucratic unresponsiveness and to call for more medicalized and individualized treatment (Tanenhaus, 2004).

In the midst of public concerns about crime and youth violence, appeals courts began to whittle away juvenile court jurisdiction. In the 1926 case *People v. Fitzgerald* involving a 16-year-old boy who had been convicted of rape in adult criminal court and sentenced to 20 years in prison, the Illinois Supreme Court ruled that, unless a youth was under age 10 or had already been ruled delinquent in juvenile court, juvenile and adult courts had concurrent jurisdiction. In subsequent 1928 and 1935 decisions, the Illinois Supreme Court bypassed the exceptions and determined that juvenile and adult courts had concurrent jurisdiction in all cases involving juveniles. This meant that adult courts could grab any case and try it under criminal, rather than juvenile, guidelines. In reality, juvenile cases in adult courts remained rare, and juvenile courts emphasized that they waived the most serious crimes to criminal courts, but the trend nonetheless undercut the unique purview of juvenile courts (Dodge, 2000; Tanenhaus, 2004).

By the 1930s, the Cook County Juvenile Court also increasingly fell under the influence of Democratic Party politics. Under Presiding Judge Frank H. Bicek, probation officers and judges—who conducted the basic work of the court—were increasingly selected on the basis of political connections. As a result, throughout the 1930s, the JPA came to criticize the politicization of the Cook County court and its shift toward focusing on crime. In 1938, the head of the JPA charged that the "approach and procedure of our Juvenile Court has become more like a Criminal than a Parental Court" (Dodge, 2000, p. 58–59).

Despite the tendency for courts to get tougher on crime, the pendulum did not completely swing away from earlier reform trends. Institutional changes such as juvenile courts and the court organization movement persisted and expanded. Moreover, the spirit of social reform also persisted in the efforts of academics and activists to study and improve urban communities. Sociologists affiliated with the University of Chicago continued to conduct studies of juvenile delinquency and urban conditions in the 1920s and 1930s, often using data generated by the Cook County Juvenile Court as well on on-the-ground observations. Perhaps most notably, Clifford Shaw and Henry McKay combined a number of sociological research techniques—analyzing offenders' "own stories" as well as mapping incidences of juvenile delinquency—to develop an ecological model of crime and delinquency that tied offenses to urban conditions and zones of the city. The juvenile court tradition of combining social research with activism also led Shaw to apply to this work to the real world. In the early 1930s, he established the Chicago Area Project, an innovative neighborhood-based effort to use the people and resources already present in communities to work with potential offenders to prevent crime. Even as the Cook County Juvenile Court became more rigid and an adjunct of Chicago party politics in the 1930s, its influence was shaping new efforts to deal with delinquency (Getis, 2000; Tanenhaus, 2004).

❖ CONCLUSION

Between roughly the 1890s and the 1920s, court systems in the United States became bigger, more elaborate, and more bureaucratic. Because courts were local institutions, the specifics varied widely, but the trend is clear. In the nineteenth century, courts were casual part-time institutions, often loose in their procedures and open to community influence. In the late nineteenth century and more so in the early twentieth century, increased caseloads and demands upon courts drove them to develop full-time professional staff and bureaucratic processes. At the same time, court reformers developed new notions of what the purposes of courts could or should be. Beyond simply administering justice, many saw courts as a means of preventing crime or rehabilitating criminals. Through means such as probation for juvenile offenders or indeterminate sentences for adults, these reformers sought to allow courts to respond flexibly to crime and to get at the root causes of criminal behavior. As a result, court reformers built a strong element of social reformism into the changed institutions, an element most obvious in juvenile courts but also apparent in specialized adult courts. At the same time, however, the expanded capabilities of the courts could just as easily be turned to more punitive crime control. The ways that modern courts functioned largely reflected their social contexts and the policy goals of the criminal justice system. During the early twentieth century, they largely sought to use their authority to reform society. In the wake of World War One and into the 1920s, courts increasingly retreated from social reform and sought instead to engage more directly in crime control. While the purposes shifted, the steady trend was the growing institutional organization and capacity of the courts.

❖ REFERENCES

Alexander, R. (1995). *The "girl problem": Female sexual delinquency in New York, 1900–1930*. Ithaca, NY: Cornell University Press.

Bernard, T. J. (1992). *The cycle of juvenile justice.* New York, NY: Oxford University Press.

Belden, E. (1920). *Courts in the United States hearing children's cases: Results of a questionnaire study covering the year 1918.* Washington, DC: United States Government Printing Office.

Breckinridge, S., & Abbott, E. (1912/1970). *The delinquent child and the home* (Reprint.). New York, NY: Arno Press.

Brumberg, J. J. (2003). *Kansas Charley: The story of a nineteenth-century boy murderer.* New York, NY: Viking.

Chauncey, G. (1994). *Gay New York: Gender, urban culture, and the making of the gay male 1890–1940.* New York, NY: BasicBooks.

Dodge, L. M. (2000). "Our juvenile court has become more like a criminal court": A century of reform at the Cook County (Chicago) Juvenile Court. *Michigan Historical Review, 26*, 51–89.

Fisher, G. (2006). Historian in the cellar. *Stanford Law Review, 59*(1), 1–21.

Freedman, E. B. (1996). *Maternal justice: Miriam Van Waters and the female reform tradition*. Chicago, IL: University of Chicago Press.

Friedman, L. M. (1993). *Crime and punishment in American history*. New York, NY: BasicBooks.

Friedman, L. M., & Percival, R. V. (1981). *The roots of justice: Crime and punishment in Alameda County, California, 1870–1910*. Chapel Hill: University of North Carolina Press.

Geis, G., & Bienen, L. B. (1998). *Crimes of the century: From Leopold and Loeb to O.J. Simpson*. Boston, MA: Northeastern University Press.

Getis, V. (2000). *The juvenile court and the progressives*. Urbana: University of Illinois Press.

Gish, C. (1999). Rescuing the "waifs and strays" of the city: The western emigration program of the Children's Aid Society. *Journal of Social History, 33*, 121–142.

Hurley, T. D. (1907). *Origin of the Illinois juvenile court law* (3rd ed.). Chicago, IL: Visitation and Aid Society.

Juvenile law is good. (1899, July 16). *Chicago Tribune*, 15.

Knupfer, A. M. (2001). *Reform and resistance: Gender, delinquency, and America's first juvenile court*. New York, NY: Routledge.

Lathrop, J. C. (1905). The development of the probation system in a large city. *Charities, 13*, 344–349.

Lindsey, B. B. (1904). The reformation of juvenile delinquents through the juvenile court. In S. J. Barrows (Ed.), *Children's courts in the United States: Their origins, development, and results*. Washington, DC: United States Government Printing Office.

Lindsey, B. B. (1905). The boy and the court: The Colorado law and its administration. *Charities, 13*, 350–357.

Mackey, T. C. (2005). *Pursuing Johns: Criminal law reform, defending character, and New York City's Committee of Fourteen, 1920–1930*. Columbus: Ohio State University Press.

Mennel, R. M. (1973). *Thorns and thistles: Juvenile delinquents in the United States, 1825-1940*. Hanover, NH: The University Press of New England.

Myers, T. (2006). *Caught: Montreal's modern girls and the law, 1869–1945*. Toronto: University of Toronto Press.

Nickerson, C. R. (1999). "The deftness of her sex": Innocence, guilt, and gender in the trial of Lizzie Borden. In M. A. Bellesiles (Ed.), *Lethal imagination: Violence and brutality in American history* (pp. 261–282). New York: New York University Press.

Odem, M. E. (1995). *Delinquent daughters: Protecting and policing adolescent female sexuality in the United States, 1885–1920*. Chapel Hill: University of North Carolina Press.

Platt, A. M. (1977). *The child savers: The invention of delinquency* (2nd ed.). Chicago: University of Chicago Press.

Rafter, N. H. (1997). *Creating born criminals*. Urbana: University of Illinois Press.

Ramey, J. (2004). The bloody blonde and the marble woman: Gender and power in the case of Ruth Snyder. *Journal of Social History, 37*, 625–650.

Robertson, S. (2005). *Crimes against children: Sexual violence and legal culture in New York City, 1880–1960*. Chapel Hill: University of North Carolina Press.

Roth, M. P. (2005). *Crime and punishment: A history of the criminal justice system.* Belmont, CA: Thomson Wadsworth.

Schlossman, S. L. (1977). *Love and the American delinquent: The theory and practice of "progressive" juvenile justice, 1825–1920*. Chicago, IL: University of Chicago Press.

Schlossman, S. L. (1998). Delinquent children: The juvenile reform school. In N. Morris & D. J. Rothman (Eds.), *The Oxford history of the prison: The practice of punishment in Western society* (pp. 325–349). New York, NY: Oxford University Press.

Schlossman, S. L. (2005). *Transforming juvenile justice: Reform ideals and institutional realities, 1825–1920.* DeKalb: Northern Illinois University Press.

Schlossman, S. L., & Wallach, S. (1978). The crime of precocious sexuality: Female juvenile delinquency in the Progressive Era. *Harvard Education Review, 48*, 65–92.

Schneider, E. C. (1992). *In the web of class: Delinquents and reformers in Boston, 1810s–1930s.* New York: New York University Press.

Sheldon, R., & Osbourne, L. (1989). "For their own good": Class interests & the child saving movement in Memphis, Tennessee, 1900–1917." *Criminology, 27*, 747–767.

Steinberg, A. (1989). *The transformation of criminal justice, Philadelphia, 1800–1880.* Chapel Hill: University of North Carolina Press.

Tanenhaus, D. S. (2000). The evolution of transfer out of juvenile court. In J. Fagan, & F. E. Zimring (Eds.), *The changing borders of juvenile justice: Transfers of adolescents to the criminal court* (pp. 13–43). Chicago, IL: University of Chicago Press.

Tanenhaus, D. S. (2004). *Juvenile justice in the making.* New York, NY: Oxford University Press.

Walker, S. (1998). *Popular justice: A history of American criminal justice* (2nd ed.). New York, NY: Oxford University Press.

Wigmore, J. H. (1924). A symposium of comments from the legal profession. *Journal of the American Institute of Criminal Law and Criminology, 15*(3), 400–405.

Willrich, M. (2003). *City of courts: Socializing justice in Progressive Era Chicago.* New York, NY: Cambridge University Press.

Wolcott, D. B. (2005). *Cops and kids: Policing juvenile delinquency in urban America, 1890–1940.* Columbus: Ohio State University Press.

Zimring, F. E. (2002). The Common thread: Diversion in the jurisprudence of juvenile courts. In M. K. Rosenheim, F. E. Zimring, D. S. Tanenhaus, & B. Dohrn (Eds.), *A century of juvenile justice* (pp. 142–157). Chicago, IL: University of Chicago Press.

4

Punishment in the Progressive Era, 1890s–1930s

Of all the elements of the criminal justice system, the process of punishment appears to be the easiest to think about historically. Just a moment's reflection can bring to mind all sorts of old punishments that have lost their place in modern criminal justice systems. Visitors to Colonial Williamsburg, for example, can observe relics of eighteenth century criminal justice—the stocks and a pillory—and marvel at how alien these forms of public corporal punishment appear. Likewise, a variety of European museums display the artifacts of medieval torture to fascinate visitors with their tales of long-ago punishments. Even where the punishments themselves remain—the prison and the death penalty, to take just two examples—older forms seem far removed from modern practice.

The past and present are, however, bound together by a continual process of reforming and reimagining punishment. In this chapter we see that, with the dawn of the twentieth century, the great challenge for Progressive Era reformers was to bring the system of punishing criminal offenders in line with the great ambitions of the era—to promote civic inclusion and responsible citizenship through systems of education and rehabilitation. Responding to this challenge, Progressives developed systems of probation and parole, designed to extend the supervision of the offender into the community and laid out ambitious plans for reforming the offender in confinement. This chapter examines the roots of the Progressive enthusiasm for reform and considers just what it was that made reformers so optimistic about the power to help the offender make good.

The changes wrought by Progressive reformers cannot simply be understood as improvements in the human condition. To be sure, there were many positive accomplishments. But this chapter also shows that actual practice during this period often fell far short of reformers' hopes. In large sections of the United States, in fact, progressive reforms never really appeared. Many prisons appeared largely unchanged from their nineteenth-century predecessors, where dull routine and harsh discipline remained the norm. Likewise, parole and probation programs often fell short, in practice, of their ambitious designs. High caseloads and minimal staff training contributed to ineffective community supervision. Failures to enact or implement reform offer a useful reminder that promising ideas are not always the most important engines of change, and that criminal justice in practice is deeply influenced by the political, social, and economic environment.

❖ THE NINETEENTH CENTURY

In the summer of 1865, just months after General Robert E. Lee's surrender at Appomattox Court House and Abraham Lincoln's assassination, the Prison Association of New York undertook a massive review of American prisons. They appointed two officers, Enoch Cobb Wines and Frederick Dwight, to undertake a review that would include visits to prisons in 18 states, the compilation of over 50 volumes of reports and data, and the 540-page *Report on the Prisons and Reformatories of the United States and Canada*. The *Report* quickly established itself as the basic text for prison reformers who shared the stated goal of Wines and Dwight: "to improve and perfect our penal and reformatory system, to impress upon it a character worthy of our civilization" (Wines & Dwight, 1867, p. 48).

When Wines and Dwight undertook their survey of American prisons and reformatories in 1865, they encountered an institutional world that looked vastly different from today's twenty-first century correctional system. The very idea of the modern prison was not very old at that point. While the first great penitentiaries—Auburn State Prison in New York and the Eastern State Penitentiary in Pennsylvania—had opened to great fanfare in the 1820s, the diffusion of the penitentiary from state to state had taken some time, and it was not until the 1850s that most states had finally constructed a recognizably modern penitentiary. Most of the 18 states they visited had only a single state prison, and even the largest states like New York had only two or three. There were virtually no specialized institutions of any kind, other than a small number of juvenile reformatories. Indeed, there was no such thing as a prison system at that time—institutions operated on a largely independent basis, with their own boards of overseers.

Behind prison walls, life was largely organized around industrial production. Most adult institutions operated under either a contract system (in which private contractors ran prison industries) or a piece-price system (in which the contractor provided the raw materials and paid a certain price per piece of finished goods produced). Indeed, the quest for employing prisoners at profitable industrial work rapidly became the primary organizing motive for most prisons. Wines and Dwight (1867) referred to the contractor as the dominant force in the prisons of 1865, the "power behind the throne greater than the throne" (p. 261).

Inmates labored long hours, six days a week, in prison factories, and found little else to alleviate the monotony of prison life. Elements of the original congregate system of the Auburn Prison remained in limited force throughout the prisons of 1865: inmates marched to and from workshops and dining halls in an artificial military lock step and the old silent system in which prisoners were forbidden to communicate with each other remained on the books, even if poorly enforced. Wines and Dwight summarized the rules in one state and observed that, "if we should give these regulations for all the state prisons, it would be seen that they are, to a great extent, transcripts the one from the other" (p. 139).

The upheavals of the Civil War shook the prison system, with Southern states largely abandoning the idea (see Chapter Five) and many in the North questioning the utility and future of the institutions. Still, as Lawrence Friedman writes, "there was no going back" to a world without prisons (Friedman, 1993, p. 159). For better or worse, the United States had committed itself to the prison as the central element in a system of punishment. Aiming to reform rather than abolish the prison, Wines and Dwight led a call for a national prison congress, which brought American and European reformers together for the first time in Cincinnati in 1870. The 40 papers presented at that pioneering meeting represented a nearly complete survey of reformist ambition at the time. The Cincinnati Congress resulted in the establishment of the National Prison Association (later known as the American Prison Association and today as the American Correctional Association). Most notable of all, this first meeting produced a Declaration of Principles, 37 propositions that served as the foundational text of modern penology (McKelvey, 1977).

In the end, though, the flourish of activity in the post–Civil War years was something of a false dawn for prison reform. Despite the ambitious agendas and international organizations, the men and women with a vision for change were largely disappointed in the final decades of the nineteenth century. Still, the visions outlined in the Declaration of Principles had an abiding influence, and it would be joined with other sorts of ideas in the Progressive Era to launch a reform movement with a more substantial impact on the organization and practice of punishment in the criminal justice system.

❖ THE PROGRESSIVE AMBITION

Historians are probably guilty of making things sound more definite than they really were when using terms like "Progressive Era"—progressivism was a term applied to a wide range of people and ideas with some common elements, and the start and end of the era are hard to pin down precisely (Dawley, 2003). While this text generally narrows the era down to roughly 1900 to 1920, it can be useful to think of the period in broader terms—many of the ideas and issues predated 1900, and the diffusion of many progressive ideas actually happened in the 1920s and 1930s (Jenkins, 1985). Reformers all shared what one historian has called a "fierce discontent" with the world they inherited, and a passion to remake the nation and the world into something closer to their own image (McGerr, 2003). For capturing the essence of progressivism in its broadest sense, historian Alan Dawley's (2003) summary is a good one: "progressivism found a certain cohesion in three overlapping aims: winning social and economic justice, revitalizing public life, and improving the wider world" (p. 3).When we consider the reformist hand in criminal justice, however, we might consider another trio of principles which, taken together, can go a long way to making sense of the progressive vision of the criminal sanction: individualization, rehabilitation, and professionalization.

Individualization

The first of the central principles progressives applied to reforming punishment was individualization. The term itself actually encompasses three basic propositions. First, progressives argued that the proper focus of the criminal justice system was more on the particular character of the criminal offender and not as much on the particular offense that had been committed. In this sense, progressives challenged the spirit of nineteenth-century classical criminological thought that emphasized the rational accounting of sanctions based on the severity of the crime itself. As in so much of the classical liberalism of the nineteenth century, the individual was viewed as a self-controlled, free willed entity—and crime, therefore, a kind of moral failing. Progressives turned this view on its head, arguing that there were many paths to crime, with many causes, and that truly just and fair forms and process of punishment should offer just as much variety in response (Rothman, 2002).

The push for individualization rested on a second critical principle—that the origins of criminal behavior were capable of being understood. Indeed, one of the hallmarks of the progressive moment was the intensely optimistic spirit (one historian calls it "stunning optimism") in which reformers sought to unravel the etiology of criminal and deviant behavior (Rosenblum, 2008, p. 74). Where did this optimistic spirit come from? It owed a great deal to the emergence of various forms of expert knowledge, each of which promised to unlock the mysteries of human behavior.

From the realm of science, inquiries into heredity helped sustain the hope that antisocial behavior could be understood as an inherited biological trait. From there, the quest was to locate those biological markers of deviance, as a way of protecting society from actual and potential offenders. For a time, the early work of Cesare Lombroso and other criminal anthropologists pointed toward a set of physical characteristics—the receding brow, the heavy jaw, the oddly shaped skull—common to criminals (an obsession with body measurement that led to the development of modern criminal identification systems)(Cole, 2001). By the twentieth century, however, the biological marker of preference was less outwardly visible—the measures of intelligence (Rafter, 1997). Henry Goddard's *The Criminal Imbecile* (1915) was, as one historian describes it "the intellectual high water mark for the conflation of mental deficiency and criminality" (Noll, 1995, p. 117). In it, Goddard warned readers that "somewhere in the neighborhood of 50% of all criminals are feebleminded" and that "we must be on the watch for symptoms of feeble-mindedness . . . when such symptoms are discovered, we must watch and guard such persons as carefully as we do cases of leprosy or any other malignant disease" (Goddard, 1915, p. 105).

Psychiatry proved to be another enduring source of optimism that the causes of criminal behavior could be understood and treated at the individual level. An influential group of psychiatrists in the United States and Europe began to argue that crime and other forms of deviant behavior had their roots in psychopathology—in mental disease, in other words, rather than the mental defects emphasized in eugenic criminology. William Healy's 1915 study, *The Individual Delinquent*, was the era's leading defense of the psychiatric diagnosis of crime (Healy, 1915; Rafter, 1997). Healy (1915), using data he collected as director of the Chicago Juvenile Psychopathic Institute, argued that "we have become certain that the development of mental tests and psychological analysis is doing more toward the establishment of true theories and of practical classification of criminals than all other methods of study combined" (p. 17).

Emerging fields like sociology and social work offered yet another apparently promising set of insights into crime, by positing that environmental factors could explain human behavior (Rothman, 2002). Progressive social science traced most forms of social disorder, including criminality, back to the dysfunctions produced by an industrializing and urbanizing society. One product of social scientific research was support for a wide range of efforts to regulate the newly complicated industrial landscape as a way of ameliorating or preventing some of the most serious harms that it created. Environmental theories of behavior also helped produce a sympathetic reading of antisocial behavior as the result of inadequate family life, educational background, vocational training or experience, and the like. The settlement houses of the late nineteenth century, such as Hull House in Chicago, formed a kind of seedbed for environmental theories of crime, which were then taken up by a pioneering generation of sociologists. Lillian Wald, in *The House on Henry Street* (published in 1915, the same year as Goddard's and Healy's books) told the story of a mother whose son was appearing in criminal court. Wald wrote, "ordinary boys and girls, she thought, could not resist these temptations [of street life] unaided; and speaking of her own boy . . . she summed up her understanding of the situation in the words: 'It's not that my son is bad; it's just that he's not a hero'" (p. 179).

The third essential premise of individualization followed from the first two: if the criminal offender, rather than the offense, was the proper object of concern, and if the roots of criminal behavior could be comprehended, then the first task of the criminal justice system was to produce an accurate diagnosis in each case. Indeed, whatever the perspective on the causes of crime—and, as we have seen, they were quite diverse—there was widespread agreement that there must be an aggressive and expended inquiry into the life and background of the offender. Indeed, progressives championed diagnosis at every stage—from preventive diagnosis of school age children, to presentencing diagnosis of convicted criminals, to ongoing assessments of those under some form of community or institutional supervision, to a final evaluation prior to release from supervision. In practice, this took the form of extensive testing and casework. Testing took all sorts of forms, though the most ubiquitous test in this era was the intelligence test. The IQ test became widely accessible to criminal justice professionals with the Stanford-Binet test (1916) and the Army Alpha and Beta tests (1917). Eventually, the IQ test would be joined by tests of vocational ability, mechanical ability, social adjustment, educational achievement, and the like.

Along with testing came the development of casework and case histories. The emerging field of social work had promoted the ideal of developing complete and comprehensive life histories of their subjects, and the criminal justice system was much affected by work like Mary Richmond's *Social Diagnosis* (1917). In this influential manual for social workers, Richmond made the case for weaving together medical, employment, educational, and family histories to achieve the proper "social treatment of individuals" (Richmond 1917, p. 38). The influence of social work on criminal justice practice can be further seen in the name of the leading social work organization—the National Conference on Charities and Corrections, where correctional reformers and administrators met side by side with those working on public health, labor conditions, social welfare, and mental illness (Recchiuti, 2007).

Historians of criminal justice should be careful not to make more out of individualization in this period than it really meant. In some ways, *classification* would be a useful term to use instead. The term classification suggests not that every individual offender was sui generis; puzzles that had to be put together one at a time. Rather, prisoners could be examined individually to see where they fit collectively, into a range of categories. For this reason, progressives strongly embraced the notion of classification of criminal offenders along different sorts of axes—classification by intelligence, for example, or classification by security risk, or classification by mental health.

Rehabilitation

At the heart of rehabilitation, there is a simple extension of the premise behind individualization—that the causes of crime lie in something beyond the simple human desire to pursue pleasure and profit. Those desires, after all, were better dealt with through systems of punishment that managed a rational calculus of pleasure and pain through deterrence. Progressives, on the other hand, were persuaded that the causes of crime were often more complex and further removed from the criminal act itself. To be sure, as noted, they rarely agreed on exactly what those causes might have been—biological, psychological, or environmental. And the term *rehabilitation* actually encompasses a Progressive Era response to the criminal offender that incorporates some distinct ideas: treatment, integration, and compassion.

As one might imagine, given the progressive emphasis on diagnosis in the new penology, formal treatment programming was one part of the rehabilitative vision. As the Prison Society of Pennsylvania (1919) noted: "the criminal is . . . a person of complex personality shaped by heredity and environment to what he is . . . demanding and deserving individual treatment according to the nature which has been developed in him" (p. 27). Fred Nelles, superintendent of the Whittier Reform School in California, established an institutional research department to provide mental testing of the young inmates and some psychiatric counseling (Schlossman, 1995), and a number of other psychiatric clinics were established around the country during this period.

The progressive vision for rehabilitation, however, tended to emphasize a more general process of community adjustment rather than specific forms of treatment and programming. In other words, the Progressive Era vision of rehabilitation was dominated by the theme of community reintegration, a term that has once again become current (Austin, 2001; Petersilia, 2003; Travis, 2005). Reintegration involved managing the offender's time in such a way as to encourage an embrace of the positive qualities of American society. As one penologist put it: "The criminal often does not see the beauty of American life, the slow, but inevitable progress of our nation and the ideals of kindness, service, and honesty which are common in many persons . . . the criminal is, by and large, the sheer individualist . . . he does not perceive the broader aspects out of which his immediate environment has been made" (Clemmer, 1958, p. 6). Interestingly, the commitment to reintegration did *not* depend on diagnosis, as reformer and administrator Howard Gill observed, "Programs of work, education, medical care, religion, recreation, and family welfare geared to solving significant problems of criminality should also be designed to *adjust the offender to the society to which he will return*, i.e. acculturation . . . treatment through problem-solving and acculturation must proceed whether or not causation can be established or dealt with" (Gill, 1970, p. 30, emphasis in original).

This image, taken from Delaware around 1905, shows a remnant of eighteenth and nineteenth century modes of punishment. At the top, two inmates stand with their heads and hands in a pillory, while an inmate below is tied to a whipping post. Delaware abolished the pillory around this time, while the whipping post remained in use until the middle of the twentieth century. Images like this one were important for the reformers of the Progressive Era, as they made their case for more humane forms of punishment.

Source: Courtesy of the Library of Congress, LC-USZ62-98905.

It should also be noted that one last element of the progressive vision was simply reforming prisons so as to make them less degrading and humiliating. It should be remembered that many prisons in the early twentieth century were still bastions of brutality. The champions of the brutal prison—those that Howard Gill called the "Old Guard"—were ever present in the minds of the reformers. Gill (1970) made the case that this approach "denied every normal basic need of the human personality and . . . fostered every pathology which results from a malfunctioning of these needs, namely, rejection, doubt, guilt, inferiority, inadequacy, diffusion, self-absorption, apathy, and despair. Is it any wonder that men left prison worse then when they entered?" (p. 30). This focus on the conditions of confinement and thereby trying to avoid additional harms arising from imprisonment itself was among the most important parts of the progressive mindset.

Case Studies in Criminal Justice: Kate Richards O'Hare, Prison Reformer

Kate Richards O'Hare was born in 1877, in Kansas. A committed socialist writer and activist, she toured the country in 1917 making speeches against the United States' entry into World War One. Arrested after one such speech in North Dakota, Kate Richards O'Hare was tried and convicted under the federal Espionage Act. Sentenced to serve a five-year term at the Missouri State Penitentiary (many federal prisoners were housed in state institutions at this time), O'Hare spent a little more than one year behind bars before her sentence was commuted.

After her release, O'Hare published an account of her time at the Missouri State Penitentiary as "federal prisoner number 21669" (O'Hare, 1923). Like many former convict authors of the time, she was unsparing in describing the harsh and degrading conditions behind bars. In a memorable passage, she describes her introduction to the prison mess hall:

"The first thing that struck me was the dead, rancid odour, the typical institution smell, much intensified. It was the concentrated odour of dead air, venerable hash, ancient stews, senile 'wienies,' and cabbage soup, mingled with the musty odour of decaying wood saturated with rancid grease and home-made soap" (p. 64).

In her book, O'Hare condemned not only the poor living conditions behind bars but also the utter absence of any positive interventions on behalf of the inmates. She described the sort of education the institution offered:

"There were no provisions in our prison for educational or vocational training. The women, at the expiration of their sentences, go out not only worn to physical depletion, but as illiterate and untrained as they entered.... In the minds of the prison officials with whom I came in contact, there was a marked antipathy to any sort of educational work among the prisoners, and seemingly a firm and deep-rooted conviction that ignorance in the prisoners is to be desired and maintained. But, while all education that might be helpful and possibly curative was relentlessly shut out, education in the ways of vice and crime and degeneracy flourished. I found learning the prison argot more interesting than any high school teacher ever made Latin" (p. 93, 95).

What makes O'Hare's stories of interest to the historian? Certainly the convict's perspective on prison life is a valuable one. O'Hare's account was part of a long history of inmate-authored works that continues today, with plenty of currently published accounts of twentieth and twenty-first century prison life (Carceral, 2004; Franklin, 1998; Martin & Sussman, 1993). Such accounts cast light onto those parts of the prison experience that might otherwise remain invisible. As always, when considering these accounts, it is important to consider how and why they were produced and how they might be representative of some larger experience.

Another interesting element to O'Hare's life story is that she chose to pursue prison study and reform after her release, much as some criminologists today began their engagement with criminal justice from the inmate's point of view. In the 1920s, she carried out an important survey of prison labor and, after moving to California, became an outspoken advocate for prison reform in the Golden State. In the most surprising turn of all, she was appointed in 1938 (at age 62) as an assistant director in the newly reorganized California Department of Corrections. O'Hare quickly helped clean house: the prison system was centralized, the board of prison directors was dismissed and replaced, abusive guards and administrators were fired, a new minimum security prison for young offenders was opened, and (closest to O'Hare's heart) many of the conditions of confinement were improved. O'Hare retired after a year. In 1943, at the invitation of Governor Earl Warren, she continued to attend meetings of the State Crime Commission, which she did until shortly before her death in 1948 (Miller, 1993).

Professionalization

What did professionalization mean to the reformers of this period? Certainly part of the idea was to open up the criminal justice system to expertise. This is no small point, for achieving the goal would mean breaking the hold on authority of various groups the reformers viewed as "nonexperts"—including (though certainly not limited to) judges, police officers and prison guards, political appointees, and politicians themselves. To allow experts some role over decision making would allow, for example, a caseworker preparing a presentencing report to claim some authority over what the sentencing judge actually did with a particular defendant. To take another example, it might allow for a prison psychiatrist to take some role in decision making regarding the punishment for rule infractions that might traditionally have been the authority of the prison guards. To be sure, this did not always (or even very often) occur in practice, but it lay at the heart of the progressive ambition.

Professionalization also meant a centralization of authority and a protection of that authority from the realm of politics and popular sentiment. It was in this way, reformers argued, that the application of expert knowledge could be guaranteed, and the operations of the criminal justice system made more orderly and rational. It might help to understand why progressives were so insistent on this to realize that the reform of state and local bureaucracies was a key part of progressive thought generally, not just in criminal justice (Recchiuti, 2007). If authority for prisons (or probation and parole) could be removed from specific localities *and* if that authority could be vested in the hands of those who possessed some expert knowledge, then one could begin the business of building a reformed system of punishment.

❖ VARIETIES OF CRIMINAL SANCTION

For all the attention paid to the place of the prison in western systems of punishment, it is helpful to remember that the prison always coexisted with noninstitutional forms of punishment. Progressive Era reformers sought to formalize and give structure to the traditional practice of watching over the offender in the community through the development of probation and parole programs (Rothman, 2002).

Probation was a term applied to a particular way of doing what criminal courts had always done in some fashion, which was to find some sort of punishment between setting a convicted person free and confining him or her to an institution. Probation would allow for continued supervision of the offender within the community for a set period of time, during which they would be obligated to follow certain rules of conduct, violations of which could result in a suspension of liberty. According to one Progressive Era account, the advantage that probation had over an older alternative like a suspended sentence was that the offender "is not excused from punishment but compelled to submit to it" (Robinson, 1923).

Of course, progressives did not invent probation per se. Many accounts credit John Augustus, a Boston boot maker often referred to as the "Father of Probation" (Inciardi 1987, p. 629). Augustus, as the story goes, was in a Boston court room one day back in 1841, when he encountered a "ragged and wretched" looking man, apparently bound for the House of Corrections. Convinced that the man's only problem was an overuse of alcohol, Augustus arranged to pay his bail and guaranteed to the judge that he would help oversee the man's conduct. At the end of the few weeks of good and sober conduct, the man was freed on the payment of a one-cent fine and court costs. Augustus was to repeat this process hundreds of times in the following years, effectively creating one of the first (albeit informal) probationary programs in the United States.

Of course, no one really invented probation, in the sense of creating something out of nothing. Historian Samuel Walker (1998) goes so far as to warn that "the colorful story of John Augustus has probably been told too many times," (p. 93) and risks misleading us as to the real history of probation—a history which does not involve any one inventor, but years of experimentation. Pioneer stories are important, but what the progressives sought to do—and did—was to systematize and centralize the practice. Massachusetts developed the first state probation law back in 1878 (even this was nearly two decades after Augustus' death), but it was not until 1899 that Rhode Island became the next state to adopt a similar law. At that point, the floodgates opened and many states adopted the practice. A National Probation Officers Association was formed in 1907, which became the National Probation Association in 1911 (and which is today the American Probation and Parole Association). By 1921, 35 states had adopted adult probation, and every state had adopted some form of juvenile probation (Robinson 1923, p. 196).

What's the Evidence?: Official Documents

One of the great dilemmas of studying the history of criminal justice is the dependence on officially produced sources to reconstruct past practice. There's little wonder these documents are often the bread and butter sources for criminal justice history–not very many participants in the criminal justice system took the time to reflect on paper their experiences. This includes criminal offenders, of course, but also the officer on the beat, the parole agent, or the prison guard, whose experiences are often lost to history. Official documents, therefore, tell us a great deal–but mostly about the point of view of the state and of those responsible for administering criminal justice institutions and programs. Most of these documents, such as annual reports, were (and still are) produced at regular intervals. Most college and university libraries house some reports from various state criminal justice agencies.

Of course, students of history who examine these sorts of documents face two problems. Do the documents tell us the kind of information we're

(Continued)

(Continued)

looking for? A prison's annual report might contain a great deal of information on the institutional farm—how many bushels of vegetables were produced, for example—but remain conspicuously silent on other issues, like discipline. Sociologist Donald Clemmer came to the same conclusion, back in 1940: "... we must give attention to the fact that the average ration is 2,675 calories per day for each inmate, yet we have more concern ... in understanding why gravy served for five consecutive breakfasts ... might precipitate a riot" (p. 59). Another question: do the documents tell us what actually happened, or are they an account of what officials intended to happen?

Here's an interesting example from a 1918 Virginia probation manual, written not long after the state had passed its first probation law. The manual describes the role of the probation officer as follows:

> "After a person is placed under his supervision, the probation officer should
>
> (1) Keep informed of the conduct and surroundings of his probationer;
>
> (2) Win his confidence, if possible. Impress upon his probationer that it is his purpose not to spy upon him, but to watch over and to help him help himself.
>
> (3) He should aid his probationer and encourage him by friendly advice and admonition, and take an active interest in reclaiming him from evil courses. Mere surveillance is ineffective; to put probation into effect the probation officer must act as a sort of father or big brother to the boy as a friendly counselor to the man. He should try to make his probationer understand that probation is not a term of punishment, but rather a period of education. He should establish friendly relations with his probationer and do whatever is most needed to strengthen his character and better his surroundings. He should secure for him employment in case the probationer is out of a job, and if necessary, obtain charitable aid, medical or psychological attention, or similar service" (State Board of Charities and Corrections [Virginia], 1918, p. 6).

Reading this excerpt might prompt some questions. The language is quite striking, particularly the repeated emphasis on the probation officer as a friend to the offender. To what extent would these affirmations of friendly relations have been borne out in practice? Similarly, one might consider the ways in which the ambitions contained in this mission statement might have fallen short in reality. What might have caused the reality of probation practice to differ from the expressed mission in this document?

Like probation, parole also has a "founding father" story: in this case, Captain Alexander Maconochie, who took charge as commandant of the English penal colony on Norfolk Island (off the coast of Australia) in 1840. Like John Augustus, Maconochie was reportedly deeply moved by the brutal conditions and disregard for humanity that he observed, and he developed a system of rewarding good conduct by prisoners. Under what he called the "mark system" prisoners would be able to progress through a series of five graded stages. The fourth of these stages was supervised release, the penultimate stage before "full restoration of liberty" (Petersilia, 2003, p. 56). By connecting release to conduct, making that release subject to the discretion of prison authorities, and requiring a period of supervision after release, Maconochie anticipated the essential form of the progressive parole system.

As with probation, this story is somewhat misleading. Various forms of supervised release, as Jonathan Simon (1993) shows, had been in existence in Western history since the medieval frankpledge and the early modern system of recognizance bonds. And, if Maconochie came up with a system that looked more recognizably modern, it is important to remember that no state government in the United States adopted a system of parole very soon after. Instead, states continued to rely on a variety of mechanisms to release inmates early, most often executive pardons and "good time" laws that allowed prisoners to earn reductions in their sentences (Blomberg & Lucken, 2000). Indeed the conditional pardon, according to historian Vivien Miller, allowed for a revocable release, dependent on behavior (Miller, 2000). Although the reformers who met at the Cincinnati Congress were well aware of the pioneering work in Australia and elsewhere, and the first institution-specific system was set up not long thereafter in 1876 by Zebulon Brockway at the Elmira Reformatory, it was not until 1907 that New York became the first state to fully adopt all the components of a parole system: indeterminate sentences, parole board controlled release, and community postrelease supervision. As with probation, the diffusion of parole was quite rapid after that, and within 20 years all but three states had adopted some form of a parole system.

So why did parole take off when it did? To be sure, the idea of parole meshed very nicely with the core elements of the progressive vision—it could be tailored to the individual, the concept centered around the notion of rehabilitation and betterment, and could be centralized and controlled by experts in the field rather than political figures. At the same time, though, reform ideas are generally adopted not on the strength of the idea but whether or not they fit a perceived need. Simon (1993) argues that the Progressive Era had new kinds of needs for which parole was well suited. In Simon's view, parole became a useful new tool for controlling inmates in an era when manual labor in prisons, which had been central to the daily operations of correctional facilities, was in rapid decline, an idea that other scholars have since developed still further (McLennan 2008). Indeed, progressive reforms were very much tied to "the domination of the labor problem" in the criminal justice system (McKelvey, 1977, p. 117).

Whatever the reason for its adoption, parole quickly emerged as one of the progressives' most politically unpopular innovations. As Joan Petersilia (2003) notes in her review of parole's history: "A Gallup poll conducted in 1934 revealed that 82% of U.S. adults believed that parole was not strict enough and should not be granted as frequently" (p. 61). Judges and police chiefs alike distrusted the parole system, acutely aware of the extent to which parole boards took into their own hands authority over the final outcome of an inmate's sentence. Advocates of parole liked to remind critics that parole was not an act "of grace" or leniency. As Sanford Bates (1936) put it: "Parole must be distinguished from pardon. Pardon involves forgiveness. Parole does not. Pardon is a remission of punishment. Parole is an extension of punishment. Pardoned prisoners are free. Parolees may be arrested and reimprisoned without a trial" (p. 248). In the end, many reformers came to share his observation that "politics is the curse of parole" (Bates, 1936, p. 261).

Notorious parole cases, like that of bank robber John Dillinger in 1933, show how public opinion could be aroused. In 1933, John Dillinger was in an Indiana State Prison with a parole date approaching. His family took the initiative to try and present the most favorable case possible to the parole board. They collected 200 signatures on a petition, secured favorable letters from upstanding local citizens, and even a supportive letter from the sentencing judge. Their efforts bore fruit, as Dillinger was released to his home on May 23. The parole board's judgment seemed misplaced, however, for Dillinger had committed a new bank robbery within two months (and there is some speculation that he may have turned back to his outlaw ways even earlier than that) (Gorn, 2009). As Dillinger went on his final, and most notorious crime spree, many commentators took the occasion to blame the parole system. Indeed, one account concluded: "the greatest enemies of the parole system have proved to be the Dillinger gangsters" (Bernstein, 1935, p. E10).

What impact did probation and parole have on the criminal justice system? Probation clearly assumed an important role as a sentencing option for judges. Lawrence Friedman and Robert Percival's exhaustive reconstruction of the operations of the criminal courts in Alameda County, California, show that while 61% of convicted felons were sentenced to state prison between 1880 and 1909, the percentage of state prison commitments dropped to 35% between 1910 and 1929 and even lower in subsequent decades. Much of the difference, according to Friedman and Percival, lay in the emergence of probation—which accounted for only 7% of felony sentences between 1880 and 1909, but jumped to one third between 1910 and 1929 (Friedman & Percival, 1987). Early probation programs in some jurisdictions may have drawn from very narrow categories of offenders, especially men charged with domestic offenses like desertion and nonsupport. It was, as historian Phillip Jenkins observes, scarcely a "revolution" (Jenkins, 1985, p. 195).

As for parole, it gradually came to assume an important if not entirely dominant place in the manner in which adult felons were released from prison. In California, the share of prison releases through parole grew from just 7% in 1907 to 35% in 1914 (Simon, 1993, p. 48). In Pennsylvania, while parole was created in 1909 with new legislation, each state institution and county house of corrections had its own parole system, until by 1921 there were as many as 70 distinct parole systems. This disorderly system, combined with the small numbers of parole supervisors and the resulting lax supervision, led one student of the system to declare that "the State of Pennsylvania has no parole system which is worthy of the name" (Jenkins, 1985, p. 186–187). Jonathan Simon (1993) reached a similar conclusion for California during the Progressive Era, arguing that reformers' ambitions in the state were never quite matched by the criminal justice bureaucracy they actually produced. Others reach the same conclusion for parole in the United States more generally, maintaining that poor parole practice repeatedly thwarted the intentions of those who designed and promoted the system (Petersilia, 2003; Rothman, 2002).

If probation and parole failed to achieve all that reformers hoped it would, it nonetheless had some impact on the criminal justice system. Unfortunately, we lack enough quantitative historical studies of either system to say for certain what the effects were. Still, historians seem to feel that parole and the indeterminate sentence may well have had the overall effect of lengthening terms of confinement for most offenders (Rothman, 2002). There is still more consensus over the idea that probation had a "net widening" impact—that it, it was less notable for diverting offenders from prison than it was in bringing into criminal justice supervision individuals who might not previously been subject to it (Rafter, 1990; Rothman, 2002).

❖ INSTITUTIONAL CONFINEMENT

For progressives, the basic challenge was to bring the prisons into line with their vision. In this quest, American reformers found themselves at a distinct disadvantage vis-à-vis their European counterparts. In the United States, institutions of confinement were hard to control centrally. Resolutely local, prisons were often supervised by individual boards of overseers, dominated by their wardens or superintendents and closely connected to city-and county-level political interests.

Therefore, one of the most important elements of progressive reform involved the creation of what one historian describes as "a bureaucratic penal state" (McLennan, 2008, p. 219). A number of states began the process in the late nineteenth century by replacing individual boards of oversight with statewide boards, theoretically less prone to the influence of local politics and individual institutional authorities (McKelvey, 1977). Early on, these statewide oversight entities were often combined boards of charities and corrections, charged with supervising all forms of institutional confinement, from poorhouses to mental asylums. The power of these early boards tended to be quite limited. Generally, they had the ability to conduct annual inspections, request institutional data, and issue public reports, but they were rarely given any operational authority over specific institutions.

The next step would come a bit later, with the creation of state-level administrative agencies charged with actually carrying out the state's institutional mission. Illinois became one of the first states to embrace this model when it established a state department of public welfare in 1917. While the Illinois model continued the older tradition of combining social welfare and correctional oversight, it was not long before states began experimenting with corrections-only agencies. New Jersey established one of the first when it created a State Board of Control in 1925. The goals of its new commissioner suggest the priorities of centralizing power: the creation of a diversified set of institutions and, most importantly, the authority to assign and transfer inmates within that system (McKelvey, 1977, p. 286). Such systems could create detailed records of individual inmates and could follow them from institution to institution. New Jersey's State Board of Control may have been novel at the time, but it became the norm in the decades that followed, as, slowly, nearly every state (and the federal government) established bureaus of prisons and departments of corrections. The process took time. In Arizona, for example, a modern state department of corrections was not created until 1968 (Lynch, 2009).

Civil service reform was another important step toward establishing central control over systems of punishment. Civil service reform—replacing politically controlled appointments with a bureaucratic, merit-based system of hiring, assignment, and promotion—began to influence the criminal justice system at the end of the nineteenth century. For progressive reformers, it represented their best hope of being able to control the type of prison guards or parole and probation officers hired, who were otherwise often political appointees with little or no training or experience. Civil service requirements and training programs helped shift the balance of power toward the state bureaucracy—but very slowly. Central training programs, for example, were scarcely in evidence before World War Two. New York, for example, created the innovative Central Guard School in 1935, but this was a lonely exception to the general rule that, where it happened, training was a localized and very limited affair (Wallack, 1938; Wilkinson, 2005).

Progressives also remade the prison itself during this period, both reordering the institutions for adult male offenders and creating new forms of correctional institutions. Certainly the progressive interest in creating more humane institutions played a role, as did the impulse to provide more educational and training opportunities for inmates. But the changes in the way prison labor was organized may well have played the most decisive role. For the average inmate, nothing was more central to their prison experience than whether or not they worked during the day and at what and under what conditions. Progressives inherited a collapsing system of contract labor and piece-price work. Organized labor unions had long objected to this system and the manner in which it undermined free labor. Beginning in New York in the 1880s, organized labor unions and their allies began to secure the upper hand, obtaining state-level legislation restricting the use of for-profit prison industries. Not surprisingly, prison officials saw the challenge to prison labor as a challenge to the very organization of the prison itself. Indeed, the National Prison Congress called an emergency meeting in 1884 to consider some of the implications to changes happening in New York.

Over the next decades, for-profit prison industries were vastly reduced. The federal Hawes-Cooper Act of 1929 gave states the right not only to bar for-profit industrial work in their own institutions but also to ban prison goods made in other states. The federal Ashurst-Sumners Act of 1935, passed in the midst of the Great Depression, effectively barred all for-profit prison industries and limited most production to goods intended for state use (with license plates, of course, being the archetypal example). The percentage of adult inmates at productive industrial work slowly declined from the 1880s through the 1920s, with the decline getting more dramatic after 1920, and again after the federal laws of 1929 and 1935 (McKelvey, 1977).

The collapse of industrial work posed a problem—for-profit labor had not only been a way of making money, it had been the central activity around which prison life had been organized. As historian Rebecca McLennan (2008) observes: "it had given rise to a distinctive corpus of customs, rules, and routines that were particularly well-suited to the needs of contractors and that served to reinforce the contract system itself" (p. 207). Into this void, to meet the threat of widespread inmate idleness, stepped a number of reformers and prison administrators who aimed to reorganize the daily life of the prison.

Some reformers took a dramatically new and even revolutionary tack. In New York State, Thomas Mott Osborne aimed to transform the prison into the site of a great experiment in democratic self-governance. A newspaper publisher and Democratic political figure in upstate New York, Osborne had been deeply influenced by experimental programs for juvenile offenders, like the George Junior Republic, which encouraged its residents to practice their own forms of governance as a way of preparing them for proper citizenship in the free world. In 1912, Osborne entered Auburn Prison anonymously under the name "Tom Brown"; the resulting account of his experience, *Within Prison Walls*, was published in 1914.

Thomas Mott Osborne poses for a photograph with a group of New York State prisoners. The image of the keeper in common cause with the kept suggests the radical vision at the heart of Osborne's idea of a democratic prison community.

Source: Courtesy of the Library of Congress, LC-B2-3310-7.

That same year, he was appointed warden of Sing Sing Prison, where he established the Mutual Welfare League, an organization designed to place some measure of prison administration into the hands of the inmates themselves. In this way, Osborne sought to turn the nineteenth-century prison on its head by replacing artificial rules and order with something approximating a real community.

Osborne's model of prison democracy was not widely replicated, however. Far more common among prisons for adult male offenders was a turn to a program-heavy focus on education, vocational training, and recreation—a new sort of institution that would become known as the "Big House" prison. It is tempting to label the period the "Big House Era" in corrections, as some historians have done (Bright, 1996; McLennan, 2008). The Big House was a far cry from the austere nineteenth-century prison and generally held far more inmates as well. Whether built new from the ground up (like Stateville in Illinois) or remade (like San Quentin in California or Sing Sing in New York), all tended to feature improvements to the basic conditions of confinement, mostly eliminating ancient striped uniforms, shaved heads, the lockstep.

Where did the Big House come from? The Michigan State Penitentiary at Jackson was one of the prototypical Big House prisons of the era. Construction on the new state prison began in 1924. Ten years later, when it was completed, it stood as the nation's largest prison, with cell space for over 5,000 inmates. Historian Charles Bright (1996) describes the mini city behind Jackson's fences: "a post office, newspaper, and radio station (with headphone receivers in every cell); a hospital with physicians, nurses, and dentists; a library, theater, bank, telephone system, bakery, garage, laundry, dairy, barber shop (with fourteen barbers), tailors, printers, carpenters, variety stores, schools, and churches (with three chaplains)" (p. 33). This was a whole new kind of institution, with a level of investment in activities and programs that would have been unknown to its nineteenth-century predecessors and which could be found in any number of similar prisons by World War Two (Blumenthal, 2004; Cox, 2009).

If the Big House aspired to manage large populations of inmates in a new way, the reformatory aspired to manage them in a distinctively new sort of institution. The reformatory idea began with a focus on juvenile offenders, as an institution to keep young people confined apart from the damaging influences of older criminals. Juvenile reformatories dated all the way back to New York's venerable House of Refuge that opened back in 1825. The House of Refuge pioneered the idea that the young offender—male or female—should be housed separately. It was the progressives, particularly with the advent of the juvenile court, who really expanded the adoption of these institutions in states across the nation. Reform schools and reformatories spread to every part of the United States, with institutions for girls experiencing particular growth in this period (Odem, 1995). While many progressive juvenile reformatories were echoes of their nineteenth-century counterparts, some genuinely innovative and experimental institutions opened, such as the Whittier State Reform School in California (Schlossman, 1995). Still, most historians continue to find a large gap between the theory and practice of juvenile reformatories, which "left the promise of the juvenile court movement not only unrealized but untested" (Pisciotta, 1996; Schlossman, 1977, p. 188).

An important outgrowth of the juvenile reformatory was the reformatory for adult offenders. The Elmira Reformatory, which opened in New York State in 1876, is widely regarded as the pioneering example of the adult reformatory. Under the long tenure of Warden Zebulon Brockway (who ran Elmira from 1876 until his retirement in 1901), the institution set the pattern for many other reformatories to come and was one of the first institutional offspring of the Cincinnati Congress and the Declaration of Principles of 1870. Elmira featured some basic reformatory elements: the selection of inmates was limited to the younger and more promising; a mark system classified inmates on the basis of behavior; inmates' progress (or lack thereof) was the basis for release, transfer, or retention; and sentencing was indeterminate, to allow for institutional discretion in managing inmates.

Even in Elmira, we see the constant mix of ideas and necessity at play. Brockway opened Elmira as a slightly modified version of the traditional industrial prison, and it is interesting to note that he only adopted the programs of military drills and educational training after New York passed legislation limiting prison industries (Schlossman & Spillane, 1992; McLennan, 2008). Elmira and Brockway were the subject of very unfavorable investigations in the 1890s, which demonstrated that Brockway's institution was held together by a system heavy on physical punishments and disciplinary cells (Pisciotta, 1996). Nonetheless, the Elmira model inspired a modest wave of reformatory construction around the country, and enshrined the concept—still widely applied today—of building institutions for the confinement of younger inmates and those with limited criminal records.

Another legacy of the Progressive Era was the opening of prisons and reformatories for women. For most of the nineteenth century, female offenders had lived in the same institutions as men, often in separate sections of a building or in distinct buildings on the same institutional campus. Progressive reformers demanded that the female criminal be treated in a manner consistent with what some scholars call "maternalist" social policy—focused on creating structures that would protect the rights and meet the needs of women and children and elevating women to important roles in the operation of those structures (Koven & Michel, 1993). In other words, female offenders were to be dealt with as a separate group, both in terms of keeping them physically apart from men, and in terms of creating a gender-specific institutional experience.

The very first women's prisons emerged as contemporaries of the Elmira Reformatory, products of the post–Civil War burst of reform energy. The earliest such institution opened in Indiana in 1873 and introduced the idea of staffing the institution with women. But it was in New York where the female prison—or at least the female reformatory—was linked to a wholly new design, the cottage system. Designed to incorporate a vision of domestic life, reformatories for women featured "cottages" spread out over rural campuses (Freedman, 1981; Rafter, 1990; Zedner, 1995). Inspired by nineteenth-century examples, most of these reformatories were not established until after 1910 (Dodge, 2006, p. 19)—and, it should be noted, the majority of female offenders, even in this era, still served their time in custodial prisons (in a number of states, still alongside men, where they handled the domestic labor for the institution).

As with probation and parole, a general consensus has emerged among scholars that the new women's institutions widened the net of state control. Most historians agree that the crimes for which women were imprisoned differed significantly from those of men and had a heavy emphasis on nonfelony sexual offenses; indeed, a 1923 federal prison census showed that only 20% of female state inmates had been sentenced for felony crimes (Dodge, 2006, p. 20). Historian Mary Odem (1995) determined, as well, that juvenile girls were far more likely to

This photo shows one of the cottages at the Federal Reformatory for Women at Alderson, West Virginia. Still in operation today as a minimum security facility, the Alderson prison began operations in 1927 as the first federal prison for women. Built on the cottage plan, the prison resembled a boarding school or a small college campus.

Source: Courtesy of the Library of Congress, HABS WVA,45-ALD.V,1-C--1.

be imprisoned during this period than boys of similar age, resulting in a surge of reformatory construction to keep up with sentencing.

Most states failed to specialize correctional institutions beyond those for adult male offenders, adult female offenders, male and female reformatories, and reform schools for male and female juvenile delinquents. In fact, a number of states failed to produce systems even this specialized during the Progressive Era. Still, some states did create very highly diversified systems that featured other types of institutions. Prisons for the mentally ill—or the criminally insane, as they were referred to—constitute one such category. New York State opened its Matteawan State Hospital in 1892 for convicted criminals judged to be insane. Institutions like Matteawan functioned, for all practical purposes, much like the mental hospitals of the period. This meant, among other things, that most inmates were held there for absolutely indeterminate periods of time. For as long as they were judged to be dangerous, offenders would be kept at these prisons, regardless of the nature of the offense for which they were first convicted.

Institutions for defective delinquents constituted another important category of new institutions in this period. The term "defective delinquent" referred to those persons judged to be mentally retarded and habitually criminal (or even at risk of being habitually criminal). Progressives created many training schools for the "feeble-minded"—in 1904, 17.3 persons labeled feeble-minded had been institutionalized per 100,000 of the general population, a figure that increased to 46.7 by 1923 (Noll, 1995). But within those training schools, administrators constantly appealed for specialized institutions for the criminally minded. By the 1920s, such institutions opened in Massachusetts, New York, Pennsylvania, and Virginia (where the State Prison Farm for Defective Misdemeanants opened in 1926) (Noll, 1995). In Massachusetts, Dr. Walter E. Fernald, who described feeble-mindedness as "the mother of crime, pauperism and delinquency," (Anderson, 1920, p. 257) helped triple the size of the Massachusetts School for the Feeble-Minded, which later became known as the Walter E. Fernald School. Like many similar institutions, the Fernald School's operations were a pale shadow of its ambitions, producing a long and troubling history of neglect and abuse (D'Antonio, 2004).

Finally, of course, there were the forgotten women and (mostly) men of institutional confinement—those who occupied space in the nation's many jails during this period. In contrast to prisons, which typically held long-term inmates, jails typically held inmates sentenced to a year or less or defendants awaiting trial. Local jails presented a bewildering variety of practices and patterns, few of them positive. As is true today, there was far less attention paid to the conditions of the jails than there was to that of prisons. Indeed, historians have been complicit in ignoring the jail—there are many more studies of prisons than there are of jails. In part, of course, this reflects the relative lack of sources. Court records are far richer for felony convictions than they are for the larger number of misdemeanor cases which were processed quickly and filled the jails. Likewise, jails rarely compiled the sorts of detailed records on their inmates that were so characteristic of Progressive Era prisons.

None of what we know about jails in this period is very positive. Conditions varied a good deal but often in the range of bad to worse. A survey of the Cook County Jail (Chicago) by noted Progressive reformer George Kirchwey (Chicago Community Trust, 1922) called the county jail "the worst feature of the American penal system" and "a convenient dumping ground for the refuse of our society." Fay Lewis' 1903 examination of the Rockford, Illinois, jail made this glum observation: "were the Prince of Peace to come again it can hardly be doubted that he would first direct his efforts against our noisome city jail" (Lewis, 1903, xxiii). The inmates at Rockford were a typical mixture. Of a total of 1,035 commitments the prior year, Lewis found that 362 were drunk, 100 disorderly, 30 drunk and disorderly, 206 lodgers, 139 vagrants—roughly 80% of the total.

Richard Serrano published a poignant account of his grandfather—arrested in Kansas City some 80 times in the 1930s and 1940s for vagrancy and public drunkenness—called *My Grandfather's Prison*. This prison was, in fact, the old Kansas City Municipal Farm completed just after World War One, and by the time Serrano's grandfather died there under mysterious circumstances, the conditions were "deplorable, unsanitary, shocking, and inhuman" (Serrano, 2009, p. 67). Serrano's grandfather spent his time at the Municipal Farm alongside hundreds of other drunks sentenced to short terms of confinement (they made up nearly 60% of all the institution's new commitments), spending most of their time just lying around and waiting for their release. He died of a broken neck while down in the jail's "dungeon," from "causes unknown"—no one ever took responsibility for the bruised and beaten man found dead alone in his isolation cell.

The Kansas City Municipal Farm was hardly exceptional. Many other city jail facilities offered their own sad echoes of these dreadful conditions. Indeed, judging by later accounts, it seems clear that Progressive Era reformers utterly failed to make substantial improvements to jail conditions in the middle decades of the twentieth century (Goldfarb, 1975).

Figure 4.1 This figure from George Kirchwey's (Chicago Community Trust, 1922, p. 21) "General Survey and Recommendations" for the Cook County Jail shows the jail population for the first Monday of each month between 1914 and 1922. Note the manner in which the jail population spiked during the cold winter months, then bottomed out during the warm summer months.

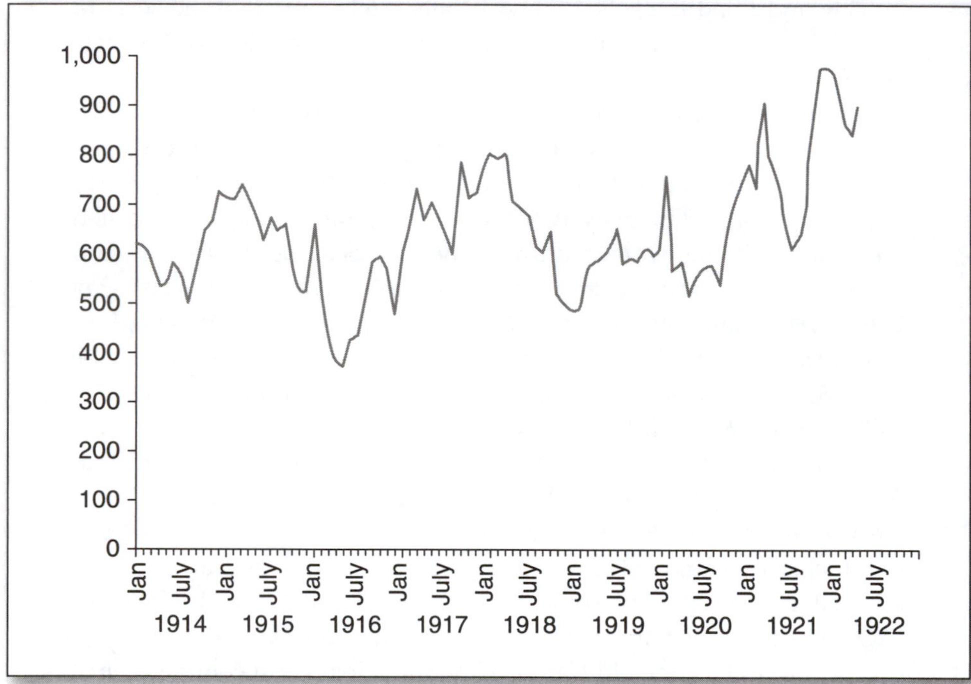

❖ THE PROGRESSIVE LEGACY

By the 1930s, it was abundantly clear that the progressives had not wholly remade the criminal justice system. The reports of the Wickersham Commission are perhaps the single best source from which to evaluate the limitations of Progressive Era reform. The Wickersham Commission was the first national crime commission, appointed by President Herbert Hoover in 1929. Formally titled the National Commission on Law Observance and Enforcement, but known by the name of its chair, George Wickersham, the commission grew out of President Hoover's concern over law breaking related to Prohibition. The Wickersham Commission quickly enlarged its mandate far beyond Prohibition, however, to examine every aspect of crime and criminal justice in the United States. In 1931, the commission released a remarkable fourteen volumes of reports, covering an astonishing range of topics: the child offender, deportation laws, alcohol prohibition, crime statistics, the costs and causes of crime, federal courts, and criminal procedure.

The Wickersham Commission also issued reports on penal institutions, probation, and parole, and these 1931 assessments offer a reasonable guide to the accomplishments and failings of the era (National Commission on Law Enforcement and Observance, 1931). On parole, the Wickersham Commission found the practice gaining some acceptance but still far from universal. The commission's survey of prisoner releases in 1927 found that only 49% of the total number had been released by parole boards, nearly the same percentage as those who departed at the maximum expiration of their sentence (Travis, 2005). Nor was the commission any more impressed with the quality of parole; in one instance, they noted that a state parole board had reviewed and decided 95 cases in just four hours (Dickey, 1993). Still, they were impressed with some systems—New Jersey, for example, impressed the Commission with its commitment to aftercare and social work techniques—and they strongly reaffirmed the premise of parole.

The commission strongly backed the premise of probation as well, noting that "probation must be considered as the most important step we have taken in the individualization of the treatment of the offender," and that "no man should be sent to a penal institution until it is definitely determined that he is not a fit person for probation" (National Commission on Law Observance and Enforcement, 1931, p. 173). Still, the commission acknowledged, "it is admitted by all concerned that probation services are almost everywhere understaffed" and that case loads were far too high to permit appropriate case work (Rothman, 2002, p. 86–87).

On prisons, the Wickersham Commission showed a mixed picture, though mostly negative. States had succeeded in diversifying their institutions, including 24 states with institutions for the criminally insane, and 18 with adult reformatories. Still, there was no escaping the tough conclusion:

> "the present prison system is antiquated and inefficient. It does not reform the criminal. It fails to protect society. There is reason to believe that it contributes to the increase of crime by hardening the criminal."

Yet, here as well, there was a call for a renewed commitment to the progressive spirit:

"we are convinced that a new type of penal institution must be developed, one that is new in spirit, in method and in objective" (National Commission on Law Observance and Enforcement, 1931, p. 170–174).

Of course, the very existence of the Wickersham Commission itself may have been the most important legacy of the Progressive Era. Reflecting the interest in strong centralized authority of the criminal justice system from state—and, in the case of the commission, even national—authorities, the Wickersham reports were a vindication of the progressive assertion that criminal justice was too important to remain a merely local concern. Moreover, with its remarkable assemblage of expert staff and advisers, the Wickersham Commission embodied the notion of professional expertise and authority, making the case that the men, women, and children traveling though the criminal justice system must be the object of attention and study. Finally, of course, the Wickersham Commission fully embraced the central tenet of progressive thought—that rehabilitation, broadly defined, was the critical purpose of any system of punishment. "The function of the penal institutions," concluded the commission, "is protection of society," a goal which could only be accomplished by "the reformation of the criminal" (Rothman, 2002, p. 144).

❖ REFERENCES

Anderson, V. V. (1920). "A state program for the custody and treatment of defective delinquents." *Proceedings of the National Conference of Social Work*. Chicago, IL: Rogers and Hall.

Austin, J. (2001). "Prisoner reentry: Current trends, practices, and issues." *Crime and Delinquency, 58*: 314–334.

Bates, S. (1936). *Prisons and beyond*. New York, NY: MacMillan.

Bernstein, V. H. (1935, July 14). "Parole system long under fire." *New York Times*, pp. E10.

Blomberg, T. G., & K. Lucken. (2000). *American penology: A history of control*. New York, NY: Aldine de Gruyter.

Blumenthal, R. (2004). *Miracle at Sing Sing: How one man transformed the lives of America's most dangerous prisoners*. New York, NY: St. Martin's Press.

Bright, C. (1996). *The powers that punish: Prison and politics in the era of the 'Big House', 1920–1955*. Ann Arbor: University of Michigan Press.

Carceral, K. C. (2004). *Behind a convict's eyes: Doing time in a modern prison*. Belmont, CA: Thomson.

Chicago Community Trust. (1922). *Reports comprising the survey of the Cook County Jail*. Chicago, IL: Calumet Publishing.

Clemmer, D. (1958). *The prison community*. New York, NY: Holt, Rinehart, and Winston

Cole, S. A. (2001). *Suspect identities: A history of fingerprinting and criminal identification*. Cambridge, MA: Harvard University Press.

Cox, S. (2009). *The Big House: Image and reality of the American prison*. New Haven, CT: Yale University Press.

D'Antonio, M. (2004). *The state boys' rebellion*. New York, NY: Simon and Schuster.

Dawley, A. (2003). *Changing the world: American progressives in war and revolution*. Princeton, NJ: Princeton University Press.

Dickey, W. (1993). Sentencing, parole, and community supervision. In Ohlin, L. E., & Remington, F. J. (Eds.), *Discretion in criminal justice: The tension between individualization and uniformity*. Albany: State University of New York Press.

Dodge, L. M. (2006). *'Whores and thieves of the worst kind': A study of women, crime, and prisons, 1835–2000*. DeKalb: Northern Illinois University Press.

Franklin, H. B. (1998). *Prison writing in twentieth-century America*. New York, NY: Penguin Books.

Freedman, E. B. (1981). *Their sisters' keepers: Prison reform in America, 1830-1930*. Ann Arbor: University of Michigan Press.

Friedman, L. M. (1993). *Crime and punishment in American history*. New York, NY: Basic Books.

Friedman, L. M., & Percival, R. V. (1987). The processing of felonies in the Superior Court of Alameda County 1880–1974. *Law and History Review, 5*: 413–436.

Gill, H. B. (1970). A new prison discipline: Implementing the Declaration of Principles of 1870. *Federal Probation, 34*: 29–33.

Goddard, H. H. (1915). *The criminal imbecile: An analysis of three remarkable murder cases*. New York, NY: The MacMillan Company.

Goldfarb, R. (1975). *Jails: The ultimate ghetto of the criminal justice system*. Garden City, NY: Anchor Books.

Gorn, E. J. (2009). *Dillinger's wild ride: The year that made America's public enemy number one*. New York, NY: Oxford University Press.

Healy, W. (1915). *The individual delinquent: A text-book of diagnosis and prognosis for all concerned in understanding offenders*. Boston, MA: Little, Brown, and Company.

Inciardi, J. A. (1987). *Criminal justice*. San Diego, CA: Harcourt Brace Javonovich.

Jenkins, P. (1985). A Progressive 'revolution'? Penal reform in Pennsylvania, 1900–1950. *Criminal Justice History, Volume VI*. Westport, CT: Meckler Publishing: 177–199.

Koven, S., & Michel, S. (1993). *Mothers of a new world: Maternalist politics and the origin of the welfare state*. New York, NY: Routledge.

Lewis, F. (1903). *The city jail: A symposium*. Rockford, IL: Calvert-Wilson Company Press.

Lynch, M. (2009). *Sunbelt justice: Arizona and the transformation of American punishment*. Stanford, CT: Stanford University Press.

Martin, D., & Sussman, P. (1993). *Committing journalism: The prison writings of Red Hog*. New York, NY: Norton.

McGerr, M. (2003). *A fierce discontent: The rise and fall of the Progressive movement in America*. New York, NY: Oxford University Press.

McKelvey, B. (1977). *American prisons: A history of good intentions*. Montclair, NJ: Patterson Smith.

McLennan, R. M. (2008). *The crisis of imprisonment: Protest, politics, and the making of the American penal state, 1776–1941*. New York, NY: Cambridge University Press.

Miller, S. M. (1993). *From prairie to prison: The life of social activist Kate Richards O'Hare*. Columbia: University of Missouri Press.

Miller, V. M. L. (2000). *Crime, sexual violence, and clemency: Florida's pardon board and penal system in the Progressive Era*. Gainesville: University Press of Florida.

National Commission on Law Enforcement and Observance. (1931). *Report on penal institutions, probation, and parole*. Washington, DC: U.S. Government Printing Office.

Noll, S. (1995). *Feeble-Minded in our midst: Institutions for the mentally retarded in the South, 1900–1940*. Chapel Hill: University of North Carolina Press.

Odem, M. (1995). *Delinquent daughters: Protecting and policing adolescent female sexuality in the United States, 1885–1920*. Chapel Hill: University of North Carolina Press.

O'Hare, K. R. (1923). *In prison*. New York, NY: Knopf.

Osborne, T. M. (1914). *Within prison walls*. New York, NY: D. Appleton and Company.

Petersilia, J. (2003). *When prisoners come home: Parole and prisoner reentry*. New York, NY: Oxford University Press.

Pisciotta, A. W. (1996). *Benevolent repression: Social control and the American reformatory-prison movement*. New York: New York University Press.

Prison Society of Pennsylvania. (1919). Report of Commission to Investigate Penal Systems. *Journal of Prison Discipline and Philanthropy, 58*: 19–46.

Rafter, N. H. (1990). *Partial justice: Women, prisons, and social control*. New Brunswick, NJ: Transaction.

Rafter, N. H. (1997). *Creating born criminals*. Chicago: University of Illinois Press.

Recchiuti, J. L. (2007). *Civic engagement: Social science and Progressive-Era reform in New York City*. Philadelphia: University of Pennsylvania Press.

Richmond, M. E. (1917). *Social diagnosis*. New York, NY: Russell Sage Foundation.

Robinson, L. N. (1923). *Penology in the United States*. Philadelphia, PA: J. C. Winston.

Rosenblum, W. (2008). *Beyond the prison gates: Punishment & welfare in Germany, 1850–1933*. Chapel Hill: University of North Carolina Press.

Rothman, D. J. (rev. ed., 2002). *Conscience and convenience: The asylum and its alternatives in Progressive America*. New York. NY: Aldine de Gruyter.

Schlossman, S. L. (1977). *Love and the American delinquent: The theory and practice of 'Progressive' juvenile justice 1825–1920*. Chicago, IL: University of Chicago Press.

Schlossman, S. L. (1995). Delinquent children: The juvenile reform school. In N. Morris, & D. J. Rothman (Eds.), *The Oxford history of the prison: The practice of punishment in Western society* (pp. 325–349). New York, N.Y: Oxford University Press.

Schlossman, S. L., & Spillane, J. F. (1992). *Bright hopes, dim realities: Vocational innovation in American correctional education*. Santa Monica, CA: RAND Corporation.

Serrano, R. A. (2009). *My grandfather's prison: A Story of death and deceit in 1940s Kansas City*. Columbia: University of Missouri Press.

Simon, J. (1993). *Poor discipline: Parole and the social control of the underclass, 1890–1990*. Chicago, IL: University of Chicago Press.

State Board of Charities and Corrections [Virginia]. (1918). *Probation manual: With an analysis of the probation laws of Virginia*. Richmond, VA: State Board of Charities and Corrections.

Travis, J. (2005). *But they all come back: Facing the challenges of prisoner reentry*. New York, NY: Urban Institute.

Wald, L. D. (1915). *The house on Henry Street*. New York, NY: Henry Holt and Company.

Walker, S. (1998). *Popular justice: A history of American criminal justice*. New York, NY: Oxford University Press.

Wallack, W. M. (1938). *The training of prison guards in the State of New York*. New York, NY: Teacher's College.

Wilkinson, R. W. (2005). In J. C.Burham, & J. F. Spillane, (eds.). *Prison work: A tale of thirty years in the California Department of Corrections*. Columbus: Ohio State University Press.

Wines, E., & Dwight, T. (1867). *Report on the prisons and reformatories of the United States and Canada*. Albany, NY: Van Benthuysen and Sons.

Zedner, L. (1995). Wayward sisters: The prison for women. In N. Morris & D. J. Rothman (Eds.), *The Oxford history of the prison: The practice of punishment in Western society* (pp. 295–324). New York, NY: Oxford University Press.

5

Dark Days in the South, 1870s–1930s

Why focus a separate chapter on the history of criminal justice in the American South? Students of contemporary criminal justice are accustomed to studying national criminal justice systems, so a chapter on a single region may seem unfamiliar. Just as comparative studies of different national systems reveal variation from country to country, we have every reason to expect that there may be subnational, or regional, variations within the nation. In fact, many contemporary criminal justice studies have shown how unique social, cultural, and political elements can produce subnational variations in criminal law and procedure (Logan, 2005, 2009), the use of imprisonment (Zimring & Hawkins, 1991; Beckett & Western, 2001), or in the use of capital punishment (Garland, 2005).

These variations are important to the history of criminal justice, for it is in the variations that we get a clearer sense of what it is that produces criminal justice systems. This chapter focuses on the unique history of crime and punishment in the American South. A purely national story can obscure what happened in the South or make uniquely southern developments seem like a mere footnote to the national story—the

South just waiting to catch up, so to speak, with the modernizing national system of criminal justice. By taking this history seriously, we gain a richer understanding of the actual lived experience of countless Americans, but we also get some insight into those factors that shape our responses to criminal behavior.

Of course, it would be a mistake to overemphasize southern distinctiveness. Matthew D. Lassiter and Joseph Crespino (2010) have recently made the case that "the notion of the exceptional South has served as a myth, one that has persistently distorted our understanding of American history" (p. 7). It is true that what makes the South worth studying is not simply the fact of racism or discrimination, which is hardly unique to the history of the American South—this echoes, after all, in United States history from the treatment of Chinese in California, Mexicans in the American Southwest, and African Americans across the urban north. Nor is the South distinctive for being dominated by rural, decentralized criminal justice, for one could find examples of this just as plentiful in the American West (Lynch, 2010).

So just what makes the southern experience distinctive? Most of us have some familiar images, endlessly recycled in popular culture, of convicts in leg irons and striped uniforms, of violent lynch mobs, inmates laboring on massive plantation-style prison farms, and so on. This chapter argues that these images are correct, in a sense. Criminal justice in the South *was* different, from policing to trial to punishment. These differences were a product of political and economic structures—the "political economy" of the South that had three core elements. First, a powerful localism to southern politics kept state-level criminal justice institutions underdeveloped and left private and local interests in charge. Second, the emergence of a one-party electoral system after Reconstruction and a legal culture of Jim Crow racial segregation built upon rhetoric of white supremacy, left little room for black political participation. Blacks had little role in the criminal justice system, other than as the primary objects of a punitive system. Finally, the distinctive, labor-intensive needs of the southern agricultural and industrial economy produced a system of labor control that was abetted by the operations of the criminal justice system.

This chapter concludes in the 1930s, a decade marked by signs of coming changes to southern criminal justice. From this decade forward, the regional distinctiveness of the South would give way to more broadly national patterns of criminal justice practice.

❖ THE PARADOX OF SOUTHERN POLICING

From the beginning, southern policing displayed an important paradox: while the policing of white crime (and, to some extent, black on black crime) was limited and ineffectual, the policing of black behavior was treated as a highly serious affair, particularly when it threatened some dimension of the established racial order. This central paradox had its origins in the antebellum slave South but remained a dominant characteristic of policing right through the 1930s.

Throughout much of the American South, slave patrols established a precedent for modern policing. As early as the 1660s, Maryland and Virginia established slave codes defining black slaves as slaves for life and making them property under the law. To enforce these laws, states with large slave populations established slave patrols between the 1690s and the 1750s. In Virginia, the House of Burgesses responded to a 1721 slave revolt by enacting plans to prevent slaves from plotting revolts during the holidays. In 1727, they sent out militias during the Christmas, Easter, and Whitsuntide holidays to disperse large slave gatherings. By 1738, the assembly operated the patrols year round and expanded their duties so that they visited slave quarters to try and find runaways. These patrols became permanent institutions, operated by the county courts, hunting for slaves who had run away or simply travelled away from their homes without passes.

By the nineteenth century, slave patrols often acted as police in towns and cities, mainly in order to monitor African Americans. By 1837, Charleston, South Carolina, operated a slave patrol with over 100 officers (Hadden, 2001; Wadman & Allison, 2004). Charleston, New Orleans, Savannah, and other southern cities, in effect, established formal policing systems well before policing is traditionally assumed to have begun in the United States (Dale, 2011; Rousey, 1996). Of course, while slave patrols and even slaveholders were operating as agents of the law and of the state, they were not wholly a part of the state. Focused on enforcing private interests, they created a system of policing less formal and less accountable than would emerge elsewhere.

Following the end of the Civil War in 1865, southern law maintained the antebellum paradox. The policing of white crime was lax, limited by weak institutional structures and a general hostility to state authority. Levels of lethal violence were particularly high in the American South, and there seems little question that the absence of strong law enforcement structures contributed to these trends. Vigilante justice also flourished where institutional structures were weak, and there was a prevalent hostility to central authority. Even many private disputes were resolved by acts of violence, most of which took place with little intervention or response from authorities. One resident of a remote portion of Kentucky-Tennessee border region recalled that the local toughs "was rough, and they'd do just about anything. Wasn't too much done about it by the law either" (Montell, 1986, p. 45).

This hostility to state authority manifested itself in other ways, including the recurring battles over the policing of the business of illicitly distilled liquor. Moonshining, as it was known, provided an important source of cash income for farmers and a common foe in federal revenue agents (who often coerced unwilling sheriffs into aiding their efforts). Whitecapping—the term used for vigilante mobs resisting outside authority—was a periodic response to moonshine policing. An effort to enhance South Carolina liquor laws contributed to the so-called Darlington Riot in 1894, in which mobs of locals shot it out with 18 constables, resulting in six deaths. William Link (1992) concludes that the Darlington Riot showed that "heavy-handed, coercive government violated traditional sensibilities about the role of government in South Carolina" (p. 314). Still later, state and national alcohol prohibition laws were also met with widespread resistance and weak local support for enforcement (Montell, 1986). When arrests were made, Montell (1986) points out that "It was not always easy to get convictions . . . as merchants and businessmen in the county seat towns relied on these sources for their own whiskey, and would speak favorably of the moonshiners to court officials" (p. 71).

Formal police organizations were fairly modest in size and scope throughout the postbellum era. Municipal police departments were vastly smaller than their northern counterparts, and investment in law enforcement at all levels—like most state investments—fell after the end of Reconstruction. County sheriffs were generally the primary institution of law enforcement, overseeing an informal group of full-time and part-time deputies. Although many of the developments in police professionalism and police technology described in Chapter Two could be found in southern law enforcement agencies, they generally appeared later and in fewer places (Rousey, 1996; Watts, 1973).

Most sheriffs, and many police departments, operated on a fee system, which dated back to the old slave patrol system and remained in place even after Reconstruction. Under the fee system, which prevailed across the South during this period, most law enforcement officers and court officials received little or no official salary, instead receiving fees according to the legal actions undertaken. Under this system, for example, when a criminal defendant was convicted, the court would assess costs. These costs would cover the costs of the court, law enforcement officers, any legal representation, and witnesses. The employment of deputies was often a private affair, funded out of the fee system. Systems which paid sheriffs per arrest, rather than per conviction, raised the prospect of large numbers of trivial cases coming before the court, while systems that paid only on conviction doubtless encouraged excessive and unfair prosecutions. Sheriffs were usually the jailers as well and were paid allowances for keeping inmates. Criminal courts still met infrequently (adjourning for weeks or months at a time) in much of the South. Frugal sheriffs that kept costs low enough to turn a profit could pack their jails with prisoners (usually black) awaiting trial.

County sheriffs' organizations and municipal police departments were virtually all white, and the end of Reconstruction in the 1870s meant an end to whatever experiments there had been in integrating police forces (Rabinowitz, 1976). In New Orleans, for example, a highly integrated police force between 1868 and 1877 quickly gave way to a nearly all-white force after Reconstruction's end (Rousey, 1986). Similar stories of black participation followed by subsequent exclusion could be found in Montgomery, Raleigh, Memphis, Jacksonville and many other cities. By century's end, black law enforcement personnel were reduced to a negligible presence, and their exclusion continued for many years. In 1924, only 13 southern cities employed even a single black police officer. As late as 1944 there was not a single black law enforcement officer in the states of Mississippi, South Carolina, Louisiana, Georgia, and Alabama (Rudwick, 1960). Where black officers were employed, it was nearly always in the policing of black neighborhoods.

The pervasive localism of southern politics showed itself in many ways, including the reluctance of states to adopt state police organizations. The state police forces adopted in much of the rest of the country—starting with the creation of the Pennsylvania State Police in 1905—had no counterpart at all in the South (save for the Texas Rangers). Indeed, most southern states did not develop state-level police forces until the 1930s and, when they did, employed the "highway patrol" model rather than the state police model. Advocates of creating an Arkansas state police spent years arguing for a centralized police authority—emphasizing everything from the dangers of crowded state highways, to moonshining in the Ozarks, to the depredations of interstate bank robbers like John Dillinger—before they finally won the day in 1935 (Lindsey, 2005). The difficult journey to the creation of an Arkansas state police force demonstrates the continued power of southern localism.

The pervasive weakness of policing white conduct had something of a parallel when it came to black-on-black crime. Many observers commented on the relative indifference of police and criminal courts to crimes in which the victims were black. Myrdal (1944) observed that many black neighborhoods suffered from a lack of police presence, "left practically without police protection" (p. 542). John Dollard, a psychologist who studied southern race relations in the 1930s, recalled:

> The white lawmen didn't regard crimes that happened between Negroes as equivalent to those that happened between whites. I sat in on a court scene where one Negro woman had shot at another about ten feet away and missed. That is an assault with a deadly weapon and probably with an intent to kill, so it's a felony. The judge's attitude was that it was all kind of funny, and he didn't keep order in the court. When the defendant, in a really exaggerated Negro dialect, said, "Well judge, she was playing around with my man," the audience, all Negro, burst into laughter. The judge then smiled behind his hand and tapped with his gavel. The defendant was fined ten dollars and put on probation (Ferris, 2004, p. 15–16).

Official tolerance of black-on-black criminality certainly had its limits, and advocates of tighter control tended to emphasize the perils of indifference for the white South. The *Birmingham News*, for example, opined in 1914:

> When criminal negroes carve up, stab and kill other criminal negroes, they rapidly develop into human tigers. The taste of blood makes them reckless. They will readily, surely give vent to their hatred of some white men, and sooner or later kill white men (Harris, 1972, p. 572).

As had been true in the antebellum slave South, black conduct in the decades after the Civil War was policed far more closely when the interests of the white South were threatened. This was especially true in the case of serious crimes involving white victims. Here, too, white southerners relied on various forms of popular justice, the most notorious and direct of which was public lynching—the practice of mobs organizing to exact lethal vengeance on one or more victims. While a good deal of lynching was done by private vigilante mobs, the most notorious and best-known cases were the mass mob lynchings, in which large numbers of people would gather for highly ritualized public torture and execution.

The removal of African Americans from the public sphere was accompanied, and to a large extent aided by, the specters of the black criminal, the black rapist, and black crime waves. Lynching, in effect, went hand in hand with the rise of political disenfranchisement and legalized racial segregation. The resultant wave of lynch justice was extensive, part of what historian C. Vann Woodward (2002) called "an intensive propaganda of white supremacy, Negrophobia, and race chauvinism" (p. 85). Historians generally agree with Woodward's assessment of the political dimensions of lynching and black crime fears. Glenda Gilmore (1996) argues "the political machine exaggerated a series of sex crimes and allegations in order to strike terror into the hearts of white voters" (p. 83).

Lynch law was justified as an appropriate expression of community sentiment and an appropriate punishment for all those thought unworthy of formal justice process. Leo Frank, a northern-born Jewish factory manager living in Atlanta, was accused in 1913 of the murder of Mary Phagan, a 13-year-old white girl who worked in the same factory. Frank was convicted and sentenced to death. After the governor commuted his sentence to life imprisonment, a mob took Frank from his jail cell and lynched him. The trial judge remarked: "I believe in law and order. I would not help lynch anybody. But I believe Frank has had his just desserts" (Dinnerstein, 1987, p. 147). It is a telling indication of official sentiment that the southern criminal justice system almost never undertook successful prosecutions for lynching in this period.

Nor was any protection for victims of mob violence forthcoming from the federal government. In the critical case of *United States v. Cruikshank* (1876), the Supreme Court asserted that the federal government lacked the authority to control private actions intended to deny civil rights. The case itself centered around a horrific racial massacre in Louisiana in which more than 60 blacks had been killed. Regardless of the severity of the conduct, the Court ruled that the federal government was only allowed to respond to state action, not private actions, thereby leaving the conduct of lynch mobs outside of federal authority.

Although the language of white supremacy and the fear of black crime could be found everywhere in the South, the political and economic forces that helped produce lynch mob violence varied over time and place (Beck & Tolnay, 1990; Tolnay & Beck, 1995). One comprehensive study argues that the Gulf Plain stretching from Florida to Texas and the cotton uplands of Mississippi, Louisiana, Arkansas, and Texas all had the highest rates of lynchings, and the common factor was large numbers of mobile African American residents not well known to the white population, together with weak local governments and law enforcement structures and relatively isolated communities (Ayers, 1984). Another important study suggests that lynching flourished where the racial order was struggling to sustain itself—in Georgia's Cotton Belt, for example, versus the commercial coast or the rural and impoverished mountain regions of the northern part of the state (Brundage, 1993). Victims of lynching were nearly always men, nearly always black, often young, loosely attached to the community, who had transgressed some aspect of southern racial codes.

Formal policing was often seen as a bulwark against vigilante justice and lynch mobs (though sheriffs not infrequently colluded with mob violence). Strict policing was fashioned as preventing or containing frightening mob violence in the name of law and order and doing so in ways that would closely reflect white interests. Indeed, the threat of mob violence could send a message to law enforcement, not unlike this one from Mississippi Governor James Kimble Vardaman: "Let there begin a most vigorous campaign against the Vagrant—the vicious Idler and the Keeper of Dives of Infamy. Let the rendezvous of the Rapist, the Murderer, the Crap-Shooter, and the Blind Tiger, be closed!" Otherwise, the Governor warned, "the mob will usurp the function which you should perform, but which you have betrayed" (Oshinsky, 1996, p. 92).

Still, police and sheriff's departments made little headway against lynch law. As one Mississippi sheriff declared, "I am ready and willing to enforce the law, but you know as well as I that unless an officer is backed up by at least some of the people, his efforts are worth very little" (Oshinsky, 1996, p. 121). Law enforcement was rarely willing to risk violence or community hostility and, in fact, officers were often on the side of the mob. Historian W. Fitzhugh Brundage (1993) observes that virtually all of the lynching he studied in Virginia involved a failure of local law enforcement to adequately protect prisoners, either because they were overwhelmed by mobs, or simply indifferent (even sympathetic) to the desire to lynch.

In the wake of the Civil War, the states of the former Confederacy created new legal instruments to control freed slaves—the Black Codes. The end of slavery upended an entire legal regime. Although many former slaves remained as tenants or hired hands where they had worked as slaves, freedom did mean an unprecedented mobility among former slaves. The Black Codes allowed southern sheriffs to arrest blacks in large numbers for a range of behaviors, from the obviously criminal offenses against persons and property to a variety of behaviors not obviously criminal—including congregating in public, use of offensive language, and certain forms of commercial enterprise.

Historians have debated the extent to which black crime actually increased in the years following slavery's end. Some see charges of theft, for example, as a mask for racial retribution and as a form of social control between white employers and black workers. Other historians assume that there were probably increases in crime like theft among impoverished, defiant, and newly mobile former slaves.

The criminal justice process offered few protections for black suspects and defendants. Police brutality and coerced confessions were among the chief complaints; and police killings were frequent. Rousey (1986) observes that "policemen killed members of the general public with something close to impunity,"—most police killings were extra-legal and most involved black victims (p. 183). Extralegal police violence was rarely punished during this period. The few federal prosecutions of such cases were largely unsuccessful (Belknap, 1989).

Among southern blacks, another important grievance was the manner in which municipal police forces policed gambling and other forms of illicit leisure. One particular source of complaint was the use of paid informants, usually black, to set up arrests in areas where white law enforcement could not otherwise penetrate. One writer, in 1904, gave voice to this widespread complaint: "the constable gives a Negro, called a "striker," money to go out and play craps. He informs the constable when and where he will gather men to play. Then the constable swoops down and arrests them. The striker gets a dividend and the constable and justice also profit by the transaction" (Du Bois, 1904, p. 58).

Criminal defendants fared little better. Southern criminal courts presented defendants with something more akin to an inquisitorial system than a true adversarial system of justice. So long as any semblance of a formal legal procedure could be justified simply by being an improvement over mob violence, defendants could expect few procedural considerations. Defense attorneys were rare, and court appointed defense attorneys very nearly nonexistent. Juries were not representative, as a brief moment of racial inclusion during Reconstruction rapidly faded in the final quarter of the nineteenth century. By century's end, juries were all white (at both the petit and grand jury levels). Even black testimony at trial was sometimes restricted. Steven Garton (2003) argues that southern criminal courts "enacted a performance designed to impress on the public the certainty of conviction and punishment. Some offenders were convicted on the flimsiest of evidence, a fact admitted by judges and juries, but the ritual of conviction was central to the court system" (p. 686).

Figure 5.1 This is a figure from W. E. B. Du Bois' 1904 study, *Notes on Negro Crime,* an early effort to apply systematic social scientific research methods to the issue of race, crime, and criminal justice. This figure shows the arrests per 1000 of "Negro" population in various U.S. cities. Note that rates of arrest were actually highest in Chicago, Cincinnati, and St. Louis, offering a useful reminder that the policing of black communities outside the Deep South was not necessarily less extensive.

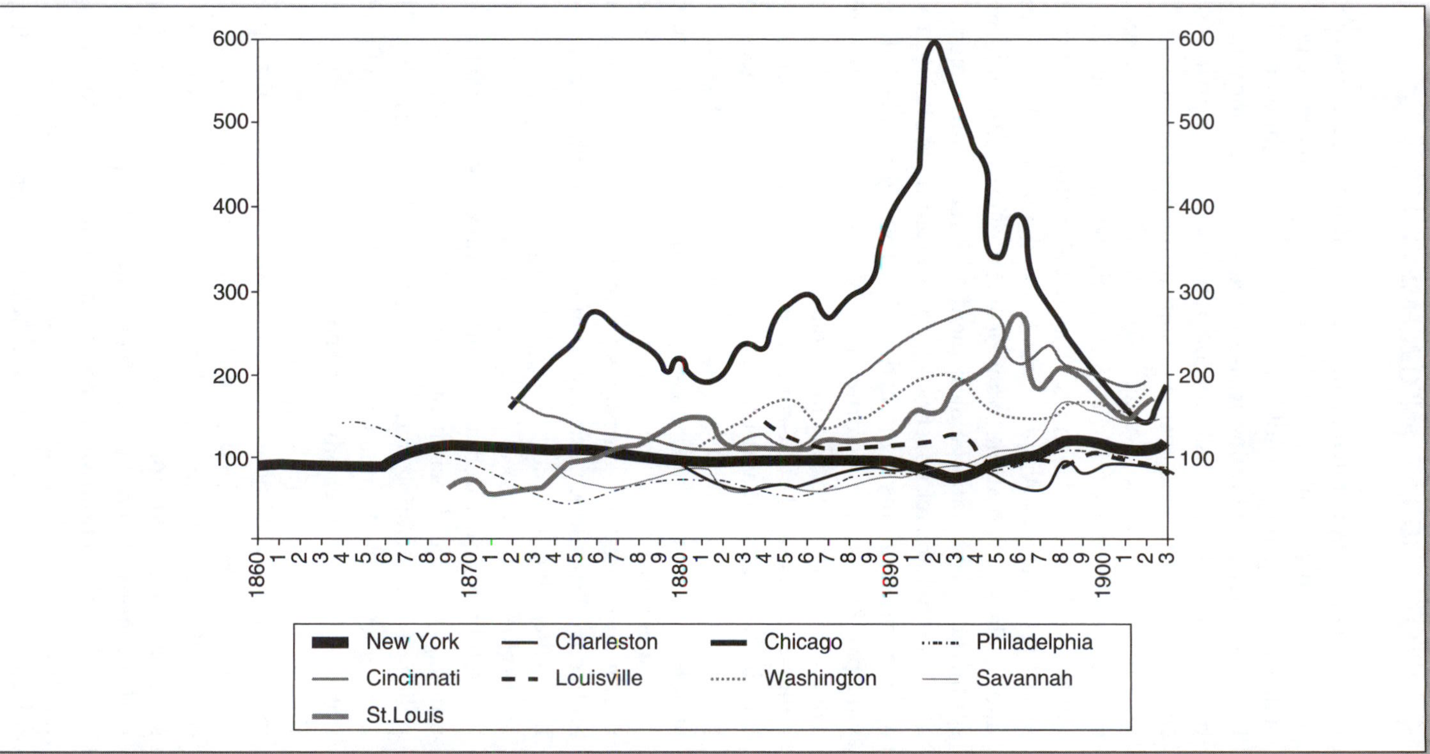

Source: W. E. B. Du Bois, Some Notes on Negro Crime, Particularly in Georgia: Report of a Social Study Made Under the Direction of Atlanta University. Atlanta: Atlanta University Press, 1904.

❖ REFORMING LAW ENFORCEMENT

Progressivism was a force in the South, as it was in the rest of the country. As elsewhere, it attempted to "selectively increase the power of the state over the private life of home and family and attempted to reform the state itself by elevating it above the sway of political interests and by increasing its responsibility for public services" (Trost, 2005, p. 23). Modernization and expansion of state authority and bureaucracy mingled with more general concerns for social justice and for social provision. To be sure, early reform efforts in the South were more limited and ran across deeper social and cultural hostility from "southern traditionalists" (as historian William Link terms them) and their antipathy to middle class, paternalistic forms of social reform. Still, reform-minded southerners were part of a movement with real political significance.

As elsewhere, reform efforts were spurred most often by campaigns against various forms of urban disorder. The fight against alcohol was a vital part of southern reform, especially its distribution through the saloon, and most especially in the black dives—the "blind tigers" where liquor was sold illegally. George Ward, elected as a reformist mayor of Birmingham, Alabama in 1904, proposed higher saloon fees and a central saloon district where the saloons could be properly policed. Worries about widespread drunkenness, prostitution, gambling, and drug use came together with a sense that political corruption encouraged their toleration to produce campaigns for more modern and efficient police and court structures. Certainly a number of southern cities—Atlanta, Louisville, Memphis, and New Orleans among them—featured police forces closely tied to local political machines.

Reformers provided an important source of external pressure on municipal police departments, often doing a far better job than did police of investigating and documenting illicit enterprise. The work and legacy of the Richmond Vice Commission offers one useful illustration. Modeled after other vice commissions around the country, the Richmond group's 1915 report to the city contained a number of important recommendations, including a demand that prohibition laws be enforced, that a Bureau of Public Morals be given responsibility over "illicit sexual immorality," that the city provide for rehabilitation services for arrested prostitutes, and that the police force be reorganized under a more powerful police chief (Link, 1992, p. 122).

Child protection was another vital interest for southern reformers. Indeed, the Richmond Vice Commission posed a pointed rhetorical question in their 1915 report: "Can parents inculcate high moral standards when across the street or down the block are houses of the red-light district?" (Shepperd, 2001, p. 119). For the dependent, neglected, or delinquent child, of course, the creation of a juvenile court was the reformers' great hope, in the South as elsewhere. Memphis created one of the first in the region, in 1910, which historian Jennifer Trost (2005) attributes to the influence of national reform networks and local middle class interests.

When court reforms did come into play, they were often implemented in highly discriminatory ways, for the racial system still prevailed. Race was still critical in southern progressivism, and leading regional reformers showed little interest in challenging the dominant structures of Jim Crow segregation. In Memphis, the juvenile court met on separate days for black and for white youth, and different court personnel were assigned for black and for white children. Memphis also provided very different levels of resources—black youth, for example, had only a single case officer assigned to the entire group of probationers, probably because probation was seen as a valuable, positive good for young delinquents. Nor did black youth in Memphis have a detention home. Instead, the court sentenced these young people to short terms in the old city jail (Trost, 2005).

Despite the inequities, progressivism did give African American reformers an opportunity and a language to push for changes, albeit with a segregated system. The creation of a whites-only juvenile detention center in Memphis was followed by a years-long quest by black Memphians to raise funds for their own detention facility. Middle class blacks pressed for these reforms in ways that largely paralleled those of white progressives (Gilmore, 1996). The growing presence of black social workers generally also included court personnel. In Virginia, the first black probation officer hired (in 1918) undertook one of the most comprehensive casework surveys of black juvenile delinquents, and the new Children's Bureau took up the cause of "dependent, neglected and delinquent colored children" (Wilkerson-Freeman, 2002, p.135). It also belies the notion that southern black communities did not want criminal justice institutions—securing properly run juvenile courts and the like were, in fact, an important part of black progressivism during this period.

❖ PATTERNS OF PUNISHMENT

Historian Blake McKelvey (1977), writing on the subject of southern penology in the post–Civil War era, claimed that the states of the former Confederacy "from a penological point of view scarcely as yet belonged to the union" (p. 197). His observation points to the most central fact of southern punishment—that the end of the Civil War and the collapse of slavery propelled the South into a different path from the rest of the nation, a path on which it would remain until the middle of the twentieth century.

Before the Civil War, southern states employed the penitentiary as an integral part of a state-level system of punishment. Indeed, the adoption of the penitentiary across much of the South was among the most notable of centralizing reforms in that region and occurred largely at the same time as in the rest of the United States. Of course, the pattern was only similar to a point. Southern prisons housed inmates from the free population, while the system of private slave ownership dealt with the remainder of the population. Still, the penitentiary was an important part of a modern vision for the antebellum South.

Following the Civil War, southern states rapidly abandoned the penitentiary system. Wartime destruction left some state penitentiaries in no condition to house sentenced criminals. In other cases, modest prison structures were maintained but reserved only for aged and infirm offenders. The economic straits of most southern states made the maintenance of expensive penitentiary systems unlikely, and no state successfully proposed the construction of a new facility in the years after the war. North Carolina did commit to the construction of a penitentiary in 1868, but delays and expenses eventually led the state in 1877 to abandon the hope of modeling a prison system on European or northern institutions. Indeed, by the start of the twentieth century, only Virginia, North Carolina, and South Carolina housed substantial numbers of prisoners in standard penitentiary buildings (although Louisiana and Alabama retained older penitentiary buildings for those too ill and infirm to be maintained elsewhere).

The alternative system of punishment to which North Carolina, and the rest of the South, first turned was the convict lease. Convict leasing refers to a system whereby convicted criminals are sentenced to work for private employers who have "leased" that labor from the state. The leasing of convicts was not, in and of itself, a southern invention. Indeed, inmates in northern prisons had been leased to private contractors for their labor for much of the nineteenth century, before the practice was largely abolished. The southern states, however, most thoroughly embraced the system. Unlike in the North, where leasing systems typically kept inmates housed in state prisons but laboring for private employers, the southern version did away with prison structures entirely, leaving the management of inmates entirely to private interests.

Convict leasing was a brutal system. As one southern-born critic of leasing described it, "The system springs primarily from the idea that the possession of a convicts' person is an opportunity for the State to make money; that the amount to be made is whatever can be wrung out of him" (Cable, 1899, p. 126). Most historians emphasize the cruelty of the system, often in connection to the old slave system, as illustrated by the title of David M. Oshinky's (1996) study *Worse Than Slavery*. Oshinsky's title is a reminder that it was the conditions attendant to the collapse of slave labor that led to the embrace of convict leasing, which served as a kind of bridge between the Old South and the New South.

As railroad networks increasingly covered the South, new agricultural and industrial enterprises emerged to take advantage of the efficiencies in transportation and access to national markets, and convicts followed. So convict leasing represented a new form of unfree labor that replaced slavery but also helped to support the industrial and commercial development of a new South. All of Alabama's male prisoners who were able to work were leased to two mining companies, the Tennessee Coal and Iron Company and the Sloss Iron and Steel Company (Curtin, 2000). In all, nearly a quarter of Alabama's coal labor was convict labor. Even when convicts labored on plantations, their work often helped support emerging commercial agriculture in places like the Mississippi Delta, where massive cotton plantations emerged in the late nineteenth century that featured labor practices that led some to describe the region as an "American Congo" after the well-known brutality of the Belgian colonial regime in central Africa (Woodruff, 2003).

Was the system really worse than slavery? Without question, leased convicts suffered terribly, and those who leased them may well have had less incentive than slaveholders to pay attention to health and welfare—a sentiment captured nicely by the titles of other historical studies of leasing: *One Dies, Get Another* and *Twice the Work of Free Labor* (Mancini, 1996; Lichtenstein, 1996). Convicts across the South—whether working in the turpentine camps of Florida, the coalmines of Alabama, or the railroads of North Carolina—performed intensely physical and dangerous work that broke down health and took many lives.

Out of sight and out of mind, convict leasing operations featured harsh discipline and shockingly bad health conditions. Flogging was the "universal punishment" (Kellor, 1901, p. 194). A description of an early prison farm in Alabama gives some sense of the oppressive means used to keep inmates in line:

> "The reports are that [Mr. Bush] often rears his horse over and against them, that he clubs them with sticks and clubs and clods of dirt and that he allows the guards to do the same . . . that he whips them unmercifully often giving them from 75 to 100 lashes, that he works them in the rain, that he gives little or no attention to the sick; that often their rations are insufficient and badly cooked" (Curtin, 2000, p. 19).

No institutions had physicians or medical care. Tuberculosis, pneumonia, and dysentery, contributed to mortality rates between 10% and 25% (Kellor, 1901, p. 202). The old penitentiary in North Carolina remained open to receive "broken" men back from railroad work. Many of these died not long after their return to the main prison, so physically deteriorated that medical interventions could not save them. Critics of convict leasing such as George Washington Cable condemned the lack of state oversight and reprinted one response from a lessee to his request for information, as a way of showing how little access the state had to information about how its prisoners were being treated (Cable, 1899, p. 125):

> *Office of Lessee Arkansas State Penitentiary,*
>
> *Little Rock, Arkansas, July 2, 1882.*
>
> *Dear Sir: Yours of ____ date to hand and fully noted. Your inquiries if answered, would require much time and labor. I am sole lessee, and work all the convicts, and of course the business of the prison is my private business. My book-keeper is kept quite busy with my business, and no time to make out all the queries you ask for. Similar information is given to the Legislature once in two years.*
>
> *Respectfully,*
>
> *Zeb. Ward*

Convict leasing was intended for both white and black offenders but, as elsewhere in the criminal justice system, there was a high degree of racial disproportion. Nearly every historical survey of leased prisoners confirms the racial disproportion in the system. One study found that nearly 90% of Alabama state convicts were black in 1890, while more than 96% of Alabama county convicts at the same time were black. Indeed, seven "black belt" Alabama counties in 1890 did not record even a single white prisoner (Curtin, 2000, p. 2). In the same vein, another study of leased Georgia and South Carolina inmates in 1880 finds that more than 90% in both states were black (Oshinsky, 1996, p. 63).

Not every connection between the criminal justice system and private employers was as explicit as the lease system. In numerous instances, local law enforcement and criminal courts administered punishments designed to assist or reinforce debt peonage—labor that was bound to their employers on account of unpaid debt. Vagrancy laws, a broad catchall concept that allowed nearly unlimited police discretion, were the primary tools for this sort of labor control. Ample evidence indicates that the emergence of parole systems in the South was at least in part an effort to help prospective employers secure workers in a time of real or perceived labor scarcity. Birmingham, Alabama, police periodically led roundups of vagrants, in which "It is a case of go to work or go to jail" (Harris, 1972, p. 579). Adults, and even youth, could be released from the criminal courts into private labor service in lieu of payment of fines. The Memphis juvenile court, for example, released black youth to the custody of white farmers (Trost, 2005). Similarly, Florida turpentine farm operators relied upon the collusion of the criminal courts to enforce unfair labor contracts and to use fines for vagrancy and other minor criminal offenses to keep laborers in camps. Camps operators would pay fines in court, whereupon laborers would be bound over to camp operators to pay off the cost of their fines (Shofner, 1981).

Florida produced one of the last and most notorious examples of the horrors of this labor system, in the case of Martin Tabert. Tabert was an adventuresome 22-years-old when he left the family farm in North Dakota in late 1921 to take a trip down South. His journey came to an end in Leon County, Florida, when he was arrested for stealing a ride on a train (Tabert had no ticket). Convicted of vagrancy, Tabert was fined $25.00 and sentenced to 90 days in the custody of the county. The sheriff then turned Tabert over to the Putnam Lumber Company, who leased inmates for $20 each per month. Tabert's parents, anxious over their son's fate, attempted to track him down but heard nothing until receiving a letter in early February from the company, informing them that Martin Tabert had died while there. Before long, stories of horrific working conditions, brutal beatings, and savage neglect emerged, along with a clear sense of the manner in which Sheriff Jones had collaborated with the company to provide a steady supply of workers by making arrests on vagrancy charges, often by sweeping arriving trains for passengers without tickets. The resultant publicity, criminal trials, and state investigations led, in 1923, to the end of Florida's county-level convict leasing programs (Carper, 1973).

Case Studies in Criminal Justice: J.C. Powell, Captain of the Florida Convict Camp

Captain Powell is one in a long line of figures in the criminal justice system who have written memoirs, or accounts of their lives and careers in the system. What makes Powell's work so fascinating and historically important is that his account is one of the very few detailed descriptions from the inside of the convict leasing system. His memoir, *The American Siberia: Or Fourteen Years Experience in A Southern Convict Camp*, published in 1891, begins with an unforgettable scene:

> "In the fall of 1876 a singular spectacle might have been observed at the little town of Live Oak, in Northern Florida. A train had just arrived, and from one of the cars some thirty odd men disembarked and formed in irregular procession by the road-side. The sun never shone upon a more abject picture of misery and dilapidation. They were gaunt, haggard, famished, wasted with disease, smeared with grime, and clad in filthy tatters. Chains clattered about their trembling limbs, and so inhuman was their aspect that the crowd of curiosity seekers who had assembled around the depot shrank back appalled" (p. 7).

Powell's shocking opening was not an indictment of the convict leasing system but of the state-run program that leasing replaced! His purpose, clearly, was to paint the leasing system as the best alternative available for the management of prisoners. As Powell recalled: "the state was poor, largely unsettled, torn with political strife . . . the horrible condition of affairs which I have outlined forced a change of some character. The building at Chattahoochee was entirely unsuited for prison purposes, and the lease system was turned to, as a last resort, very much as was the case when Georgia was saddled with that institution" (p. 8).

Powell, along with his brother, was employed by Major H.A. Wise to take charge of the very first group of leased inmates. The opening scene at the railroad depot turns out to be the moment at which Powell meets up with his new charges. His account provides many important details of camp operations and of camp life, which would otherwise be lost to historians. Powell tells of the way in which the strap was used for discipline, for example:

> "It consists of a section of tough leather about a foot and a half long by three inches broad, and attached to a wooden handle. The castigation is applied below the loins, and the convict place upon his knees with his palms on the ground . . . During the time that I was at the head of the lease system, I allowed no one else to administer punishment, as

> the matter was always unavoidably the source of more or less outside criticism, and I did not wish responsibility to be divided" (p. 21).

Of course, when reading these sorts of memoirs and accounts, historians must be attentive to the perspective of the author. This is as true for the stories of the keepers as it is for the kept. In Powell's case, one is alert to the purpose here, which is both to tell a gripping story but also to justify the system in which he worked. Consider this extended passage from *The American Siberia*, and the manner in which it treats the leasing system, the prisoners, and reaction of local African Americans to the arrival of a camp of prisoners:

> "The news of the change of lease was received with rejoicing by the prisoners of the turpentine camps. A convict is invariably anxious for a change of some sort, and is willing to take chances of getting out of the frying-pan into the fire. And the fact was that the work at the pine woods, particularly the chipping, had broken down most of the long-time men; they were eager to exchange the hack and dipper for the plow and hoe . . . we went to work at once and the process of selection proved tediously long. It was concluded at dark, and before day-light next morning I started for Live Oak with our prisoners. They included all the sick, the decrepit and the women, and several wagons were used to carry those unable to walk and the baggage and camp equipment. It was a long line, patrolled by guards at each side, and moved slowly through the woods toward town. We found a large crowd waiting at Live Oak, where we took the train . . . Early in the afternoon we reached the station where a number of four-mule wagons were waiting to convey the party to the camp, about twelve mile distant. The convicts were bundled in, the guards formed as before, and the procession started."

> "In order to appreciate the curious demonstration which followed us clear to our destination, it must be understood that the rich agricultural region in this part of the state is thickly settled by negroes, who live the most primitive of imaginable lives, and most of whom have never been out of Jefferson County. To these simple folks the spectacle that we formed was one of surpassing interest. They flocked from far and wide and lined the road-side. Almost as far as one could see there was a vista of open mouths and uplifted hands. At one point they brought out a gigantic bass drum, and a darky musician beat the long-roll as we hove in sight. The convicts caught the spirit of the occasion and sang and yelled at the top of their voices. One of them thrummed a guitar, and altogether it was like a nightmare of minstrelry" (Powell 1891, p. 341, 345–346).

By the time Martin Tabert had the fatal misfortune of arriving in Florida, the system of convict leasing had already disappeared from most of the South. To some extent, convict leasing faded away because of a reaction to the horrors of the system—the high mortality rates among leased inmates, the free use of corporal punishment, and the ghastly physical conditions of the camps. Critics such as George Washington Cable (1899) condemned this "shameful and disastrous source of revenue" (p. 128). More often, however, convict leasing faced opposition from private workers increasingly campaigning against the practice, which took away jobs and wages from the workforce through the unpaid use of unfree labor. Mine workers in Alabama, for example, vigorously opposed a system that kept wages suppressed and took many jobs from free labor. Populist politicians, for their part, drummed up a white working class furor over the exploitation of this resource by the wealthy elite.

One response was the birth of the state prison farm system, nowhere better represented than in the creation of Mississippi's Parchman Farm. Located on 20,000 acres in the Mississippi Delta, Parchman Farm was the brainchild of Governor James Kimble Vardaman. Champion of the white farmer and laborer, and unabashed racist, Vardaman proclaimed the prison farm to be the solution to the problem of corrupt moneyed interests' involvement in the criminal justice system and an appropriate place of labor for the state's convicts.

The language of prison programming, reform, and rehabilitation was barely, if at all, present in prison farms. In fact, one could question whether the language of reform had any greater place in prison farms than in the old convict leasing system. The largest farms, such as Parchman in Mississippi or Angola in Louisiana, operated in ways that would have seemed familiar to operators of massive slave plantations. Inmates at Parchman Farm, for example, were spread out over 15 field camps. Each of the field camps had a central barracks (known as "the cage") where inmates were housed and fed. An appointed superintendent ran Parchman, and he oversaw the sergeants who ran each of the field camps. Two assistants (or "drivers") in each camp assisted the sergeants. The real day-to-day work of governance at Parchman was controlled by convict trusties—who numbered as many as one in five inmates—who carried out the supervision of work and even carried the guns that kept the rest of the inmates in line as they toiled in long lines in the field. The inmates, known as "gunmen" at Parchman because they labored under the gun, began their days before sunrise, as they were marched to the fields to being producing their daily quota.

Another response to the abuses of the convict leasing system was the chain gang. In this case, prisoners did not work on massive prison farms but on smaller road camps that could be scattered throughout the state. Counties also adopted the chain gang system to take advantage of inmate labor and end the control of private interests over their labor. North Carolina, Georgia, Florida all had extensive chain gang systems, as did most counties. Even city jails employed convict labor. Birmingham's convicts "cleaned and repaired city streets ten hours a day" (Harris, 1972, p. 582). This system was invaluable for places like Birmingham, where grave limits on available financial resources would have made it difficult to pay for a comparable amount of free labor. The roughly one hundred men working on Birmingham's streets on any given day—80 to 90 of which would have been black—were impossible to pay for.

South Carolina county chain gang inmates at work chopping wood in 1934. This photograph, taken by musicologist Alan Lomax during his travels through the South, shows a line of black inmates swinging axes. Note the huge piles of wood in the background of the photo.

Source: Courtesy of the Library of Congress, Prints & Photographs Division, Lomax Collection, LC-DIG-ppmsc-00419.

As in the convict-leasing era, women made up a small but consistent proportion of the inmate population, and were generally housed along with the male prisoners. Mary Ellen Curtin (2000) observes that "until 1888, state female prisoners in Alabama cooked, cleaned, and worked as servants for prison contractors at the same mining camps and farms that employed male prisoners" (p. 4). When they were finally removed into a separate facility—and Alabama was one of the first southern states to put women into their own facility—it was more out of concern for women's behavior in the common camps than any concern for their own safety and well-being. At Parchman Farm, women never comprised more than 5% of the inmate population and were kept hard at work making clothes and bedding, sometimes canning vegetables, and occasionally working the cotton fields. It should be noted that, if the overall number of women inmates was low, the numbers of white women were even smaller. At Parchman Farm, for example, white women were barely a presence at all, averaging between zero and five in number. Perhaps for this reason, few southern states adopted separate women's camps or prisons during this period.

Juveniles also labored alongside adults on the prison farms and chain gangs of the South, where the creation of separate juvenile institutions lagged far behind the rest of the country. Although the earliest juvenile reformatories appeared in the early part of the nineteenth century elsewhere in the country, among southern states only Texas, Tennessee, and Kentucky had established state-level juvenile custodial facilities by 1890. Likewise only Birmingham, Augusta and Richmond had city reformatories for boys, although Columbia, South Carolina, did have a private home for delinquent boys. Race was undoubtedly a factor in the late adoption of juvenile institutions, as a 1904 report suggested: "The movement for juvenile reformatories in Georgia would have succeeded some years ago, in all probability, had not the argument been used: it is chiefly for the benefit of Negroes" (Du Bois, 1904, p. 8).

In the absence of such facilities, young men ended up alongside older and more experienced criminals, as one account from Augusta, Georgia lamented:

> "Sad to say that among the so-classed criminals are many young boys who are not criminals in the true sense of the word. There is the offending boy caught for throwing rocks, or spinning his top, or pitching his ball in the street. While some of these young boys are pardoned, a large number are fined; and as these fines cannot always be paid, they are therefore 'sent up' and thereby classed as criminals" (Du Bois 1904, 54).

The presence of young boys on county chain gangs and state farms served as one of the greatest sources of black anger and discontent with the criminal justice system.

Forms of community supervision that were hallmarks of progressive reform in the rest of the country penetrated southern criminal justice systems only slowly. Adult probation, which was a hallmark of progressive reform in many states, made very halting progress. The first southern state to adopt an adult probation law was Georgia, in 1913—by which time they were the 25th state to embrace probation. By 1938, 38 of the 48 states had adopted probation, with southern states conspicuous among the nonadopters: Alabama, Arkansas, Florida, Louisiana, Mississippi, South Carolina, and Texas.

Parole, another progressive innovation, made slightly greater inroads into the South, but the diffusion of parole laws and the use of parole still lagged the rest of the United States. Virginia, Florida, and Mississippi still did not have adult parole systems by the start of World War Two. Most inmates released from the massive prison farms, state road camps, or prisons were simply sent home—little concern for what became of them, and not much attention to what today might be termed reintegration. Where parole did not exist, early release was often a matter for executive clemency, a highly paternalistic process in which a small number of inmates could bargain for mercy (Miller, 2000).

Some states, like Georgia, came to embrace parole. Even here, parole did not arrive until 1908, well after half of the United States, and it operated on a very modest scale for some time. Parole cases in Georgia began with petitions, which generally addressed the questions of postrelease work and family life. Combined with a review of behavior and conduct while imprisoned, this information provided the basis for parole decisions. Blacks had to "involve themselves and their families in complex relationships with whites to have any chance of parole or pardon success" (Garton, 2003, p. 682). State parole files indicate "that many convicts, including African Americans . . . were being released well before the expiry of their sentence and before the minimum time to be served with good behavior." Mercy and brutality worked hand in hand: "For black families white paternalism offered a small window of opportunity to assert some agency to mediate the harshness of the criminal justice system. . . . The price of this agency was social and economic indebtedness, in extreme cases peonage, to white masters. Far from being the antidote to brutality, mercy was its support" (Garton, 2003, p. 76).

❖ THE BEGINNING OF THE END IN THE 1930S

In June of 1933, pioneering musicologist John Lomax set out on a journey across the South to collect recordings of traditional songs under the auspices of the Library of Congress. Accompanied by his son Alan, John Lomax headed to the prison farms—one of the places where they felt some sort of authentic black culture could be captured, set apart and isolated from the modern world. Hauling cumbersome recording equipment, they collected prison work songs, beginning an engagement with the southern prison that would take them to countless farms and camps during the remainder of the decade. But even as they undertook their journey, they were conscious of the forces of modernity that were bringing to an end the era they sought to record. By the time Alan Lomax returned to Parchman Farm in Mississippi in 1947 and 1948 to make a series of famous recordings, the old prison songs were already fading into memory (Lomax, 1993). The slow fade of the prison song was matched by the gradual fading of a distinctive criminal justice system.

The irony of Lomax's recordings—the use of the most modern audio recording technology to try and capture songs and sounds fading away in the modern world—points to the first important element in the transition of southern criminal justice, growing outside scrutiny. This was most obviously true in the case of lynching, which declined notably during the 1930s. The response to the terrible lynching of Claude Neal in 1934 illustrates some of these changes. Claude Neal, a black laborer, had been accused of raping and murdering a white woman, the daughter of one of his employers. A mob in rural northwest Florida seized the fugitive Neal across the border in Georgia, brought him back to Florida, and tortured him to death in a gruesome public display of violence. The case quickly drew national attention and condemnation, as the anonymity enjoyed by lynch mobs began to fade in the growing spotlight of modern communication technology. News services could report to a national audience, and photos and film could and did capture more immediately and widely the horror of mob murder. Even the first lady, Eleanor Roosevelt, commented on the Claude Neal lynching, noting that it was "a horrible thing" (Cook, 1999, p. 243).

What's the Evidence?: Newspapers

For students of criminal justice history, newspapers can be among the most useful primary sources. Today, a great many historical newspapers are available to students interested in studying aspects of criminal justice. Many libraries, for example, subscribe to various electronic databases of newspapers, which allow the user to search the full text for various subjects and key words. Many other databases are free, such as the newspapers that are part of "Chronicling America: Historic American Newspapers 1880-1922" from the Library of Congress, or the Google News Archive. A good list of these may be found here: http://www.researchguides.net/newspapers.htm.

Of course, newspapers are useful for helping us to establish the answers to "what happened?" sorts of questions. But they don't always report events in the same way. Those differences, of course, can be helpful to the historian as well, for they serve as an invaluable guide to the ways in which public opinion was expressed and shaped. Consider two different ways in which newspapers covered the 1930 mob lynching of Jimmy Levine in the town of Ocilla, Georgia. The first, in an editorial entitled, "Georgia Slips Back" was published in the *Pittsburgh Press* on February 5, 1930: "The latest lynching in Georgia therefore will come as a shock to those who had hoped that this most horrible of all forms of murder was passing . . . If telegraphic accounts are correct, the mob exhibited unusual barbarity. After Georgia's last lynching, seventeen men were indicted and sixteen were sent to prison. It is to be hoped the authorities will display equal zeal in the present instance, thereby serving notice that rule of lynch law is not to be resumed (p. 8). The *Ocilla Star*, on the other hand, published a very different sort of editorial: "When this kind of crime is committed, whether it be in Georgia or in Maine, men are going to see that the offender gets his punishment without waiting for the courts. Wrong, of course, but it will nearly always be done. This paper does not condone lynching, but so long as this crime is committed, so long may criminals expect mob violence." (*Ocilla Star*, as reported by the *Macon Telegraph* and reported in the *Afro-American*, February 22, 1930, page 18.)

The same glare of national publicity began to shine on the discriminatory practices of southern police and criminal courts. The decade's great controversy and cause was the case of the so-called "Scottsboro Boys" in Alabama. Local police pulled nine young black men from a train, accusing them of raping two white girls. Despite scant evidence supporting the claims that they had committed a crime, the young men were quickly sentenced to death in the proceeding that featured inadequate counsel, coerced and tortured confessions, and almost nothing that resembled a legitimate adversarial trial. The drama of numerous trials, appeals, and re-trials riveted public attention between 1931 and 1937 (Carter, 1979).

Prison farms and chain gangs also began to draw high levels of critical national attention. Frank Tannenbaum (1924), in his widely read popular work *Darker Phases of the South*, began his chapter on "Southern Prisons" in this fashion: "Please, reader, do not read this chapter unless you can steel your heart against pain. It is not a kindly tale. If you are sensitive it will give you sleepless nights and harrowing dreams" (p. 74). The publication of Robert Burns' 1932 memoir, *I Am a Fugitive From a Georgia Chain Gang* and the release that same year of the Warner Brothers' film *I Am a Fugitive from a Chain Gang* more directly captured the public imagination. Burns' story began with his being sentenced to six to 10 years of chain gang labor for armed robbery. He escaped and made his way to Chicago, where he became a successful editor and publisher. When he was reported to authorities as a fugitive, Burns returned to Georgia on the promise that he would serve only a short amount of time, off the chain gang. Instead, the state reneged on its promises, and in 1930 Burns once again escaped, this time ending up back in his home state of New Jersey. Not long after his memoir and the film appeared in 1932, he was rearrested once more as a fugitive. This time, the state of New Jersey refused to extradite him, citing the brutal conditions of the chain gang.

The federal government and national criminal justice organizations also played a critical role in the centralizing tendencies of southern justice. A federal antilynching measure, the Wagner-Costigan bill, came very near of passage in 1935, as did similar bills in 1938 and 1940. The Wagner-Costigan bill promised "equal justice to every race, creed, and individual" and would penalize a state or local government if a lynching went unprosecuted for 30 days. In those instances, federal law enforcement would intervene and charge local officials whose indifference or collusion made them responsible for the delay. They could receive a fine of up to $5,000 and/or a jail term of up to five years. By 1939, the Justice Department had established a Civil Liberties Unit (later designated the Civil Rights Section) with the intention of investigating violations of constitutional rights. In July 1942, President Franklin Roosevelt instructed the Justice Department to automatically investigate apparent mob killings of blacks in order to assess whether there might be a basis for asserting federal jurisdiction (Belknap, 1989).

National police and prison organizations played an important role in promoting national criminal justice standards and practices. When the National Prison Association—today's American Correctional Association—held its annual meetings in Nashville in 1889 and Austin in 1897, the meetings scarcely challenged the predominant systems in the South and, indeed, most of the assembled representatives agreed that the southern black population required a distinctive form of confinement (Curtin, 2000). By the 1930s, however, pressure from the same organization for states to adopt standard practices was far greater than it had been, and there was little evidence of an inclination to grant the southern argument that its needs were truly exceptional.

Of course, in telling this story, one should be careful not to overemphasize the role of external forces. Some of the most important voices of criticism and reform continued to come from modernizing southerners (those living in the South and expatriates elsewhere). Some strategies for reform were self-consciously "southern" in their focus, such as the antilynching campaign of Jessie Daniel Ames's Association of Southern Women for the Prevention of Lynching (ASWPL). Ames organized southern women to fight against what she called the "false chivalry" of lynching, radically undermining the defense of white womanhood that had so long been used as a justification for mob violence. The ASWPL undertook sophisticated grassroots campaigns, often pressuring local sheriffs and law enforcement officers to sign a statement that lynchings were never justified and that lynchers should be prosecuted (Hall, 1993).

Local prison reformers in the South looked to build bridges with their counterparts elsewhere. The files of Austin MacCormick, head of the reformist Osborne Association headquartered in New York City, contain numerous letters from southern correspondents, imploring him to come to the state to bolster their efforts. A Dallas attorney wrote to MacCormick in 1945: "Barbarism is being practiced in our prisons now, every day, and not a hand is raised. . . By chance I read of the Osborne Association and then of you." Likewise, a Birmingham attorney wrote to MacCormick in 1949 seeking information on model prison legislation, and to complain that the "Prison Reform Bill" in Alabama was the victim of "malicious attacks" from those who claimed reformers wanted to "make a country club and tea room out of the prisons . . . that the women wanted to get control of the prison system and serve roses to all the prisoners."

Blacks also fought the injustices of the criminal justice system and challenged it to reform and modernize. Many voices highlighted the hypocrisy of fighting against fascism and racism abroad even as lynch law and mob violence prevailed at home (Gilmore, 2009). The National Association for the Advancement of Colored People (NAACP) increasingly employed high profile cases involving the mistreatment of criminal suspects and criminal defendants to change southern racial practices. At the same time, NAACP antipeonage efforts continued to highlight the role of southern law enforcement and criminal courts in supporting retrograde labor practices.

All of these forces of change apparent by the 1930s should certainly not erase the powerful legacy of the southern experience to that point. The criminal justice system had proved a powerful tool for the preservation of a white-dominated racial order, and it had helped to sustain a system of segregation that had still not yet been successfully challenged. More important, the legacy of racial bias and disproportion continued (and continues) to haunt the criminal justice system to this day. Indeed, it is probably useful to recall the relatively shallow roots of rehabilitative language in some parts of the United States—while conventional "national" histories suggest, for example, that the middle decades of the twentieth century were dominated by "broadly accepted and unquestioned" reform experiments, liberal corrections, and commitments to clinical and rehabilitative criminal justice, that these elements had only shallow roots in much of the United States, where a more punitive and racially discriminatory criminal justice approach held sway and was only lightly touched by these more reformist currents (Lynch, 2010).

❖ REFERENCES

Ayers, E. L. (1984). *Vengeance and justice: Crime and punishment in the American South*. New York, NY: Oxford University Press.

Beck, E. M., & Tolnay, S. (1990). The killing fields of the deep South: The markets for cotton and the lynching of blacks, 1882-1930. *American Sociological Review*, 55, 526–539.

Beckett, K., & Western, B. (2001). Governing social marginality: Welfare, incarceration, and the transformation of state policy. In D. Garland (ed.), *Mass imprisonment: Social causes and consequences*. Thousand Oaks, CA: Sage.

Belknap, M. R. (1989). *Federal law and southern order*. Athens: University of Georgia Press.

Brundage, W. F. (1993). *Lynching in the new South: Georgia and Virginia, 1880–1930*. Chicago: University of Illinois Press.

Burns, R. E. (1932). *I am a fugitive from a Georgia chain gang!* New York, NY: Vanguard Press.

Cable, G. W. (1899). *The silent South*. New York, NY: Charles Scribner's Sons.

Carper, N. G. (1973). Martin Tabert, martyr of an era. *The Florida Historical Quarterly*, 52, 115–131.

Carter, D. T. (1979). *Scottsboro: A tragedy of the American South*. Baton Rouge: Louisiana State University Press.

Cook, B. W. (1999). *Eleanor Roosevelt: 1933–1938*. New York, NY: Viking.

Curtin, M. E. (2000). *Black prisoners and their world, Alabama, 1865–1900*. Charlottesville: University of Virginia Press.

Dale, E. (2011). *Criminal justice in the United States, 1789–1939*. New York, NY: Cambridge University Press.

Dinnerstein, L. (1987). *The Leo Frank case*. Athens: University of Georgia Press.

Du Bois, W. E. B. (1904). *Some notes on negro crime, particularly in Georgia*. Atlanta, GA: The Atlanta University Press.

Ferris, W. R. (2005). John Dollard: Caste and class revisited. *Southern Cultures, 10*, 7–18.

Garland, D. (2005). Capital punishment and American culture. *Punishment & Society, 7*, 347–376.

Garton, S. (2003). Managing mercy: African Americans, parole and paternalism in the Georgia prison system 1919–1945. *Journal of Southern History, 36*, 675–699.

Gilmore, G. E. (1996). *Gender and Jim Crow: Women and the politics of white supremacy in North Carolina, 1896–1920*. Chapel Hill: University of North Carolina Press.

Gilmore, G. E. (2009). *Defying Dixie: The radical roots of civil rights, 1919–1950*. New York, NY: W.W. Norton.

Hadden, S. E. (2001). *Slave patrols: Law and violence in Virginia and the Carolinas*. Cambridge, MA: Harvard University Press.

Hall, J. D. (1993). *Revolt against chivalry: Jessie Daniel Ames and the women's campaign against lynching*. New York, NY: Columbia University Press.

Harris, C. V. (1972). Reforms in government control of negroes in Birmingham, Alabama, 1890–1920. *Journal of Southern History, 38*, 567–600.

Kellor, F. (1901). *Experimental sociology: Descriptive and analytical: delinquents*. New York, NY: The Macmillan Company.

Lassiter, M. D., & Crespino, J. (2010). *The myth of southern exceptionalism*. New York, NY: Oxford University Press.

Lichtenstein, A. (1996). *Twice the work of free labor: The political economy of convict labor in the new South*. London, UK: Verso.

Lindsey, M. G. (2005). Localism and the creation of a state police in Arkansas. *Arkansas Historical Quarterly, 64*, 352–380.

Link, W. A. (1992). *The paradox of southern progressivism 1880–1930*. Chapel Hill: University of North Carolina Press.

Logan, W. A. (2005). Horizontal federalism in an age of criminal justice interconnectedness. *University of Pennsylvania Law Review, 154*, 257–334.

Logan, W. A. (2009). Contingent constitutionalism: State and local criminal laws and the applicability of federal constitutional rights. *William & Mary Law Review, 51*, 143.

Lomax, A. (1993). *The land where the blues began*. New York, NY: Pantheon.

Lynch, M. (2010). *Sunbelt justice: Arizona and the transformation of American punishment*. Stanford, CA: Stanford Law Books.

Mancini, M. (1996). *One dies, get another: Convict leasing in the American South 1866–1928*. New York, NY: Columbia University Press.

McKelvey, B. (1977). *American prisons: A history of good intentions*. Montclair, NJ: Patterson Smith.

Miller, V. M. L. (2000). *Crime, sexual violence, and clemency: Florida's pardon board and penal system in the Progressive Era*. Gainesville: University Press of Florida.

Montell, W. L. (1986). *Killings: Folk justice in the upper South*. Lexington: University Press of Kentucky.

Myrdal, G. (1944). *An American dilemma: The negro problem and modern democracy*. New York, NY: Harper & Row.

Oshinsky, D. M. (1996). *Worse than slavery: Parchman Farm and the ordeal of Jim Crow Justice*. New York, NY: Simon & Schuster.

Powell, J. C. (1891). *The American Siberia*. Chicago, IL: W. B. Conkey.

Rabinowitz, H. N. (1976). The conflict between blacks and the police in the urban South, 1865–1900. *Historian, 39*, 62–76.

Rousey, D. C. (1996). *Policing the southern city: New Orleans, 1805–1889*. Baton Rouge: Louisiana State University Press.

Rudwick, E. M. (1960). The negro policeman in the South. *Journal of Criminal Law, Criminology, and Police Science, 51*, 273–276.

Shepperd, S. C. (2001). *Avenues of faith: Shaping the urban religious culture of Richmond, Virginia*. Tuscaloosa: University of Alabama Press.

Shofner, J. H. (1981). Postscript to the Martin Tabert case: Peonage as usual in the Florida turpentine camps. *The Florida Historical Quarterly, 60*, 161–173.

Tannenbaum, F. (1924). *Darker phases of the South*. New York, NY: Putnam.

Tolnay, S. E., & Beck, E. M. (1995). *A festival of violence: An analysis of southern lynchings, 1882-1930*. Chicago: University of Illinois Press.

Trost, J. (2005). *Gateway to justice: The juvenile court and progressive child welfare in a southern city*. Athens: University of Georgia Press.

Wadman, R. E., & Allison, W. T. (2004). *To protect and to serve: A history of police in America*. New York, NY: Prentice Hall.

Watts, E. J. (1973). The police in Atlanta, 1890–1905. *Journal of Southern History, 39*, 165–182.

Wilkerson-Freeman, S. (2002). The creation of a subversive feminist dominion: Interracialist social workers and the Georgia New Deal. *Journal of Women's History, 13*, 132–154.

Woodruff, N. E. (2003). *American Congo: The African American freedom struggle in the delta*. Cambridge, MA: Harvard University Press.

Woodward, C. V. (2002). *The strange career of Jim Crow*. New York, NY: Oxford University Press.

Zimring, F. E., & Hawkins, G. (1991). *The scale of imprisonment*. Chicago, IL: University of Chicago Press.

6

Criminal Justice Research and Professionalism, 1920s–1960s

Criminal justice research and professionalism, at the start of the twenty-first century, have each reached a level of mature development. Since the 1960s, criminal justice has built for itself an established presence within higher education, in which colleges and universities around the world have developed academic centers, departments, and schools dedicated to training and research. Every year, publishing houses produce dozens of texts (including this one) that cover every aspect of crime, criminal law, and the justice system. Academic journals feature hundreds of criminal justice-related articles each year, and major professional associations such as the Academy of Criminal Justice Sciences and the American Society of Criminology hold huge annual meetings that attract thousands of criminal justice researchers and practitioners. Criminal justice professionalism seems as well established as the research field, and it is now taken for granted that the various criminal justice occupations—work in law enforcement, corrections, probation, and so on—will require specific training and credentialing. Each area of criminal justice work has its own well-developed professional organization and detailed standards for professional conduct.

What may be less clear today is the process by which we came to this point. How did criminal justice come to be a subject for extensive research and scholarly investigation? And how did the process of professionalization take hold in the field? The two areas were rooted in shared assumptions about criminal justice, and changes in one area tended to reinforce those in the other. This chapter reviews the interconnected history of both developments, starting with their first flourishing in the 1920s through their substantial growth and maturation by the 1960s.

❖ MOVING BEYOND SPECULATION: THE CRIMINAL JUSTICE SURVEYS

In 1920, the good citizens of Cleveland, Ohio, suffered a serious crisis of confidence in their criminal justice system. Details of an embarrassing crime scandal involving the chief judge of the municipal courts held the city's attention most of the summer and fall. The lurid details of the case—the chief judge being implicated in a murder and shown to have had many underworld connections—moved some to try and restore confidence in the system. The Cleveland Foundation, a civic foundation established in 1914 to help the city evaluate a variety of social problems, commissioned a study to be directed by leading legal scholars Roscoe Pound and Felix Frankfurter.

The principles of the study were fairly simple. First, too little was known about the functioning of the criminal justice apparatus, and what was "known" was often based on sensational (and non-representative) cases. As Frankfurter (1922) wrote in the preface to the final study, "the system is judged not by the occasional dramatic case, but by its normal, humdrum operations" (p. v). Second, to properly understand the criminal justice system required a comprehensive collection of empirical data, undertaken in an objective and nonpolitical fashion. Independent collection of data was particularly important, since contemporary researchers understood that most records in criminal cases "were atrocious" (Fuller, 1931, p. 143). Third, criminal justice was, in fact, a "system" whose parts operated in meaningful concert with one another, just like many other complex public and private bureaucratic structures; the authors of the Cleveland survey produced a diagram of the system, called "the path to justice" (Pound & Frankfurter, 1922, p. 238). Thinking about criminal justice as a system promoted greater efficiency in the processing of cases.

Fourth, proper study of the criminal justice system could lead to suggestions for reform, but these must follow from the actual results of the research and not be seen as overtly political or detached from the investigation itself. As the survey authors noted "facts have a reforming power of their own" (Pound & Frankfurter, 1922, p. 85).

The resulting publication, *Criminal Justice in Cleveland*, was a massive (729 pages) overview of every aspect of the system. The report exposed many of the dark corners of the criminal justice system, with which the general public was almost entirely unfamiliar. Investigators for the crime survey went to the criminal courts to see some of the "rough justice" that was being meted out. There, large numbers of drunks and traffic violators were processed side by side with more serious offenders—all at a rate of two and a half minutes per case! Investigators for the crime survey ventured to the city jail ("a dark, dingy place") and the Warrensville Workhouse to better understand conditions of confinement.

The Cleveland survey also exposed hidden criminal justice system practices that were not formally rooted in the criminal law. One such practice was the habit of "no-papering" in the prosecutor's office. No-papering meant that no criminal charges were ever filed, as opposed to nolle prosequi, in which charges would be formally filed before the case was dropped for lack of adequate proof. As one court official told the survey: "If Burns is arrested and when the officer comes down here he finds that somebody knows Burns and that he has lived around Cleveland for a while, is a pretty good fellow, and will probably never be in trouble again, we simply decide never to go ahead with the case, and the case is marked 'no papers'" (Pound & Frankfurter, 1922, p. 143). Likewise, the survey highlighted the judicial use of the "motion in mitigation" that allowed judges to defer the execution of a criminal sentence and which, according to the survey, "makes a farce of judicial business" (Pound & Frankfurter, 1922, p. 285).

The survey even employed some innovative original research on media coverage of crime and criminal justice (Pound & Frankfurter 1922, p. 515–555). Felix Frankfurter personally directed this aspect of the study, which featured qualitative analysis of the city's newspaper coverage of crime and a quantitative analysis of the inches of newspaper column space dedicated to felony crimes. This attention reflected a general concern that media coverage distorted public perceptions of the criminal justice system and improperly influenced system actors. As Raymond Moley, then director of the Cleveland Foundation, would later argue, "public service has always suffered from the inexorable rule of newsgathering that the thing which is most worthy of notice is the unusual" (Moley, 1929, p. 77).

The best-known dimension of the Cleveland project, however, was the extensive use of statistical data to show how the criminal justice system actually processed cases. Here, the survey tended to rely upon official statistics for much of its report data, without careful questioning of the manner in which these statistics were collected, what sort of activity was hidden or missing from this data, or what bureaucratic agendas might underlie the production of this data. Still, the survey's statistical approach to documenting criminal justice practice was hugely influential.

Figure 6.1

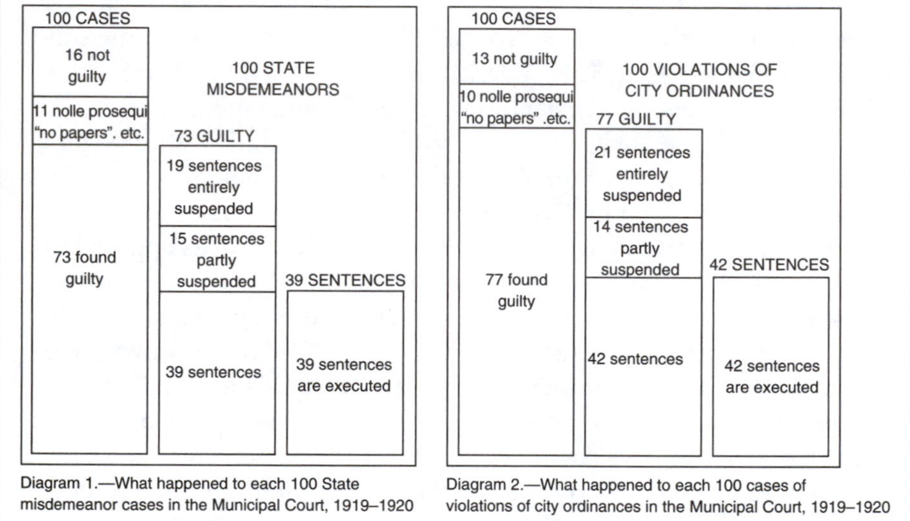

Diagram 1.—What happened to each 100 State misdemeanor cases in the Municipal Court, 1919–1920

Diagram 2.—What happened to each 100 cases of violations of city ordinances in the Municipal Court, 1919–1920

These figures from the Cleveland survey are a typical early effort to describe the processing of cases. A variation on the "mortality table," the figures revealed outcomes of lower-level criminal cases in the Municipal Court at each stage of the process.

Source: Criminal Justice in Cleveland: Reports of the Cleveland Foundation Survey of the Administration of Criminal Justice in Cleveland, Ohio. Cleveland, OH: Cleveland Foundation, 1922.

As Figure 6.1 suggests, one concern of the survey was the extent to which the system was "inefficient" in processing cases that came to the Municipal Court, with the ratio of convictions relative to cases being taken as a key efficiency indicator.

Criminal Justice in Cleveland did not, of course, appear out of nowhere. Pound, Frankfurter, and Moley were all products of a progressive reform tradition that linked improvements in public administration to greater sophistication in the empirical study of social problems and police responses. The Cleveland survey reflected the progressive tradition of legal realism, which emphasized the need to study law in action, and which generally regarded traditional legal philosophy as staid, inefficient, and corrupt. Legal realists felt strongly that legal institutions must adapt themselves to changing social environments. Moley (1929) would later elaborate on this theme that the failures of criminal justice were generally failures of adaptation. In a chapter titled "The Medieval Colleagues of the Prosecutor," Moley imagined the twelfth-century British monarch Henry II paying a visit to a modern American courthouse and being comforted in finding familiar characters such as the sheriff still roaming the landscape of criminal justice. For Moley, the point was that American criminal justice had utterly failed to keep up with current social conditions.

If criminal justice had failed to keep up with the times, progressives like Moley, Pound, and Frankfurter felt they knew why—old-fashioned and corrupt politics. The cause of backwardness, they argued, was essentially political in nature. Political interests tended to corrupt and thwart the efficient operations of the criminal justice system. That the Cleveland survey began with stories about a corrupt judge, or that it tended to expose instances of corruption and political influence, helps explain why it took such an interest in the statistical summaries of official case processing—the so-called mortality tables. A failure to successfully prosecute and convict appeared to be a political failure of the system, and the authors took it for granted that an increase in the number of convictions was desirable.

In diagnosing political influence as the primary cause of inefficiency, the progressives also offered up a cure, which was to remove politics from public administration. Indeed, they began to make an innovative distinction between professional administration and politics. That building up the independence of the former would reduce the influence the latter became fundamental to the worldview of progressives. Public administration would provide "a nonpartisan, maximally efficient means to deal with the purely technical problems of running city services" (Ciepley, 2006, p. 59). Herbert Croly's *Progressive Democracy* (1914) offered up one of the earliest and most influential American arguments for an independent, professional public administration, what he called "a body of permanent officials to assist him [the political executive] in converting his program into well-framed and well-administered laws and to carry on the business of the state in an efficient manner" (p. 356). Criminal justice reform was, then, very much a call for criminal justice professionalism. The Cleveland Survey demanded greater attention be paid to the "training of workers and experts . . . in connection with the schools and universities of the community" and that "special courses be offered to social workers, parole and probation officers, police officers, teachers, and nurses" (p. 485).

Of course, the autonomous professional state was hardly close to reality yet, so progressive reformers like the authors of the Cleveland survey often turned to private sources of support for their research and reform efforts. In doing so, they built upon a tradition of privately funded research efforts that included studies of urban life conducted by settlement house workers, investigations of vice conducted by antiprostitution organizations, and surveys of crime conditions by child-saving organizations (Fronc, 2006; Robertson, 2009). A good example of this early work is Sophonisba Breckenridge and Edith Abbott's *The Delinquent Child and the Home* (1912), a remarkable study of Chicago's juvenile court which drew upon the resources of the privately funded Chicago School of Civics and Philanthropy (where both authors taught) and the Russell Sage Foundation (founded in 1907 to support the development of social scientific research on critical social problems).

The Cleveland survey was followed by a long series of similar studies. The best-known of these were the Missouri Crime Survey (1926) and the Illinois Crime Survey (1929). These criminal justice surveys continued to be produced until World War Two, although the greatest number were produced between 1926 and 1931. Like the Cleveland study, much of the outpouring of criminal justice research before World War Two was supported by private organizations. Private research foundations were emerging in this period as major sources of support for individual researchers and research projects that governments or universities were not yet willing or able to support (Zunz, 2000). More importantly, foundations helped to bring research on social problems out of the strict confines of the academic world and encouraged a practical and problem-solving orientation to scholarly inquiry. It was the foundations that promoted the survey approach to studying social problems which the criminal justice surveys would embrace; in its first seven years, the Russell Sage Foundation supported roughly 140 surveys, on subjects as diverse as public health, housing, school reform, and recreation (Zunz, 2000, p. 35).

In addition to the general surveys, private support was critical in the development of surveys in specific criminal justice areas. The work of two scholars—Bruce Smith in policing and Austin MacCormick in corrections—illustrates these pre-1940 developments. Bruce Smith began his research career with the privately funded New York School of Municipal Research in 1916 (working with director Charles Beard) and conducted his first survey of a police department (in Harrisburg, Pennsylvania) that same year. In 1921, the Municipal Research entity became the Institute of Public Administration, and Smith served as its first manager. Associated with the Institute until his death in 1955,

Table 6.1 Crime Commissions in the United States, 1919–1931

Chicago Crime Commission	1919
Law Enforcement Association of Kansas City, Missouri	1920
Cleveland Crime Commission	1921
Minnesota Crime Commission	1922
Baltimore Criminal Justice Commission	1923
Crime Commission of Los Angeles	1923
Crime and the Georgia Courts	1924
California Commission for Reform of Criminal Procedure	1925
National Crime Commission	1925
Missouri Association for Criminal Justice	1926
Illinois Association for Criminal Justice	1926
Nebraska Crime Commission	1926
Kentucky Commission to Study the Causes of Crime	1926
New York State Crime Commission	1926
Massachusetts Crime Commission	1926
New Hampshire Crime Commission	1926
Report on a Minor Survey of the Administration of Criminal Justice—Hartford, New Haven, and Bridgeport, Connecticut. American Institute of Criminal Law	1926
Report of the Crime Survey Committee of the Law Association of Philadelphia	1926
New Jersey Commission to Investigate the Subject of Crime	1927
Minnesota Crime Commission	1927
California Crime Commission	1927
Report of the Commission of Inquiry into Criminal Procedure, State of Michigan	1927
A Study of Crime in the City of Memphis, Tennessee. American Institute of Criminal Law and Crime	1928

(Continued)

(Continued)

Report of the Criminal Law Advisory Commission to the General Assembly of Rhode Island	1928
Michigan State Crime Commission	1929
California Crime Commission	1929
National Commission on Law Observance and Enforcement [Wickersham Commission]	1929
Report to the General Assembly of the Commonwealth of Pennsylvania of the Commission Appointed to Study the Laws, Procedures, etc., relating to Crime and Criminals	1929
Virginia Commission on Crimes and Prisons	1930
Philadelphia Criminal Justice Commission	1930
Hawaii Governor's Advisory Committee on Crime	1931
Oregon Crime Commission	1931
California Crime Problem Advisory Committee	1931
Preliminary Report of the Survey of Criminal Justice in Oregon	1931
Criminal Justice in Virginia	1931

Source: American Bar Foundation (1955, p. 5–6).

Smith produced surveys of roughly 50 police departments and 18 state law enforcement organizations (Smith, 1930, 1932, 1941, 1946). His studies promoted effective police organization and bureaucratic structure; efficiency in crime control, police training, and professionalism; the reduction of corruption and third-degree tactics; and the development of comprehensive crime statistics and reporting.

The career of Austin MacCormick in corrections also shows the development of criminal justice research in the prewar period. Attracted to the pioneering work of Progressive Era prison reformer Thomas Mott Osborne, MacCormick joined Osborne in conducting a survey of the United States Naval Prison at Portsmouth, New Hampshire, in 1917 (not long after MacCormick had graduated from college). Their work at Portsmouth initiated a collaboration that would continue until Osborne's death in 1926. Together, using private funds that Osborne raised, they founded the National Society of Penal Information (NSPI) in 1922. The purpose of the NSPI was to conduct survey research of the nation's prisons, reformatories, and jails. For much of the twenties, MacCormick and other NSPI researchers traveled the United States, documenting conditions in state correctional systems. NSPI studies provided some of the first comprehensive studies of actual prison conditions and became a vital source of information and support for those who wished to centralize and professionalize corrections (NSPI 1926, 1929).

It is telling that the work of Smith and MacCormick, both of whom were regarded as leading experts in their fields of inquiry, was largely conducted through private organizations, outside of university settings. Another important institutional setting for the support and dissemination of research were the emerging professional organizations. The National Probation Association (NPA; later the National Probation and Parole Association) offers a good example. The organization had a very modest beginning as a gathering of 14 probation officers at the 1907 annual meeting of the National Conference of Charities and Corrections (notice that "corrections" was still largely subsumed under the larger organizational framework of social welfare and social work). Not until 1915 did this informal organization acquire an executive secretary and begin the process of formalizing its operations. Four decades later, the membership had grown to 31,000, with a national office that housed a large clerical and professional staff. As it grew, the NPA was able to secure funds for its own research projects from sources like the Milbank Memorial Fund and the Commonwealth Fund (Krisberg, Marchionna, & Baird, 2007, p. viii). In 1952, after the NPA had merged with the American Probation and Parole Association, it began sponsoring the publication of a journal, *Crime and Delinquency*.

Case Studies in Criminal Justice: Charles L. Chute, Probation Professional

Charles L. Chute is not a name well known to many in criminal justice today, but his work in the field of probation and parole is an outstanding illustration of the developments in research and professional expertise in the period before World War Two. Chute's ambitions provide insight into the development of an emerging scholarly field, and his writings show the spirit of excitement and optimism typical of the era.

Charles L. Chute graduated from the New York School of Social Work in 1910 and was immediately appointed a field agent of the National Child

(Continued)

(Continued)

Labor Society. In 1913, he became executive secretary of the New York State Probation Commission and still later took up the leadership of the emerging National Probation Association, which he led until 1948. Chute was a leading force in lobbying for the first federal probation law, passed in 1925 in the midst of Prohibition and over the objections of anti-alcohol forces (including the powerful Anti-Saloon League) who felt that probation would allow Volstead Act violators to escape punishment too readily (Dressler, 1959, p. 24). Despite an assistant attorney general who proclaimed probation to be "all part of a wave of maudlin rot of misplaced sympathy for criminals," Chute was able to prevail and secure passage of the Federal Probation Act (Dressler, 1959, p. 24). Later, Chute traveled the country, advocating for the adoption and improvement of probation systems (Chute & Bell, 1956).

Like his contemporaries, Chute believed that criminal justice systems could be reorganized in a rational way that would ultimately allow society to solve the problems of crime and delinquency. In an essay (published in 1923) called "Rational Crime Treatment" Chute spelled out some of the requirements of this new system:

> "We are just beginning to build up a science of human behavior which alone will make it possible for us to understand the so-called criminal . . . as yet few grasp the significance of the scientific approach to this problem. The great mass of people are still hopelessly irrational and unscientific in their consideration of it—more so, perhaps, than in almost any other field of human experience. Why is this so? Because it is a field in which emotions have long ruled—primitive emotions: fear, hatred, revenge. Then, too, it is a field largely monopolized by that most conservative of all professions, the law. Treatment of crime has been largely hampered by rigid criminal codes, based upon outworn principles of equal responsibility, 'punishment to fit the crime,' and the essentially unjust and discredited principle of the need for severe punishment to deter others. Through inertia, conservatism and the accumulated fears and prejudices of generations, the law has changed but little, although increased knowledge and social advances have made fundamental changes imperative. . . Besides the probation system and the court clinic, which adapt themselves to all courts dealing with delinquency, the movement for special socially organized courts is also a hopeful factor in the situation. . . This scientific plan of crime treatment, whose

aim is to lift up and save rather than to crush down and destroy, should prove not only more successful and more safe, but also more just. How prone are we to forget that the debt is not all on one side! Every delinquent child, every criminal adult, no matter how deliberate may seem his offending, is to some extent at least the victim of bad social conditions for which society and all of us as members thereof are surely to blame. . . We are so far today from the rational program of crime treatment outlined that it will take time to attain it, but progress should be more rapid than at any previous time in history because of this growing scientific spirit and approach to the problem . . . . Why do we not adopt such a program at once? Because of inertia and conservatism; the many selfish interests involved in the present system; the incompetency of many public officials, hampered by politics and the distrust in which they are held by the public; ignorance of the scientific gains in this field; persistence of the instinctive emotions of fear and hatred of the criminal and the primitive demand for vengeance. Last, and perhaps most of all, comes out 'penny-wise' economy—the objections of the taxpayer to the outlay necessary to establish through probation systems, special courts, and the diversified institutions required. This last and greatest objection will be overcome, however, as will the others, by greater public knowledge, as unquestionably the expenditure will prove an investment in manhood and womanhood bringing large social returns. 'The greatest enterprise in the world,' says Emerson, 'for splendor, for extent, is the upbuilding of a man.'" (Chute, 1923, p. 5–8)

Charles L. Chute is just one of many figures in the history of criminal justice who sought to understand how the process of criminal justice actually worked. Like those of his era, he was moved to action by the hope that studying the system would ultimately bring forth a more modern, bureaucratic, and efficient system. How do Chute's confident words of 1923 read today? Should we admire him for his great optimism and for his words of hope and compassion for the criminal offender? Should he, on the other hand, be criticized for failing to see all the potential obstacles and limitations to realizing this vision? And, if we do criticize, do we see his failure to recognize limitations as the product of a naïve person, who was unaware of the roadblocks that awaited reforms in the real world? Or, perhaps, was this a willful effort to "sell" new programs to the public, even at the expense of covering up the less desirable truth? There is no easy answer to these questions for historians who study the careers of reformers in criminal justice.

Law school faculty generated most of the university-based criminal justice research before World War Two (reflecting the ongoing interest in examining "law in action" in criminal justice), with a smaller proportion coming from within programs in public administration (reflecting the interest in criminal justice as a problem of efficient state and local governmental administration). The few early experiments in situating distinct programs in criminal justice studies within universities included police administration programs at places like Michigan State, San Jose State, and Washington State. These early programs tended to be organized in the spirit of vocational training for police officers and failed to greatly advance the idea of criminal justice as an academic field (Morn, 1995; Foster, Magers, & Millikin, 2007).

One of the most critical early steps in establishing a distinct presence for criminal justice research in American higher education came with the creation in 1950 of the School of Criminology at the University of California, Berkeley. The School was organized out of the older Bureau of Police Organization, which had been established at Berkeley in 1932 by August Vollmer, with support from the Rockefeller Foundation. The Berkeley School of Criminology adopted the reformist but practical orientation of the prewar criminal justice surveys, deemphasizing criminological theory in favor of a curriculum that focused on the problems of criminal justice administration (Bopp, 1977, p. 75). In many ways, the Berkeley program was the high-water mark for the practical, efficiency-minded approach to criminal justice research. Its first dean, O. W. Wilson, was selected precisely because of his background in criminal justice administration, rather than for any interest or expertise in the study of crime causation. Wilson recruited a few standard bearers of their fields, including Austin MacCormick in corrections. Other faculty tended to come from the ranks of criminal justice professionals and did not necessarily need to possess a doctorate—practical experience, however, was essential. Wilson took the position that "professional training cannot be provided exclusively by instructors who use knowledge from a book in lieu of actual experience in the field" (Morn, 1995, p. 65).

The Berkeley program was not without its detractors. By the 1960s, a new generation of critical criminologists would call into question the close relationship between the Berkeley faculty and the institutions of criminal justice. One recalled the school in this way: "[it] trained middle-management personnel in the arts of police and correctional administration, stressing business management, Taylorism, and professionalism. It was a program of good old-fashioned law and order, albeit [August] Vollmer's reformist brand, and it had little patience even for the niceties of liberal social science" (Platt & Shank, 1976, p. 1–3). Although the Berkeley program, as it had been devised by Wilson, did not outlive his departure in 1960, its ambitions for research in service to the practical problems of criminal justice administration continued on in other institutional settings, including the John Jay College of Criminal Justice and the Academy of Criminal Justice Sciences (founded as the International Association of Police Professors in 1963) (Morn, 1995; Hale, 1998).

❖ THE ROOTS OF PROFESSIONALIZATION

The effort to professionalize criminal justice work emerged hand-in-hand with the development of criminal justice research. This isn't surprising when one considers all of the shared assumptions between the two movements: that politics should be removed from the system (recall that the authors of the Cleveland Crime Survey called political appointments "an absurd piece of inefficiency"; Frankfurter & Pound, 1922, p. 215); that decision-making within the criminal justice system could be standardized and based on empirical research; and that expert knowledge about the criminal justice system could be used to develop sets of "best practices" that could then be used to appropriately train new police officers, probation and parole workers, and prison guards.

Advocates of professionalization shared something else with the early survey researchers—they generally felt that existing practices were far below appropriate standards, and that there was a great deal of work to be done before the practice of criminal justice met their expectations. Patrick Murphy (1977), who would later go on to a distinguished career as a police administrator, recalled leaving the Navy as a young man to join the New York City Police Department (NYPD) in 1946: "I suddenly realized how unfair the comparison between the military and the domestic police had been to the Navy: the Catch-22s and other instances of irrationality and insanity which I found in the Navy were but minor irritants compared to the wholesale inefficiency, inept management, and sometimes maddening corruption that I was to find in the New York Police Department, and then later in police departments everywhere" (p. 27).

Patrick Murphy and other contemporary champions of professionalizing criminal justice were right. The NYPD, and most criminal justice agencies, suffered from a host of problems. Stories of systemic corruption, from the highest levels of administration to the cop on the street, could be found in any number of law enforcement organizations. Police organization in many cities was an oddly decentralized throwback that reflected the power of highly local ward politics. For their part, prisons in all regions of the United States remained isolated kingdoms unto their own, often administered by political appointees with no practical experience and little interest in running their institutions effectively (Edgerton, 2004). And, in both law enforcement and correctional settings, front line workers were rarely, if ever, given any kind of training. Whatever officers learned was acquired on the job.

The push for professionalization demonstrated what historian Samuel Walker (1998) calls "a divided soul"—divided between the social welfarist aspects of reform, in which criminal justice professionals could become agents of rehabilitation and effective social change and the quest for a more effective and efficient crime-fighting apparatus (p. 131). Walker's observation is helpful—although these two impulses were not mutually exclusive, neither did they co-exist easily together. The police officer could be seen as a helpful social worker or a tough-minded crime fighter, but it was hard to be both at the same time. Even where some level of peaceful co-existence between the two roles could be sustained, sooner or later one ended up prioritized over the other. And, in the mid-twentieth century, the search for efficiency in crime control generally won the day among professionalization's advocates.

The career of O. W. Wilson shows this divided soul as well as the ultimate emphasis on crime control. Wilson was a longtime police administrator who began his career in law enforcement as a protégé of August Vollmer, the quintessential Progressive Era police reformer and frequent advocate of the social worker role. Wilson's career leading police forces began in Wichita, Kansas, in 1928 and would take him most famously to the head of the Chicago Police Department from 1960 to 1967. Some of Wilson's innovations tended toward the progressive social work component of police professionalism, such as his effort in Wichita to make certain that police handling juvenile cases would first investigate the child's home situation and coordinate their efforts with various city social services.

On the other hand, much of Wilson's career was dedicated to the search for more efficient crime control through a professional police force. In 1941, Wilson published a manual on how departments could efficiently allocate patrol officers according to calls for service; in 1950, he published the first comprehensive textbook on police administration (Wilson, 1941, 1950). Wilson promoted one of the earliest university-based training programs for police officers; created a training academy for police cadets; helped develop a law enforcement code of ethics and fought corruption; improved police record keeping and communications; and developed widely-used measurements of officer productivity.

To achieve professionalization, criminal justice programs advanced reforms along three critical lines. First, reformers sought to make improvements in the selection and training of criminal justice personnel. Second, criminal justice systems sought to centralize and bureaucratize their operations. Third, criminal justice embraced new technologies designed to make their work more efficient. Not all these elements were present in every new program or package of reforms, but collectively they represent much of what professionalism meant in this era.

The effort to improve the quality of criminal justice personnel was perhaps the most critical of the three threads. Reformers placed a great faith in the ability of competent workers (by which they meant intelligent, properly trained, and inclined to follow the rule of law) to improve the functioning of the criminal justice system. The Cleveland survey, addressing police detective work, concluded that it "requires some men of scientific training—men having the educational foundation that will permit them to develop scientific methods of operation" (Frankfurter & Pound, 1922, p. 71). In that spirit, the Cleveland survey researchers conducted intelligence testing of the city's current police officers, using the fairly new Army Alpha Intelligence Examination (which had been developed during World War One) and discovered that the officers scored somewhat below the wartime Army subjects.

Improving the quality of criminal justice personnel was not simply a matter of screening for intelligence and basic competencies; it was also a matter of providing suitable training. The campaign for professional competency manifested itself early on in the field of social work, where Mary Richmond's (1917) landmark work, *Social Diagnosis*, aimed to put the field on a more scientific footing. Still, even in social work, there was resistance and old habits: "while we spoke of casework techniques and psychiatric interpretations of behavior, a great deal of the professional literature of the 1930s was still nonscientific in outlook. There was much inspirational material based on hunch rather than evidence. A certain intransigence developed between those who wanted proof and those who insisted their asserted facts were self-evident" (Dressler, 1959, p. 127).

Criminal justice training programs moved forward at the same slow and halting pace. Local police departments saw only limited practical changes. The creation of the National Police Academy by the FBI in 1935 was a well-publicized step, but this had little influence on similar developments at the state and local level. A 1929 survey of cities found that only 31 of 47 responding cities even had a training program

(Ragsdale, 1929). If police training remained limited at midcentury, corrections training was even further behind. Virtually all prison guards received basic, on-the-job training, often little more than being allowed to follow more senior personnel for a short period of time. The Federal Bureau of Prisons, the New York City Department of Correction, and the New York State Department of Corrections established three of the earliest formal centralized training programs during the 1930s. These early models did not immediately inspire many imitators, and the New York State Central Guard School was closed during the early 1940s because of wartime budget restrictions. World War Two had a negative impact on training programs generally—with the war taking many police officers and prison guards into military service, there was little time to prepare the new recruits that would take their place. New York State did not reestablish a central training academy for correctional officers until the early 1970s. Similar efforts to standardize and regularize the rules of probation and parole supervision were slow in coming. California, one of the leaders in professionalization, did not publish a parole agent manual until 1954. Designed so that each parole agent could readily understand the administrative expectations for his or her work performance, the manual was an important effort to see to it that criminal justice workers operated upon a common set of work standards (Simon, 1993).

The second target of reformers was the organization of criminal justice agencies. Generally, policing and corrections were highly decentralized operations at the start of this period. Urban law enforcement generally devolved significant authority to the local precinct level, while individual prisons and reformatories operated with relatively little supervision from central state departments. Organizational weakness meant, among other things, that criminal justice operations remained highly vulnerable to political influence. Even in the 1920s and 1930s, for example, police departments continued to serve a political function by aiding in the repression of labor activism. Acting at the behest of powerful business and economic interests, the police in many American communities acted as the strike breaking "shock forces" of the business community (Monkkonen, 1992; Fogelson, 1977; Johnson, 2003).

The growing push for a professional, crime-control focus meant removing departments from this political vulnerability, by creating stronger and more centralized bureaucracies. The Los Angeles Police Department (LAPD) under William Parker, chief between 1950 and 1966, serves as a good example. Historian Edward Escobar (1999) points out that the department began to separate itself from the interests of the city's business community after 1938, gaining statutory control over all internal disciplinary decisions, disbanding its antilabor Red Squad, and seeking to eliminate corrupt officers. Even as a young man joining the LAPD in the late 1920s, Parker reportedly refused to tolerate the corruption of his fellow cops or to look the other way when he became aware of a crime. Stories in national magazines the *Saturday Evening Post* and the *Reader's Digest* claimed that, as police chief, Parker cleaned up a corrupt and vice-ridden city, driving organized crime out of town and leaving the remaining con artists and prostitutes confused and alone (Detzer, 1960; Jennings, 1960). According to the *Reader's Digest* portrait, "he has set an example of stiff-necked integrity, of refusal to compromise, that now reaches down through the ranks to the newest recruit on the beat. This has earned him the respect of most good citizens of Los Angeles, and the undying hatred of the underworld" (Detzer, 1960, p. 240).

The key to Parker's strategy was applying modern business management techniques to police administration. Under his leadership, the LAPD established a Research and Planning division to improve operations by analyzing crime patterns, streamlining processes, and deploying officers more efficiently. Parker also consolidated his command structure by merging divisions and implemented much more extensive training programs intended to make his officers more professional. These changes were intended to support a more authoritative style of law enforcement. In contrast to an earlier goal of maintaining public order, Parker's LAPD focused on fighting crime, still a relatively new objective for police following World War Two. Under Parker, the LAPD embraced tactics such as conducting intensive patrol of high-crime neighborhoods and stopping and frisking suspicious persons (Domanick, 1994). That a highly centralized interventionist organization would promote better police work was a matter of faith. As one biographer observed of the similarly minded O. W. Wilson: "In his view, law enforcement should be organized along semi-military lines. It was a philosophy that assumed a major structural reform of police agencies would ensure a change in institutional values. Thus, pride would be developed in the ranks, honesty and integrity would naturally follow, and the quality of police service would ultimately be improved" (Bopp, 1977, p. 72).

The push for centralization is equally obvious in the correctional field, since prison and reformatory systems were nominally state-directed enterprises to begin with. The creation of state-level correctional systems began in New York, where one was established in 1926; in California, the critical reforms took place a decade later, and most other states embraced the department of corrections model during the 1940s and 1950s. Even more striking were efforts by correctional bureaucracies to gain some centralized control over decisions relating to the commitment of inmates to particular

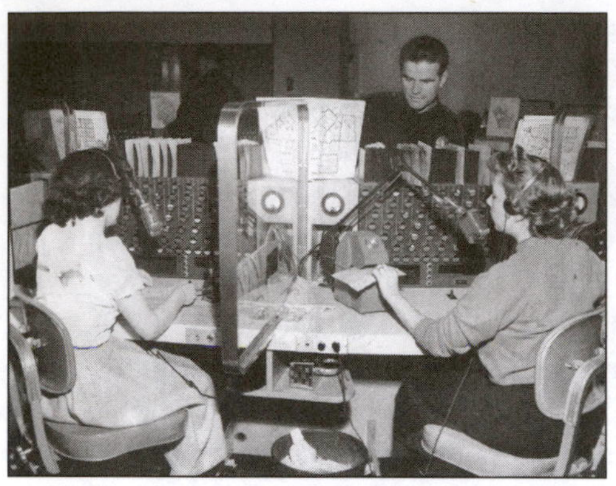

This 1956 photograph shows some of the LAPD's 85 police radio telephone operators at work. Images like these highlight the department's public emphasis on using communication technology to maximize speed and efficiency.

Source: Los Angeles Public Library Photo Collection. Photographer: Bill Walker.

institutions as well as parole and release decisions. The American Law Institute developed a model Youth Authority Act, which spurred the creation of the California Youth Authority in 1941; in New York, the Elmira Reception Center was given statutory authority in 1945 to receive, evaluate, and assign all sentenced felons between 16 and 21 years of age.

Technology formed the third thread of the professionalization movement. Historians of policing have long acknowledged the central role of the "big three" advances in technology—the patrol car, the two-way radio, and the telephone. The embrace of new technologies went hand-in-hand with other changes. Consider, for example, the extent to which the use of patrol cars equipped with two-way radios could allow for a consolidation and centralization of police stations and make police departments less reliant in smaller precinct stations (Monkkonen, 1992). Federal Bureau of Prisons chief Sanford Bates hailed "science to the rescue" in corrections. He claimed, for example, that the lie detector could take the place of the crude and unprofessional use of the third degree. Even more important, technology would be the servant of professional and enlightened administration. Bates (1936) observed that

> "in our Federal penal institutions we have installed high-powered electric floodlights, automatic telephones with special cut-in emergency devices, radio communicators, automatic annunciators; tool proof or unsalable steel bars; harmless tear gas"

all of which could work with the tools of psychology and the social sciences to

> "rescue the prisons of the country from the slough of despond of hit-or-miss, politically controlled, unintelligent stagnation in which they have been immersed and raise them to the level of intelligently conducted business enterprises" (p. 115, 126).

What's the Evidence?: Popular Culture

It isn't hard to recognize that much of what the public knows about today's criminal justice system is mediated by the many cultural representations of crime and criminal justice. Indeed, researchers have noted what they refer to as the "CSI Effect" to describe the impact of twenty-first century television dramas about criminal investigators on the perceptions of jurors in actual criminal trials. Though not everyone is certain that the "CSI Effect" actually exists (Shelton, 2008), there's no question that culture plays an important role in how we comprehend our justice system.

But what is that role? Some would argue that cultural representations are simply a mirror to society—casting back at us a reflection of their place and time. Other scholars are less certain of the mirror image effect, arguing that cultural representations are less than perfect mirrors—that there are always elements of distortion, bias, and omission. Still others argue that culture should not be thought of simply as a mirror—perfect or imperfect—because culture not only represents reality, it helps to shape that reality by influencing social knowledge and practice.

Few moments of modern criminal justice took on as much resonance in post–World War Two popular culture as police professionalism, with the rise of the police procedural story. Before World War Two, the private detective had reigned supreme; from the more formal English detective fiction of Agatha Christie and Dorothy Sayers to the gritty "hardboiled" American detective stories created by Dashiell Hammett and Raymond Chandler, the heroes did their work against the backdrop of ineffectual and obstructionist police forces (or, in the case of the American stories, actively corrupt police as well). While the fictional private detective did not disappear after World War Two (the popularity of Mickey Spillane's tough-guy detective, Mike Hammer, is an outstanding postwar example), crime fiction in the postwar period witnessed the triumph of the police procedural.

The heroes of the police procedural were rarely the colorful characters of private detective stories. Indeed, in the age of police professionalism, they were often notable for how little their personal lives and characters played a role in the stories that were told. Two examples from this period—from different genres—represent the model. Dick Tracy, the police hero of newspaper comic strips, emerged in the 1940s as the nation's most visible and popular crime fighter. Though the series had its start back in the 1930s,

(Continued)

(Continued)

the heyday of Chester Gould's creation was the 1940s, when Dick Tracy faced off against a series of unlikely criminal villains. While the villains were always wildly grotesque characters (which reflected Gould's own criminological take–normal looking people were apparently not as likely to end up as criminals), Dick Tracy and his fellow officers were resolutely professional, and their private lives largely mainstream and out of view. *Dick Tracy* introduced the idea of technology and formal investigations as the key to crime fighting. Gould's "Crimestoppers" feature–with crime prevention tips for young readers–found real-world parallels with the LAPD's Deputy Auxiliary Police (DAPS), which was focused on "predelinquent" Mexican-American Youth, who visited crime labs, attended lectures, and studied police procedure (Escobar, 1999, p. 264).

Beginning on radio in 1949, and appearing on television in 1951, came another famous police procedural series, *Dragnet*. Starring its creator Jack Webb, *Dragnet* ran on television from 1951 until 1959 (and reemerged in the late 1960s in an updated version with Harry Morgan with which today's students–and certainly their instructors–are probably most familiar). Like Chester Gould, Jack Webb strongly identified with the police subjects of his series, spending considerable time with actual officers at work, attending police academy courses, and employing technical advisors from the LAPD. Webb's character, LAPD Detective Joe Friday, was the consummate police professional. Few cases were solved without technical and forensic evidence, and Friday himself made famous his signature line, "just the facts" when witnesses would introduce opinions and ideas beyond the scope of his investigation. It is little surprise that the LAPD endorsed the series.

For historians, the move to professionalization in criminal justice presents a challenge of interpretation. The first generations of criminal justice reformers were completely convinced of the merits of their goals; if actual practice fell short of those goals, and it often did, those failures were failures of implementation, not conception. By the 1960s and 1970s, new generations of reformers, along with the first generation of criminal justice historians, took a more skeptical view of professionalization itself. The critical perspective was most pronounced in the police field, where administrators of professionalized departments were roundly criticized as being too far removed from the concerns of ordinary rank-and-file workers and detached from the communities they hoped to serve. As one text described it, professionalism "had worked too well": "With this strong commitment to professionalism and growing elitism, police began to lose touch with the citizens they were charged to protect and serve. The desire for cost-efficient police service overshadowed the immeasurable value of police-community interaction" (Wadman & Allison, 2004, p. 141, 145).

Patrick Murphy (1977) offered a similar assessment, from the perspective of a long-time police administrator. He observed in the 1970s that "neighborhood law enforcement" would avoid the sins of professionalization, including "overcentralization, insensitivity to local variations in crime problems, headquarters abstractions, and bureaucratic immobility" (p. 27). Mark Moore and George Kelling, scholars of policing, offered their own critique in a famous 1983 article, "To Serve and Protect: Learning from Police History," in which they argued that a reliance on technology and the tools of professionalization had weakened police ties to local communities, while having no demonstrable effect on crime rates.

These early critics generally argued that the reformers had actually reshaped criminal justice practice, even as they argued against the changes. Other historians, however, took a different approach, questioning whether reform rhetoric really had much impact on actual practice. Particularly in the field of correctional history, scholars attacked professionalization rhetoric as superficial and cosmetic, producing only marginally improved prisons while concealing the fact that operations generally continued much as they had before. These historians tended to stress the continuity in criminal justice practice, heaping scorn on rhetorical changes they believed masked underlying stagnation—changes like the transformation of *prisons* into *correctional institutions* and *prison guards* into *correctional officers* (Rothman, 2002).

Even more recently, however, a new generation of historians has begun to consider whether the push for professionalization might have had some positive dimensions after all. Not that older generations of scholars had ignored this entirely; Moore & Kelling (1983) readily conceded, for example, that professional standards had reduced corruption, improved some of the basic procedures provided to criminal suspects, and produced better-trained officers. Other historians find themselves attracted by the reformers' optimism. Mary M. Stolberg's account (2002) of the vision of Detroit Police Commissioner George Edwards praises his efforts at inculcating respect for civil liberties and racial fairness in the early 1960s, noting that his vision "stands in stark contrast to our own era's pessimism about hard-core problems of crime, race, and urban renewal" (p. 14).

❖ NEW RESEARCH PERSPECTIVES: THE FIELD RESEARCH EXPLOSION

As noted earlier, the early crime surveys were primarily focused on examining official data to discern the functioning of the system, using efficiency as a measuring stick (Remington, 1990). Within a number of these studies, however, was the genesis of a new research concept, one which relied less on reported statistics and more on observational data collected by independent investigation. In this emerging view, mortality tables and efficiency studies failed to tell the complete story of criminal justice practices. Hugh Fuller's 1931 study of criminal justice in Virginia put it directly:

> The Study of what the courts did with the cases filed is not so much a test of the efficiency of the courts as it may be the beginning of an appreciation that there were reasons why the cases were so disposed of and that these reasons are often complex, requiring for their complete understanding a much deeper and more thorough insight into practices and motives then a mere preparation of a series of mortality tables (p. 75).

Fuller was hardly the only prewar researcher to notice the complexity of criminal justice decision making. Raymond Moley (1929) observed that criminal practice was

> seriously involved in a deep cultural stratum . . . it is idle to say that the administrator is concerned only with the application of a fixed criminal law, with the philosophy of which he is not concerned. The law in fact is not so fixed as it appears and in its application the prejudices and preconceptions of the administrator may enjoy quite ample scope. Legislator, judge, and prosecutor, quite without realizing it, apply their own conceptions of punishment or treatment. To this confusion is added the pervasive influence of politics with a resulting brew that does not subject itself to simple definition (p. 222, 225–226).

The critical question was if actual practice was rooted in an ever changing "strange brew" of personal predilection, organizational imperative, and political influence, how should researchers undertake to study the criminal justice system? One of the most influential early researchers to make the case for field research was Donald Clemmer. In his 1940 study, *The Prison Community*, Clemmer told readers: "The survey type of study will tell us that prison walls are thirty feet high, but it will not usually reveal that when an inmate sees and learns about a certain wall, attitudes inimical to reformation develop . . . our major concern is with the 'unseen environment'" (p. 59).

After World War Two, the call for independent and critical assessments of the criminal justice system began to bear fruit, with a wave of field research initiated in the 1950s. Caleb Foote's (1956) studies of the Philadelphia police were among the earliest influential projects. A committed pacifist, Foote had been convicted of draft evasion in 1943, and served six months in a federal prison camp (followed by another year's imprisonment in 1945). Following the war, his experience working with Japanese-American detainees during war, and his disgust with the American practice of detention, led him to pursue a law degree from the University of Pennsylvania Law School, where he eventually joined the faculty. During his time as a law student, and later as a faculty member, Foote helped organize some of the earliest research on police discretion and behavior.

To examine police arrest practices, two students in Foote's research group attended preliminary hearings at Divisional Police Courts, reviewed trial transcripts, collected data from citizen watchdog groups, and accompanied the "Motor Bandit Patrol" on an eight-hour tour of duty. Their aim was to review the laws of Pennsylvania on arrest, and then to have "the law and the practice . . . compared to see whether there are gaps between the two." The gaps they found were very considerable. For example, Pennsylvania law required that an arrest precede a formal search for evidence, and that such searches could not be used to discover a cause for arrest. Yet, the authors reported, the Philadelphia police "made virtually no effort to observe this command; they regularly use the search to turn up the evidence on which to base their arrests . . . they make numerous 'spot checks' (random arrests) in the 'dope areas' of Philadelphia" (Markowitz and Summerfield 1952, 1192). Even worse, they reported: "Negroes who assert their rights against the police apparently do so in some cases at the risk of arrest. According to the records of one organization, arrests of Negroes for disorderly conduct have been made solely for such reasons as: protesting, at the police station, an illegal entry and beating; objecting to an unauthorized search of the person and being struck; or inquiring why a friend was in the police wagon" (Markowitz & Summerfield, 1952, p. 1202). Clearly, these sort of observational studies revealed aspects of practice for which statistics were not helpful or even available.

Foote and his students introduced into academic scholarship the kind of monitoring of day-to-day police practice pioneered by the National Association for the Advancement of Colored People (NAACP) and other civil rights organizations in the 1930s and 1940s. In New York

City and other large cities, civil rights investigators reported extensively on routine police practice, including indiscriminate searches, the use of the third degree, and lethal police violence (Biondi, 2003; Johnson, 2003). In Los Angeles, the role of the police in the 1943 "zoot suit riots" (days of violent clashes between Navy personnel and Mexican-American youth that featured many instances of police misconduct, and during which the police generally appeared to tolerate violence by sailors against youth) spurred the creation of the Coordinating Council for Latin American Youth (CCLAY) in monitoring police abuses (Escobar, 1999). The American Civil Liberties Union (ACLU) began pushing for systematic data collection on police brutality even before the 1931 publication of the Wickersham Commission's study *Lawlessness in Law Enforcement*; in the wake of the report, the ACLU proposed a third-degree complaint bureau in New York City to monitor police practice (Johnson, 2003). Collectively, these efforts created an early fieldwork infrastructure, with which later academic investigators like Caleb Foote could collaborate.

Civil rights groups provided the clearest evidence to date that actual criminal justice practice could depart significantly from the formal rule of law, in ways that could not be fixed by, but which would require the assertion of constitutional rights by suspects and criminal defendants against "presumptions of guilt, police brutality, coerced confessions, inadequate counsel, discriminatory jury selection, and 'mob-dominated trials'" (Gilmore, 2008, p. 334). Individual cases were used to indict the systemic racism of everyday practice; a Workers Defense League flier regarding the 1940 Odell Waller case (a black sharecropper accused of murdering his abusive white landlord) made the argument that "Waller is a typical victim of the planter justice which has ground down the poor people, white and colored, of the Southern states for generations. He was tried in a court presided over by a judge who made no attempt to conceal his anti-Negro bias and condemned by a jury consisting of a businessman, a carpenter, and ten landlords. Sharecroppers had no place on the jury list which was made up of those who paid the $1.50 Virginia state poll tax" (Gilmore, 2008; Sherman, 1992, p. 42; Heard, 2010; Zarnow, 2008; Rise, 1995).

The Philadelphia research conducted by Foote and his students with the assistance of the city's NAACP chapter attracted the notice of a research team being assembled in 1953 by the American Bar Foundation (ABF) to undertake a comprehensive examination of criminal justice administration. Much like prewar studies, the ABF project was supported by private foundation funding—in this case, the Ford Foundation. Unlike the prewar studies, which were often conducted on a shoestring budget, the generous funding provided by the Ford Foundation allowed the ABF to assemble an impressive research team. Eventually, the researchers embraced the observational and critical approach pioneered in the Philadelphia research and self-consciously rejected the earlier "survey" approach and the assumptions of professionalization advocates. As historian Samuel Walker (1992) finds, while

> The Survey staff could have embraced the long-standing recommendations for better leadership, higher personnel standards, the application of modern management techniques, and so on . . . " they "embraced a new paradigm in which the substantive criminal law was often viewed as problematic in and of itself, and daily administration managed the conflicts and contradictions as best it could (p. 58–59).

The resulting projects quickly became the most influential field research studies of criminal justice. The major volumes to come out of the ABF project include *Sentencing* (Dawson, 1969); *Arrest* (LaFave, 1965); *Prosecution* (Miller 1970); *Conviction* (Newman 1966); and *Detection of Crime* (Tiffany, McIntyre, & Rotenberg, 1967).

The ABF studies, and those it inspired, established a series of propositions that would inform decades of criminal justice research to come. One was that decision making was highly discretionary at every level of the criminal justice system, and therefore highly contingent on individual predilection and institutional culture (Reiss & Black, 1970; Piliavin & Briar, 1964; Westley, 1955). As one review put it, "In short, the system of criminal justice administration turned out to be infinitely more complicated than anticipated, which meant that research methods and aims had to be re-evaluated" (Armstrong, 1968, p. 262). A second proposition held that discretionary decision making was often "low visibility" and not readily captured except by direct observation (Goldstein, 1960; Skolnick, 1966).

The third proposition held that informal bargaining and negotiation were prevalent in the criminal justice process. Dorothy Miller and Michael Schwartz's (1966) study of mental health commitment hearings showed quite clearly the extent to which the subjects of the hearings would influence the outcome based on their attitude. In their work, they classified the subjects of the hearings as taking one of four approaches to the hearing (defiance; bewilderment; no-participation; volunteer). The defiant subjects were the most likely to be released. The nonparticipants were the most likely to be committed, while the volunteers were sorted out between the genuinely sick and those who wanted commitment for malingering, like "a middle-aged women, who had previously been committed as an alcoholic, wanted to return to the hospital ward where she had made friends and where she had found some relief from the deadly boredom of living with a 'dull' husband or a man who was under indictment for writing bad checks and sought commitment in preference to going to jail" (p. 33) (a choice not unlike, the authors suggestively noted, the choice made by Big Red in Ken Kesey's novel *One Flew Over the Cuckoo's Nest*).

A fourth conceptual contribution of these early field studies was to consider the various roles (and role conflicts) of criminal justice system personnel (Ohlin, Piven, & Pappenfort, 1956). William A. Westley's (1955) influential article "Violence and the Police: A Sociological Study of Law, Custom, and Morality" argued that community hostility produced among police "a close, social group, in which collective action is organized for self-protection and an attack on the outside world" (p. 110). Role conflict—a circumstance in which criminal justice professionals perceived conflicting or incompatible expectations for the performance of their duties—assumed a prominent role in studies of probation, parole, and correctional officers as well as police. Role conflict studies contributed to doubts that professionalization standards could easily be translated into actual practice.

A final conceptual contribution of the field studies was a skepticism regarding the mission of criminal justice system and its function, a skepticism they inherited from the civil rights investigations of the 1930s and 1940s. The role of police-community conflict in sparking the destructive 1943 riots in Detroit and Harlem, to say nothing of the long history of police complicity in repressing black political activity and maintaining white supremacy in the South, sparked a general questioning of law's justification. This would eventually extend to any number of elements of the criminal law. What did laws regarding juvenile justice, drug use, vagrancy, drunk and disorderly, prostitution, and gambling *really* intend to accomplish? This critical stance received expression in later work such as Herbert Packer's *The Limits of the Criminal Sanction* (1968), which posed the direct questions: "What are we trying to do by defining conduct as criminal and punishing people who commit crimes? To what extent are we justified in thinking that we can or ought to do what we are trying to do?" In the end, this skepticism would help to spur what Lawrence Friedman (1994) called the "constitutionalization" of criminal procedure (see Chapter 7).

❖ TIME TO COUNT

The application of statistical analysis and sophisticated program evaluation techniques to the practice of criminal justice emerged in the wake of the first generation of survey research, promoted by the growing ranks of academic researchers and supported by professionalizing administrators. The interest in better data and data analysis grew out of a pointed critique of existing knowledge. By the early 1930s, some scholars argued that the survey studies suffered from poor research methods, narrowness of scope, and poor data on actual practice. In a widely read indictment, Jerome Michael and Mortimer J. Adler (1932) told readers:

> Most of the quantitative (statistical) research, completed and projected, is not only insignificant; it is also unnecessary and pretentious. It is unnecessary because, since we cannot interpret it significantly, it has little practical utility, and because accurate non-quantitative descriptive knowledge . . . is sufficient . . . it is pretentious in its meretricious limitation of scientific method; the quantitative character of its findings should not conceal its true nature as undirected descriptive work of indeterminate validity (p. 315).

Michael and Adler pulled no punches in describing existing quantitative data as useless. Yet, even as they wrote, new fields of statistical work in criminal justice prediction and evaluation were emerging; fields that would revolutionize practice.

Not surprisingly, prediction came before evaluation. The ambition to develop reliable measures of risk prediction became one of the central animating features of criminal justice research. Not that everyone believed that prediction could ever be removed from the realm of subjective human judgment. As one parole expert put it at midcentury:

> Prediction tables may someday replace the human judgments of parole boards, but if this is to be so, the tables will need to be refined . . . while the tables rate past and present, they cannot hope to do much about rating the immediate future. What measurement device can evaluate such intangibles as the effect it may produce upon the newly released parolee if he finds his job offer is not bona fide? Who can place a plus or minus value on the personality of the parole officer who will take the released man's arrival report? Who can measure the effect upon a particular man of discovering that his wife intends to divorce him, but had not told him so while he was incarcerated? . . . We have not yet found a

way of predicting the possibilities of such eventualities or surmising the part they will play in recidivism or nonrecidivism (Dressler, 1959, p. 115).

In spite of the skeptics, the goal of infusing criminal justice decision making with actuarial precision won many adherents. After all, prediction in criminal justice was a logical extension of the progressive notion of individualization—the idea, as we have seen, that the system should respond to the particular circumstances of each criminal. Indeed, there would be no need for prediction at all without the discretionary decision making progressives introduced into criminal justice through parole and the indeterminate sentence. Historian Bernard Harcourt (2007) has coined the term *actuarial impulse* and traces it back to the 1920s. One of the most enthusiastic promoters was sociologist Ernest W. Burgess; his massive 1928 study of parole in Illinois sought to predict success on supervised release from prison through the use of a basic predictive scale. Still influential today, the Burgess scale simply scored inmates on a series of risk factors, awarding one point for each positive factor result—parolees with higher scores were therefore more likely to succeed, those with lower scores were at greater potential risk for being returned to prison (Harcourt 2007). As a result, advocates of statistical prediction claimed, parole boards might be able to employ "the same scientific procedure employed by insurance companies when they estimate the probable cost of insuring new applicants on the basis of their experience with the part death rates of insured persons of similar characteristics" (Harcourt, 2007, p. 39).

Burgess' pioneering study generated numerous follow up academic studies on prediction in the criminal justice systems. During the 1930s, academic dissertations appeared with titles like "Prediction Methods and Parole," "A Study of Success and Failure of One Thousand Delinquents Committed to a Boys' Republic," and "A Technique for Developing a Criteria of Parolability" (Harcourt, 2007). Criminal justice and legal journals published a tremendous amount of theoretical and experimental research from the 1930s through the 1950s. Still, it is important not to overstate the immediate influence of statistical prediction. Despite the flurry of academic interest, real-world applications of these methods lagged. Indeed, following the publication of Burgess' 1928 study, Illinois was the only state to fully integrate prediction instruments in formal decision making until the 1960s.

At the start of the decade in an article called "It's Time to Start Counting," clinical psychologist J. Douglas Grant (1962) issued a call for greater investment in predictive instruments to inform and assess criminal justice decision making. Grant was the first head of the California Department of Corrections research unit—created in 1958—and deeply committed to improving criminal justice outcomes. He argued that, "when you can measure what you are speaking about and express it in numbers, you know something about it, but when you cannot measure it, when you cannot express it in numbers your knowledge is of a meager and unsatisfactory kind" (Grant, 1962, p. 264).

Grant caught the temper of his times, for the 1960s featured a number of new, real-world applications of prediction research (Kahn, 1964). Among the most famous examples was the Manhattan Bail Project of the Vera Foundation, begun in 1961. A chemical engineer, Louis Schweitzer, became interested in bail problems and established the Vera Foundation, a nonprofit research agency focused on criminal justice issues. Project staff consisted mostly of New York University law students given quarters in the Criminal Courts building, from which they could interview inmates in the detention pen. Staff members would interview jail inmates regarding a variety of potential risk factors (such as employment and community attachment), quickly translate the responses to a numerical score that assessed the likelihood a defendant would abscond, and rush the completed results to a judge prior to arraignment. The results were widely credited to have been a success, bringing specific research results into practice. It stimulated similar projects in other cities, and led to a National Conference on Bail and Criminal Justice, held in 1964, and then to a national bail reform act the following year (Botein, 1965; Vera Institute of Justice, 2003).

The second emerging field for quantitative criminal justice research was program evaluation. By the middle of the twentieth century, formal program evaluations were still largely nonexistent. Put another way, no one in federal, state, and local criminal justice systems had any real idea whether new policies worked any better than old policies or whether their efforts worked to prevent recidivism. One critic reviewed the theoretical differences among psychological caseworks, noting that "it should be possible to establish that one orientation yields more effective results than the other" but that "despite three decades of philosophical dispute" no side had "presented any research evidence to back up their claims" (Dressler, 1959, p. 133). Another review of correctional programs at midcentury concluded: "most treatment programs are based on hope and perhaps informed speculation rather than on verified information" (Bailey, 1966, p. 157). Still later, the authors of the Kansas City Preventive Patrol Experiment (1972–1973) would assert that, "the history of policing is a chronicle of unchallenged assumptions" (Kelling, Pate, Pieckman, & Brown, 1974).

A 1966 meta-analysis of correctional program evaluations, reviewing 100 studies published between 1940 and 1960, gives us a good sense of the field's growth (Bailey, 1966). Eleven of the studies were published between 1940 and 1944, eight studies between 1945 and 1949, 21 studies between 1950 and 1954, and 58 studies between 1955 and 1959 (two program evaluations from before 1940 were also included). In other words, more than half of the studies had been published in the last five years under review, and more than two-thirds in the last decade. This review also found a general lack of quality. Of the 100 evaluations, 52 were found to have employed "nonsystematic empirical study designs" (meaning that they lacked any sort of selection control or control groups for comparison). Another 26 employed some control procedures, but no actual control groups, while only 22 employed fully experimental designs (Bailey, 1966, p. 153). The small numbers and poor quality of evaluation studies would become, by the 1970s, a leading source of criticism of rehabilitative programming, while newer evaluation studies would cast doubt on the ability of new criminal justice programs to have an appreciable effect on criminal behavior (see Chapter 7).

❖ CODA: THE PRESIDENT'S COMMISSION ON LAW ENFORCEMENT AND THE ADMINISTRATION OF JUSTICE

Fifty-five years after a crisis of confidence led Clevelanders to initiate a survey of criminal justice practice in their city, a national crisis of confidence precipitated the largest criminal justice research survey yet conducted. In 1965, President Lyndon Johnson, responding to the growing political salience of the crime issue and public concerns over rising crime rates and perceived lawlessness, proposed the creation of a President's Commission on Law Enforcement and Administration of Justice. Noting that, "we must arrest and reverse the trend toward lawlessness," President Johnson instructed the Commission to study the problems of crime and criminal justice, to find a more "fair and effective" plan of attack.

The Commission quickly determined that its mission would be to "distill and set forth extant knowledge about our system of criminal procedure." In doing so, the Commission and its various task forces eventually published a massive public report in 1967, which became a best-selling book in 1968. Over 800 pages long, *The Challenge of Crime in a Free Society* was, more than anything, a product of the developments in research and professionalism in the decades since the Cleveland survey. The commission argued that, "a significant reduction in crime is possible" if criminal justice systems met the following seven objectives:

1. The prevention of crime
2. The development of a far broader range of alternatives for dealing with offenders
3. Eliminating unfairness and injustice
4. Improving the levels of knowledge, expertise, initiative, and integrity of criminal justice personnel
5. Devoting greater resources to research
6. Higher levels of funding for criminal justice
7. Community involvement in criminal justice planning

Notice that points #4 and #5 speak directly to the quest for improved research and professionalism; points #1, #2, and #3 were to be made possible through these things; point #6 was largely aimed at securing them. Only point #7—the call for community involvement—struck a slightly different note, questioning the manner in which criminal justice professionals routinely excluded community input and participation.

The Challenge of Crime in a Free Society was a coming of age of sorts for professionalization and criminal justice research. Where the early criminal justice surveys just began to mark the outlines of the vast system of justice, the Commission's work confidently mapped out an interconnected system. Indeed, its mapping is still used today by students of criminal justice. With the publication of the report, criminal justice research and professionalism advanced farther than ever before and entered the very heart of the national political conversation about criminal justice. The coming decades would test President Johnson's optimistic statement that "new knowledge, new techniques, and new understanding" would provide the keys to solving the problems of crime.

❖ REFERENCES

American Bar Foundation. (1955). *The administration of criminal justice in the United States: Plan for a survey.* Chicago, IL: American Bar Foundation.

Armstrong, W. P., Jr. (1968). Administration of criminal justice: The American Bar Foundation project. *American Bar Association Journal, 54,* 261–263.

Bailey, W. C. (1966). Correctional outcome: An evaluation of 100 reports. *Journal of Criminal Law, Criminology, and Police Science, 57*, 153–160.

Bates, S. (1936). *Prisons and beyond.* New York, NY: Macmillan.

Biondi, M. (2003). *To stand and fight: The struggle for civil rights in postwar New York City.* Cambridge, MA: Harvard University Press.

Bopp, W. J. (1977). *O.W. Wilson and the search for a police profession.* Port Washington, NY: Kennikat Press.

Botein, B. (1965). The Manhattan bail project: Its impact on criminology and the criminal law processes. *Texas Law Review, 43*, 319–331.

Breckenridge, S. P., & Abbott, E. (1912). *The delinquent child and the home.* New York, NY: Charities Publication Committee.

Chute, C. L. (1923). Rational crime treatment. *Review of Reviews, 67*, 521-526.

Chute, C. L., & Bell, M. (1956). *Crime, courts, and probation.* New York, NY: Macmillan.

Ciepley, D. (2006). *Liberalism in the shadow of totalitarianism.* Cambridge, MA: Harvard University Press.

Clemmer, D. (1940/1958). *The prison community.* New York, NY: Holt, Rinehart and Winston.

Croly, H. D. (1914). *Progressive democracy.* New York, NY: Macmillan.

Dawson, R. O. (1969). *Sentencing: The decision as to type, length, and conditions of sentence.* Boston, MA: Little, Brown.

Detzer, K. (1960, March). Why hoodlums hate Bill Parker. *Reader's Digest, 76*, 239–246.

Domanick, J. (1994). *To protect and to serve: The LAPD's century of war in the city of dreams.* New York, NY: Pocket Books.

Dressler, D. (1959). *Practice and theory of probation and parole.* New York, NY: Columbia University Press.

Edgerton, K. (2004). *Montana justice: Power, punishment, & the penitentiary.* Seattle: University of Washington Press.

Platt, T., & Shank, G. (1976). In S. Dod, M. Fuller, M. Hannigan, H. Nawy, G. McLauchlan, T. Platt, H. Schwendinger, G. Shank, A. Snare., & P. Takagi (Eds.). Berkeley's School of Criminology, 1950–1976. *Crime and Social Justice 6 (1976)*: 1–3.

Escobar, E. J. (1999). *Race, police, and the making of a political identity: Mexican Americans and the Los Angeles Police Department, 1900–1945.* Berkeley: University of California Press.

Fogelson, R. M. (1977). *Big city police.* Cambridge, MA: Harvard University Press.

Foote, C. (1956). Vagrancy-type law and its administration. *University of Pennsylvania Law Review, 104*, 603.

Foster, J. P., Magers, J. S., & Mullikin, J. (2007). Observations and reflections on the evolution of crime-related higher education. *Journal of Criminal Justice Education, 18*, 123–136.

Friedman, L. M. (1994). *Crime and punishment in American history.* New York, NY: Basic Books.

Fronc, J. (2006). *New York undercover: Private surveillance in the Progressive Era.* Chicago, IL: University of Chicago Press.

Fuller, H. N. (1931). *Criminal justice in Virginia*. New York, NY: The Century Company.

Gilmore, G. E. (2008). *Defying Dixie: The radical roots of civil rights, 1919–1950*. New York, NY: W. W. Norton & Company.

Goldstein, J. (1960). Police discretion not to invoke the criminal process. *Yale Law Journal, 69*, 543–594.

Grant, J. D. (1962). It's time to start counting. *Crime & Delinquency, 8*, 259-264.

Hale, D. C. (1998). Criminal justice education: Traditions in transition. *Justice Quarterly, 15*, 385–394.

Harcourt, B. E. (2007). *Against prediction: Punishing and policing in an actuarial age*. Chicago, IL: University of Chicago Press.

Heard, A. (2010). *The eyes of Willie McGee: A tragedy of race, sex, and secrets in the Jim Crow South*. New York, NY: Harper Collins.

Jennings, D. (1960, May 7). Portrait of a police chief. *Saturday Evening Post, 232*, 45, 84–89.

Johnson, M. (2003). *Street justice: A history of police violence in New York City*. Boston, MA: Beacon Press.

Kahn, A. J. (1964). Public policy and delinquency prediction. *Crime & Delinquency, 11*, 218–228.

Kelling, G. L., Pate, T., Pieckman, D., & Brown, C. E. (1974). *The Kansas City preventive patrol experiment: A technical report*. Washington, DC: Police Foundation.

Krisberg, B., Marchionna, S., & Baird, C., eds. (2007). *Continuing the struggle for justice: 100 years of the National Council on Crime and Delinquency*. Thousand Oaks, CA: Sage.

LaFave, W. R. (1965). *Arrest: The decision to take a suspect into custody*. Boston, MA: Little, Brown.

Markowitz, P. R., & Summerfield, W. I., Jr. (1952). Philadelphia police practice and the law of arrest. *University of Pennsylvania Law Review, 100*, 1182–1216.

Michael, J., & Adler, M. J. (1932). *An institute of criminology and criminal justice*. New York, NY: Bureau of Social Hygiene.

Miller, D., & Schwartz, M. (1966). County lunacy commission hearings: Some observations of commitments to a state mental hospital. *Social Problems, 14*, 26–35.

Miller, F. W. (1970). *Prosecution: The decision to charge a suspect with a crime*. Boston, MA: Little, Brown.

Moley, R. (1929). *Politics and criminal prosecution*. New York, NY: Minton, Balch.

Monkkonen, E. H. (1992). History of urban police. *Crime and Justice: A Review of Research, 15*, 547–580.

Moore, M. H., & Kelling, G. L. (1983). To serve and protect: Learning from police history. *The Public Interest, 70*, 22–48.

Morn, F. (1995). *Academic politics and the history of criminal justice education*. Westport, CT: Greenwood Publishing Group.

Murphy, P. V., & Plate, T. (1977). *Commissioner: A view from the top of American law enforcement*. New York, NY: Simon and Schuster.

National Society of Penal Information. (1926). *Handbook of American prisons and reformatories*. New York, NY: National Society of Penal Information.

National Society of Penal Information. (1929). *Handbook of American prisons and reformatories*. New York, NY: National Society of Penal Information.

Newman, D. J. (1966). *Conviction: The determination of guilt or innocence without trial*. Boston, MA: Little, Brown.

Ohlin, L. E., Piven, H., & and Pappenfort, D.M. (1956). Major dilemmas of the social worker in probation and parole. *National Probation and Parole Association Journal, 2,* 211–225.

Packer, H. L. (1968). *The limits of the criminal sanction*. Palo Alto, CA: Stanford University Press.

Piliavin, I., & and Briar, S. (1964). Police encounters with juveniles. *American Journal of Sociology, 70,* 206–214.

Pound, R., & Frankfurter, F., (eds.). (1922/1968). *Criminal justice in Cleveland*. Montclair, NJ: Patterson Smith.

Ragsdale, G. T. (1929). The police training school. *Annals of the American Academy of Political and Social Science, 146,* 170-176.

Reiss, A. J., Jr., & Black, D. J. (1970). Police control of juveniles. *American Sociological Review, 35,* 63–77.

Remington, F. J. (1990). Development of criminal justice as an academic field. *Journal of Criminal Justice Education, 1,* 9–20.

Richmond, M. E. (1917). *Social diagnosis*. New York, NY: Russell Sage Foundation.

Rise, E. W. (1995). *The Martinsville seven: Race, rape, and capital punishment*. Charlottesville: University of Virginia Press.

Robertson, S. (2009). Harlem undercover: Vice investigators, race, and prostitution, 1910–1930. *Journal of Urban History, 23,* 486–504.

Rothman, D. J. (2002). *Conscience and convenience: The asylum and its alternative in progressive America*. Hawthorne, NY: Aldine de Gruyter.

Sherman, R. B. (1992). *The case of Odell Walker and Virginia justice, 1940–1942*. Knoxville: University of Tennessee Press.

Shelton, D. E. (2008). The CSI effect: Does it really exist? *NIJ Journal, 259,* 1–6.

Simon, J. (1993). *Poor discipline: Parole and the social control of the underclass, 1890–1990*. Chicago, IL: University of Chicago Press.

Skolnick, J. (1966). *Justice without trial: Law enforcement in democratic society*. New York, NY: John Wiley & Sons.

Smith, B. (1930). *A reorganization plan for the Chicago Police Department: Report No. 4*. Chicago, IL: Citizens Police Committee.

Smith, B. (1932). *A regional plan for Cincinnati and its environs*. New York, NY: Institute of Public Administration.

Smith, B. (1941). *The Baltimore police survey*. New York, NY: Institute of Public Administration.

Smith, B. (1946). *The New Orleans police survey*. New Orleans, LA: Bureau of Governmental Research.

Stolberg, M. M. (2002). *Bridging the river of hatred: The pioneering efforts of Detroit Police Commissioner George Edwards*. Detroit: Wayne State University Press.

Tiffany, L. P., McIntyre, D. M., & Rotenberg, D. L. (1967). *Detection of crime: Stopping and questioning, search and seizure, encouragement and entrapment*. Boston, MA: Little, Brown.

United States President's Commission on Law Enforcement and Administration of Justice. (1967). *The challenge of crime in a free society: A report*. Washington, DC: U.S. Government Printing Office.

Vera Institute of Justice. (2003). *A short history of Vera's work on the judicial process*. Retrieved from http://www.vera.org/content/short-history-veras-work-judicial-process

Wadman, R. C., & Allison, W. T. (2004). *To protect and serve: A history of police in America*. Upper Saddle River, NJ: Pearson/Prentice Hall.

Walker, S. (1992). Origins of the contemporary criminal justice paradigm: The American Bar Foundation survey, 1953–1969. *Justice Quarterly, 9*, 47–76.

Walker, S. (1998). *Popular justice: A history of American criminal justice*. New York, NY: Oxford University Press.

Westley, W. A. (1955). Violence and the police. *American Journal of Sociology, 59*, 34–41.

Wilson, O. W. (1941). *The distribution of police patrol force*. Chicago, IL: Public Administration Service.

Wilson, O. W. (1950). *Police administration*. New York, NY: McGraw-Hill.

Zarnow, L. (2008). Braving Jim Crow to save Willie McGee: Bella Abzug, the legal left, and civil rights innovation, 1948–1951. *Law & Social Inquiry, 33*, 1003–1041.

Zunz, O. (2000). *Why the American century?* Chicago, IL: University of Chicago Press.

7

Liberalism's Twin Revolutions, 1930s–1970s

The most fundamental questions about the criminal justice system include the following: What is its purpose? What are its goals? How best can these goals be achieved? Of course the criminal justice system seeks to protect society from crime, but how best can it do that? These issues underwent implicit but serious reevaluation in the middle of the twentieth century. Different sets of experts addressed these questions from two different angles. Both conceived of themselves as liberals—people who shared common broad beliefs in the importance of liberty and equality and in the ability of government to create positive change—but they had different professional orientations and concerns. As a result they championed very different outcomes.

First, from the 1930s to the 1970s, social scientific inquiry drove change in the criminal justice system. Reformers drew on a pervasive therapeutic ethos to experiment with new approaches to corrections. Because many states applied medical frameworks to adult corrections and sought to utilize various remedies to reintegrate offenders into society, the process of rehabilitation increasingly came to parallel the medical process of diagnosis and treatment, offering the same promise of a cure.

Second, more or less simultaneously, a series of landmark decisions by U.S. federal appeals courts and the Supreme Court redefined criminal defendants' rights. Increasingly skeptical about the good intentions of law enforcement and corrections officers, federal judges used the Fourteenth Amendment to selectively incorporate into state criminal court proceedings elements of the Bill of Rights such as the right to counsel and protection against unreasonable search and seizures. By clarifying what due process meant and extending federal constitutional protections to state and local jurisdictions, the courts required police and prosecutors to be more accountable for the legality of their investigations, forced prisons to observe minimum standards, severely curtailed the death penalty, and challenged the protective premises of juvenile justice.

Liberalism's twin revolutions were, however, antithetical to one another in important ways. Advocates of both believed in their ability to achieve positive social change. While advocates of the rehabilitative ideal believed strongly that through discretion and expert judgment they could improve offenders, advocates of due process in the law questioned both the effectiveness of professional discretion and the premise of rehabilitation. In addition, both of the twin revolutions encountered increasing resistance over time and discovered the limits to just how much fundamental change could be implemented in the criminal justice system.

❖ THE REHABILITATIVE IDEAL

The revolution in criminal justice treatment programs of the midtwentieth century has been called many things: the rehabilitative ideal, the medical model, therapeutic justice, clinical corrections, and more. The underlying impulse—that all criminal offenders were, in fact, persons in need of some kind of treatment intervention—was deeply rooted in the traditions of progressive reform. But midcentury advocates of treatment programming pushed that vision further than their Progressive Era predecessors had been willing or able to go. In their quest to solve the problem of criminality, advocates of rehabilitation expanded upon progressive ideas and, in many cases, helped develop entirely new types of intervention programming. And, where progressive reformers often sought to let the institutions of work, family, and community perform much of the rehabilitative work, midcentury criminal justice professionals increasingly made the case that real cures for crime could come from professional interventions. To be sure, the goal of transforming criminal justice into a massive treatment enterprise was never fully realized. Many criminal offenders at midcentury languished in jails, prisons, and reform schools that would have been indistinguishable from those of earlier decades, while probationers and parolees dealt with agents with little interest in the therapeutic aspects of their work. Still, the rehabilitative ideal *did* influence a great deal of practice and, more importantly, it came to define for professionals and the general public just what a modern criminal justice system was supposed to be doing.

The unprecedented commitment to treatment programs at midcentury was the product of an odd mixture of anxiety and confidence. Perhaps the greatest source of anxiety was the suspicion that the traditional sources of order and conformity, such as the family, the church, or industrial labor, were increasingly proving to be weak and unreliable. Therefore, criminal offenders could not simply be reintegrated into their families or communities; rather, the hard work of changing behavior would have to be undertaken by criminal justice professionals themselves (Simon, 1993). Advocates of rehabilitative programming benefitted from other kinds of anxiety, especially periodic bursts of public concern with specific crimes. In the United States, the public furor over sex crimes in the 1930s (Galliher & Tyree, 1985), juvenile delinquency during the 1940s, and heroin addiction in the 1950s each provided treatment-oriented professionals an opportunity to advance their presence within the criminal justice system.

Anxieties alone, of course, could not have produced a commitment to rehabilitation without the confidence that these new interventions could be made to work. Particularly in the United States, the experience of the Great Depression and World War Two had left liberals increasingly confident in the capacity of a vastly enlarged state to exercise power in the name of preserving domestic and international order. Little wonder, then, that the capacities for state intervention would be extended to the criminal offender as well. New investments in criminal infrastructure were made possible by postwar economic growth, which provided states with the opportunity to make expensive commitments to treatment programs. National and state governments made these kind of investments not simply because they had the resources but because of the widespread public confidence in the capacity of the medical and social sciences to unlock the sources of deviant behavior and to treat the underlying issues.

Leading the charge were the fields of psychiatry and psychology, which reached a pinnacle of public influence in the postwar years (Herman, 1995; Capshew, 1999). Dr. Karl Menninger, one of the best-known advocates of applying the tools and insights of psychiatric knowledge to the criminal justice process, made a forceful case for employing the "scientific method" in dealing with the criminal offender, as opposed to "obsolete methods based on tradition, precedent, and common sense." Common sense, Menninger (1968) felt, was only the best society could do until it learned better and developed the "uncommon sense" that only expert study and investigation could provide (p. 3).

Treatment advocates took a highly critical stance toward anything resembling a punitive approach toward the criminal offender. Menninger condemned what he felt were the traditional values of criminal justice: "Catch criminals and lock them up; if they hit you, hit them back." "This is common sense," Menninger concluded, "but it does not work." Experts in rehabilitative fields were united in their opposition to punishment practices they felt originated from untrained and emotional popular impulses toward revenge and retribution. Menninger and many of his fellow treatment advocates, for example, were resolute opponents of the death penalty: "I don't know of a single argument for capital punishment . . . murder is murder regardless of who does it." Proponents of rehabilitation and treatment tried hard to distance themselves from the idea that they were even involved in *punishing* the criminal offender. One institutional psychiatrist put it this way: "I don't believe in punishment. I don't think in those terms. I think that people who commit crime should be treated until they are capable of going out into society again" (Stanford, 1972). This redefinition of terms translated into a broad-based set of rhetorical changes in the criminal justice system, designed to downplay punishment and foreground treatment. In 1954, the American Prison Association became the American Correctional Association and advised their members to make similar sorts of changes. In due course, many prisons became correctional institutions, prison guards became correctional officers, and punishment cells became adjustment centers (Mitford, 1973).

Critics of the rehabilitative ideal sometimes charged that it operated *only* on the level of rhetoric, and that reformers were simply slapping fancy new labels onto the same old criminal justice practices. There is certainly some truth to this charge—changing labels, after all, was an easy and inexpensive way to try to demonstrate a commitment to treatment without having to do much else. On the other hand, the rehabilitative impulse undeniably produced tangible changes in criminal justice practices. Four, in particular, stand out for their importance.

First, the rehabilitative ideal produced an extensive commitment to the diagnosis and classification of the adult criminal offender. Classification had been a hallmark of Progressive Era planning for criminal justice, but the study and diagnosis of the offender had largely been limited to the juvenile offender. Even in juvenile justice, study and diagnosis were rarely integrated into actual institutional practice. Among adult offenders, classification remained a rarity, save for efforts to classify prisoners by security level (Sullivan, 1990). In the 1930s, Superintendent Howard Gill of the Norfolk Prison Colony in Massachusetts developed one of the first comprehensive classification schemes for a single correctional institution. Norfolk, under Superintendent Gill, embraced the idea that prisoners were "socially maladjusted human beings . . . who need help, understanding and guidance in rebuilding their lives and characters" (Rothman, 2002, p. 386). Toward that end, Gill developed the SCAMP plan of classification (Situational Cases; Custodial Cases; Asocial Cases; Medical Cases; Personality Cases) for sorting prisoners based on treatment categories. Each category carried with it a specific set of therapeutic interventions, based on the nature of the prisoner's problems.

Classification emerged as a programmatic tool in other areas as well, including parole. In California, the Special Intensive Parole Unit (SIPU) was developed in four phases between 1953 and 1964. The first two phases focused largely on the effects of smaller caseload sizes for parole agents, with the postrelease behavior of SIPU parolees being compared to control groups in regularly sized caseloads. Phase three introduced some attention to the problem of classification by classifying cases by risk level, in order to see whether smaller caseloads might be more or less effective among different parolee risk levels. Phase four introduced the most ambitious classification element into the program, by testing all parolees using a five-stage scale of maturity level. Parole agents were also classified, on the basis of their "orientation to their work," as either internal (meaning they focused on the internal thoughts and feelings of parolees) or external (meaning they tended to focus on parolees' work and other external activities). Low-maturity parolees were then matched with external agents, and high-maturity parolees with internal agents, with both kinds of matches tested in both small and regular caseload sizes (Glaser, 1995; Simon, 1993).

A second manifestation of the rehabilitative ideal was the development of centralized reception and diagnostic centers within state juvenile and adult correctional systems. One major 1938 indictment of the manner in which young adult offenders were handled by the criminal justice system, *Youth in the Toils*, pleaded for a new approach that would aim for "the unmaking of youthful criminal careers, not retributive punishment" (Harrison & Grant, 1938, p. 7). Toward that end, the authors of *Youth in the Toils* argued, the criminal justice system should employ "new methods" and "new machinery," including centralized correctional bureaucracies run by experts (Harrison & Grant, 1938, p. 130–161). The book's publication inspired the American Law Institute (ALI) to establish, that same year, a working committee on criminal justice that featured a virtual who's who of liberal criminal justice thought. In 1940, the committee proposed some "new machinery": a Model Youth Correctional Authority Act. The proposed Youth Authority would be an autonomous administrative entity responsible for the correctional treatment of serious offenders, including the operation of a centralized reception and classification center. Although no state adopted the ALI proposal in its entirety, its publication gave a boost to state-level efforts to create reception centers (Tappan, 1957).

In New York, the ALI plan helped to inspire the opening of the Elmira Reception Center (ERC) in November of 1945. Adult felony offenders aged 16 to 30 were committed to Elmira from the criminal courts, where they spent 60 days undergoing a series of examinations. As it was originally constituted, the ERC program had four stages: reception (2–3 days), orientation (2–3 days), examination (7–10 days), and program. ERC staff made the case that the inmate should "make time serve him" by using these two months of assessment to explore his interests and capacities. In theory, the conclusion of this evaluation period would then produce a "classification and recommendations" report indicating the optimal institutional assignment. The report consisted of a summary sheet for the receiving prison, which highlighted the psychologist's report, the psychiatrist's report, the general education report, the vocational education report, the physical education report, the religion report, the custodial report, treatment recommendations, and general parole recommendations. The recommendations in turn grouped inmates into one of several classes that suggested either longer or shorter periods of confinement.

A third element of rehabilitative programming at midcentury was a commitment to indeterminate sentencing and predictions of future dangerousness. Here, too, the roots of indeterminate sentencing and prediction went back to the Progressive Era, but with greater confidence came greater commitment to holding offenders until they were ready to be released. *Youth in the Toils* devoted hundreds of pages to the call for treatment and compassion, but concluded with the following words: "If, however, the offender is either unwilling or unable to seize an opportunity fairly given, the gates of prison or penal camp must be closed upon him and stay closed. Segregation of those who are either too weak or have become too vicious to discharge their obligations toward a free society would be fully justified" (Harrison & Grant, 1938, p. 167). Karl Menninger, America's best-known proponent of indeterminacy in service to scientific treatment, put it this way:

> If we were to follow scientific methods, the convicted offender would be detained indefinitely pending a decision as to whether and how and when to reintroduce him successfully into society. All the skill and knowledge of modern behavioral science would be used to examine his personality assets, his liabilities and potentialities, the environment from which he came, its effects upon him, and his effects upon it (Murphy, 1973, p. 136).

Of course, many offenders under indeterminate sentences served only short periods of time, and the evidence is mixed as to whether the average length of stay was longer under indeterminate versus determinate sentencing. Still, true indeterminacy held out, for every offender, the prospect that institutional confinement or criminal justice supervision could extend far longer than under determinate systems, based solely on diagnosis and assessment rather than actual criminal offense.

A fourth and final hallmark of the medical model involved the introduction of therapeutic interactions in the criminal justice setting. Some of these interactions came through a renewed commitment to employing mental health professionals toward treating, and not simply diagnosing, the criminal offender. Individual counseling, of course, was an expensive proposition to undertake; far more often, institutions undertook group therapy and counseling efforts as a means of treating the individual. At the Fairfield School for Boys (Ohio), a state reformatory for young men aged 15 to 19, inmates placed in an experimental therapy group were enrolled in a twice-weekly group psychotherapy group along with a one-hour weekly individual psychotherapy session for 20 weeks. Another group was placed in a control group, for comparison purposes. Trained mental health professionals directed the Fairfield experiments, but more typically institutional teachers, counselors, and even other inmates led "group therapy" sessions (Persons, 1966).

Every function of criminal justice supervision was to be directed toward therapeutic ends. Jonathan Simon details the efforts in California to reorient its parole programs around clinical methods and therapeutic ends. Here, too, midcentury reformers were often repeating Progressive Era ideas—in this case, the value of scientific casework and therapeutic relations between caseworker and client—but giving them their fullest expression to date in criminal justice practice. In California, the new parole manual for 1959 emphasized to agents that their ultimate goal was "influencing, motivating, or treating parolees" (Simon, 1993, p. 76).

It was not long before advocates of therapy began to criticize the traditional institutions of criminal justice as inadequate or even antithetical to therapeutic results. New settings for treatment emerged during this period, designed to promote a more positive environment for treatment. One important innovation was the therapeutic community. Designed to provide a highly structured environment emphasizing group interactions and personal responsibility, the therapeutic community concept emerged following World War Two, heavily promoted by widely read publications such as Maxwell Jones' *The Therapeutic Community: A New Treatment Method in Psychiatry* (1953).

Applications of the therapeutic community concept appeared throughout the criminal justice system between the 1950s and 1970s. One of the most publicized experiments from this period came from the "Highfields experiment" in New Jersey. There, group-based interaction was designed to promote the rehabilitation of juvenile offenders, borrowing concepts from other group-based therapeutic programs like Alcoholics Anonymous (McCorkle, Elias, & Bixby, 1958). Highfields (opened in 1950) was a home for 16 year olds and featured minimal personnel and short-term intensive residence periods. Its therapy centered on "guided group interactions," which claimed to achieve major improvements in offender attitudes, adjustment, and postrelease reoffending (McCorkle, Elias, & Bixby, 1958). As one evaluator described it: "the boys do ventilate; they do get support from one another; they do achieve awareness of their problems and of the problems of others" (Weeks, 1958, p. 161).

An experimental program for delinquent youth, begun in Provo, Utah in 1956, employed a similar intensive treatment model of guided group interactions, in which "the absence of formal structure . . . has the positive effect of making boys more amenable to treatment." In the Provo case, young men lived at home, spending part of every day at a group home with fellow offenders. The program placed great confidence in the power of the group dynamic to change behavior: "Only through a group and its processes can a boy work out his problems. From a peer point of view it has three main goals: (1) to question the utility of a life devoted to delinquency; (2) to suggest alternative ways for behavior; and (3) to provide recognition for a boy's personal reformation and his willingness to reform others" (Empey & Rabow, 1961).

Figure 7.1 Note that the Provo experiment drew from a random selection of both reformatory and probation cases, which also served as the "control" groups to the "treatment" group that took part in the Pinehills program.

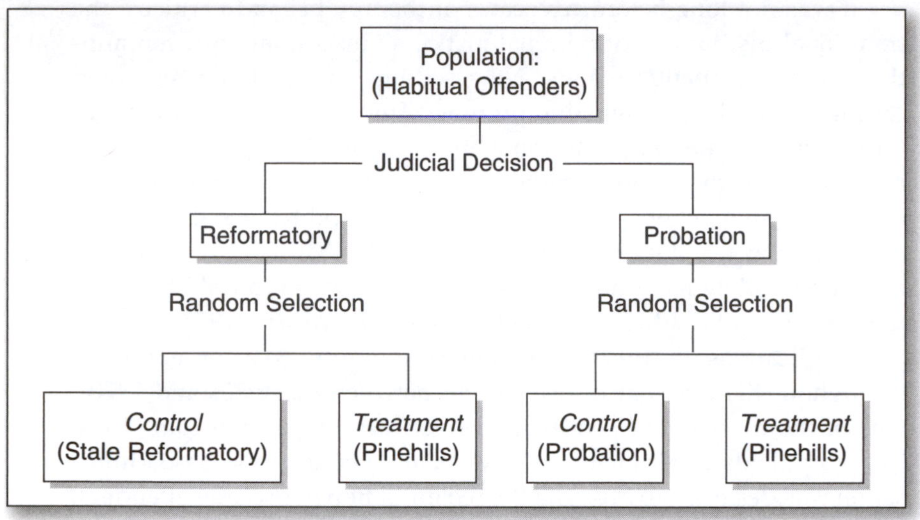

Source: LaMar T. Empey and Jerome Rabow, "The Provo Experiment in Delinquency Rehabilitation," American Sociological Review (October, 1961) 26: 679–696.

Even where therapeutic communities were not employed, reformers embraced the idea of relocating treatment interventions outside the traditional institutional setting. In California, the California Youth Authority embraced community-based rehabilitation efforts on a statewide scale, launching the Community Treatment Project (CTP) in 1961. As Schlossman (1995) observes: "As much as any single event, the creation of the CTP inaugurated the commitment to desinstitutionalization and to community treatment movements in American juvenile corrections" (p. 346). By the late 1960s, the focus on community and residential treatment found its way into the President's Crime Commission report ("Institutions tends to isolate offenders from society, both physically and psychologically") and encouraged the development of halfway houses, work release programs, and prison furlough programs (Latessa & Allen, 1982).

The Medical Model at Work: Three Cases

Three specific areas of criminal justice practice illustrate the rehabilitative impulse at work. Each reflects the distinct combination of public anxiety over a particular aspect of criminal behavior with professional confidence in the capacity of scientific interventions to diagnose and treat the criminal offender.

The first area involved state responses to the so-called *defective delinquent*—a Progressive Era term that never had a precise meaning but that generally referred to criminal offenders diagnosed with subnormal intelligence or some mental abnormality. New York State opened the nation's first institution for defective delinquents in 1921. In 1926, the state of Virginia established the State Prison Farm for Defective Misdemeanants, staffed by "such trained and expert medical and mental assistants as . . . deemed necessary to carry out the corrective and reformative purposes of the farm" (Noll, 1995, p. 117–121). Other states followed with separate institutions or special programs for defective delinquents within larger institutional settings. Maryland's Defective Delinquent Law (1951) was the nation's most comprehensive legislation and employed an expansive definition of a defective delinquent: "one who by the demonstration of persistent aggravated antisocial or criminal behavior, evidences a propensity toward criminal activity, and who is found to have either such intellectual deficiency or emotional unbalance, or both, as to clearly demonstrate an actual danger to society so as to require such confinement and treatment, when appropriate, as may make it reasonably safe for society to terminate the confinement and treatment."

The development of specialized programs for the so-called sexual psychopath represents another important focus of the rehabilitative model. By 1960, 26 states (along with a number of western countries) had introduced sexual psychopath laws. As with the defective delinquent, there was no precise definition of the subject. Sutherland (1950) pointed out a series of varied definitions, from the very simple—"lack of power to control his sexual impulses"—to the exceedingly broad—"emotional instability or impulsiveness of behavior, or lack of customary standards of good judgment, or failure to appreciate the consequences of his acts, or a combination of such conditions." Although critical of such laws, Sutherland conceded that their passage had been closely tied to "the trend toward treatment and away from punishment."

Sexual psychopath laws reflected the same combination of anxiety and confidence expressed in the medical model more generally. On the one hand, the impetus for the laws arose out of a nationwide panic, starting in the 1930s, over sex crimes and predatory repeat offenders (Freedman, 1987). On the other hand, the laws also provided for indeterminate commitment to psychiatric treatment facilities, rather than prisons, and allowed medical authorities to determine when offenders ought to be released. Although confinement until "fully and permanently recovered" meant that some offenders might be placed under permanent restraint, sexual psychopath laws nonetheless proceeded from the confident assumption that all of those released would leave the institution having been fully and permanently cured of their underlying problems (Pratt, 1998).

California was among those states that passed sexual psychopath legislation. A state official described the purpose of the law as a "curative and remedial means of treating the sexually deviated offender by way of psychiatric approach" (Hacker & Frym, 1955, p. 766). In 1954, California opened the Atascadero State Hospital, a facility specifically designated for receiving offenders designated as sexual psychopaths. Criminal defendants considered by the courts as probable candidates for the sexual psychopath designation were committed to Atascadero (the commitment was a civil, rather than a criminal, procedure—although the odd combination of criminal and civil produced a sort of hybrid process) for a 90-day period of observation and evaluation. At the end of the observation period, offenders were either returned to court for a resumption of their criminal proceedings or committed to Atascadero for treatment. Generally, about half of the cases were returned and half were committed (Rood, 1960). Those offenders committed to Atascadero remained for an indefinite period of time—until they were cured—and were subject to the full range of midcentury psychiatric therapies: primarily group counseling and behavioral therapy but also including psychiatric drugs, electroshock treatments, and even psychosurgery (lobotomy).

The *Atlanta Georgian* newspaper marked the opening of the United States Narcotic Farm with this striking image, showing a line of drug addicts headed toward a cure, thanks to the enlightened work of treatment providers.

Source: Atlanta Georgian, 1906–1939.

The problem of drug addiction presented yet another opportunity for the medical model to assert itself in the criminal justice system. Here, too, the advance of the therapeutic model was aided by a combination of public anxiety over the dangers of drug addiction and the confidence that scientific knowledge would advance a solution. The most important monument to this combination of hope and fear was the United States Narcotic Farm, opened in 1935 at Lexington, Kentucky. A combination of hospital and prison, the facility served as the primary source of publicly funded treatment for addicts referred from the criminal courts. Voluntary admissions were also accepted. Federal prisoners sent to Lexington were to be called *patients* and were provided a highly structured program of recreation, vocational therapy, and psychotherapy (Campbell, Olsen, & Walden, 2008).

Following World War Two, successive waves of heroin use sparked the creation of various state treatment programs for the drug-addicted offender. New York City opened a treatment program in 1952 for youthful addicts at Riverside Hospital on North Brother Island in the East River, which included spaces for delinquent youth sent by court order. State level treatment programs connected to the criminal courts emerged with full force during the 1960s, with the development of massive civil commitment programs for drug-addicted offenders. New York State created the Narcotic Addiction Control Commission in 1966, a treatment-oriented program to which those arrested for drug-related crimes could be civilly committed for a period of three to five years. In California, the Civil Addict Program (CAP) was begun in 1961, to provide treatment and to control the addict "for the prevention of contamination of others and the protection of the public" (McGlothlin, Anglin, & Wilson, 1976). Individuals committed to CAP spent some time in an institutional setting engaged in group therapy, followed by a multiyear program of community supervision by specially trained parole agents (Simon, 1993, p. 85–94).

The Critique of the Medical Model and the Rehabilitative Ideal

The ambition and scope of midcentury rehabilitation programs was not enough to spare them from devastating criticism. As we see in Chapter 9, the rise of get-tough law and order politics in the 1960s targeted treatment-oriented criminal justice programs for coddling offenders who needed (or deserved) harsher treatment. But many of the strongest challenges to the medical model came from within the ranks of liberal reformers.

The most common criticism of rehabilitative programming pointed to massive problems with implementation. Simply put, critics charged that there was a huge disparity between what the state was promising to do with the criminal offender and the programs that it actually delivered. Prison educational and vocational programs, for example, were hampered by a lack of funding, an inability to attract qualified professional staff, and poor or nonexistent evaluation methods (Irwin, 1980; Sullivan, 1990, p. 65). Evaluations of treatment-oriented institutions found them frequently overcrowded and understaffed; group therapy sessions were not run by mental health professionals, and patients suffered from neglect and inattention (Cole, 2000). For all of the intensity of midcentury rhetoric, actual practice fell well short. Small wonder that two prominent criminologists concluded, "The Era of Treatment remains stalled at the threshold, an age still clamoring to be born" (Korn & McCorkle, 1959; Sullivan, 1990, p. 75).

Other critiques went deeper than problems of implementation, attacking the medical model for being poorly conceptualized and inadequate to fulfill its promises. An early critical study of sexual psychopath laws described sexual psychopathy as an "inadequate, confusing, and obsolete medical term" loaded with "ambiguities, uncertainties, and arbitrariness." This same study concluded that psychiatry was simply not ready to meet its own goals: "under prevalent conditions of examination and treatment, valid and objective scientific criteria for commitment or for discharge of the patient do not exist" (Hacker & Frym, 1955, p. 777). Michael Hakeem (1958) excoriated the criminal justice system for privileging psychiatric knowledge:

> The courts and correctional agencies should not persist in giving legal and official support and sanction to the almost universal fallacy of considering psychiatrists to be experts on human behavior, motivation, personality, interpersonal relations, problems of social organization, emotional reactions, crime and delinquency, other social problems, and similar nonmedical topics. It is astounding that judges and correctional officials continue to view psychiatrists as experts on human behavior when there is considerable experimental and other research which shows laymen to be superior to psychiatrists and associated personnel in the judgment of peoples' motives, emotions, abilities, personality traits, and action tendencies (p. 682).

A study of Maryland's Patuxent Institution for defective delinquents in 1976 attacked the overly broad concept of defective delinquency, concluded that the professional staff could not reliably predict future dangerousness, and produced a recidivism level "only marginally" superior to other state prisons (Courtless, 1998, p. 144–146). In similar fashion, some studies of the United States Narcotic Farm at Lexington showed more than 90% of all inmate-patients relapsed to drug addiction after release. Critics charged that existing expert knowledge was simply inadequate to comprehend the nature of drug addiction.

The failures of rehabilitative programs like the one at Lexington led directly to another point of criticism: that rehabilitation was ultimately subordinated to punishment in the criminal justice system. For some liberal critics, this was a deliberate decision by criminal justice systems, which employed the mask of rehabilitative rhetoric to conceal the underlying focus on punishment. The ranks of these early critics included legal scholars such as Francis Allen (1959), who warned, "under the dominance of the rehabilitative ideal, the language of therapy is frequently employed, wittingly or unwittingly, to disguise the true state of affairs that prevails in our custodial institutions and at other points in the correctional process . . . too often the vocabulary of therapy has been exploited to serve a public-relations function" (p. 229). Herbert Wechsler (1959) who similarly cautioned, "the danger rather is that coercive regimes we would not sanction in the name of punishment or of correction will be sanctified in the name of therapy without providing the resources for a therapeutic operation" (p. 4).

For other critics of the rehabilitative impulse, the subordination of treatment to punishment was not simply a masking device—rather, the primacy of punishment was built into the system, and no amount of commitment to treatment or therapy could overcome this essential nature. The pioneering work of sociologist Erving Goffman gave this critical perspective an important theoretical basis. Institutions of confinement, Goffman (1957) argued, possessed "encompassing tendencies" that worked against the goals of rehabilitation. In what he called "total institutions," all aspects of inmates' lives were placed under rigid authority, and compliance with that authority became the primary requirement. "In fact," Goffman wrote, the claim of rehabilitation "is seldom realized and even when permanent alteration occurs, these changes are often not of the kind intended by the staff." Critics like David Rothman (1978) employed Goffman's "strong and compelling theoretical analysis" in advancing the claim that "incarceration by its very nature will inevitably infantilize the inmate and make his future adaptation to society more problematic" (p. 83).

What's The Evidence?: Program Evaluations

No single publication has been more closely associated with the critique of rehabilitation than Robert Martinson's 1974 essay "What Works?—Questions and Answers About Prison Reform," published in *The Public Interest*. The origins of Martinson's essay dated back to the initiation in 1966, by the New York State Governor's Special Committee on Criminal Offenders, of a broad review of the criminal justice literature on rehabilitation. Martinson was one of the criminologists hired by the committee to conduct the study, led by Douglas S. Lipton, which surveyed 231 published and unpublished evaluations of rehabilitation programs completed between 1945 and 1967. When the study had been completed, however, New York officials were no longer

(Continued)

(Continued)

interested in publishing the findings. Martinson's frustration at what he regarded as the suppression of research findings led him to independently publish a version of the study's conclusions in the 1974 essay (the full study was finally published one year later).

Martinson's version of the study's conclusions was highly damning to the rehabilitative enterprise, placed up front in the essay and italicized by the author for emphasis: "*With few and isolated exceptions, the rehabilitative efforts that have been reported so far have had no appreciable effect on recidivism*" (Martinson, 1974). Martinson used this stark conclusion to justify a larger political point, that society must de-emphasize the place of institutional confinement for the criminal offender. Rather than, "a more full-hearted commitment to the strategy of treatment," Martinson (1974) argued—in other words, a focus on problems of implementation—society had to consider whether or not "the prison has become an anachronism and can be replaced by more effective means of social control" (p. 49-50).

Subsequent assessments of the "What Works?" essay make it clear that, in making his political point, Martinson almost certainly overstated the extent to which rehabilitative programs had failed. Martinson himself partly revised his pessimistic assessment in a later article (Martinson, 1979). No one, however, has really quarreled with Martinson's observation that most so-called evaluation studies published before 1967 were deeply flawed in methodological terms. In fact, one response to Martinson's essay has been a renewed interest in the development of more sophisticated and reliable methods for evaluating criminal justice programs. Criminologist Doris MacKenzie (2006), for example, has made a forceful case that "strategies for reducing crime should be based on scientific evidence," employing the term "evidence-based corrections" to describe "the need to use scientific evidence to make informed decisions about correctional policy" (p. 20).

If Martinson's essay has been treated as a call to action by contemporary criminologists, it offers a different sort of challenge for historians of criminal justice; namely, how do we think carefully about ideas like success and failure? Historians of nearly every major rehabilitative undertaking can find, in print, reports and studies praising their effectiveness or urging greater commitment of resources to build upon promising beginnings. And, less often but still quite commonly, historians can find criticisms and attacks on those very same programs. What to make of all the positive and negative evaluations? Historians should take care to consider the sources of the evaluations in every case, and to consider the kinds of methodologies that the authors employ.

❖ THE JUDICIAL REVOLUTION

The second major factor driving change in the criminal justice system in the middle of the twentieth century was the elaboration of concepts of due process and equal protection in the legal system. This resulted in what has been termed a *judicial revolution*, a series of decisions mainly handed down by the U.S. Supreme Court that reshaped the operation of American law. The judicial revolution affected many aspects of American life—it undermined the legal basis of racial segregation, it expanded the right to privacy, it placed new barriers between church and state—but in the case of criminal justice it reshaped the ways that institutions operated and forced them to adhere to much more rigorous procedural standards than they had in the past.

In the middle of the twentieth century, federal courts primarily used the Fourteenth Amendment to the U.S. Constitution to extend federal protections to state and local criminal procedures. In particular, the courts increasingly maintained that the clause declaring that a state could not "deprive any person of life, liberty, or property, without due process of law; nor deny to any person within its jurisdiction the equal protection of the laws" meant that many of the protections laid out in the first 10 amendments to the Constitution applied to state and local governments as well as the federal government. These protections included security against unreasonable searches and seizures, the right to legal counsel in trials, and protection against self-incrimination. Although the federal courts only gradually and selectively incorporated federal constitutional rights into the law, this nonetheless had the effect of imposing a new set of standards on local law enforcement agencies and courts. The creation of new federal standards was often met with recalcitrance on the part of state and local law enforcement, which had until then largely been able to control their work.

The judicial revolution was rooted in the concept of legal liberalism, the belief that courts and the law could make positive social change. Legal liberalism, however, was not simply an imposition by a small handful of judges, as it sometimes is thought to have been, nor was it simply a product of a more general liberalism common in the 1960s. Instead, the judicial revolution and the legal liberalism that helped spawn it were built upon changing viewpoints within the legal profession and external pressures by people seeking to use the courts to achieve social change.

The leadership of Chief Justice Earl Warren pushed the Supreme Court and the federal courts to expand protections of civil rights and civil liberties. Warren exemplifies the changing viewpoints within the legal profession. He had been a leading Republican politician in California, serving as district attorney in Alameda County in the 1920s and 1930s, state attorney general from 1938 to 1942, and governor from 1943 to 1953. In these positions he maintained a hard-line stance on crime and civil liberties, giving anticrime speeches to police groups and supporting the World War Two-era internment of Japanese-Americans. As he moved onto a national stage, however, running for vice president in 1948 and seeking the presidential nomination in 1952, Warren became increasingly concerned about issues of race and civil rights. Appointed chief justice of the Supreme Court in 1953, Warren led the court in its dismantling of the legal structures of racial segregation. In *Brown v. Board of Education of Topeka* (1954), one of the first major cases of his tenure, Warren convinced the court to rule unanimously that racial segregation of schools was inherently unequal and thereby unconstitutional. This pattern of using court rulings to expand civil rights and civil liberties—particularly for African Americans—would also characterize the Warren Court's rulings on criminal justice issues as well (Powe, 2000; Walker, 1998).

The model of legal liberalism exemplified by the Warren Court was also partly premised on skepticism about the rehabilitation that experienced its heyday at the same time. Liberal judges and attorneys embraced many of the critiques of the rehabilitative model: that implementation was poor, that treatment was poorly conceptualized, and that punishment was built into the system. This is perhaps most evident in the area of juvenile justice where, since the beginning of the century, procedures had been highly informal. Juvenile courts had operated on the premise that one of their main goals was to offer treatment to young offenders and that to do so they needed a great deal of procedural informality. Juvenile courts did not require evidence beyond a reasonable doubt to adjudicate a child delinquent; they did not need to inform a child or family of the charges or keep a hearing transcript; they did not utilize trials by jury. By the middle of the twentieth century, however, legal scholars increasingly questioned this model. For example, in his textbook *Juvenile Delinquency*, legal scholar Paul Tappan (1949) criticized juvenile courts for violating presumptions of innocence. In their efforts to help young offenders, he argued, juvenile courts neglected to provide due process, assumed that children before them had done what they were accused of, and focused mainly on methods of treatment. Critics arguing along a similar line maintained that, since juvenile courts and criminal courts had similar functions and similar power to incarcerate, they should operate with similar standards. By 1966 one of the most thorough critiques—published in the *Harvard Law Review*—questioned juvenile courts for both their procedural informality and their tendency to discourage attorneys from intervening on behalf of accused youth. Moreover, this study questioned the rehabilitative premise of juvenile courts, asserting that, "The judge as an amateur psychologist, experimenting upon the unfortunate children who must appear before him, is neither an attractive nor a convincing figure" (quoted in Manfredi, 1998, p. 41).

The judicial revolution that culminated in the 1960s resulted from external pressures by activists focused on the ways in which due process in criminal courts was intertwined with issues of civil rights. Beginning as early as the 1920s, the Legal Defense and Education Fund (LDF) of the National Association for the Advancement of Colored People (NAACP) took up cases of African Americans accused of crimes under circumstances that seemed racially discriminatory. For example, in 1925 the LDF helped coordinate the defense of Dr. Ossian Sweet after he was accused of shooting two men outside of his Detroit home (see Chapter 2; Boyle, 2004). By the 1930s, the LDF—in coordination with the American Civil Liberties Union (ACLU)—began to win important victories in the Supreme Court protecting the civil rights of criminal defendants. In *Powell v. Alabama* (1932), the Supreme Court overturned the conviction of one of the Scottsboro boys—African American youths who had been sentenced to death for raping a white woman (see Chapter 5)—by determining that legal counsel was necessary for poor defendants in capital cases (Geis & Bienen, 1998; Gottschalk, 2006). Not only did these cases highlight the ways in which external entities such as the LDF increasingly acted on behalf of criminal defendants—particularly African Americans—whose civil rights may have been violated, they also illustrated the ways in which federal courts—and particularly the Supreme Court—began to intervene in state criminal proceedings, selectively applying federal protections articulated in the Bill of Rights to local criminal prosecutions.

External pressures from the Civil Rights movement and other activists had an even greater impact following World War Two. Between the 1920s and the 1970s, the number of African Americans incarcerated grew from roughly one-third of the total U.S. prison population to over one-half. As a result, the incarceration of African Americans became increasingly intertwined with other issues of civil rights (Gottschalk, 2006). In particular a religious movement called the Nation of Islam (also known as the Black Muslims) exercised influence in the legal system as a result of its active recruitment of African American men in prison between the 1940s and 1960s. Under the leadership of Elijah Muhammad and his most famous minister, the prisoner-turned-activist Malcolm X, the Nation of Islam mingled traditional Sunni Islam faith with American notions of black nationalism. By the late 1950s and early 1960s, Black Muslims in prison sued for rights to religious freedoms such as wearing religious hair styles and traditional dress, having access to their own ministers, and eating special diets. In response to a case brought by a Black Muslim alleging that he had been denied permission to buy religious publications, the Supreme Court decided in *Cooper v. Pate* (1964) that inmates in state prisons had standing to sue in federal courts and that, by implication, state prisoners had rights protected under the federal constitution (Christianson 1998; Walker 1998).

By the early 1960s, a more generalized prisoners' rights movements emerged in conjunction with the Civil Rights movement. Again the LDF and the ACLU actively pursued cases dealing with both conditions and racial segregation in prisons. By the middle of the 1960s, federal district courts of appeal increasingly overturned lower court decisions and established protections for inmates. In *Jordan v. Fitzharris* (1966), the United States District Court for the Northern District of California found that the implementation of solitary confinement at California's Soledad prison constituted cruel and unusual punishment. Marking the close connections between issues of prison conditions and social inequality, the U.S. Supreme Court in *Lee v. Washington* (1968) found racial segregation in state prisons to be unconstitutional. By the early 1970s decisions by federal courts across the country reshaped prison administration by imposing a new layer of legal regulation, forcing prisons to improve conditions under the threat of federal sanctions. In this way, external pressures by activists helped to transform legal thinking, which in turn reshaped criminal justice practice (Christianson, 1998; Walker, 1998).

Case Studies in Criminal Justice: Clarence Earl Gideon, Criminal Defendant

Clarence Earl Gideon (1910–1972) spent much of his adult life moving from job to job, serving time in prison on five different occasions for felonies such as gambling and theft. Despite his humble circumstances, he became the key litigant in one of the most important Supreme Court cases of the twentieth century. He illustrates the way that an ordinary person can exemplify larger issues in the history of criminal justice.

Gideon was arrested in 1961 for breaking and entering into a pool hall in Panama City, Florida, where he had occasionally worked and run a floating poker game. At his trial in April 1961, he specifically requested that the court appoint a lawyer to represent him. The court, however, maintained that under Florida law it was only required to appoint legal counsel in capital cases. Forced to conduct his own criminal defense, Gideon was convicted and sentenced to the Florida State Prison in Raiford. Gideon applied to the Florida Supreme Court in October 1961 for a writ of habeas corpus—an order freeing him on the grounds that he had been illegally imprisoned—but his application was denied. He did not stop there. In January 1962, Gideon sent a handwritten application to the United States Supreme Court, requesting that his case be heard on the grounds that he had been denied due process of law because he had been denied an attorney. The Supreme Court decided to take up his case (Lewis, 1964).

DIVISION OF CORRECTIONS
CORRESPONDENCE REGULATIONS
MAIL WILL NOT BE DELIVERED WHICH DOES NOT CONFORM WITH THESE RULES

No. 1 -- Only 2 letters each week, not to exceed 2 sheets letter-size 8 1/2 x 11" and written *on one side only*, and if ruled paper, do not write between lines. *Your complete name* must be signed at the close of your letter. *Clippings, stamps, letters* from other people, *stationery* or *cash must not be enclosed* in your letters.
No. 2 -- All *letters* must be addressed in the *complete prison name* of the inmate. *Cell number*, where applicable, and *prison number* must be placed in lower left corner of envelope, with your complete name and address in the upper left corner.
No. 3 -- *Do not send any packages without a Package Permit.* Unauthorized *packages* will be destroyed.
No. 4 -- *Letters* must be written in English only.
No. 5 -- *Books, magazines, pamphlets*, and *newspapers* of reputable character will be delivered *only if* mailed direct from the publisher.
No. 6 -- *Money* must be sent in the form of *Postal Money Orders* only, in the inmate's complete prison name and prison number.

INSTITUTION ______ CELL NUMBER ______
NAME ______ NUMBER ______

In The Supreme Court of The United States
Washington D.C.
clarence Earl Gideon
Petitioner | Petition for a writ
vs. | of Certiorari Directed
H.G. Cochran, Jr., as | to The Supreme Court
Director, Divisions | State of Florida.
of corrections State |
of Florida | No. 890 Misc.
OCT. TERM 1961
U. S. Supreme Court

To: The Honorable Earl Warren, Chief Justice of the United States
Comes now the petitioner, Clarence Earl Gideon, a citizen of The United states of America, in proper person, and appearing as his own counsel. Who petitions this Honorable Court for a Writ of Certiorari directed to The Supreme Court of The State of Florida. To review the order and Judgement of the court below denying The petitioner a writ of Habeus Corpus.
Petitioner submits That The Supreme Court of The United States has The authority and jurisdiction to review The final Judgement of The Supreme Court of The State of Florida The highest court of The State Under sec. 344(B) Title 28 U.S.C.A. and Because The "Due process clause" of the

Clarence Earl Gideon prepared this handwritten petition to the United States Supreme Court in 1961. Although the case had national impact, it began with a simple letter from a man who "always believed that the primarily [sic] reason of trial in a court of law was to reach the truth" (Lewis, 1964, p. 78).

Source: Petition for a Writ of Centiori from Clarence Gideon to the Supreme Court of the United States, 06/05/1962 . National Archives.

Gideon's application came at the conjunction of two critical moments in the Supreme Court's judicial revolution. First, in the middle of the twentieth century, the Supreme Court was in the midst of redefining the function of habeas corpus. For most of the nineteenth century, the protection had only applied to pretrial detention. The logic was that habeas corpus protected against illegal arrest and unlawful custody but that once a person was convicted of a crime their imprisonment by definition became legal. In the twentieth century, however, courts began to apply habeas corpus rules to

(Continued)

(Continued)

federal cases where procedures fell outside of constitutional boundaries. Under Earl Warren, the Supreme Court began to apply habeas corpus guidelines to state courts as well and to take up petitions like that of Gideon who claimed to have been denied due process. Second, the existing precedent on the issue of legal counsel, *Betts v. Brady* (1942), did not seem to be working. The Betts decision set the rule that legal counsel was not constitutionally necessary except in capital cases or under special circumstances such as a defendant being illiterate. Every time a litigant brought a claim of special circumstances before the Supreme Court, however, the Court affirmed it. The precedent itself seemed to be increasingly meaningless and potentially unfair to any future litigant in whose case special circumstances were *not* found. The Gideon case—involving a defendant who was indigent but otherwise capable—offered an opportunity for the Supreme Court to address directly the question of a right to counsel in criminal cases (Lewis, 1964; Powe, 2000).

To argue Gideon's case, the Supreme Court appointed Abe Fortas, one of the leading attorneys in Washington, DC at the time. Fortas—who would himself be appointed to the Supreme Court in 1965—built a case designed to direct the Court to consider the constitutional issues at its core. Gideon himself provided much of the raw material for the case, explaining his life story in a long letter to Fortas as he was preparing the brief to be presented to the Supreme Court. First, Gideon maintained his innocence throughout, proclaiming "I did not break into this building nor did I have to I had the keys to the building..." (Lewis, 1964, p. 78). Moreover, Gideon's main position also became key for Fortas. Gideon declared "There was not a crime committed in my case and I don't feel like I had a fair trial. If I had a attorney he could brought out all these [various aspects that demonstrated innocence] in my trial" (Lewis, 1964, p. 79). Fortas, in crafting the case, argued that the Fourteenth Amendment requires that an attorney be appointed to represent indigent defendants in all cases involving serious crimes. Although Gideon had sought to make his own case and the trial judge had even tried to help him, the transcript of his case revealed that mistakes had been made and opportunities to defend himself missed. Only a competent attorney could be expected to provide an adequate defense.

In the end, the Supreme Court agreed, ruling in *Gideon v. Wainwright* (1963) that the Sixth Amendment right to counsel was incorporated in the Fourteenth Amendment and that hence legal representation was necessary in all cases—federal and state—that involved serious offenses. Unlike many of the other criminal justice cases of the 1960s, the Gideon decision was reasonably popular. Most states already provided some degree of legal counsel for poor defendants, so the outcome forced relatively few to change their procedures. In addition, upon retrial, Gideon was found not guilty; the fact that he was innocent of the crime for which he had spent two years in prison made the outcome more palatable to the public.

The case itself illustrates the many factors that often came together in some combination each time judicial precedent changes: a potentially sympathetic defendant; a compelling constitutional issue; defense attorneys capable of highlighting the critical issues; and a federal court ready to alter existing law. The judicial revolution of the 1960s was not simply the result of federal courts making unilateral decisions but instead the outcome of the frequent congruence of factors such as these.

The Rights of People Accused of Crimes

In the 1960s the Supreme Court reached the apogee of its incorporation of greater civil rights and due process into criminal law. One key turning point was the Court's decision in *Mapp v. Ohio* (1961). In 1957, Dollree Mapp was arrested by Cleveland police officers for possession of obscene materials after they entered her home without a warrant in pursuit of a different suspect for a different offense. The Supreme Court overturned her conviction by a 6-3 vote, declaring that "all evidence obtained by searches and seizures in violation of the Constitution is . . . inadmissible in a state court" (quoted in Walker, 1998, p. 181). At first glance, this ruling simply rearticulated the U.S. Constitution's Fourth Amendment protection that "the right of the people to be secure in their persons, houses, papers, and effects, against unreasonable searches and seizures, shall not be violated." Prior to the *Mapp* decision, the exclusionary rule that illegally obtained evidence could not be used had only clearly applied to the federal courts. The *Mapp* decision marked a key change in jurisprudence in that the Supreme Court now used the Fourteenth Amendment's due process and equal protection clauses to apply the exclusionary rule to state governments as well. In terms of constitutional law, the Court selectively incorporated elements of the Bill of Rights into the Fourteenth Amendment to extend these rules to states and localities. As a practical matter, the extension of the exclusionary rule to local law enforcement forced police to adhere to higher standards in seeking suspects and to be more accountable for their actions.

By clarifying the right to counsel first articulated in the *Gideon* case, the Supreme Court also forced police and prosecutors to be much more dutiful to the law in obtaining confessions. *Escobedo v. Illinois* (1964) involved a criminal suspect who had been interrogated in a police station without an attorney, despite the defendant's request for legal counsel and the fact that his lawyer was present in the building demanding to see his client. Under a rule that the right to attorney attached to cases at a "critical" stage, the Supreme Court decided that suspects should be permitted legal counsel during interrogations. In *Miranda v. Arizona* (1966), the Supreme Court went further, determining that police needed to advise suspects at the time of their arrest both of the right to an attorney and to their protection under the Fifth Amendment against self-incrimination. With these decisions, the Court reacted strongly against the history of police and prosecutors extracting confessions via deception, intimidation, and the third degree. It questioned the methods by which state and local law enforcement had, until then, frequently operated and sought to force police and prosecutors to build cases in more professional and fair ways (Powe, 2000; Walker, 1998).

The Supreme Court's criminal justice decisions in the 1960s generated widespread popular opposition. Critics claimed that the Supreme Court was siding with criminals against victims of crime, a perception that was particularly galling in the context of increasing crime rates. Many law enforcement officials and politicians encouraged this view. Los Angeles Police Chief William Parker, for example, asserted that the *Escobedo* decision was "handcuffing the police." Likewise Republican presidential candidate Barry Goldwater responded to *Escobedo* by observing that, "no wonder our law enforcement officers have been demoralized and rendered ineffective in their jobs" (Powe, 2000, p. 391). Criticism of the *Miranda* decision was even more extensive. Boston police commissioner Edmund McNamara said as result of *Miranda*, "criminal trials no longer will be about a search for truth, but search for technical error" (Powe, 2000, p. 399).

These decisions, however, should be viewed in light of what came before. They were intended to balance out earlier practices in which police and prosecutors were given a more free hand to enforce the law as they saw fit. In many ways, unfettered discretion for law enforcement officers contributed to discrimination and unequal justice. In addition, the decisions of the Warren Court also sought to maintain some discretion for police. In *Terry v. Ohio* (1968), for example, the Supreme Court ruled that police officers could stop and frisk individuals on the basis of suspicion even if the officers did not have probable cause to make an arrest. The cumulative practical effect of these decisions, despite their unpopularity, was to help establish procedural guidelines that reflected the incorporation of Bill of Rights protections into state and local law, and protected the interests of both defendants and society.

The Death Penalty

Midcentury debates about capital punishment linked many of the trends seen in the judicial revolution more generally. The issue brought together efforts by activists to use constitutional law as a vehicle for social change and efforts by the federal judiciary and legal profession to standardize criminal procedure and to minimize racial discrimination.

The United States experienced a long decline in the number of times the death penalty was actually carried out from the 1940s to the 1960s. As historian David M. Oshinsky (2010) writes, "The numbers were startling; the United States saw 153 executions in 1947, 65 in 1957, and only 2 in 1967" (p. 11). A number of factors drove this trend. Public opinion gradually shifted away from supporting the death penalty. A number of books appeared in the 1950s criticizing the death penalty as inconsistent with American moral standards, unfair in terms of racial and class discrimination, and ineffective as a deterrent of crime. In addition, high-profile individual cases directed public attention to the issue of capital punishment. For example, Caryl Chessman, a bandit and rapist condemned to die, transformed himself into a prominent antideath penalty activist by smuggling out of prison manuscripts highlighting his cause. Although he won eight stays of execution and became a celebrity, Chessman was nonetheless put to death in the gas chamber in California's San Quentin prison amidst political controversy in 1960. Courts became increasingly willing to hear appeals at midcentury, particularly in capital cases. As legal scholar Stuart Banner (2002) writes, "Annual petitions for a writ of habeas corpus, the vehicle by which state prisoners can ask federal courts to review their convictions, nearly quadrupled between 1952 and 1962" (p. 246). The appeals process dramatically increased the amount of time that elapsed between convictions and executions, and the death rows of prisons in the United States gradually filled with convicts seeking to postpone the carrying out of their sentences.

These appeals, however, did not focus on the fundamental acceptability of the death penalty. Instead they tended to focus on one of three issues. First, had the trial procedures been fair? Chessman's appeals mainly addressed the inadequate transcript of his original trial. Second, did the method of execution cause unnecessary pain and suffering? In the middle of the twentieth century, a number of cases addressed the constitutionality of the electric chair and the gas chamber. Third, was it fair to execute people for crimes other than murder? In the 1950s several states—particularly in the South—condemned people to die for rape and occasionally theft. These sentences raised questions not only about whether the punishment was proportionate to the crime but also—due to the fact that many of the condemned were African American—whether the sentences were racially discriminatory (Banner, 2002; Oshinsky, 2010).

As with other elements of the judicial revolution, the reconsideration of the death penalty accelerated due to the influence of the Civil Rights movement. In the 1960s, both the LDF and the ACLU actively adopted the issue of capital punishment, noting its disproportionate application to African Americans. Los Angeles attorney Gerald Gottlieb provided one critical new piece of the intellectual puzzle by publishing an article called "Testing the Death Penalty" in the *Southern California Law Journal* in 1961. Gottlieb argued, based on earlier non-capital cases that had found punishments disproportionate to the crimes they were associated with, that capital punishment might be disproportionate to *any* crime. What Gottlieb (1961) termed "evolving standards of decency" might make the death penalty per se fall under the category of "cruel and unusual punishment" prohibited under the Eighth Amendment. This concept particularly influenced Arthur Goldberg, appointed to the Supreme Court in 1962. Goldberg responded by circulating among the other justices a memo drafted by his law clerk Alan Dershowitz (who would later become a prominent activist attorney) endorsing the notion that evolving standards of decency opened capital punishment to question. Goldberg's memo went one step further, however, explicitly suggesting that executions were a disproportionate penalty for rape. Although Earl Warren prevailed upon Goldberg not to publish his memo, Goldberg did express its core ideas in a dissent to the Supreme Court's decision not to hear *Rudolph v. Alabama* (1963) (Banner, 2002; Oshinsky, 2010).

Cases involving rape revealing a striking pattern regarding the death penalty: it was disproportionately applied to African Americans, particularly those accused of crimes against white people. A 1951 case involving seven African American men sentenced to die in Virginia introduced statistical data demonstrating this trend: all 45 men executed for sexual assault in Virginia since 1908 were African American. While the Virginia appeals court hearing the case dismissed this pattern as not demonstrating conscious discrimination, this type of pattern attracted the interest of legal activists such as the LDF and the ACLU (Oshinsky, 2010).

Goldberg's dissent sent a signal that some members of the Supreme Court were willing to reconsider the death penalty and provided ammunition for the LDF and the ACLU to organize against it. They employed what has been called a moratorium strategy. As Stuart Banner (2002) describes it, "By raising every plausible constitutional claim in every possible case, the LDF hoped to force the machinery of execution to grind to a halt for the claims to be resolved" (p. 252). In fact the number of executions decreased sharply in the 1960s and ceased entirely after 1967, although the LDF's strategy may have simply helped accelerate a long-term trend. The main accomplishment of the LDF and of the ACLU was to help select cases to bring death penalty issues before the Supreme Court (Banner, 2002).

By the early 1970s, after the departures of several justices including Warren and Goldberg and the appointment of their successors by Republican president Richard Nixon, the Supreme Court actively sought death penalty cases that would help it resolve the issues that kept coming before it. In early 1972, the Supreme Court selected four death penalty cases to hear, out of nearly 200 before it. Two cases involved rape—to highlight the question of whether the death penalty was too severe for crimes that did not result in the victim's death—and two involved murder. One of the murder cases was that of William Henry Furman, who fired a shot that killed the owner of a home he had been burglarizing. Furman's case encapsulated central debates about the death penalty. He was convicted of felony murder, a capital case in which intent to kill did not have be proven; in fact, Furman only learned of the death of his victim after his arrest. Furman was also African American, while his victim was white. Other than that, however, little differentiated Furman's case from numerous others that did not lead to capital sentences. Arguing for Furman and the others, Anthony Amsterdam, the lead attorney for the LDF, maintained that the infrequency and inconsistency with which the death penalty was applied made it cruel and unusual. Moreover, this very inconsistency permitted racial discrimination in the selection of cases to which capital punishment would be applied (Banner, 2002; Oshinsky, 2010).

The Supreme Court's five-votes-to-four decision in *Furman v. Georgia* (1972) rendered the death penalty unconstitutional, but in a very narrow way. Unable to reach consensus, all nine justices wrote separate opinions. Only two, Thurgood Marshall and William Brennan, found capital punishment inherently unconstitutional. Even they disagreed as to why; Marshall found the death penalty to violate the prohibition on cruel and unusual punishments, whereas Brennan accepted the notion of evolving standards of decency. The other three who sided with them focused on the implementation of capital punishment. William O. Douglas emphasized its implicit racial discrimination, and Potter Stewart emphasized its inconsistent application. Stewart famously wrote, "These death sentences are cruel and unusual in the same way that being struck by lightning is cruel and unusual . . . I simply conclude that the Eighth Amendment cannot tolerate the infliction of a death sentence . . . so wantonly and freakishly imposed" (Banner, 2002, p.263; Oshinsky, 2010, p. 52). As is discussed in Chapter 9, the nature of the Furman decision left the door open for legislatures to bring back the death penalty by trying to mitigate its randomness.

As Stuart Banner (2002) argues, the debates about the death penalty in the late 1960s and early 1970s highlight three key trends in constitutional law of the time. First, they reflect the notion from legal liberalism that the courts represent a means of implementing social change. Second they also reflect the efforts to achieve greater standardization of criminal procedure, particularly at the state and local level. Third, they incorporate the concern about racial discrimination that seemed to underlay much of the judicial revolution. While few justices used race as a legal rationale, it seems clear that in the death penalty cases and other decisions that the federal judiciary sought to reduce the amount of criminal justice discretion that could be translated into racial inequality.

The Judicial Revolution in Juvenile Justice

As with other areas of criminal and constitutional law, the Supreme Court's interventions in juvenile justice in the 1960s and 1970s reflected both the expansion of due process and the limits on this process. The notion that juvenile courts offered young offenders treatment had traditionally justified a highly discretionary approach to decision making, governed by far fewer procedural rules than was the case in adult criminal procedure. By the 1960s, however, significant elements of the legal profession actively questioned both the rehabilitative premise of juvenile courts and the courts' procedural informality.

On June 8, 1964, 15-year-old Gerald Gault from Globe, Arizona, was arrested after he and a friend purportedly made an obscene telephone call. After two hearings before Judge William McGee—in which no witnesses were sworn, no transcript was made, and the complainant did not appear—Gault was sent to a juvenile reform school to begin an indeterminate sentence. Gault could theoretically have been institutionalized for six years—until he reached age 21—for an offense that would have warranted a 30-day jail sentence for an adult. Gault's parents reached out to an attorney who filed a habeas corpus petition on their behalf. The case eventually reached the Arizona Supreme Court, which concluded that the Arizona juvenile court law was constitutional and that Judge McGee had followed minimal procedural standards. Despite the fact that Gault had in fact been released from reform school by this time, the defeat in the Arizona Supreme Court created a basis for his attorneys—in conjunction with the ACLU—to appeal the case to the United States Supreme Court (Manfredi, 1998; Tanenhaus, 2011).

By the mid-1960s, the federal government took an increasing interest in juvenile justice. In 1961, President John Kennedy created the President's Committee on Juvenile Delinquency to investigate the issue and signed legislation authorizing $30 million in federal money for local community prevention programs. The resulting Office of Juvenile Delinquency sponsored numerous studies of juvenile courts that would inform the conversation about juvenile justice in the 1960s. In addition, in 1964, Earl Warren delivered a speech before the Annual Conference of Juvenile Court Judges signaling his willingness to consider juvenile justice issues in the Supreme Court. Warren did not indicate how he would rule but he suggested that he would consider issues such as children's right to counsel, standards of evidence in juvenile court, and due process requirements. Finally, an earlier case before the Supreme Court, *Kent v. United States* (1966), provided a rehearsal for several issues raised in Gault's case. The substance of the Kent case involved the transfer of a juvenile offender to an adult criminal court in Washington, DC. Because the case was in the District of Columbia courts, it was automatically under federal appeals jurisdiction and had little impact on states and localities. The issues the *Kent* case raised, however, were national in scope: to what degree did juvenile courts need to observe constitutional protections? The Supreme Court ruled that such protections were necessary, at least within federal jurisdiction. Writing for the majority, Abe Fortas—at this time a member of the Supreme Court—argued, "There is evidence . . . that the child [in juvenile court] receives the worst of both worlds: that he gets neither the protections accorded to adults nor the solicitous care and regenerative treatment postulated for children" (Bernard, 1992; Manfredi, 1998; Tanenhaus, 2011, p. 58).

In arguing Gault's case before the Supreme Court, the ACLU lawyers representing him decided to focus on a limited number of constitutional provisions, rather than the entire constitutionality of juvenile courts. They argued that since juvenile courts were functionally similar to criminal courts—both decided questions of guilt and had the authority to imprison defendants—they should have similar procedural protections, such as the rights to an attorney, to a transcript, and to confront witnesses. Gault's attorneys also sought to counter the argument that greater procedural formality would undermine the rehabilitative goals of juvenile courts by pointing out that adult criminal justice was becoming increasingly treatment oriented with no loss of legal protections for defendants (Manfredi, 1998; Tanenhaus, 2011).

The Supreme Court's majority opinion in *In re Gault* (1967)—again written by Abe Fortas—used the Fourteenth Amendment to selectively incorporate Bill of Rights protections into juvenile courts. Fortas' opinion strongly criticized the discretionary nature of juvenile court proceedings, arguing that, "Departures from established principles of due process have frequently resulted not in enlightened procedure, but in arbitrariness" (quoted in Manfredi, 1998, p. 120). Moreover, Fortas also raised questions about the effectiveness of rehabilitation offered by juvenile courts. Fortas argued that more thorough observance of due process would actually improve treatment by allowing the courts to more accurately gather information about youths and by improving the legitimacy of court decisions in the eyes of their clients. "The observance of due process standards," Fortas wrote, "will not compel the States to abandon or displace any of the substantive benefits of the juvenile process" (quoted in Manfredi, 1998, p. 120). The Supreme Court's decision mandated that juvenile courts incorporate due process protections that were required of criminal courts: the right to notice, the right to have legal counsel, the right to confront witnesses and to cross-examine them, and the privilege against self-incrimination. In so doing, the Supreme Court undercut some of the protective assumptions of juvenile courts and brought many of the adversarial elements of criminal courts into them (Bernard, 1992; Manfredi, 1998; Tanenhaus, 2011).

Despite enthusiasm for the *Gault* decision in legal circles, the implementation of it was neither immediate nor complete. The Supreme Court issued the *Gault* decision during the height of public backlash against liberal rulings following the *Miranda* case and in the midst of increasing crime rates. As a result, it was easy for critics to see *Gault* as one more imposition by a Court regarded as out-of-touch with reality. In addition, the Supreme Court's personnel also changed dramatically in the late 1960s. Earl Warren retired in 1968 in the expectation that President Lyndon Johnson, a Democrat, would be able to select his successor. Johnson's nomination of Fortas to be chief justice failed, however, and Fortas ultimately resigned from the Supreme Court also. In 1969, Richard Nixon, a Republican, ended up selecting

Warren Burger to be chief justice, giving the court a more conservative orientation (Tanenhaus, 2011).

These changes affected the jurisprudence around juvenile justice because *Gault* left many issues unresolved. In 1970, the Supreme Court heard *In re Winship*, a case involving a 12-year-old New York City boy who had been found delinquent by a judge using a loose standard that the "preponderance of evidence" was enough to demonstrate guilt. The court ruled that using a "preponderance of evidence" standard was sufficient in cases involving status offenses—those that were defined by the status of being a juvenile—but that a standard derived from criminal courts that guilt must be proven beyond a reasonable doubt was necessary in criminal cases. In *McKeiver v. Pennsylvania* (1971), the Supreme Court determined that jury trials were *not* necessary in delinquency hearings. The *McKeiver* decision helped define the outer limits of how much the Supreme Court wanted to incorporate criminal proceedings into juvenile courts and reasserted a fundamental distinction between the two (Bernard, 1992; Manfredi, 1998; Tanenhaus, 2011).

In practice, *Gault* and subsequent decisions did not affect juvenile courts as much as their advocates expected. Many juvenile courts complied poorly with the post-*Gault* procedural requirements, particularly with the requirement that youths be given access to legal counsel. One study of three urban juvenile courts conducted soon after the *Gault* decision found that one court informed just over half of juveniles of their right to counsel, a second court informed less than 5%, and a third did not inform any juveniles of the right to counsel (Lefstein, Stapleton, & Teitelbaum, 1969). The Supreme Court justices and civil liberties attorney who rendered decisions such as *Gault* valued the extension of due process, believing that it would make court procedures more fair and permit higher-quality treatment. Many of the judges and probation officers who operated local juvenile courts, however, continued to believe in the importance of discretion in achieving the proper outcome for young offenders and believed that the Supreme Court had gone too far in importing procedures from criminal courts. As a result, many juvenile courts resisted implementing post-*Gault* reforms (Bernard, 1992; Manfredi, 1998; Tanenhaus, 2011).

In addition, Fortas' ideal of retaining and improving rehabilitation services offered through the courts also proved to be problematic in the environment of increased skepticism about rehabilitation in the 1970s. Critics in state legislatures increasingly sought to revise juvenile court laws to be more like criminal laws and hence more punitive (see Chapter 9). Skepticism from liberals about rehabilitation had been one of driving forces leading to *Gault*. As it turned out, skepticism about rehabilitation also became one of the driving forces contributing to efforts to make juvenile courts get tough on young offenders in the 1970s and beyond (Feld 1999).

❖ CONCLUSION

The twin liberal revolutions in mid-twentieth-century criminal justice resolved questions involving the purposes and goals of criminal justice in different ways. This outcome is not terribly surprising in large part because the two reform movements started from different premises. Advocates of rehabilitation believed strongly in the ability of the state—and particularly in the ability of the social and medical sciences—to diagnose and treat the fundamental causes of criminal behavior. Advocates of the judicial revolution, by contrast, were most concerned about overreaching by agents of the state. They believed that vigorous protection of due process rights in legal proceedings was necessary to ensure that the government did not abuse criminal defendants, even when the intentions of the government were helpful. Advocates of judicial liberalism also reflected the strain of skepticism about rehabilitation that increasingly characterized discussion of it by the 1960s and 1970s. To be sure, some advocates tried to reconcile the twin revolutions. Justice Fortas, for example, argued in his *Gault* opinion that improving due process protections would increase the accuracy and legitimacy of rehabilitative interventions and thereby make them more effective. But for the most part, these two trends were at odds with one another. Moreover, both encountered increasing resistance and limitations over time. As crime rates increased and conservatives called for increasingly punitive approaches to criminal justice, neither rehabilitation nor due process extended quite as far as their advocates had hoped. Both helped transform the criminal justice system at midcentury but neither was fully implemented nor fully successful.

❖ REFERENCES

Allen, F. A. (1959). Criminal justice, legal values and the rehabilitative ideal. *Journal of Criminal Law & Criminology, 50*: 226–232.

Banner, S. (2002). *The death penalty: An American history*. Cambridge, MA: Harvard University Press.

Bernard, T. J. (1992). *The cycle of juvenile justice*. New York, NY: Oxford University Press.

Boyle, K. (2004). *Arc of justice: A saga of race, civil rights, and murder in the jazz age*. New York, NY: Henry Holt.

Campbell, N. D., Olsen, J. P., & Walden, L. (2008). *The Narcotic Farm: The rise and fall of America's first prison for drug addicts*. New York, NY: Abrams.

Capshew, J. H. (1999). *Psychologists on the march: Science, practice, and professionalism in America, 1929–1969*. New York, NY: Cambridge University Press.

Christianson, S. (1998). *With liberty for some: 500 Years of imprisonment in America*. Boston, MA: Northeastern University Press.

Cole, S. A. (2000). From the sexual psychopath statute to 'Megan's Law': Psychiatric knowledge in the diagnosis, treatment, and adjudication of sex criminals in New Jersey, 1949–1999. *Journal of the History of Medicine & Allied Sciences, 55*: 292–314.

Courtless, T. F. (1998). *Corrections and the criminal justice system: Laws, policies, and practices*. Belmont, CA: Wadsworth.

Empey, L. T., & Rabow, J. (1961). The Provo Experiment in delinquency rehabilitation. *American Sociological Review, 26*: 679–696.

Feld, B. C. (1999). *Bad kids: Race and the transformation of the juvenile court*. New York, NY: Oxford University Press.

Freedman, E. B. (1987). 'Uncontrolled desires': The response to the sexual psychopath, 1920–1960. *Journal of American History, 74*: 83–106.

Galliher, J. F., & Tyree, C. (1985). Edwin Sutherland's research on the origins of sexual psychopath laws: An early case study in the medicalization of deviance. *Social Problems, 33*: 100–113.

Geis, G., & Bienen, L. B. (1998). *Crimes of the century: From Leopold and Loeb to O.J. Simpson*. Boston, MA: Northeastern University Press.

Glaser, D. (1995). *Preparing convicts for law-abiding lives: The pioneering penology of Richard A. McGee*. Albany, NY: SUNY Press.

Goffman, E. (1957). *Characteristics of total institutions*. Symposium on Preventive and Social Psychiatry conducted at Walter Reed Army Institute of Research.

Gottlieb, G. H. (1961). Testing the death penalty. *Southern California Law Review, 34*.

Gottschalk, M. (2006). *The prison and the gallows: The politics of mass incarceration in America*. New York, NY: Cambridge University Press.

Hacker, F. J., & Frym, M. (1955). The Sexual Psychopath Act in practice: A critical discussion. *California Law Review, 43*: 766–780.

Hakeem, M. (1958). A critique of the psychiatric approach to crime and correction. *Law and Contemporary Problems, 23*: 650–682.

Harrison, L. V., & Grant, P. M. (1938). *Youth in the toils*. New York, NY: The Macmillan Company.

Herman, E. (1995). *The romance of American psychology: Political culture in the age of experts*. Berkeley: University of California Press.

Irwin, J. (1980). *Prisons in turmoil*. Boston, MA: Little, Brown.

Jones, M. (1953). *The therapeutic community: A new treatment method in psychiatry*. New York, NY: Basic Books.

Korn, R. R., & McCorkle, L. W. (1959). *Criminology and penology*. New York, NY: Henry Holt.

Latessa, E., & Allen, H. E. (1982). Halfway houses and parole: A national assessment. *Journal of Criminal Justice, 10*: 153–163.

Lefstein, N., Stapleton, V., & Teitelbaum, T. (1969). In search of juvenile justice: Gault and its application. *Law and Society Review, 3*: 491–562.

Lewis, A. (1964). *Gideon's trumpet*. New York, NY: Random House.

MacKenzie, D. L. (2006). *Evidence-based corrections: Reducing the criminal activities of offenders and delinquents*. New York, NY: Cambridge University Press.

Manfredi, C. P. (1998). *The Supreme Court and juvenile justice*. Lawrence: University Press of Kansas.

Martinson, R. (1974). What works?—Questions and answers about prison reform. *The Public Interest, 35*: 22–54.

Martinson, R. (1979). New findings, new views: A note of caution regarding sentencing reform. *Hofstra Law Review, 7*: 242–258.

McCorkle, L. W., Elias, A., & Bixby, F. L. (1958). *The Highfields story: A unique experiment in the treatment of juvenile delinquents*. New York, NY: Henry Holt.

McGlothlin, W. H., Anglin, M. D., & Wilson, B. D. (1976). Outcome of the California civil addict commitments: 1961–1972. *Drug and Alcohol Dependence, 1*: 165–181.

Menninger, K. (1968). *The crime of punishment*. New York, NY: Viking.

Mitford, J. (1973). *Kind and usual punishment: The prison business*. New York, NY: Knopf.

Murphy, J. G. (1973). *Punishment and rehabilitation*. Belmont, CA: Wadsworth.

Noll, S. (1995). *Feeble minded in our midst: Institutions for the mentally retarded in the South, 1900–1940*. Chapel Hill: University of North Carolina Press.

Oshinsky, D. M. (2010). *Capital punishment on trial: Furman v. Georgia and the death penalty in modern America*. Lawrence: University Press of Kansas.

Persons, R. W. (1966). Psychological and behavioral change in delinquents following psychotherapy. *Journal of Clinical Psychology, 22*: 337–340.

Powe, L. A. (2000). *The Warren Court and American politics*. Cambridge, MA: Belknap Press of Harvard University Press.

Pratt, J. (1998). The rise and fall of homophobia and sexual psychopath legislation in postwar society. *Psychology, Public Policy, and Law, 4*: 25–49.

Rood, R. S. (1960). California's program for the sexual psychopath. *Cleveland-Marshall Law Review, 9*: 462–466.

Rothman, D. J. (1978). The state as parent: Social policy in the progressive era. In W. Gaylin, I. Glasser, D . Marcus, & D. Rothman, *Doing good: The limits of benevolence*. New York: Pantheon.

Rothman, D. J. (2002). *Conscience and convenience: The asylum and its alternatives in progressive America* (Rev. ed.). New York, NY: Aldine de Gruyter.

Schlossman, S. L. (1995). Delinquent children: The juvenile reform school. In N. Morris & D. J. Rothman (eds.). *The Oxford history of the prison: The practice of punishment in Western Society*. New York, NY: Oxford University Press.

Simon, J. (1993). *Poor discipline: Parole and the social control of the underclass, 1890–1990*. Chicago. IL: University of Chicago Press.

Stanford, P. (1972, September). A model, clockwork-orange prison. *New York Times Magazine*, 9, 71–74, 76, 78–80, 84.

Sullivan, L. E. (1990). *The prison reform movement: Forlorn hope*. Boston, MA: Twayne.

Sutherland, E. H. (1950). The sexual psychopath laws. *Journal of Criminal Law and Criminology*, *40*: 543–554.

Tanenhaus, D. S. (2011). *The constitutional rights of children:* In re Gault *and juvenile justice*. Lawrence: University Press of Kansas.

Tappan, P. W. (1949). *Juvenile delinquency*. New York, NY: McGraw-Hill.

Tappan, P. W. (1957). Young adults under the youth authority. *Journal of Criminal Law, Criminology, and Police Science*, *47*: 629–646.

Walker, S. (1998). *Popular justice: A history of American criminal justice* (2nd ed.). New York, NY: Oxford University Press.

Wechsler, H. (1959). Law, morals, and psychiatry. *Columbia Law School News*, *18*: 2, 4.

Weeks, H. A. (1958). *Youthful offenders at Highfields*. Ann Arbor: University of Michigan Press.

8

The Expanding Federal State, 1920s–1990s

One of the most significant changes in twentieth-century criminal justice has been the expanding role of the federal government. For most of United States history, criminal justice has been primarily local. This pattern emerged from the American colonies, where individuals could only rely on assistance from nearby authorities. Even after the creation of the United States, states and localities created most criminal laws, and local officials enforced them. In the twentieth century, however, the federal government assumed new law enforcement functions, and the criminal justice system itself assumed a much more national character.

In many ways, this shift parallels the changing nature of federal government in the United States. Under a federal system, individual states are understood not as subordinate units of the national government but instead as distinct entities having separate existences and particular responsibilities. The national or federal government is an overarching entity, having its own powers and responsibilities. Both state and national governments are understood to derive their authority from the will of the people. In early United States history, the federal government was sometimes understood to be a voluntary association that states entered into, but following the Civil War in the 1860s the federal government came to function as the central unifying entity to which the states were subordinate. Moreover, in the latter half of the nineteenth century, the federal government enlarged its administrative capacity and assumed new regulatory functions that individual states could not address on their own (Skowronek, 1982).

Political scientists sometimes describe the increasing authority of central governments—in the United States as well as other countries—as an expanding state. This is confusing in the United States, because the term *state* usually refers to state governments. In this context, however, an expanding state refers to a larger set of government arrangements and the greater capacity of governments to take action. Because the federal government in the United States drove this change, we refer to it as an expanding federal state.

In the twentieth-century United States—and particularly after the 1930s—the power and capacity of the federal government increased dramatically. In the realm of criminal justice, this shift is most clearly evidenced by the growth of federal agencies. Most obviously, the Federal Bureau of Investigation (FBI) became the nearest thing to a national police force. In similar fashion, federal correctional systems, drug control agencies, and the federal criminal law all helped shape national practice, either by setting the standard for state-level criminal justice or by actively shaping the national policy agenda.

One irony of the transformation of federal criminal justice institutions is that the process does not really follow patterns normally associated with politics in the United States. Today, liberal approaches to politics are often associated with a large government that provides generously for the welfare of its people, whereas conservative approaches to politics are often associated with a smaller government. In the area of criminal justice, both approaches—liberal investments in rehabilitative programming and conservative commitments to law and order—have resulted in the expansion of the national state's role and capacity.

❖ THE GROWTH OF THE FBI AND THE WAR ON CRIME

The federal government had a hand in criminal justice since its founding, creating the U.S. Marshals service in 1787. In the nineteenth and twentieth centuries, it created new agencies under the aegis of the Treasury Department, using its authority to regulate interstate commerce and collect taxes as the basis for criminal investigations. Most notably, in the 1920s, it operated the Bureau of Prohibition to enforce the ban on the manufacture, sale, and distribution of alcohol (see Chapter 2). The federal government also created the Border Patrol in 1924, following passage of more restrictive immigration legislation, to try to police the flow of illegal immigrants into the United States (Hernandez, 2010).

The growth of the federal role in criminal justice, however, accelerated sharply in the 1930s. Since 1929, the United States had been in the midst of the Great Depression, a lasting and devastating economic downturn. In response, the administration of President Franklin D. Roosevelt—coming into office in 1933—launched a series of initiatives called the New Deal intended to bring the nation out of its economic slump, change the role of the federal government, and restore public confidence. While the Roosevelt administration is probably best remembered for its economic recovery policies, it also staked out a greater claim of federal responsibility for crime control. Responding to worries over Depression-era lawlessness, Roosevelt determined to increase the duties, functions, and prominence of the FBI.

The groundwork for this war on crime was established earlier. President Theodore Roosevelt issued an executive order in 1908 establishing the agency that would become known as the FBI. [From its founding until the spring of 1934, this agency was known as the Bureau of Investigation; from 1934 to the fall of 1935 it was called the Division of Investigation; after 1935, it was known as the FBI. For the sake of clarity, this chapter will refer to it as the FBI throughout.] As shown in Chapter 2, the FBI had a somewhat limited law enforcement role in the 1910s but became more actively involved in national security investigations during and following World War One. By the early 1920s, the FBI was enmeshed in corruption. Director William Burns, a former private detective, was forced to resign in 1924 for failing to disclose the role of his agents in a scandal involving federal leases on oil reserves at the Teapot Dome Oil Field in Wyoming. In his place, Attorney General Harlan Fiske Stone selected J. Edgar Hoover to be the head of the FBI (Jeffreys-Jones, 2007; Potter, 1998; Powers, 1987; Theoharis, 2004).

Hoover's appointment—to a post that he would hold from 1924 until his death in 1972—initiated an era of professionalization at the FBI. This professionalization, in turn, laid the foundation for a much stronger national security state. Hoover joined the FBI in 1917 and led its Radical Division, coordinating its investigations of peace advocates, socialists, and communists during and after World War One and playing an instrumental role in the Palmer raids (see Chapter 2). He kept his job during upheavals in the FBI and the Department of Justice by emphasizing his managerial abilities. As the head of the FBI, Hoover presented himself, in the words of biographer Richard Gid Powers (1987) as "one of a new breed of progressive managers who were applying the methods of science to the old problems of government" (p. 145). In the 1920s, Hoover sought to shift the FBI from functioning like autonomous private detectives to functioning more like professional bureaucrats. He sought to improve his agency's efficiency by reducing the number of personnel, tightening supervision of his staff, and improving recordkeeping and documentation. Hoover's FBI also tended to hire and promote agents much like himself: young, college-educated, often unmarried, white males who shared a belief in the power of organization (Potter, 1998; Powers, 1987; Theoharis, 2004).

Hoover's initial reforms in the 1920s helped establish the FBI's national leadership within law enforcement. These reforms included new training programs, dress requirements, and codes of conduct that distinguished FBI agents as professionals. In addition, the FBI assumed a central role in criminal identification. In 1924, it consolidated two existing sets of fingerprints, one previously maintained by the International Association of Chiefs of Police (IACP) and the other collected on federal prisoners, into a single repository maintained by the FBI. This expanded into a national collection of fingerprint information by the 1930s. Similarly, the FBI also assumed responsibility for collecting crime data from local police, consolidating and analyzing it, and publishing the results in its Uniform Crime Reports beginning in 1930. These new functions helped make the FBI a central clearinghouse of information for law enforcement nationwide. By making data available to other agencies and cooperating with them, Hoover's FBI built a supportive constituency among local police leaders and the IACP. In addition, Hoover overcame negative images associated with federal law enforcement. The intelligence work of World War One and the Palmer raids had suggested that the FBI mainly engaged in repression, while scandals in the early 1920s had implied that federal law enforcement was filled with corruption. Hoover put these images in the past—at least temporarily—by cultivating an image of the FBI as the consummate professional agency. His reforms also emphasized that the organization itself—not any single individual—was the key to law enforcement (Jeffreys-Jones, 2007; Potter, 1998; Powers, 1987; Theoharis, 2004).

Further change in federal law enforcement emerged partly in response to changes in crime in the 1920s and 1930s. First, in the context of Prohibition—the federal ban on producing, selling, and distributing alcohol that went into effect in 1920—organized criminal syndicates gained increased prominence. By establishing a market for illegal alcohol, gangsters transformed themselves into large-scale illegal enterprises. In Chicago, racketeer Al Capone's organization established control over the liquor business through a combination of business savvy and ruthless violence against its competitors. Federal agents estimated that, by 1927, the Capone organization earned over $60 million from selling illegal alcohol. Moreover, many gangsters presented themselves as very public figures. Capone frequently appeared in the newspapers and newsreels of the day and became a popular icon. Although Capone was arrested by Treasury Department agents in 1929 on charges of income tax evasion and convicted in 1931, he and others like him helped establish both large-scale criminal businesses and an image in the public mind that organized crime had become a pervasive element in American life (Ruth, 1996; Walker, 1998, p. 158–159; Ward, 2009).

Second, the crime of kidnapping exploded both in frequency and public perception in the early 1930s. Racketeers frequently used abduction to settle disputes with their fellow gangsters or to collect debts, while criminals kidnapped businessmen to collect ransoms. The prominence of kidnapping increased dramatically when, on March 1, 1932, the infant son of world-famous aviator Charles Lindbergh was taken from the family's country home in rural New Jersey, prompting a highly publicized search for the child and whoever had taken him. While local law enforcement retained jurisdiction over the case, President Herbert Hoover tasked J. Edgar Hoover and the FBI with coordinating federal assistance in the investigation. In this particular case, the FBI provided minimal aid, instead engaging in jurisdictional squabbles with the New Jersey state police. Moreover, despite the payment of a ransom, Lindbergh's son was not returned; he was instead found dead more than two months after the kidnapping just four miles from Lindbergh's home, having probably died the night he was taken. The case generated an outpouring of public reaction. Citizens flooded the FBI and the Department of Justice with letters, offering assistance and demanding action. This response provided momentum for the passage of a new federal kidnapping law in June 1932 (generally called the Lindbergh Law), giving the FBI jurisdiction over many kidnappings and establishing the death penalty in federal kidnapping cases (Geis & Bienen, 1998; Potter, 1998; Powers, 1987). Kidnappings—and the Lindbergh case in particular—also increased calls for a greater federal role in policing. The *Camden* (New Jersey) *Courier Post* opined in May 1932, "this crime shows that America needs a system of state 'Scotland Yards'—with a central organization at Washington" (quoted in Powers, 1987, p. 175).

Third, a wave of high-profile bandits actively robbed banks, stole payrolls, and carried out kidnappings in the 1930s. More or less simultaneously, John Dillinger, Charles Arthur "Pretty Boy" Floyd, George "Machine Gun" Kelly, Lester Gillis (better known as Baby Face Nelson), the Barker-Karpis Gang (including Alvin Karpis, Kate "Ma" Barker, and Arthur "Doc" Barker), and Bonnie Parker and Clyde Barrow were all active—mainly in the Midwest—between 1930 and 1935. Unlike the largely ethnic organized criminal syndicates of the day, these bandits were typically white and native-born. They turned to crime in the context of the hard times of the Great Depression. They also had greater mobility than earlier criminals, being able to move from place to place rapidly due to the availability of automobiles and the development of highways. Also unlike the criminal syndicates, which increasingly operated like businesses and, after the arrest of Capone, sought to avoid notoriety, these bandits largely operated on their own and frequently sought attention. Bonnie Parker, for example, sent poems glamorizing her exploits to newspapers and Pretty Boy Floyd developed a reputation for giving some of his takings to families facing economic distress. Because they operated across state lines—and hence some of their crimes fell under federal jurisdiction—and because of their prominent public profile, these bandits all but demanded the attention of the FBI (Burrough, 2004; Potter, 1998).

An attack on federal law enforcement agents provided the impetus for the FBI to launch its New Deal-era war on crime. On June 17, 1933, in a train station parking lot in Kansas City, Missouri, four bandits armed with machine guns ambushed four FBI agents and three local police officers who had been transporting an escaped bank robber, Frank "Jelly" Nash, to the federal prison in Leavenworth, Kansas. They opened fire, killing Nash and three of the law enforcement officers and severely wounding two others. The attackers—who may have included Pretty Boy Floyd—may have been trying to rescue Nash, or they may have been trying to prevent him from informing on others. The attack—which became known as the Kansas City Massacre—prompted an immediate mobilization of law enforcement to catch the killers and it created the pretext for the federal government to expand its law enforcement powers (Burrough, 2004; Potter, 1998; Powers, 1987).

The Kansas City Massacre occurred at almost precisely the moment that the new Roosevelt administration—inaugurated just three months earlier—was already in the midst of reorganizing the Department of Justice and considering major new initiatives against crime. Attorney General Homer Cummings told reporters that the killing of a Department of Justice agent represented the underworld's "declaration of war" against the United States government (quoted in Powers, 1987, p. 184). In a series of speeches in the summer and fall of 1933, Cummings announced that the government was launching its own war on crime.

The Department of Justice's metaphorical declaration of war helped mobilize the public to support new initiatives and Congress to take action. As the journal *Law and Contemporary Problems* put it in 1934, "Until very recent days . . . crime was almost exclusively a local phenomenon. . . . But so dramatic have been the recent depredations of organized criminal bands [that] the aid of the federal government has first been besought" (Cavers, 1934, p. 399). That same year Cummings announced a series of new laws that would ultimately be enacted as an omnibus crime bill in May. This legislation made law and order central to New Deal politics. The laws defined a variety of interstate crimes that fell under federal jurisdiction, authorized federal agents to carry guns and make arrests (rather than relying on local authorities to do so, as they had until then), and clarified hiring rules for FBI agents in order to further professionalize the bureau (Jeffreys-Jones, 2007; Potter, 1998; Powers, 1987).

The FBI's manhunt for bandit John Dillinger in 1934 became the most prominent early conflict in the war on crime and helped reinforce the agency's central role in policing. In May 1933, a 30-year-old Dillinger had been released after serving nine years in prison and almost immediately began robbing banks and stores across the country. Dillinger gradually came to public attention as witnesses to his robberies commented on his cheerful manner and fashionable clothing. The start of his crime spree also coincided with the start of the federal government's war on crime. Dillinger almost flaunted his notoriety. Arrested in Arizona in January 1934 and extradited to a jail in Crown Point, Indiana, upon his arrival he posed for photographs with his arms around the prosecutor and sheriff. On March 3, 1934, he escaped from jail using a piece of wood shaped to look like a pistol, stole the sheriff's car, and fled across state lines. The Crown Point escape added to Dillinger's fame, but it also prompted the federal government to pursue him. In addition the escape provided Cummings with further ammunition to argue for his federal crime bill, maintaining that the escape highlighted the inability of local officials to handle modern crime and the need for federal intervention. Agents from the FBI's Chicago field office led by Melvin Purvis tracked Dillinger to the Little Bohemia Lodge in northern Wisconsin in late April but botched their raid. In the ensuing gun battle Dillinger and his gang escaped, killing one agent in the process. The affair at Little Bohemia embarrassed the FBI, but it provided Cummings and Roosevelt enough momentum to convince Congress to pass the crime bills. Ultimately Purvis' team got a second shot at Dillinger. After arresting and interrogating Dillinger's associates and his girlfriend, they tracked him to Chicago. Then on July 21, 1934, a tip informed Purvis that Dillinger would be going to the movies that night at the Biograph Theater. After the movie ended, agents led by Purvis surrounded Dillinger on the street and shot him dead. Dillinger's dramatic and public death increased not only his own fame but also that of the agency that had taken him down (Burrough, 2004; Potter, 1998; Powers, 1987).

Beginning in 1933, the Department of Justice initiated publicity campaigns presenting crime as a national, rather than local problem, and the FBI as the key to a solution. Efforts by Attorney General Homer Cummings to publicize his war on crime led to greater attention to public relations within the FBI. The agency encouraged a series of articles by freelance reporter Courtney Riley Cooper, mainly published in *American Magazine* between late 1933 and 1935. These stories built a narrative emphasizing the professional competence of the FBI but linking the daring of agents and the technical skills of the organization all back to Hoover as its mastermind. Although this view contradicted Hoover's own earlier efforts to elevate the organization over any individual, it also established Hoover in the public eye as the key figure in the war on crime in a way that was very useful to him. This publicity campaign culminated in 1935. That year Cooper released a book version of his articles called *Ten Thousand Public Enemies* which used a dramatic narrative to promote an image of the FBI as a crack team of scientific investigators led by Hoover. That same year, Hollywood film studios released a wave of motion pictures about the FBI that also highlighted government crime fighting. Most notably, *G-Men* (starring James Cagney) focused on Hoover himself, presenting him as the originator of the war on crime, appearing before Congress to argue for the crime bills actually advocated by Cummings. These stories and movies helped build a public willing to support the FBI as a national law enforcement agency, first by providing glimpses into the criminal underworld that seemed to threaten ordinary people and then by presenting the FBI as a modern agency able to protect them (Burrough, 2004; Potter, 1998; Powers, 1987; Theoharis, 2004).

By 1935 the FBI also increasingly concentrated power to itself, in part because it distrusted local law enforcement. To a degree, this was justified by events (Bomar, 1934). When in 1933 St. Paul, Minnesota, brewery heir William Hamm was kidnapped by members of the gang led by Alvin Karpis and Fred and Doc Barker, details of the negotiations kept leaking back to the kidnappers. After Hamm was recovered, FBI investigators subsequently learned that several police officials had been receiving money from the underworld, and that Hamm himself may have had more knowledge of the affair than he acknowledged. Subsequently, rather than collaborate with local police as it had done in the 1920s, the FBI's approach to crime control increasingly involved extracting what information it could from local law enforcement and trying to assume control of cases under their own authority. The search for the Barker-Karpis gang—and other bandits of the New Deal era—also relied on information provided by criminal's associates. In addition to informants who volunteered, bandits' girlfriends, wives, families, friends, landlords, and doctors also gave up information when the FBI threatened them with prosecution. In 1935, FBI agents used surveillance to track Doc Barker to Chicago, where they arrested him on January 8. Just one week later, other informants led FBI agents to Fred Barker and his mother, Kate "Ma" Barker, in a cabin near Ocala, Florida, where the agents killed both Barkers in a gun battle. Karpis, the ringleader of the gang, remained on the run for more than another year. When the FBI finally tracked him down in New Orleans in April 1936, Hoover arranged to be there to arrest him personally (Burrough, 2004; Potter, 1998; Powers, 1987).

Karpis's arrest marked the apogee of this phase of the federal war on crime. The last major bandit of the Great Depression had been apprehended, while Hoover basked in the publicity of the arrest. Moreover it marked the ascent of the FBI as the nation's premier law enforcement organization. Ironically, even though the FBI emphasized cooperation with local police and scientific detection, the final victories in the war on crime emerged from centralizing control over its investigations and relying on coercing information from often uncooperative witnesses. The 1930s war on crime was built on creating stronger federal agencies, centralizing authority, and utilizing repressive measures against criminals' contacts. Moreover it succeeded in part by convincing the public that they wanted these measures in order to control crime.

This photograph shows weapons seized from the cabin where FBI agents killed Fred and Kate Barker in 1935. The FBI used photographs like this one to illustrate the threat to public safety posed by criminal gangs, to highlight the effectiveness of law enforcement, and to justify FBI actions when agents used lethal violence.

Source: Federal Bureau of Investigation.

Case Studies in Criminal Justice: Melvin Purvis, FBI Agent

Melvin Purvis (1903–1960), one of the best-known FBI agents of the 1930s, exemplified the transformations of the agency and of federal law enforcement during the first two decades of Hoover's administration. A young attorney from Timmonsville, South Carolina, Purvis joined the FBI late in 1926, just two years after Hoover became the agency's director. Purvis attracted Hoover's attention and rose quickly through the ranks. Purvis became the assistant Special Agent in Charge (SAC) of the FBI's Chicago office in 1929, then in 1931 became the SAC of first the Cincinnati office and then the Washington, DC, office, where Hoover monitored him closely. On November 17, 1932, Hoover appointed Purvis SAC of the Chicago office.

During the reform phase that characterized Hoover's first decade as FBI director, Purvis embodied many of the qualities that characterized agents in general. Young, driven, and from a privileged southern background, Purvis had a professional education as a lawyer rather than experience in law enforcement. In his autobiography, Purvis described special agents—many of whom were bachelors, like himself and Hoover—as being married to their jobs. He wrote that, "the special agent works hard and long. He is subject to call at any time during the twenty-four hours of a day . . . in many instances in recent years, so much continuous application of duty has been necessary that to many of us it seemed foolish to go home" (Purvis, 1936, p. 25–26). Purvis (1936) also emphasized the importance of character for special agents, writing that, "there are three qualities that most special agents have in common: courage, intelligence, and resourcefulness" (p. 53). Like many FBI agents of his day, Purvis represented the replacement of the detectives who had been central to early federal law enforcement efforts with professionals who dedicated themselves to a bureaucracy.

Purvis gained national prominence when his Chicago office was put in charge of the 1934 manhunt for John Dillinger. Even though he and his men had limited contacts in the underworld and little practical skill with investigations, Purvis's agents managed to track him down. Later in 1934, the FBI also brought in Purvis to supervise the manhunt for Pretty Boy Floyd, whom they eventually killed in East Liverpool, Ohio. Purvis (1936) characterized these adventures by writing that, "it is difficult to believe that many men's lives are more intense, active and exciting than were the lives of special agents during the early '30s. Our business was man hunting, and for three years I was on the firing line of the greatest and most successful drive against crime this country has ever seen" (p. 244).

(Continued)

(Continued)

Purvis's relationship with Hoover and the FBI deteriorated, however, while the war on crime was still taking place. Journalists gravitated toward Purvis as the face of the war on crime following the Dillinger killing, and to some degree Purvis encouraged this by dramatizing his encounters with public enemies. On the one hand, in his autobiography, Purvis (1936) pushed aside the notion of individual credit for himself or for any agent by writing that "Special agents cut no notches on their guns; no one will ever know, so far as I am concerned, who sent Dillinger and Floyd to their eternal rewards" (p. 248). On the other hand, he reminded readers that he was present for both killings. Marginalized from subsequent investigations, Purvis resigned from the FBI in 1935. The FBI, with its emphasis on bureaucratic professionalization and the centrality of Hoover, had no place for a famous individual agent. Hoover reportedly viewed the 1936 publication of Purvis's autobiography, *American Agent*, as a snub because it glamorized Purvis's contributions, acknowledged local law enforcement, and failed to mention Hoover by name. In subsequent years, Purvis found work—often as a result of his previous career in the FBI—but interventions by the Bureau discouraged employers from hiring him for sensitive positions in intelligence or security. Purvis eventually committed suicide in 1960 (Burrough, 2004; Potter, 1998; Powers, 1987; Purvis, 1936).

To the extent that Purvis rose within the FBI, he represented what Hoover wanted a special agent to be. During the Dillinger investigation, however, Purvis became almost as prominent as the agency itself. Purvis's departure and the FBI's subsequent efforts to prevent him from working in related fields shows how the midcentury agency could not tolerate an operative whom could not easily be folded into its bureaucratic ethos and public image.

❖ ALCATRAZ AND THE WAR ON CRIME

The federal government also made significant changes to its prison system in the 1930s to support the war on crime, opening a new maximum-security prison on Alcatraz Island in San Francisco Bay in the summer of 1934. The federal penitentiary at Alcatraz served both the practical function of housing the bandits and gangsters arrested during the 1930s and the symbolic function of embodying the toughness of the federal government in the war on crime. Established at the same time as the rise of the FBI and the passage of the 1934 crime legislation, Alcatraz reinforced the message that the federal government had developed an increased administrative capacity to fight crime.

The federal prison system was troubled in the 1920s and early 1930s. The three existing federal prisons at the time—at Atlanta, Georgia; Leavenworth, Kansas; and McNeil Island, Washington—all experienced a series of embarrassing escapes in the early 1930s. Prison authorities struggled to hold their most desperate inmates at a time when criminal networks provided logistical support for their members in jail, ill-paid and ill-trained guards could often be bribed, and criminals were willing to use violence to escape. When the California bandit Roy Gardner—famous for twice escaping from federal marshals—was taken to McNeil Island, he told the warden that he "would not be staying long." Five months later he escaped. In addition, the prisons also struggled with corruption and scandal. In the early 1930s, the Bureau of Prisons faced public embarrassment when newspaper reports revealed that Al Capone enjoyed special treatment at the federal penitentiary in Atlanta and continued to direct criminal operations on the outside. Under the circumstances, leaders in the Department of Justice such as Cummings, Hoover, and Bureau of Prisons Director Sanford Bates worried about both their ability to retain custody of high-profile inmates and to maintain control of the prisons (Ward, 2009).

On October 12, 1933, Homer Cummings announced that the federal government would open a new prison at Alcatraz Island as part of the larger war on crime. The new prison would house the prison system's most prominent criminals, greatest escape risks, and biggest troublemakers. As Cummings said, "Here may be isolated the criminals of the vicious and irredeemable type so that their influence may not be extended to other prisoners who are disposed to redeem themselves" (quoted in Ward, 2009, p. 49). Opening Alcatraz also represented an element of the Roosevelt administration's campaign to build public confidence in its ability to manage the crime problem. Given the failings of existing prisons and the negative publicity surrounding them, Cummings believed that the federal government needed a new prison that was highly secure and disciplined. The Department of Justice selected a former military prison on Alcatraz Island in San Francisco Bay as the site precisely because it was on a small island. From a practical perspective, it was relatively easy to secure and, from a public relations perspective, it conveyed a sense of isolation and punishment. Within a year, the Bureau of Prisons retrofitted the existing facility into a modern prison and opened it for inmates in June 1934.

At a time when the progressive emphasis on rehabilitation exerted tremendous influence in correctional policy elsewhere, Alcatraz adopted an entirely different approach. Intended for the worst of the worst inmates, Alcatraz was designed to incapacitate and to punish. It was also intended to deter other criminals, representing a symbol of the treatment that could await future offenders. The Bureau of Prisons set up a regime where escape was intended to be impossible and inmates were kept to strict schedules and allowed minimal privileges. Staff members were required to live on the island but barred from any but the most basic interactions with inmates in order to minimize the opportunities for them to help connect prisoners to the outside world.

The Bureau of Prisons intended the initial inmates at Alcatraz to be the worst offenders in the current federal prison system. In its early years, the roster of Alcatraz inmates included Doc Barker and other members of the Barker-Karpis gang, Al Capone and other organized crime figures from Chicago, New York, and Detroit, and other well-known bandits, bank robbers, and kidnappers.

The administration at Alcatraz imposed tight restrictions on inmates, partly to maintain control of the institution and partly to project a harsh public image intended to deter crime. More so than other prisons, Alcatraz kept its inmates on a highly regulated timetable highlighted by 16 hours each day in cells and multiple counts during the eight hours in which inmates had meals or work duties. It also sharply limited the goods that inmates were allowed to keep in their cells and strictly enforced rules against contraband. In addition, Alcatraz staff members were prohibited from communicating anything to the public about the operations of the prison (Ward, 2009).

This secretiveness became a problem for the Bureau of Prisons by the late 1930s as former inmates who had been released or transferred elsewhere began to talk to the press about their experiences at Alcatraz. In 1938, one former inmate, Roy Gardner, published an account of his experiences called *Hellcatraz: The Rock of Despair*. In it, he described Alcatraz as "the toughest, hardest place in the world" (quoted in Ward, 2009, p. 184). The Bureau of Prisons allowed the book to go to press and issued no rebuttals, apparently assuming that the book reinforced the image that it intended to convey. These reports, however, helped to generate debates both in the press and within the Department of Justice over whether the methods of control at Alcatraz were too harsh. The 1941 murder trial involving Henry Young, an inmate who killed a fellow prisoner, exposed day-to-day conditions at the prison to public light. Young's defense admitted that he had committed the crime, but argued that he had been temporarily insane due to such harsh conditions. Initial testimony by prison officials revealed the use of solitary confinement in cells in the prison basement with minimal amenities; subsequent testimony by disgruntled inmates described staff indifference to inmates' suffering. Young was ultimately convicted of involuntary manslaughter (rather than the more serious charge of first-degree murder) and the prison itself suffered condemnation in the press.

Despite its efforts to control its inmates, Alcatraz experienced repeated strikes, resistance, and escape attempts almost from its opening. The most severe occurred in May 1946 when a group of prisoners—all of whom had previously tried to escape—captured firearms and took guards hostage, intending to use their captives to secure passage to the mainland. While they broke out of their cells, they were unable to get out of the cellblock. The response from the prison staff was poorly organized, but gunfire from outside—directed at both the escapees and at other cellblocks where no one had escaped—kept the escapees contained and eventually allowed guards to recapture them. In the course of this so-called "battle of Alcatraz," two prison officers were killed and 13 guards were wounded; three inmates died, and two others were later executed for their roles in the escape. This uprising led to another in a series of investigations into conditions at the prison; Warden James Johnston was removed from his post, and the Bureau of Prisons quietly began to phase out Alcatraz as the warehouse for the worst of the worst offenders (Ward, 2009).

Alcatraz in the 1930s and 1940s served dual functions that were not necessarily congruent, both trying to discipline the worst criminals in the U.S. prison system and symbolically demonstrating the strength of the federal state. The administrators at Alcatraz usually prioritized the practical matter of managing their inmates, but they often did not succeed. Instead, Alcatraz had greater success in the symbolic function of physically embodying the war on crime.

❖ THE FBI, DOMESTIC SECURITY, AND CIVIL RIGHTS

In the midst of the 1930s war on crime, the FBI also assumed a new role in ensuring domestic security. By expanding its intelligence gathering activities—and blurring the line between actual threats and potential political opponents—the FBI contributed to the growth between the 1930s and the 1960s of increasingly powerful and more elaborate federal mechanisms for domestic surveillance.

The FBI and its predecessors had been concerned with gathering intelligence and ensuring domestic security throughout its history, notably seeking to prevent subversion during and after World War One (see Chapter 2). After a relative lull in the 1920s, these efforts increased again in the 1930s. Soon after taking office in 1933 (the same year that Adolf Hitler's Nazi Party took power in Germany), Franklin Roosevelt began asking the FBI for information on Nazi groups in the United States. As international tensions increased in the 1930s, Roosevelt increasingly turned to the FBI to monitor domestic threats. On August 24, 1936, Hoover met privately with Roosevelt and reported that communists were seeking to infiltrate both American labor unions and federal government agencies. Soon after the August 24 briefing, Roosevelt and Secretary of State Cordell Hull verbally authorized Hoover to expand FBI intelligence gathering. This provided the legal authority for Hoover to establish general intelligence operations that persisted for decades. It also helped introduce an important distinction between the FBI's investigative work—focused on specific violations of the law—and its intelligence work—focused on collecting information about potential threats to national security. By the late 1930s and early 1940s, the FBI gathered intelligence not only on fascist and communist infiltrators in the United States but also on opponents of the United States' intervention into World War Two, some of Roosevelt's political rivals, and African American civil rights activists (Jeffreys-Jones, 2007; Powers, 1987; Theoharis, 2004).

Although the FBI played only a highly circumscribed role in foreign and military intelligence during World War Two, the bureau expanded its domestic counterespionage work. In 1939, Roosevelt authorized the FBI to take charge of investigations of domestic subversion and directed local law enforcement to forward any relevant information to the FBI. In addition the FBI coordinated efforts by members of the American Legion—a military veterans' organization—to monitor suspicious activities in defense factories or in their communities. Also beginning in September 1939, Hoover established a "Custodial Detention" index of people thought likely to engage in actions contrary to the national interest who could be detained in the event of war. Following U.S. entry into the war in December 1941, Attorney General Francis Biddle authorized that German and Italian aliens listed in the index should be detained. In July 1943, Biddle determined that the Custodial Detention program was unreliable and ordered that all persons detained to be released and that the FBI destroy the listing. According to historian Athan Theoharis, however, Hoover retained the list and ordered his agents to continue confidential intelligence gathering. These actions helped establish the precedent for more systematic domestic intelligence operations by the FBI following the war (Powers, 1987; Theoharis, 2004, p. 52–55).

The FBI and Anticommunism

As early as 1945, renewed U.S. concern about communism provided new direction for the FBI. Following World War Two, the United States and the Soviet Union—which had been wartime allies against Germany—increasingly saw each other as fundamentally opposed to one another. As the Soviet Union imposed its communist system on satellite states in Eastern Europe, U.S. policy makers came to see Soviet communism as fundamentally expansionist and threatening. The hardening of positions on each side led to the Cold War—an ongoing diplomatic and political confrontation between the United States and the Soviet Union—lasting from the 1940s until the late 1980s. In this context, the FBI—the federal agency chiefly responsible for domestic security—took the initiative to fight both espionage by Soviet agents and subversion by Americans sympathetic to communism. This mission grew logically out of both federal law enforcement's history of battling militant elements within the United States and Hoover's own deep opposition to radicalism and desire for order (Powers, 1987; Schrecker, 2002). In 1947, Hoover appeared before the House Un-American Activities Committee (HUAC), a congressional committee already investigating domestic communist subversion, to express his positions and to form an alliance. Hoover asserted bluntly that the American Communist Party "stands for the destruction of our American form of government; it stands for the destruction of American democracy; it stands for the destruction of free enterprise" (quoted in Schrecker, 2002, p. 127). In so doing, Hoover helped to articulate concerns that already existed, and sought to mobilize congressional and popular support for an anticommunist campaign. He stated, "I feel that once public opinion is thoroughly aroused as it is today, the fight against Communism is well on its way. Victory will be assured once Communists are identified and exposed, because the public will take the first step of quarantining them so they can do no harm" (quoted in Schrecker, 2002, p. 133).

From the end of World War Two, the FBI vigorously sought to expose purported Soviet spies in the United States government. Hoover sent the White House a series of reports accusing government officials of espionage and grew increasingly frustrated that they generated little response from President Harry Truman's administration. While a few of these reports were based on genuine evidence, most involved unprocessed rumors and allegations similar to the accusations that critics of the New Deal had been making for over a decade. Nonetheless, Truman's inaction frustrated Hoover and prompted allegations from critics that

Truman was soft on communism. To quell the threat of possible subversion and to quiet his opponents, in 1947 Truman initiated a Loyalty Security Program. This authorized the FBI to investigate whether current federal government employees posed security risks. While the program did not go as far as Hoover wanted, it nonetheless launched years of inquiries into the affiliations, activities, and even reading habits of ordinary government workers (Powers, 1987; Schrecker, 2002).

The FBI also targeted suspected radicals and the American Communist Party. In early 1946, the FBI revived its Custodial Detention Program, this time making preparations to arrest enemy sympathizers on the basis of ideology. Although the Justice Department would not pursue legislation to allow preventive detentions, the FBI nonetheless sought a legal precedent that would allow it to go forward. To this end, in 1948 they launched prosecutions of 12 leaders of the Communist Party under the Smith Act (also known as the Alien Registration Act), a 1940 law that outlawed advocating the overthrow of the U.S. government. In the 1949 trial, the government argued that communist doctrine itself represented a threat and brought forward former communists and informers planted within the party to testify against party leaders. The trials resulted in convictions, but the biggest damage to the Communist Party resulted from creating a fear within the party that it was infiltrated with FBI informers and agents (Powers, 1987).

The FBI's approach might be seen as an effort to raise public awareness of what it considered subversion. Beginning in 1947, it provided information to HUAC to assist its investigations of communists in government, in the Hollywood film industry, and in other aspects of American life. Likewise in the 1950s, it informally passed information to Senator Joseph McCarthy (the most prominent anticommunist of his day) and to Senate committees investigating the apparent threat of communists in government. Although the FBI typically asked that its information be used as background, members of Congress would often take raw unanalyzed information and publicly release it as fact (Jeffreys-Jones, 2007, p. 155–157; Theoharis, 2004, p. 88–96). In a similar fashion, a 1950 Senate investigation linked homosexuality to Cold War politics, suggesting that government employment of gay men and lesbians posed a threat to national security because homosexuals were vulnerable to blackmail by communist spies. In response the FBI established a "Sex Deviate" program in 1951 to investigate the sexuality of past and present government workers. As a result, government agencies increasingly dismissed workers for homosexuality and barred suspected gay men and lesbians from employment. The FBI, moreover, leaked accusations that public figures were homosexuals to congressional committees if it seemed to serve the agency's interests (Jeffreys-Jones, 2007, p. 158–159; Johnson, 2004; Theoharis, 2004, p. 96–100). These FBI efforts tended to blur homosexuality and communism into undifferentiated but vague threats to national security. They also expanded the role of the FBI from law enforcement to policing political and personal behavior in the perceived interest of national security.

The FBI and Civil Rights

The midcentury FBI also expanded its investigations of civil rights violations, particularly of violence against African Americans. By no means did it become a champion of civil rights, and Hoover and the agency did not become committed to the cause. Nonetheless, from the later years of Franklin Roosevelt's administration onward, pressure from the Department of Justice prompted the FBI to take a more active role in civil rights cases. Moreover, this shift resulted from an emerging sense that the federal government was the only body capable of investigating civil rights violations, particularly if state and local governments were indifferent or even responsible. The expanded role for the federal government in civil rights cases is one more example of the ways in which changes in criminal justice apparatus reflected the expansion of the federal state, a process most evident in the New Deal. At the same time, it is also an example of the reluctance and hesitation that sometimes accompanied this expansion.

The expanded role of the FBI in civil rights cases is most evident in its investigations of lynching. Despite the frequency of lynching in the late nineteenth and early twentieth centuries, the federal government was reluctant to intervene against the practice (see Chapter 5). The 1876 Supreme Court decision *United States v. Cruikshank* only permitted the federal government to respond to state actions violating civil rights, not the actions of private individuals. In addition to the constitutional question, federal officials were reluctant to openly challenge those writers and legal scholars who defended lynching and vigilantism as legitimate if these actions had community support or took the place of inefficient or ineffective local courts. In the 1930s, despite a decrease in lynching, the Roosevelt administration still did not endorse the National Association for the Advancement of Colored People's (NAACP's) calls for an antilynching law for fear of alienating white southern voters. Throughout the 1930s, however, legal reformers lobbied the Department of Justice to more actively pursue antilynching interventions. Soon after the 1939 appointment of progressive former

Michigan governor Frank Murphy as attorney general, the Department of Justice embraced this cause by establishing a Civil Rights Unit (later renamed the Civil Rights Section). This new pressure from the Department of Justice helped to overcome the FBI's reluctance to intervene in civil rights cases. In 1940, newspaper reports that an Atlanta police detective tortured an African American suspect into confessing a burglary spurred the local federal prosecutor and FBI office into investigating in a case called *United States v. Sutherland*. This case established a pattern of the Civil Rights Section and the FBI acting vigorously if police or other state actors were suspected of being involved or complicit in racial violence. The *Sutherland* case also illustrates the limits of federal authority. Despite the increased federal commitment, the Department of Justice remained hamstrung in its ability to investigate civil rights violations by private citizens; they could not investigate private citizens involved in a larger resurgence of the Ku Klux Klan. Furthermore, when they did get cases to court, southern juries could not be counted on to return guilty verdicts (Jeffreys-Jones, 2007, p. 93–96; Waldrep, 2008).

As campaigns for African American civil rights accelerated in the 1950s and 1960s, the FBI remained slow to pursue violations of civil rights and violence against the movement. Agents hesitated to conduct inquiries with limited chances of convictions and to investigate local police officers with whom they had to work. In addition, in the early 1960s the FBI rarely protected civil rights activists from violent resistance, despite pressure to do so from Attorney General Robert F. Kennedy. Hoover maintained that the FBI was an investigative agency, not a peacekeeping one. Hoover himself had little enthusiasm for the civil rights movement, seeing it as a challenge to established authority and a potential source of communist subversion. Moreover, Hoover came to believe that civil rights leader Martin Luther King Jr., was acting under communist influence. The FBI used surveillance and wiretapping to gather incriminating evidence about King's personal life but, despite floating rumors about him, was never able to undermine his public standing (Powers, 1987).

Nonetheless, in the mid-1960s, President Lyndon Johnson mobilized Hoover and the FBI to actively pursue civil rights issues. Following the disappearance of three civil rights workers in Mississippi in 1964, Johnson and Robert Kennedy used federal power to fight civil rights violations in much the same way that Roosevelt and Cummings had used federal power to fight crime in 1933. Kennedy ordered Hoover to treat the disappearances as kidnappings and Johnson signaled that the crime represented an attack on federal authority. Hoover personally travelled to Mississippi to announce that the FBI was opening a new office there and deploying over 150 agents. While Hoover remained personally indifferent to the cause of civil rights, he was, according historian Richard Gid Powers (1986, p. 407–412), driven to act by the threat to federal authority, the drama of the crisis, and the explicit engagement of the president.

The FBI Campaign Against Radical Subversion

Hoover and the FBI continued to see maintaining domestic security against radical subversion as one of the agency's major functions in the 1950s and 1960s. In this way, the FBI's purview expanded beyond crime control and law enforcement. In addition, the agency came to see the traditional tools of law enforcement as inadequate for this function. In 1956, the FBI launched a new program to battle the Communist Party called COINTELPRO (or Counter Intelligence Program). This effort sought to destroy the Communist Party from within by planting agents inside the organization, intercepting mail, conducting electronic surveillance, and fomenting divisions within the group. The FBI subsequently launched COINTELPRO programs aimed at a splinter communist group called the Socialist Workers' Party in 1961, against white hate groups such as the Ku Klux Klan in 1964, against black nationalist groups in 1967, and against student radicals and the New Left in 1968 (Cunningham, 2003, 2004; Jeffreys-Jones, 2007, p. 169–170; Powers, 1987, p. 336–343; Theoharis, 2004, p. 120–124).

Applying a counterintelligence strategy to white hate groups made sense, given the Ku Klux Klan's challenge to established law and order and the difficulty that federal prosecutors had in gaining convictions in earlier civil rights cases. Once the FBI engaged in the issue of civil rights, it sought to undermine hate groups by placing informants within them. By the mid-1960s, the FBI had approximately 2,000 informants in the Ku Klux Klan, accounting for one-fifth of the group's total membership. With this influence, the FBI sought to guide Klan activity and disrupt its internal organization, severely weakening the group within a few years (Cunningham, 2003; Powers, 1987, p. 412–415).

It is also not surprising that in the contentious 1960s the FBI targeted black nationalists and student radicals. Like the Klan but with a different political perspective, leaders and the bureau perceived them also to be threats to domestic security. During the urban riots of the 1960s, Lyndon Johnson specifically directed Hoover to investigate the riots' causes. The FBI could find no evidence of any coordinating organization among rioters, but it did find African American resentment. By 1967, Hoover authorized the creation of a COINTELPRO operation to undermine black nationalist leaders' efforts to gain political respectability and form effective coalitions. Likewise during the escalating student protests against the Vietnam War, the FBI similarly targeted groups such as Students for a Democratic Society (SDS) that styled themselves a "New Left." Hoover worried that they would align themselves with the "Old Left" of communists and socialists but also abhorred their rejection of conventional order. The New Left COINTELPRO sought to place informants within activist groups and tarnish their public image by promoting violent protests. In these operations the FBI moved well beyond its law enforcement function, seeking instead to pursue its own vision of domestic security (Cunningham 2003, 2004; Powers, 1987, p. 422–433).

From the mid-1960s to the early 1970s, the FBI also provided intelligence work for the White House. Hoover and Johnson had an exceptionally close relationship, so Johnson was able to use the FBI to gather information on his political opponents. By contrast, Hoover clashed with Johnson's attorneys general (Robert F. Kennedy, Nicholas Katzenbach, and Ramsay Clark) over their anticrime initiatives and responses to urban riots. As a result, the FBI increasingly sidestepped the normal Department of Justice hierarchy and responded directly to the president. When Richard Nixon became president in 1969, he further expanded FBI intelligence gathering. In order to try to stop information leaks from within the Nixon administration, the FBI conducted surveillance and wiretapping on selected State and Defense Department officials, White House appointees, and reporters. By the early 1970s, however, Hoover became increasingly reluctant to expand intelligence operations further, judging that their exposure could be politically devastating (Powers, 1987; Theoharis, 2004).

The FBI changed dramatically in the early 1970s. First, J. Edgar Hoover's death on May 2, 1972, initiated a period of rapid turnover and instability among FBI leadership. Second, investigations of the June 1972 break-in of the Democratic National Committee's headquarters in the Watergate Hotel revealed the extent to which the Nixon administration sought to use the FBI for political investigations. Third, congressional inquiries between 1974 and 1976 exposed many of the FBI's intelligence gathering activities, including the COINTELPROs. As a result, the FBI went through a period in the 1970s of internal demoralization and contraction, sharply curtailing its domestic surveillance work and rigorously avoiding political operations. At the same time, it also engaged in internal reforms, hiring more women and African Americans and seeking greater collaboration with the Department of Justice and Congress (Jeffreys-Jones, 2007; Powers, 1987;

Theoharis, 2004). Nonetheless, the story of the FBI under Hoover's 48 years of leadership remained one of a remarkable concentration and expansion of federal power. With the FBI as its key instrument, the federal government assumed a far more prominent role in law enforcement than had been possible earlier. In addition, it developed a capacity to engage in domestic intelligence gathering and security operations inconceivable at the beginning of the century.

❖ THE LONG WAR ON DRUGS

During the middle of the twentieth century, the federal government also built up its bureaucratic capacity to combat the distribution and use of certain drugs. As with other aspects of law enforcement, federal efforts to interdict drugs expanded alongside increasing local efforts. By the middle of the century, however, the federal government clearly set the agenda for the fight against drugs.

In the early part of the twentieth century, a patchwork of local, state, and federal laws regulated drugs. The Harrison Narcotic Act of 1914 (see Chapter 2) established a structure for the federal government to restrict the distribution of cocaine and narcotics. It also prompted the development of a federal Narcotics Division within the Treasury Department (Spillane, 2004). For the most part, however, local conditions regulated local drug markets. In Chicago, for example, Progressive Era reformers exerted sufficient public pressure to drive sales of morphine, heroin, and cocaine into acknowledged vice districts; one 1912 investigation found that 43 of 44 known outlets for drug sales were in three neighborhoods. The fact that drug sales were restricted to a relatively finite number of fixed locations like cigar stores, brothels, and private homes—all of which required connections to gain access to—kept drug distribution relatively contained to a fairly small network of people. A high profile campaign to shut down Chicago's vice district in 1914 largely eliminated these particular drug outlets but also prompted new drug outlets to spring up in an overwhelmingly African American district on Chicago's South Side. Increased legal pressure from city officials and police in the 1920s and 1930s forced drug selling into more transient locations such as cheap hotels and street corners but still kept it contained within relatively limited portion of the city (Spillane, 1998).

Increasing concern in the 1920s about a national drug problem led the federal government to establish a new narcotics bureau within the Treasury Department in 1930. In the 1920s, in the contexts of Prohibition and a perceived increase in crime, popular newspapers and magazines increasingly presented narcotics as a threat to the social order and drug addicts as potential criminals. One magazine article in the *Literary Digest* asserted that, "Drug addiction is responsible for some of the most atrocious crimes on record" (quoted in Speaker, 2001, p. 600). At the same time, scandals revealed that agents of the Narcotics Division in New York City were closely tied to drug traffickers. To battle the illegal enterprises that were increasingly asserting control over the drug trade, Congress established a new Federal Bureau of Narcotics (FBN) in 1930 (Jonnes, 1999).

The first commissioner of the FBN, Harry J. Anslinger, dominated drug control in the United States from the formation of the agency in 1930 to his retirement in 1962. Anslinger played a role similar to that of J. Edgar Hoover. Like Hoover, Anslinger was also a long-tenured progressive manager who believed in the power of organization. Anslinger worked his way up through the federal bureaucracy in the 1910s and 1920s, taking posts abroad in the Netherlands, Germany, and Venezuela where he frequently dealt with narcotics issues. In 1929, he became an assistant commissioner of the Prohibition Bureau. This experience helped shape Anslinger's approach to controlling narcotics. As FBN commissioner, Anslinger drew on what he considered to be lessons of Prohibition's failure. He avoided interfering with the personal lives of most ordinary citizens, favoring local prosecutions over federal intervention for possession of minor drugs and eschewing federal regulation of pharmaceuticals such as barbiturates and amphetamines. Instead in the 1930s, Anslinger and the FBN targeted more serious drugs such as opium and heroin, seeking to prevent them from entering the United States. Anslinger and State Department officials worked closely with an international convention organized by the League of Nations to establish rules to control the distribution of drugs abroad. At the same time, the FBN also

This photograph of federal agents destroying seized narcotics in 1920 illustrates early efforts by the federal government to control the flow of drugs into the United States. The image itself also illustrates the manner in which federal law enforcement tried to project a public image of calm professionalism.

Source: Courtesy of the Library of Congress, LC-DIG-npcc-29153.

pressured European nations to crack down on opium and heroin production within their borders, in the interest of preventing its spread to the United States (Carroll, 2004a; Jonnes, 1999; Musto, 1999).

The FBN's position on marijuana changed sharply during the early years of Anslinger's leadership. In the early 1930s, marijuana was not regulated under federal law and Anslinger viewed it as a nuisance drug. Following his experience in the Prohibition Bureau, Anslinger understood that federal courts did not want to hear minor drug possession cases and preferred to let the states regulate marijuana. At the same time, however, states increasingly turned to the federal government to do something. In the 1920s and 1930s, state and local officials and the popular press increasingly complained that marijuana use brought increased crime. Around 1936, Anslinger shifted his position on marijuana, calling for federal regulation. Not only did this shift respond to external calls for action, it also helped protect the FBN from a 1936 proposal to eliminate the agency. Soon after the introduction of the bill, Anslinger began to speak out strongly against the perceived menace of marijuana, justifying the FBN's continued existence. In both congressional testimony and a series of magazine articles, he presented marijuana as addictive, a gateway to more serious drugs like heroin, and a source of crime (Carroll, 2004a; Jonnes, 1999; Musto, 1999). Anslinger's horror stories included one co-authored in a 1937 *American Magazine* article called "Marijuana: Assassin of Youth," in which he described one Los Angeles youth wandering the city while high on marijuana. "Suddenly, for no reason, he decided that someone had threatened to kill him and that his life . . . was in danger. Wildly he looked about him. The only person in sight was an aged bootblack. Drug-crazed nerve centers conjured the innocent old shoe-shiner into a destroying monster. Mad with fright, the addict hurried to his room and got a gun. He killed the old man, and then babbled his grief over what had been wanton uncontrolled murder. . . . That's Marijuana!" (quoted in Speaker, 2001, p. 600).

In this context, the Treasury Department proposed a new transfer tax to regulate marijuana. Using the taxing power provided a means for the federal government to take action without usurping the traditional state and local jurisdiction in criminal justice matters. Under the Marijuana Tax Act—which went into effect on October 1, 1937—anyone who grew, possessed, transported, prescribed, or sold marijuana had to pay a $1 tax; any nondoctor who sold marijuana had to pay a $100 tax every time the drug was transferred to another person's hands. The tax act had the effect of making legitimate exchanges of marijuana impossible, either making sellers register with the federal government and announcing their exchanges to state governments that had already passed laws against marijuana or forcing them to violate federal law by not registering. Enforcement remained the job of local police, with occasional aid from FBN officers. (Carroll, 2004a; Jonnes, 1999; Musto, 1999).

Following World War Two, a larger drug culture emerged, particularly in northern cities. Heroin became more accessible. In addition, it became more strongly associated not only with the emerging subculture of hipsters and jazz musicians but also with a segment of the African American population brought to increasingly crowded cities by the Great Migration (Jonnes, 1999).

In response to the drug problem, the federal government increasingly focused on interdiction and penalties. Two laws—the Boggs Act, passed in 1951, and the Narcotics Control Act of 1956—first established and later toughened federal mandatory minimum sentences for drug possession and trafficking. Anslinger in particular advocated for these changes; as had Hoover and the FBI, Anslinger and the FBN worked very closely with politicians of both parties to help advance agency interests. In 1951 testimony before both the Senate Special Committee to Investigate Organized Crime in Interstate Commerce (the Kevauver Committee) and before a House committee considering the Boggs Act, Anslinger sought simultaneously to downplay public fears of a narcotics epidemic but also to gain tools to fight the drug problem such as more FBN agents (Carroll, 2004a; Jonnes, 1999; Musto, 1999). In his congressional testimony, Anslinger compared the current situation to "using blotting paper on the ocean." He maintained that, "we can catch them—the smugglers, the syndicates, the pushers, the wholesalers, and the users." But without longer sentences "we can't keep them in. . . . We put one crowd in jail, then start on another one. By the time we get the second one, the first is out working again. So it's just a merry-go-round." (quoted in Carroll, 2004a, p. 86).

Passage of the Boggs Act shows us another dimension of federal leadership in criminal justice, namely its role in standardizing state criminal law. Anslinger and the FBN encouraged states to pass what became known as "little Boggs" acts, largely to ensure that state-level sanctions were increased to match the new federal law. Seventeen states and the territory of Alaska passed little Boggs Acts, using statutory language provided to them directly from the FBN (Bonnie & Whitebread, 1970, p. 1074). This informal process of creating uniform legislation continued in the drug field; when Congress passed the Controlled Substances Act in 1970, the Justice Department also drafted a Uniform Controlled Substances Act for the states. Today, every U.S.

state has passed this legislation, ensuring that the federal government sets the terms of drug control. The same trend, toward uniform state laws based on federal models, may be seen in many areas of criminal law and procedure, the most notable being the development (starting in 1952) of the American Law Institute's Model Penal Code, designed to standardize state practice.

Through the 1950s, Anslinger's fundamental positions remained hugely influential. In numerous public statements, he argued that increased punishment was the single best deterrent to drug use and that approaches such as education about narcotics and treatment outside of residential facilities would do more harm than good. Anslinger also sought to discourage public debate that presented alternative points of view. For example, the American Bar Association (ABA) and the American Medical Association (AMA) formed a joint committee in 1955 to study the narcotics problem and existing drug laws. In 1958, the committee issued an *Interim Report* that questioned existing punitive approaches and that tentatively proposed new experiments in drug education and non-residential treatment. The FBN responded by issuing its own report that publicly condemned the ABA-AMA report, recapitulated the established argument for punishment, and engaged in personal attacks on members of the joint committee (Carroll, 2004b; Musto, 1999).

By the 1960s, however, an interdiction-only approach to drugs was increasingly difficult to sustain. The emerging influence of the mental health profession presented an alternative approach to the problem of narcotics. Moreover, the increasingly widespread use of marijuana and narcotics created a reality that undermined Anslinger's horror stories about them. At roughly the same time as Anslinger's 1962 retirement diminished the influence of the FBN, a model of drug treatment focused on health and welfare gained the support of John Kennedy's administration. The final ABA-AMA report was published in 1961, a White House Conference on Drug Abuse met in 1962, and a Presidential Commission on Narcotic and Drug Abuse issued a report in 1963, recommending relaxation of mandatory minimum sentences and more research into and treatment of drug addiction. By the later 1960s, the federal government increasingly devoted resources to a more medicalized approached to illegal drugs, emphasizing treatment, education, and the epidemiology of addiction (Musto, 1999).

That said, Anslinger's decades as head of the FBN had a remarkably lasting influence. Although his FBN did not endure in quite the same way as Hoover's FBI, Anslinger did establish the parameters for a federal commitment to policing drugs and laid the groundwork for the expansion of drug control in the 1970s and beyond. In 1967, the last year the FBN was in existence, it featured a staff of 300 drug agents. Its successor agency, the Bureau of Narcotic and Dangerous Drugs (BNDD) employed 1,446 agents in 1973; that year it was replaced by the Drug Enforcement Administration (DEA) which employed 2,117 agents in 1976 (Nadelmann, 1993, p. 140–141). Conversations about drug policy continued to divide into a debate over interdiction versus education and treatment but in official circles would rarely question the appropriateness of the federal government as the leader in waging a war on drugs.

What's The Evidence?: Federal Records

For many decades, the internal records of federal agencies involved in law enforcement were extremely difficult to obtain. The FBI, for example, essentially maintained closed records until the mid-1970s, not releasing any documentation to the National Archives. During the investigations of the FBI and other intelligence agencies, however, Congress amended the Freedom of Information Act (FOIA) in 1974 to make it possible for researchers to request specific records. The congressional hearings and reports between 1974 and 1976 also quoted FBI records extensively. Even so, researchers struggled mightily against the complications and expense of obtaining information via FOIA requests. Only in recent decades did the FOIA require the FBI to establish a "reading room"—both physically at FBI headquarters in Washington, DC and electronically on the Internet—containing some of the most often requested files. The electronic reading room—now containing FBI files on dozens of figures and organizations, and open for anyone to read—can be accessed at http://vault.fbi.gov. Finally in the 2000s, significant collections of FBI records were transferred to the National Archives and Records Administration (NARA), where they are now available to researchers at the NARA facility in College Park, Maryland (Theoharis, 2004; U.S. Department of Justice, Federal Bureau of Investigation, 2010).

Much of the twentieth-century debate over the federal role in criminal justice played out in public, however, particularly in hearings before congressional committees. For students interested in researching debates over federal law enforcement and the evolution of particular agencies, the published records of these hearings and the printed reports that resulted from them represent easily accessible sources of evidence. The most complete one-stop source to find listings of congressional hearings and reports is the Library of Congress catalog, currently available online at http://catalog.loc.gov/. But students do not need to actually go to the Library of Congress to access these records. Many congressional hearings and reports are available in major university and local libraries that participate in the Federal Depository Library program, housing copies of government documents.

These congressional hearings and reports encapsulated many of the major debates over crime and justice. For example, in the early 1950s, the U.S. Senate Special Committee to Investigate Organized Crime in Interstate Commerce conducted a long-lasting investigation that brought organized crime to public attention. Its hearings and a subsequent report were printed (U.S. Senate Special Committee to Investigate Organized Crime in Interstate Commerce, 1950a, 1950b), and highlights were released the subsequent year for popular consumption, edited by the committee's chair, Tennessee Senator Estes Kefauver (1951). Similarly, the subcommittee hearings over the question of tightening drug regulations that ultimately led to the 1951 and 1956 drug control acts have also been published (U.S. House Committee on Ways and Means, Subcommittee on Narcotics, 1951; U.S. Senate Committee on the Judiciary, Subcommittee on Improvements in the Federal Criminal Code, 1956). These hearings feature the testimony of Harry Anslinger and other FBN officials as well as that of other stakeholders in the debate over drug policy.

As with any other primary source, the testimony from these hearings and reports should be placed in context and compared against other sources, not just read as literal truth. As the term *stakeholder* implies, each of the participants had a stake in the issues and policy outcomes they thought beneficial. Often committee members and their staffers arranged these hearings as a kind of theater to dramatize particular interpretations of issues. Agencies like the FBN supplied committees with many of their witnesses, carefully chosen to highlight the agency's agenda. As another example, Kefauver's Senate Subcommittee to Study Juvenile Delinquency highlighted the rather narrow issue of the influence of comic books on juvenile crime. Focusing on the sensational may not have done much to solve problems but it drew public attention to issues, particularly when committee hearings were televised. Only by examining the perspectives of the speakers, the contexts in which they were speaking, the goals they were trying to achieve, and the audiences they were trying to reach can students really evaluate seemingly straightforward sources like congressional hearings.

❖ THE EXPANDED FEDERAL ROLE IN CRIMINAL JUSTICE AFTER 1970

The enlarging role of the federal government in criminal justice continued to be a major trend in the late twentieth century. Although criminal justice remained at heart the province of local and state officials, the federal government exerted an increasingly strong influence through mechanisms such as presidential commissions, funding for particular programs, and sentencing guidelines. The main vehicle driving this trend was a series of federal omnibus crime bills passed between the 1960s and 1990s that consciously sought to respond to local crime.

The federal government assumed a more direct role in routine law enforcement with the passage of the Omnibus Crime Control and Safe Streets Act in 1968. Proposed by the Johnson administration mainly to provide aid to local police, the law created the Law Enforcement Assistance Administration (LEAA). This agency funneled grants to cities and states, providing funding for police, corrections, and social services related to crime. As the bill evolved in Congress, however, politicians reshaped it so that it reflected more of a conservative crime control agenda than the Johnson administration's liberal approach. In addition to creating the LEAA, the final bill also expanded federal wiretapping authority—a provision opposed by the Johnson administration—and sought to restrict the federal judiciary's authority to review criminal cases—a clear slap at the Warren Court (Flamm, 2005; Gest, 2001; Walker, 1998).

During its relatively short existence, the LEAA exerted a tremendous influence on new directions in criminal justice. Established in 1968, the LEAA had its functions absorbed by the National Institute of Justice in 1979 and was ultimately abolished in 1982. During this time, the LEAA experienced frequent changes of leadership and of visions of what its role should be. As a result, although it distributed millions of dollars per year, it did so in a frequently incoherent fashion. In addition, members of Congress sought to use LEAA funding to support isolated projects for their districts. As it worked in reality, local police agencies were most aggressive in applying for LEAA grants and ended up receiving the largest shares of money. Police, however, could only spend a limited share of the LEAA money on salaries, so they used the cash on training and equipment. The availability of federal money subtly influenced police and other agencies to improve transportation and communications but to pay less attention to improving their practices (Gest, 2001). Moreover, the LEAA highlights a way in which the expanding federal role in fighting crime existed in an uneasy balance with the ideal of local and state control of criminal justice. While federal funding could influence criminal justice practice, the LEAA in reality exercised only limited control over what was done with the money.

In the 1970s and beyond, the federal government did assume a more assertive role in dealing with organized crime. Under J. Edgar Hoover's leadership, the FBI was curiously passive about organized crime, with Hoover often denying that national criminal networks existed. Despite the attention that Senator Estes Kefauver's hearings in the Senate Special Committee to Investigate Organized Crime in Interstate Commerce brought to the issue in the 1950s, the FBI engaged with it in only a limited fashion. Historians such as Richard Gid Powers (1987, p. 332–335) and Athan Theoharis (2004, p. 130–135) have suggested that pursuing organized crime would have forced the FBI to give up some of its autonomy by collaborating with other law enforcement agencies and distracted it from its perceived core mission of maintaining domestic security. The FBI tended to collect intelligence on organized crime activities rather than to pursue prosecutions. By the 1960s, however, increasing evidence of the influence of organized crime and pressure from attorneys general Robert F. Kennedy and Ramsay Clark pushed the FBI to take action. The expansion of wiretapping authority under the 1968 crime bill and new powers granted by the Racketeer Influenced and Corrupt Organizations (RICO) Act of 1970—which allowed prosecutions for illegal enterprises, not just individual criminal acts—gave the FBI new tools to fight organized crime. As a result, FBI investigations of organized crime expanded dramatically in the 1970s and 1980s. By the 1990s, the increased use of electronic surveillance and of criminal informants led to a series of successful prosecutions of mobsters (Jeffreys-Jones, 2007; Theoharis, 2004).

The federal government also became more actively involved in firearms regulation in recent decades. In this case, the goal of more extensive gun control resulted from the initiative of liberal reformers rather than advocates of stronger national security or tougher crime control, but the outcome was nonetheless similar: greater federal involvement in criminal justice. The 1968 crime bill imposed some modest restrictions on guns, such as a ban on mailing guns across state lines and restrictions on some imports of inexpensive firearms. By the 1970s and 1980s these regulations became a target of criticism by the National Rifle Association (NRA), a gun rights advocacy group that maintained that any restrictions on firearms represented a first step toward an outright ban on gun ownership. The NRA enjoyed extensive influence, but incidents such as the 1981 shooting of President Ronald Reagan gave political momentum to gun control advocates. James

Brady—Reagan's press secretary who had been severely wounded in the assassination attempt—and his wife Sarah Brady allied themselves with liberal gun control advocacy groups such as Handgun Control, Inc. In 1987, their allies in Congress introduced the Brady Bill to impose mandatory waiting periods and background checks before purchasers could buy guns. The Brady Bill initially made little progress in Congress due to stiff opposition from the NRA and its supporters. This gradually changed, however, as police organizations—interested in keeping guns off the streets—came out in favor of it. The 1992 election of Democrat Bill Clinton as president gave the law further momentum. The Brady Handgun Violence Prevention Act passed Congress in November 1993 and went into effect on February 28, 1994. It mandated background checks on gun purchasers and prohibited sales to people convicted of felonies and those who had been committed to mental institutions, among others (Gest, 2001).

As the example of the Brady Bill indicates, liberals as well as conservatives contributed to the expansion of the federal role in criminal justice. During the 1992 presidential campaign, Clinton called for hiring an additional 100,000 new police officers to put on the nation's streets. This call for more police resonated with many Americans in part because it came at a time when rates of violent crime—particularly in big cities—were quite high and polls showed that crime was a major public concern. In 1994, the Clinton administration successfully passed the Violent Crime Control and Law Enforcement Act, appropriating funds to hire the first of the promised 100,000 police. This law also authorized additional funding for prison construction, created new federal criminal offenses that could be subject to the death penalty (including terrorism, murder of law enforcement officers, and drug trafficking), and imposed a temporary ban on assault weapons. In addition, the 1994 Crime Act included the Violence Against Women Act, which provided $1.6 billion to support shelters for battered women and a domestic violence hotline (Gest, 2001; Gottschalk, 2006, p. 151–153; Mauer, 2006, p. 68–81). While the Clinton administration implemented crime control solutions favored by liberals such as community policing and gun control, it nonetheless approached criminal justice in a fashion similar to its more conservative predecessors, using expanded federal participation to expand the influence of criminal justice institutions in American life.

In the late 1990s, the ABA determined that the federal criminal codes included several thousand offenses, and that 40% of all federal criminal laws added since the Civil War had been enacted since 1970. As a result, many crimes that had previously been the responsibility of local law enforcement also came to fall under federal codes, creating overlapping jurisdictions. For example, the Armed Career Criminal Act of 1984 gave the federal government the option of prosecuting local offenders and enhancing their sentences if they committed firearms offenses after three previous felony convictions. While the impact of this law was small—only about 2,000 criminals were convicted under it between 1984 and the late 1990s—the overall impact of federalization was tremendous (Gest, 2001). Direct federal spending on criminal justice rose by over 600% between 1982 and 2003 and the number of inmates in federal prison increased from approximately 35,000 in 1985 to almost 180,000 in 2005 (Hughes, 2006, 2; Maguire, 2012, table 6.13.2010). In short, the trend toward an increased federal role in criminal justice—and expanded state power—that became prominent between 1930 and 1970 accelerated further after 1970.

❖ CONCLUSION

In the middle third of the twentieth century, crime was reconceptualized as a national problem. Actual offenses of course remained local, and local and state agencies retained jurisdiction in the vast majority of cases, but the federal government increasingly claimed overall responsibility for criminal justice. Elements of this shift can be seen long before the twentieth century, but the process accelerated sharply in the 1930s with the New Deal's war on crime.

In addition, the federal government developed not only a larger role in criminal justice but also a more elaborate administrative arm to take action. It expanded its law enforcement powers and prison system, to be sure, but also created more elaborate data collection instruments and mechanisms to affect local practice. As examples, the fingerprint files of the 1920s and 1930s, the surveillance programs of the 1940s, 1950s, and 1960s, and the federal funding initiatives of the 1960s and 1970s all increased the information in the hands of federal agencies and their capacity to act. This shift, however, should not be seen solely in terms of an increasingly punitive or repressive state. Nor should it be seen as the product of just one ideological perspective. The growing federal capacity in criminal justice was prompted by both liberal and conservative administrations and congresses that operated on relatively similar assumptions about the importance of maintaining order and domestic security. Moreover the outcomes of the expanded federal state included not only more police power but also an increased capacity to protect civil rights. The midcentury expansion of the federal government's role in criminal justice is not really a story of changing goals or directions. It is a story of the ways in which the federal government's set of tools changed.

❖ REFERENCES

Bonnie, R. J., & Whitebread, C. H. (1970). The forbidden fruit and the tree of knowledge: An inquiry into the legal history of American marijuana prohibition. *Virginia Law Review, 56*.

Bomar, H. L. Jr. (1934). The Lindbergh law. *Law and Contemporary Problems, 1*, 435–444.

Burrough, B. (2004). *Public enemies: America's greatest crime wave and the birth of the FBI, 1933–34*. New York, NY: Penguin Press.

Carroll, R. (2004a). Under the influence: Harry Anslinger's role in shaping America's drug policy. In J. Erlen & J. F. Spillane (Eds.), *Federal drug control: The evolution of policy and practice* (pp. 61–100). New York, NY: Pharmaceutical Products Press.

Carroll, R. (2004b). The Narcotics Act triggers the great nondebate: Treatment loses to punishment. In J. Erlen & J. F. Spillane (Eds.), *Federal drug control: The evolution of policy and practice* (pp. 101–144). New York, NY: Pharmaceutical Products Press.

Cavers, D. F. (1934). Foreword. *Law and Contemporary Problems, 1*, 399.

Cunningham, D. (2003). Understanding state responses to left- versus right-wing threats: The FBI's repression of the New Left and the Ku Klux Klan. *Social Science History, 27*, 327–370.

Cunningham, D. (2004). *There's something happening here: The New Left, the Klan, and FBI counterintelligence*. Berkeley: University of California Press.

Flamm, M. W. (2005). *Law and order: Street crime, civil unrest, and the crisis of liberalism in the 1960s*. New York, NY: Columbia University Press.

Geis, G., & Bienen, L. B. (1998). *Crimes of the century: From Leopold and Loeb to O.J. Simpson*. Boston, MA: Northeastern University Press.

Gest, T. (2001). *Crime & politics: Big government's erratic campaign for law and order*. New York, NY: Oxford University Press.

Gottschalk, M. (2006). *The prison and the gallows: The politics of mass incarceration in America*. Cambridge, MA: Cambridge University Press.

Hernandez, K. L. (2010). *Migra!: A history of the U.S. Border Patrol*. Berkeley: University of California Press.

Hughes, K. A. (2006). *Justice expenditure and employment in the United States, 2003* (No. NCJ 212260). Bureau of Justice Statistics Bulletin. Washington, DC: Bureau of Justice Statistics.

Jeffreys-Jones, R. (2007). *The FBI: A history*. New Haven, CT: Yale University Press.

Johnson, D. K. (2004). *The lavender scare: The Cold War persecution of gays and lesbians in the federal government*. Chicago, IL: University of Chicago Press.

Jonnes, J. (1999). *Hep-cats, narcs, and pipe dreams: A history of America's romance with illegal drugs*. Baltimore, MD: Johns Hopkins University Press.

Kefauver, E. (1951). *Crime in America*. Garden City, NY: Doubleday.

Mauer, M. (2006). *Race to incarcerate*. (2nd ed.). New York, NY: New Press.

Maguire, K. (Ed.). (2012). *Sourcebook of criminal justice statistics* Retrieved from http://www.albany.edu/sourcebook/

Musto, D. F. (1999). *The American disease: Origins of narcotic control* (3rd ed.). New York, NY: Oxford University Press.

Nadelmann, E. A. (1993). *Cops across borders: The internationalization of U.S. criminal law enforcement*. University Park: Pennsylvania State University Press.

Potter, C. B. (1998). *War on crime: Bandits, g-men, and the politics of mass culture*. New Brunswick, NJ: Rutgers University Press.

Powers, R. G. (1987). *Secrecy and power: The life of J. Edgar Hoover*. New York, NY: Free Press.

Purvis, M. (1936). *American agent*. Garden City, N.Y: Doubleday, Doran, & Co.

Ruth, D. E. (1996). *Inventing the public enemy: The gangster in American culture, 1918–1934*. Chicago, IL: University of Chicago Press.

Schrecker, E. (2002). *The age of McCarthyism: A brief history with documents* (2nd ed.). Boston, MA: Bedford/St. Martin's.

Skowronek, S. (1982). *Building a new American state: The expansion of national administrative capacities, 1877–1920*. New York, NY: Cambridge University Press.

Speaker, S. L. (2001). The struggle of mankind against its deadliest foe: Themes of countersubversion in anti-narcotics campaigns, 1920–1940. *Journal of Social History, 34*, 591–610.

Spillane, J. F. (1998). The making of an underground market: Drug selling in Chicago, 1900–1940. *Journal of Social History, 32*, 27–48.

Spillane, J. F. (2004). Building a drug control regime, 1919–1930. In J. Erlen & J. F. Spillane (Eds.), *Federal drug control: The evolution of policy and practice* (pp. 25–60). New York, NY: Pharmaceutical Products Press.

Theoharis, A. G. (2004). *The FBI and American democracy: A brief critical history*. Lawrence: University Press of Kansas.

United States Congress, House Committee on Ways and Means, Subcommittee on Narcotics. (1951). *Control of narcotics, marijuana, and barbiturates: Hearings before a subcommittee of the Committee on Ways and Means, House of Representatives, Eighty-second Congress, First Session, on H. R. 3490 and H. R. 348, April 7, 14, and 17, 1951*. Washington, DC: Government Printing Office.

United States Congress, Senate Committee on the Judiciary. Subcommittee on Improvements in the Federal Criminal Code. (1956). *Narcotic Control Act of 1956. Hearing before the subcommittee on Improvements in the Federal Criminal Code of the Committee on the Judiciary, United States Senate, Eighty-Fourth Congress, Second Session, on S. 3760, a bill to provide for a more effective control of narcotic drugs*. Washington, DC: U. S. Government Printing Office.

United States Congress, Senate Special Committee to Investigate Organized Crime in Interstate Commerce. (1950a). *Report*. Washington, DC: U. S. Government Printing Office.

United States Congress, Senate Special Committee to Investigate Organized Crime in Interstate Commerce. (1950b). *Investigation of organized crime in interstate commerce. Hearings Before a special committee to investigate organized crime in interstate commerce, United States Senate, Eighty-First Congress, Second Session, Pursuant to S. Res. 202*. Washington, DC: U.S. Government Printing Office.

United States Department of Justice, Federal Bureau of Investigation. (2010). *A guide to conducting research in FBI records*. Washington, DC.: FBI History Program, Office of Public Affairs. Retrieved from http://www.fbi.gov/foia/a-guide-to-conducting-research-in-fbi-records

Waldrep, C. (2008). National policing, lynching, and constitutional change. *Journal of Southern History, 74*(3), 589–626.

Walker, S. (1998). *Popular justice: A history of American criminal justice* (2nd ed.). New York, NY: Oxford University Press.

Ward, D. A. (2009). *Alcatraz: The gangster years*. Berkeley: University of California Press.

9

The Politics of Law and Order, 1960s–2000s

Historians tend to focus on big moments of change. After all, change is more dramatic than continuity and change helps delineate one period from another. When historians of the future look back at major changes in U.S. life in the late twentieth century, it is likely that one central topic will be the massive expansion of the criminal justice system in an effort to get tough on crime.

The most obvious manifestation of the growth of the criminal justice apparatus is the startling growth of the U.S. prison population between 1970 and 2010, resulting in what could be called mass incarceration. While this growth slowed somewhat in the decade between 2000 and 2010, the United States maintained an incarceration rate far higher than at any earlier point in its history, or in other comparable nations. Criminal justice scholar Travis Pratt (2009, p. xiii) asserted that, "At the beginning of 2008, the United States had 1% of its population behind bars. Our incarcerated population is larger than China's (a nation that dwarfs us in overall population size) and our rate of incarceration is higher than for nations such as . . . Iran . . . where one can earn a stint in incarceration for merely holding certain political views." Historian Heather Ann Thompson (2010, p. 703) wrote that ". . . at no other point in its past had the nation's economic, social, and political institutions become so bound up with the practice of punishment."

Despite the change, it is important not to overemphasize the ways in which the expansion of criminal justice represents a departure. Instead, this expansion built upon earlier trends in U.S. history of the increasing reach of criminal justice agencies and the enlarging role of the federal government. It would also be a mistake to view the growth of criminal justice in purely critical terms. Changes in the late twentieth and early twenty-first centuries brought with them greater degrees of professionalism and accountability and more effective techniques for controlling crime. This chapter explores how and why criminal justice changed in this period. First, it describes the broad outlines of the changes. Second, it analyzes the historical factors contributing to these changes. And third it assesses some of the specific ways that patterns of change have played out in different sectors of the justice system.

❖ THE SCALE OF MASS INCARCERATION

At the end of the year in 2007, federal and state prisons in the United States held approximately 1.6 million people. This worked out to a rate of 506 people imprisoned for every 100,000 in the U.S. resident population, or about 1 in every 198 persons being held in federal or state prisons (West & Sabol, 2008). These numbers seem large, but they become astonishing in a longer term perspective. As Figure 9.1 indicates, the U.S. imprisonment rate remained relatively constant for decades from when these numbers were first collected in 1925 until the early 1970s, hovering around 100 per 100,000 people. But in the early 1970s, the pattern shifted dramatically. U.S. imprisonment rates began to move sharply upward so that by 2007—the year rates peaked—the imprisonment rate was five times higher than it had been in 1970. In absolute numbers, the difference is even starker. The 1.6 million people imprisoned in 2007 were more than eight times the roughly 196,000 imprisoned in 1970. The state of California alone has the largest prison system in the Western industrialized world, holding more inmates than do Great Britain, France, Germany, and the Netherlands combined (Donziger, 1996; Gottschalk, 2006; Mauer, 2006; Pratt, 2009; Schlosser, 1998).

What did all these inmates do to end up in prison? Someone unfamiliar with how criminal justice works might conclude from these high incarceration rates that the United States had become a very dangerous country indeed. In reality, however, incarceration for nonviolent

Figure 9.1 Prisoners Incarcerated in State and Federal Institutions, 1925–2010

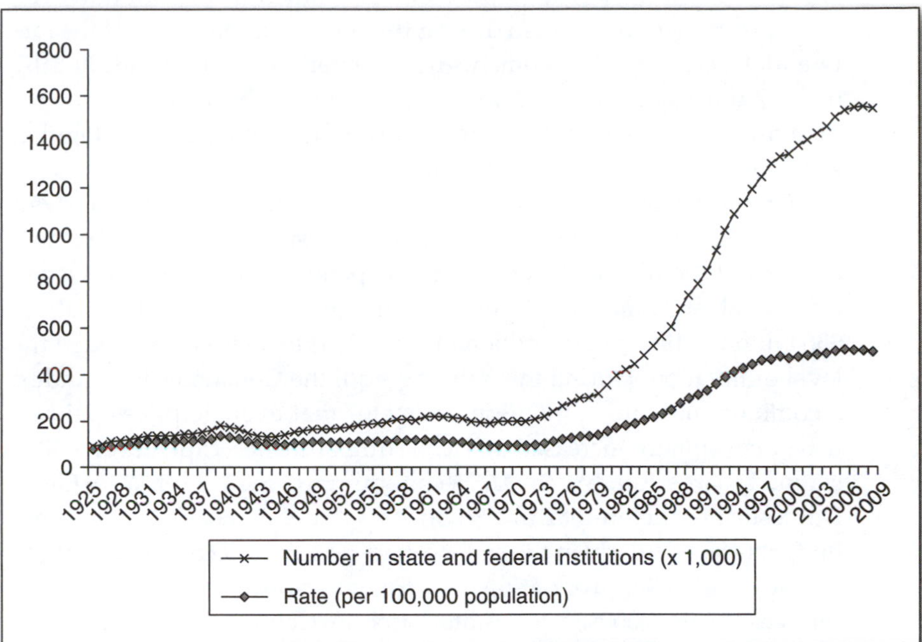

offenses largely fueled the expansion of the prison population. As Marc Mauer (2006, p. 30–35) calculated, the number of new sentences to state prisons increased by 101% from 1985 to 2000. Broken down by offense, however, new sentences for violent crimes increased by a more modest 45%, but new sentences for drug offenses increased by a whopping 402%. Similarly, the number of inmates incarcerated in federal prisons for violent crimes increased 77% from 1985 to 2000, but the number incarcerated in federal prisons for drug offenses increased 683%.

The demographics of the U.S. prison population also become starkly different from the demographics of the U.S. population as a whole. Hispanics and African Americans both comprise about 13% of the U.S. population, yet Hispanics comprise about 20% of federal and state prisoners and African Americans about 38%. In 2007, roughly 481 of every 100,000 white males were imprisoned in state and federal prisons, whereas 1,259 of every 100,000 men of Hispanic origin were, and 3,138 African American men were (West & Sabol, 2008, p. 4). As a result, incarceration became far more pervasive among Hispanics and African Americans than among whites (Donziger, 1996; Gottschalk, 2006; Mauer, 2006; Pratt, 2009; Schlosser, 1998).

In addition, the U.S. prison population is overwhelmingly male, with roughly 13 times more men than women held in state and federal prisons in 2008. The population of women in prison, however, grew faster than that of men during the incarceration boom of the late twentieth century. For women, the incarceration rate multiplied by over 12 times between 1970 and 2007, while the incarceration rate for men multiplied by only four times during the same period (Maguire, 2012, table 6.28.2010; West & Sabol, 2008).

One result of the expansion of criminal justice and particularly of incarceration has been a massive increase in spending. In the last two decades of the twentieth century, total spending on the justice system by federal, state, and local governments increased 418%, from about $36 billion in 1982 to $185 billion in 2003. This increase far exceeded the level of inflation. During this same period, the Consumer Price Index, a common measure of inflation, indicates that average prices paid by urban consumers increased 184%. Criminal justice expenditures also claimed a larger share of the U.S. economy, growing from 1.1% of Gross Domestic Product in 1982 to 1.8% in 2003 (Hughes, 2006). Government budgets—particularly in the states—had to shift to accommodate these increases, often appropriating less for education and social welfare services. In the 2000s, a few states such as California were spending more on corrections than on higher education (Pratt, 2009).

Even so, the speed at which the prison population grew seems to have peaked around the year 2000 and to have leveled off later. From 2000 to 2009, the average annual growth rate of the population in federal and state prisons was 1.8% per year, as compared to an average annual growth rate of 6.5% per year in the 1990s. In 2010, the overall U.S. prison population declined for the first time since 1972 (Guerino, Harrison, & Sabol, 2011). It is possible that the boom era in incarceration is drawing to a close, or at least that large-scale expansion is reaching a plateau. Crime and justice became less compelling public issues in the 2000s, and the economic downturn of the latter part of the decade made it difficult for many state governments to afford an ever-expanding prison population. Nonetheless, the result of four decades of growth is a massive criminal justice system and an enormous prison population, both of which continue to shape U.S. society.

❖ THE ORIGINS OF MASS INCARCERATION

What led to this burst of incarceration? An easy answer would be that the growth of the criminal justice system was a straightforward response to an increase in crime. Crime, however, is only part of the explanation, and perhaps not the most important part. Instead, the growth of the criminal justice system emerged out of the particular political, social, intellectual, and economic trends of the late twentieth century.

Increased Fear of Crime

The amount of serious crime in the United States increased sharply between the early 1960s and the early 1990s. According to the FBI's Uniform Crime Reports (UCR), the rate per resident population of eight serious index crimes reported to the police—murder and non-negligent manslaughter, rape, robbery, aggravated assault, burglary, larceny-theft, motor vehicle theft, and arson—increased by 215% between 1960 and 1980. These serious crimes remained at an elevated level in the 1980s before beginning to drop in the early 1990s (Maguire, 2012, table 3.106.2010). Critics such as Mauer (2006), however, question the early UCR data, pointing out that many police departments did not participate or provide complete data, so the apparent sharp increase in crime in the 1960s may be a simple result of including more information. The National Crime Victimization Survey (NCVS), a household survey of people ages 12 and over conducted by the U.S. Census Bureau twice a year since 1973 and generally considered a more accurate gauge of crime, suggests that rates of crime victimization rates were relatively constant from the early 1970s to the early 1990s.

What did change was the amount of homicide. Murder is the most easily measured crime because friends and relatives almost always report it and evidence in the form of a dead body is almost always left behind. The U.S. murder rate doubled in the 1960s, from less than 5 homicides per 100,000 people in 1960 to more than 10 homicides in 1970. The murder rate fell back a little in subsequent years but again exceeded 10 per 100,000 from 1979 to 1981 and from 1990 to 1993 (Bureau of Justice Statistics, 2010). Looking at these numbers with a long-term perspective, estimates created by Douglas Eckberg (1995) suggest that the murder rates of the 1960s through the early 1990s were quite comparable to murder rates from the early 1900s through the early 1930s. But examined with a narrower perspective, the murder rates of the 1960s through the early 1990s represent a dramatic increase over those of the 1940s and 1950s (Lane, 1997). Moreover, examined on an international scale, overall late twentieth-century U.S. rates of crime victimization were slightly lower than those of developed countries such as Great Britain and Australia, but U.S. homicide rates more than doubled those of other comparable countries (Mauer, 2006; Zimring & Hawkins, 1997).

Intertwined with actual changes in crime rates, public perceptions of crime also changed between the 1960s and the 1990s. Many Americans increasingly came to believe that they could become victims of crime, particularly violent crime. Much of this concern revolved around U.S. cities, which underwent profound transformations in this period. Since the 1910s, African Americans—mainly southern and rural—moved into northern and western cities in a process known as the Great Migration. This process accelerated in the 1940s with the World War Two-era industrial boom and continued through the 1960s. In Detroit, for example, the African American population grew exponentially from less than 6,000 people in 1910 to over 660,000 in 1970. Beginning in the 1940s, however, large numbers of white residents began to move out of American cities, particularly in the North and East, relocating to suburbs or, increasingly, pursuing new jobs in the South and West. Detroit's white population peaked in 1950 and declined thereafter. Moreover, the industrial base of northern cities—the engine of jobs and prosperity—began to decline. While the 1950s are often perceived as the high point of American prosperity, that decade actually saw the beginnings of contractions in automobile manufacturing and other heavy industries and the relocation of factories from the urban North to locations elsewhere that offered lower taxes and less expensive labor (Sugrue, 1996). As a result, by the 1960s, many American cities filled with large populations of unskilled migrants who arrived just as the jobs that sustained previous generations moved away. These migrants ended up contributing disproportionately to the increase in crime in the 1960s.

From the perspective of the largely white population that moved to the suburbs, it seemed that the cities were no longer safe. Famous crimes—covered intensely in the media—further fueled this perception. For example, the 1964 murder of Kitty Genovese in New York City fostered the idea that cities had become highly dangerous. Genovese, a young white woman, had been followed home to her quiet residential neighborhood by an African American man and stabbed repeatedly outside of her apartment building. Even as neighbors watched the attack and heard her screams, no one called the police. Advocates of tougher law enforcement used incidents like this one to paint a picture that cities had become perilous places where only vigorous policing could keep people safe (Johnson, 2003, p. 245).

A series of urban race riots in the 1960s intensified public concerns that something had to be done about crime. The riots—in Harlem in 1964, in the Watts section of Los Angeles in 1965, in dozens of cities in 1966, and in over 100 cities during the "long hot summer" of 1967—followed very similar patterns. African Americans frustrated with continued inequality protested against specific problems, confrontations escalated, and local law enforcement struggled to restore order. In many cases, police actions or brutality precipitated the uprisings. The 1964 Harlem riot followed the shooting of a black teenager by plainclothes New York City police officers. The 1965 Watts riot likewise followed the botched arrest of an African American driver for a traffic offense. These riots often led to large-scale killing and physical destruction of communities. The 1967 Detroit riot caused 43 deaths (including killings of 30 African Americans by law enforcement officers) and the looting or burning of over 2,500 buildings. While the riots were exceptional events rather than ordinary crime, they nonetheless contributed to a perception that neither local law enforcement nor the federal government was capable of restoring stability (Flamm, 2005; Lane, 1997; Sugrue, 1996). A frustrated public responded by demanding more vigorous government action. One constituent wrote to New York Governor Nelson Rockefeller saying, "This letter is written to you by a law-abiding citizen who feels she is discriminated against in favor of dope addicts and welfare cheats. I am a widow who lives alone, works every day, pays taxes, and lives by the rules. I get very little from my taxes when I can no longer walk on the streets and when I am afraid in my own house" (quoted in Kohler-Hausmann, 2010, p. 77).

This photograph from the 1965 Watts riot in Los Angeles shows predominately white police officers frisking a group of African American men. It illustrates the racial divisions that characterized urban policing in the 1960s and that contributed to the rioting.

Source: Los Angeles Public Library Photo Collection. Photographer: Cliff Wesselmann.

What's the Evidence?: Official Crime Data

Since the 1970s, the amount of quantitative data about the criminal justice system compiled and made available by governments at the federal, state, and local levels has expanded exponentially. Several factors have contributed to this. First, the public interest in criminal justice and the

(Continued)

(Continued)

expanded federal role have prompted the federal government to increasingly collect and release information. The Omnibus Crime Control and Safe Streets Act of 1968 and its subsequent amendments created federal agencies to coordinate data collection and dissemination. Second, since the 1960s and 1970s, social scientific research has increasingly come to rely on analysis of quantitative data, and computer technology has made it possible to store and analyze increasingly large datasets. Third, since the 1990s, the emergence of the Internet has facilitated the dissemination of information. Quantitative data that, a few decades ago, could only have been acquired through hours of hunting in a research library, can now be acquired online in a few moments. At the same time, users of the data should still be aware of how the data is generated and how its nature contributes to its strengths and limitations.

The FBI's Uniform Crime Reporting program is the longest-running effort to collect statistics about crimes known to police and law enforcement responses. It was first conceived by the International Association of Chiefs of Police in 1929 and implemented in the early 1930s. This program produces several annual publications, including the comprehensive volume now known as *Crime in the United States* that are available online at http://www.fbi.gov/about-us/cjis/ucr/ucr. Its methodology has changed several times, however, so data from different periods cannot always be directly compared, and critics charge that the inclusion of more jurisdictions in periods such as the 1960s artificially increase reported crime rates.

The Bureau of Justice Statistics (BJS), an agency under the federal Department of Justice, has the broader mission of collecting, analyzing, and disseminating information about crime and the operations of justice systems at all levels of government. Established in 1979, it collects data and generates reports on an astonishing array of topics. If, for example, you wanted to know how many executions took place in a given year and how that compared to a previous year, the best place to start would be the BJS annual publication, "Capital Punishment." BJS data and publications currently can be accessed at http://bjs.ojp.usdoj.gov/index.cfm.

Areas that government reports do not cover are often addressed by scholarly agencies. Most prominently, the Sourcebook of Criminal Justice Statistics, produced by the Hindelang Criminal Justice Research Center at the University at Albany's School of Criminal Justice, assembles data about many aspects of criminal justice. Since it was established in 1973, the

Sourcebook has produced a thick volume of data tables that represent perhaps the best one-stop shopping location for criminal justice data. With the expansion of the Internet, the Sourcebook has migrated online and can currently be accessed at http://www.albany.edu/sourcebook/index.html.

This explosion of criminal justice data represents something of a double-edged sword from a historical perspective. On the one hand, a tremendous amount of information is now available. On the other hand, these data tend to focus on very recent years and, to the extent that they deal with trends over time, tend to focus on relatively short periods. The information that is available before even the 1990s remains less complete and more difficult to acquire than is recent information. The nature of the data thus contributes to a tendency to think about criminal justice in very contemporary terms. To put the recent data in a historical context, users should look to find ways to acquire data covering longer spans of time and seek to compare information from past and present. In addition, considering how the information was created helps illuminate both what the data reveal and what it does not.

Political Change

Criminal justice assumed an increasingly central role in U.S. politics in the 1960s. The Great Migration, the deindustrialization of cities, and the rise in crime all helped create an environment in which politicians' calls for increased law and order resonated. Law and order also provided an issue upon which conservative politicians could challenge more liberal rivals. In their 1964 runs for the presidency, both Alabama Democratic Governor George Wallace and Arizona Republican Senator Barry Goldwater made crime and justice key themes in their campaigns. Wallace presented his campaign as an insurgency against incumbent Democratic President Lyndon Johnson, trying to win white blue-collar votes by linking Johnson to the African American civil rights movement and linking the civil rights movement to risks to voters' personal safety. Goldwater's campaign, both more subtly and more expansively, argued that the United States was experiencing a moral crisis. He suggested that the welfare state—which reached its apogee with the liberal Johnson administration's promise to create a Great Society—had, in reality, coddled criminals, fostered indiscipline in homes and society, and thereby promoted crime. These political campaigns, of course, failed. Wallace ran a distant second in the

Democratic primaries, and Johnson defeated Goldwater in the 1964 general election. In some ways, however, the rhetoric of these campaigns succeeded in giving substance to new ideas. The campaigns suggested that presidents and the federal government had a key role to play in fighting crime and fostered a compelling notion that tougher government policies could help restore a sense of law and order (Flamm, 2005).

The Johnson administration responded by trying to implement its own strategy to control crime. In the spring of 1965, Johnson convinced Congress to create the Office of Law Enforcement Assistance, an agency to fund federal assistance to local police. He also announced the creation of the President's Commission on Law Enforcement and the Administration of Justice. This Crime Commission's final report, *The Challenge of Crime in a Free Society*, released in spring of 1967, broke new ground by treating crime and criminal justice not as isolated elements but as a complex interconnected system (see Chapter Six). It offered over 200 specific recommendations for reducing crime and for improving the operations of police, courts, and prisons. The report's emphasis on sociological solutions and greater research and resources reflected the larger optimistic and liberal assumptions of the Great Society that more government intervention in society could help solve social problems. In doing so, however, it angered both conservatives, who saw the Crime Commission's report as insufficiently focused on immediate problems, and radicals, who saw the report as deliberately ignoring inequalities and power relations in society. As a result, the Crime Commission failed to recapture the larger public debate over law and order (Flamm, 2005; Gest, 2001).

A second presidential commission—this one to investigate the urban riots—even more clearly demonstrated the liberal uncertainty about how to address crime and violence. In 1967, in the wake of the Detroit riot, Johnson announced the appointment of the National Advisory Commission on Civil Disorders, known as the Kerner Commission after its chair, Otto Kerner. The commission's 1968 report reflected scholarly understandings of collective violence as political acts aimed at social change and offered a detailed analysis of the social conditions that led to violence. But the clearest message of the report, stated on the first page of the introduction, was that "white society is deeply implicated in the ghetto. White institutions created it, white institutions maintain it, and white society condones it" (quoted in Flamm, 2005, p. 107). While the report recommended spending and social services to mitigate the problem, it failed to offer solutions, or even a thorough analysis of how white racism operated. Conservatives condemned the report; one columnist wrote that it placed "blame everywhere but where it belongs, everywhere, that is, except upon the rioters and upon the liberals who . . . prepared the way for the riots" (quoted in Flamm, 2005, p. 108).

By the mid-1960s, conservative politicians adopted crime and justice as a signature issue. In 1966, conservative Republican candidate Ronald Reagan won the California governor's office over incumbent liberal Democrat Edmund G. "Pat" Brown largely by promising to restore law and order. Reagan blamed both the Watts riots and student protests at the University of California at Berkeley on small minorities of malcontents and agitators. In each case, he promised that, as governor, he would not tolerate law breaking under the guise of civil disobedience, and that he would respond to crises by deploying the National Guard (Flamm, 2005). Calls for law and order also shaped political outcomes when New York City voters decisively rejected a civilian police review board in a 1966 referendum. Liberal Republican Mayor John Lindsay expanded the authority of a racially diverse board of civilians that heard complaints about police misconduct and could impose discipline. In response, the Patrolmen's Benevolent Association initiated a referendum to abolish the board. The subsequent campaign drew strongly on the themes of public safety and street crime, suggesting that a civilian review board would tie the hands of police. One poster depicted a young woman emerging nervously from a subway onto a dark street and declared, "The Civilian Review Board must be stopped . . . Her life . . . your life . . . may depend on it." The logic of the advertisement was that a "police officer must not hesitate. If he does . . . the security and safety of your family may be jeopardized" (Flamm, 2005, p. 76–80; Johnson, 2003, p. 241–251).

By the end of 1968, Republican Richard Nixon successfully used the issue of law and order to help win the presidency. In the course of that year, the assassination of Martin Luther King Jr., in April, the killing of Robert F. Kennedy in June, and protests at the Democratic Party National Convention in Chicago in August all helped keep the focus of public opinion on the problems of disorder, violence, and crime. Nixon succeeded in appropriating conservative law and order ideas in a way that appealed to middle-class white voters. He critiqued the Johnson administration's focus on poverty as the source of crime and its supposed weak commitment to law enforcement, challenged the Warren Court's decisions (see Chapter Seven), and promised expanded programs aimed at crime prevention and deterrence. Although Nixon did not propose any particularly new initiatives, he did manage to capture a political advantage by articulating a position of favoring practical measures to control crime. In doing so he helped establish a template for subsequent politicians to succeed by being tougher on crime than their opponents (Flamm, 2005; Gest, 2001; Pratt, 2009).

Mounting violence in prisons provided politicians with another justification to impose harsher crime control measures. By the late 1960s and early 1970s, prison inmates increasingly rioted to demand better conditions, with the number of major uprisings growing from five in 1967 to 27 in 1970, 37 in 1971, and 48 in 1972. Most notably, inmates at the Attica Correctional Facility in New York occupied a wing of the prison and took 40 workers hostage on September 9, 1971. During the prison takeover, the news media managed to get reporters, microphones, and cameras inside the prison, providing a public forum for the rioters to issue their demands. The inmates' goals paralleled those of the larger prisoners' rights movement: a minimum wage for work, religious freedom, a better diet, better education, and a generally greater level of respect (see Chapter 7). The situation, however, became an occasion for political leaders to draw a hard line against disorder. Governor Nelson Rockefeller refused to make concessions. After the inmates threatened to execute hostages, Rockefeller authorized state police and prison guards to launch an armed assault to recapture the prison by force. They succeeded but the assault killed 43 people, including 10 hostages (Christianson, 1998; Gottschalk, 2006; Walker, 1998). In the short term, the violent suppression of the Attica uprising generated support for the prisoners' rights movement. The 1972 New York State Special Commission on Attica, also known as the McKay Commission, condemned the use of force to retake the prison and highlighted the legitimacy of inmates' demands. But in the long term, prison riots fostered a backlash. A vocal element of the public supported Rockefeller's firm stance and recoiled at prisoners' use of violence. Despite the investigations and reforms that followed the Attica uprising, the riots contributed to a conservative narrative that criminals were out of control and could only be managed through new measures to get tough on crime.

Intellectual Shifts

In the 1970s, scholars of criminal justice also began to rethink many of their earlier assumptions. The resulting research tended to undercut many existing rehabilitation-based approaches to criminal justice and instead to provide ammunition for advocates of greater use of incarceration.

Marvin Wolfgang, Robert M. Figlio, and Thorsten Sellin's *Delinquency in a Birth Cohort* (1972) highlighted how much crime was the work of repeat offenders. This study traced all males born in Philadelphia in 1945 through when they turned 18 in 1963. The authors used police and school records to reconstruct the criminal careers of 9,945 of these youths. They found that over one-third of juveniles in their sample had at least one official contact with the police. Of these, almost half of the group that had contact with the police had only one, and a significant share had only between two and four contacts. However, 6% of the original cohort had five or more contacts with police and were responsible for the over half of the total offenses committed by this cohort. This study gave substance to anticrime rhetoric that hard-core or career criminals committed most crime. The policy implications were staggering—if police and prosecutors could get these 6% off the streets, overall crime rates would decline markedly (Walker, 1994, p. 56–59).

The publication of leading criminal justice scholar James Q. Wilson's book *Thinking About Crime* (1975) helped establish a new intellectual paradigm. Wilson's book—written for general audiences and published with a commercial press—probably had greater influence with policymakers and the public than it did with other researchers. In it, Wilson argued for a rejection of both the anti-poverty approaches to reducing crime associated with liberals and harshly punitive approaches associated with conservatives. In developing his argument, Wilson strongly critiqued the community-based crime prevention programs and decarceration movement developed in the 1960s and 1970s. Instead he focused on using tough measures to fight serious crime by repeat offenders, explicitly citing Wolfgang's work. Arguing that, "Wicked people exist. Nothing avails except to set them apart from innocent people" (Wilson, 1975, p. 209), he strongly endorsed building more prisons and renewing efforts to identify and incarcerate the small percentage responsible for the majority of crimes. Wilson advocated the idea that "the rate of serious crime would be only one-third what it is today if every person convicted of a serious offense were imprisoned for three years" (p. 202).

These ideas prompted tremendous enthusiasm for new models of punishment, such as "selective incapacitation," by which the system focused on imprisoning repeat offenders. The goal of incarcerating the right "wicked people" became something of a holy grail. Subsequent research, however, has shown that selective incapacitation is highly problematic for several reasons. First, the amount of crime selective incapacitation reduces may be exaggerated. Second, it turns out to be extraordinarily difficult to predict in advance who will become repeat offenders. Third, the cost of imprisonment presents a barrier to implementing selective incapacitation (Walker, 1994; Pratt, 2009). Nonetheless, the idea that it would be possible to lock up the wicked people became pervasive in policy circles and public discussions in the late twentieth century. This notion, combined with skepticism about liberal rehabilitation programs highlighted by the 1974 publication of Robert Martinson's "What Works" (see Chapter 7), helped provide an intellectual justification for large-scale incarceration and policies promoting law and order.

Mandatory Sentencing

Various forms of mandatory sentencing laws that emerged from the 1970s to the 1990s also contributed to the growth of prison populations. These laws imposed strict guidelines on judges requiring them to sentence persons convicted of particular crimes to mandatory minimum terms in prison. Mandatory sentencing laws succeeded in part because they seemed to satisfy the demands of a wide range of interests. To some extent, these laws helped implement notions of selective incapacitation. To a greater extent, however, they also responded to calls for law and order. Many conservative critics complained that the indeterminate sentencing laws that prevailed for most of the twentieth century allowed too much discretion for judges to issue lenient sentences and too much opportunity for criminals to leave prison early. Victims' rights advocates pointed to cases of convicted offenders who were released and offended again. They argued that mandatory sentences would keep known criminals off the streets. These arguments dovetailed with liberal critiques of indeterminate sentencing. In the 1960s and 1970s, critics inspired by the civil rights movement argued that indeterminate sentences offered too much flexibility to the criminal justice system and created the possibility that offenders could spend excessive amounts of time in prison. They pointed to cases like that of George Jackson, an African American inmate who became a prominent prisoners' rights activist. At age 18, Jackson had been convicted of stealing $70 in a gas station holdup and sentenced to an indeterminate sentence of one to seventy years in prison (Mauer, 2006; Walker, 1998).

In this context, various mandatory sentencing laws passed with bipartisan support. For example, between 1975 and 1990, Florida passed ten separate mandatory sentencing provisions, assigning required minimum sentences in crimes involving drugs, firearms, and repeat offending (Walker, 1994). The federal government also began drawing up sentencing guidelines following the passage of a 1984 crime law. Initially, both Republicans and Democrats sought to rationalize an existing hodgepodge of federal criminal law and lessen the ability of judges to make arbitrary decisions. In the end, the resulting guidelines—which went into effect in 1987—tended to make federal law more punitive. The guidelines embraced the concept of "truth in sentencing," which reduced the range of possible sentences and eliminated discretionary parole release. As a result, the typical stated length of federal sentences got shorter, but the amount of time served got longer. These changes provoked widespread criticism from federal judges, who felt that rigid guidelines restrained them from making decisions appropriate to individual offenders. In 2005, the Supreme Court found large portions of the guidelines to be unconstitutional on technical grounds, but by then the guidelines had helped drive the massive expansion of the federal prison system (Gest, 2001; Mauer, 2006; Walker, 1994).

Despite the growth of incarceration, a common perception persisted that criminals often left prison after serving a short term. By the 1990s, the best known policy response to this became known as "three strikes, you're out." The idea of three strikes combined a goal of protecting society with a sense of retribution and a crude sort of selective incapacitation: offenders convicted of three felonies should be sentenced to long—possibly life—terms in prison. In 1993, the kidnapping and murder of 12-year-old Polly Klaas gave increased momentum to state-level campaigns to establish three strikes laws. Klaas had been abducted from her home in Petaluma, California, by Richard Allen Davis, a career criminal who had twice before been convicted of kidnapping. Following the Klaas killing, both conservative and liberal politicians embraced three strikes as a means of controlling repeat offenders such as Davis. President Bill Clinton endorsed three strikes laws in his January 1994 State of the Union address (Gest, 2001).

Between 1993 and 1995, at least 24 states and the federal government enacted some form of a three strikes law. California's was among the broadest and best known. In California, a second conviction for particularly serious felony offenses—such as rape and robbery—would double the sentence. A third conviction—for any felony—would result in a life sentence, with the possibility of parole after 25 years. While three strikes laws pulled in some of the worst offenders, they filled prisons with less dangerous criminals as well. In California in 1994, 70% of second-and third-strike cases involved nonviolent offenses. In California and elsewhere, three strikes laws culminated a long-term shift away from indeterminate sentencing toward a much more rigid model. While the indeterminate sentences of midcentury may have suffered from an excess of discretion, the highly determinate sentences of the late twentieth century suffered from a lack of flexibility. States and localities found themselves locked into a situation where they had to build more prison cells and house more long-term inmates whether or not they posed actual threats to society (Donziger, 1996; Gest, 2001; Schlosser, 1998).

The War on Drugs

Efforts to prevent and punish the use of illegal drugs also drove the expansion of the criminal justice system in the latter third of the twentieth century. At the federal level, Richard Nixon's presidential administration devoted more attention to drugs than did its predecessors. In part, this emerged from the "law and order" focus of Nixon's 1968 campaign for the presidency. It also resulted from changes in drug use in the 1960s. Serious narcotics such as heroin were increasingly pervasive in inner cities, where they were widely reported to contribute to the upsurge in violent crime, and among U.S. soldiers fighting in Southeast Asia. In addition, milder drugs such as marijuana also became more common and accepted among young people. Whereas earlier in the twentieth century marijuana had been mainly used by minority subcultures—musicians, artists, urban African Americans, Hispanic laborers—by the 1960s it was increasingly used by white middle-class youth (Goldberg, 1980; Jonnes, 1999; Kohler-Hausmann, 2010).

The Nixon administration's strategy for controlling the drug problem took two parallel tracks, focusing on reducing both demand for drugs—through addiction treatment—and supply—through interdiction. On the demand side, in 1971 the Nixon administration created a new executive agency, the Special Action Office for Drug Abuse Prevention (SAODAP), to coordinate federal drug use prevention programs and to fund new state and local treatment programs. The number of federally-funded drug treatment centers expanded to nearly 4,000. Many used methadone maintenance to help heroin addicts. Although Nixon's rhetoric presented drug abuse as a grave threat, his administration nonetheless supported treatment to a surprising degree. On the supply side, the Nixon administration consolidated its domestic drug enforcement agencies. First it replaced the Federal Bureau of Narcotics with the Bureau of Narcotics and Dangerous Drugs (BNDD) in April 1968. Then in July 1973 it consolidated the BNDD and other federal agencies dealing with illegal drugs into the Drug Enforcement Agency (DEA). The federal government also increased funding for drug control from roughly $80 million in 1969 to $730 million in 1973. By 1973, the Nixon administration seemed to achieve some short-term success in reducing heroin use. Scattered evidence reported increased heroin prices, fewer overdoses, and fewer arrests for heroin possession (Goldberg, 1980; Jonnes, 1999).

Highly punitive drug laws became an important indicator of toughness in the war on drugs. In a January 1973 address, New York Governor Nelson Rockefeller asked his state legislature to establish mandatory minimum sentences of life terms in prison without the possibility of parole for all illegal drug dealers. The actual law enacted later in the year was somewhat less harsh, but it was still widely considered the nation's toughest drug law; it imposed a sentence of 15 years to life for possession of four ounces of an illegal drug, or selling two ounces (Schlosser, 1998; Walker, 1998). The Rockefeller Drug Laws had the effects of jamming New York's court system (due to an initial ban on plea bargaining), with little appreciable impact on drug usage. Nonetheless, other states and the federal government followed New York's example; in the subsequent decade, 48 states imposed some form of mandatory minimum sentences for drug violations (Kohler-Hausmann, 2010). In addition, more incarceration for drug offenses helped prompt more prison construction. In the wake of the Rockefeller Drug Laws, New York engaged in a wave of prison building in the 1980s and 1990s in rural areas upstate. Hit hard by long-term economic transformations, these upstate communities welcomed the new prison construction because they expected the prisons to bring investment, infrastructure development, and jobs (Donziger, 1998; Schlosser, 1998).

In the 1980s, the drug war continued to expand but with a new focus: cocaine. Three major factors helped direct attention to cocaine. First, powerful and violent international trafficking organizations attracted a great deal of notoriety, especially as related problems like drug killings and money laundering spilled over into ports of entry in the United States. Second, a series of celebrity deaths from cocaine use attracted public attention to the drug. In 1982, comedian John Belushi died from an overdose of cocaine and heroin. More shockingly, in 1986, two young athletes—Len Bias, a basketball player from the University of Maryland who had been drafted by the Boston Celtics and Don Rogers, a football player for the Cleveland Browns—both died separately but in rapid succession from cocaine overdoses. Third, a new, much more affordable, form of cocaine called crack became available in the early 1980s. Unlike the traditional powdered form of cocaine, crack was processed into a crystalline rock that could be smoked in a pipe and deliver a powerful high. Crack's affordability made it accessible to people of limited means. The drug was disproportionately used by African Americans in big cities, spreading outward from New York City and Los Angeles and quickly became associated with inner city violence and poverty. By 1986, crack became the target of intense media attention; both *Time* and *Newsweek* ran cover stories on crack and the CBS and NBC television networks ran prime time news investigations (Jonnes, 1999; Reinarman & Levine, 1997).

Seizing upon growing antidrug sentiment, in the late 1980s the federal government aggressively expanded its role in fighting illegal drugs. President Ronald Reagan embraced his wife Nancy's campaign to encourage young people to "just say no" to drugs. He stated at a 1986 press conference, "Starting today, Nancy's crusade to deprive drug peddlers and suppliers of their customers becomes America's crusade" (quoted in Jonnes, 1999, p. 399). In response, Congress enacted the Anti-Drug Abuse Act of 1986, expanding funding for both drug enforcement and drug treatment. The 1986 law also introduced stiff mandatory minimum sentences for drug possession and, in particular, created penalties for possession of crack cocaine far more severe than penalties for the same quantity of powdered cocaine. A second Anti-Drug Act, passed in 1988, doubled federal funding for drug enforcement and mandated the appointment of a Cabinet-level drug czar to coordinate federal drug control efforts. Reagan's successor, George H. W. Bush, continued the war on drugs. In September 1989, he addressed the nation about the ongoing problem of drug abuse, claiming that crack was so common that it could be purchased in Lafayette Park across the street from the White House. In many ways, Bush's antidrug strategy represented a new gloss on existing efforts, promising more intensive street-level policing, increased cooperation between different law enforcement agencies, tougher sentencing, and greater antidrug education (Gest, 2001; Jonnes, 1999; Walker, 1994).

Much of the public attention on drugs in the 1980s and early 1990s focused on crack. Media reports characterized it as highly addictive and widespread, using metaphors like "plague," "epidemic," and "flooding America" to describe its impact. However, while crack certainly devastated many neighborhoods and lives, official statistics do not support this image of a national epidemic. National Institute on Drug Abuse surveys showed a downward trend in both overall drug use and cocaine use between 1986 and 1993. Specific surveys indicate that, at the height of crack use in 1986, about 4% of high school seniors tried crack in the previous year. In 1992, only about 3% of adults ages 18 to 34 had ever used crack, and only 0.4% had used it in the past month. Critics such as Craig Reinarman and Harry G. Levine (1997) use these data to argue that the crack epidemic was overstated. Instead, they suggest that the federal government's campaign against drugs—particularly crack—emerged out of an effort to gain political advantage by taking measures deemed tough on crime.

The war on drugs has had a disproportionate impact on minority groups. While most studies showed that roughly the same percentages of white people and African Americans used drugs in the 1980s, African American arrest rates, conviction rates, and incarceration rates for drug offenses were far higher than those for whites (Alexander, 2010; Donziger, 1996). Social structures may have made it easier for law enforcement officers to target African American drug use. While most drug use among white people took place behind closed doors, the fact that much drug dealing in urban, disproportionately African American neighborhoods took place in public generated complaints and allowed police to more easily identify perpetrators (Mauer, 2006). A typical tactic was the New York City Police Department (NYPD)'s Operation Pressure Point beginning in 1984, in which the NYPD flooded police officers into an open-air drug market in order to make arrests and scare off dealers and buyers. In addition, the federal sentencing disparities for crack cocaine—more often used by African Americans—versus powdered cocaine—more often used by white people—also contributed to more African Americans serving longer terms in prison (Donziger, 1996; Walker, 1998). The war on drugs not only expanded the justice system, it also contributed toward the justice system disproportionately targeting African Americans and members of other minority groups.

Victim's Rights and Women's Rights

Two other related trends of the latter third of the twentieth century—the movements for victims' rights and women's rights—affected the criminal justice system in complex ways. On the one hand, they expanded the social services provided by the justice system, forcing law enforcement and the courts to become more professional and more responsive to the communities they served. On the other hand, they also contributed to increasingly punitive responses to crime.

Concerns about crime victimization emerged alongside the publication of the first real data about it in the late 1960s. The Johnson administration's Crime Commission conducted pilot studies using surveys of victims to determine the actual extent of crime. These eventually led to the launch of the National Crime Victimization Survey (NCVS) in 1973. Also in the early 1970s, the Law Enforcement Assistance Administration (LEAA), facing criticism for funneling an excessive share of its resources to law enforcement, began funding programs to help compensate victims and protect witnesses of crime. A series of

LEAA-funded training and educational conferences for social service providers coalesced into the National Organization for Victim Assistance (NOVA) in 1975. An umbrella organization for various local victims' assistance groups and programs, NOVA became an advocate for increased federal support for victims' services (Gottschalk, 2006).

The intersection of victims' rights and fear of crime provided momentum for both. The impact of real increases in crime in the 1970s was compounded by extensive coverage in the news media and in television and film dramas. Local television news programs routinely began their broadcasts with crime stories, and one survey found that one-third of all stories on 100 local news programs dealt with crime-related issues (Donziger, 1996; Pratt, 2009). Tragedies such as the 1981 kidnapping and murder of 6-year-old Adam Walsh in Florida also contributed to concerns about victimization. Following Adam Walsh's death, his father, John Walsh, helped organize a national movement to draw attention to the problem of child kidnapping. Walsh became the host of the television show *America's Most Wanted*, dedicated to publicizing and apprehending fugitives. In 1984, Walsh also cofounded the National Center for Missing and Exploited Children with funding from the federal government. Established in frustration over the limited ability of local law enforcement to deal with the horror of a lost child, the resulting group helped organize resources and pass laws to facilitate children's recovery (Donziger, 1996).

In the 1980s, the federal government embraced the cause of victims' rights. In 1981, the Reagan administration announced National Victims' Rights Week to draw attention to the issue. In 1982, Congress enacted the Victim Witness Protection Act, which allowed restitution for victims and statements of how crimes had impacted victims in federal cases. In 1984, Congress passed the Victims of Crime Act, which established a fund for victims' compensation and for child abuse prevention and treatment. Subsequent laws in 1990 and 1994 gave victims further rights to participate in the sentencing phases of trials and expanded funding for restitution and victims' services. States also embraced victims' rights. In 1979, Wisconsin established the first bill of rights for victims. In 1982, California became the first state to amend its constitution to recognize victims' rights. By the end of the 1980s, 44 states had victim compensation programs (Gottschalk, 2006; Walker, 1994).

Evaluations of the impact of victims' rights vary. On the one hand, most commentators acknowledge that providing social services and restitution for victims is a positive step. Providing these services may not do much to reduce crime, but it validates victims' experiences and helps them move on. Protecting victims from intimidation also makes them more likely to testify as witnesses in criminal trials and thereby smooths the operations of the court system. On the other hand, many proposals to defend victims' rights rely on limiting the rights of defendants. The rhetoric of victims' rights seems constructed in contrast to the rights of the accused already in the Constitution. Moreover, incorporating victim impact statements into sentencing—which became common in the 1990s—helped re-introduce elements of retribution into court decisions (Gottschalk, 2006; Walker, 1994). The harshest views of the victims' rights movement suggest that it contributed directly to the expansion of a penal state in the 1980s and 1990s. As Marie Gottschalk (2006) writes, the victims' rights movement "was remarkably in sync with the ascendant conservative forces and relatively immune from critical examination" (p. 114).

In a parallel manner, elements of the women's movement also acted in ways that supported a more punitive approach to criminal justice. In the 1970s, as women's groups established rape crisis centers to provide social services for sexual assault victims, they turned to the LEAA and other public funding for financing. In so doing, they gradually emphasized a law enforcement response to rape, rather than advocating a more fundamental challenge to gender relations. For example, in the 1970s and 1980s, a group of Los Angeles area rape crisis centers expanded their facilities and offered a wider array of social and mental health services—particularly for African American and Hispanic women—due to funding from California's Office of Criminal Justice Planning (OCJP), initially channeling grants from the LEAA. In so doing, they developed closer ties to law enforcement. As the first director of the OCJP's Sexual Assault Program explained, "I was always trying to think of new angles to get money. . . . So I came up with this idea, well, let's look at it in terms of high crime area and minority representation, and mainly with Republicans you talk high crime" (Gottschalk, 2006, p. 128). Similarly, advocacy to enact rape shield laws—laws that limited the admissibility of evidence about the character and sexual history of victims—also entailed alliances between antirape activists and law and order advocates. Many of the changes in rape laws that passed in the 1970s and 1980s were parts of larger anticrime measures (Gottschalk, 2006).

Likewise the movement against domestic violence also converged with the shift toward law and order. Police had traditionally regarded violence against women by spouses and domestic partners as a low priority, one that they often sought to resolve with personal intervention rather than arrest. The emergence of the modern feminist movement in the 1960s and 1970s, however, focused new attention on the problem and fostered activists specifically concerned with protecting battered women. As with the antirape movement, in the 1970s the battered women's movement also turned to the LEAA and other public agencies for funding to open and expand shelters for victims of domestic abuse. This funding, however, came with the string attached that the shelters had to work closely with the police and the criminal justice system to help ensure prosecution of batterers. In addition, a series of lawsuits filed by and on behalf of battered women in New York City, Oakland, and Connecticut changed how law enforcement agencies dealt with domestic violence incidents. The 1984 Connecticut decision *Thurman v. City of Torrington* required a local police department to pay the plaintiff $2.6 million for violating her civil rights by failing to protect her from her husband's abuse. These cases led cities and states across the country to adopt policies requiring police to arrest all suspects in felonious domestic assaults. These changes mandated that police and courts take violence against women seriously and respond to it professionally. At the same time, these changes also reinforced a public perception that arrest and prosecution represented the best solution to social problems. Critics argue that, in this way, the women's movement had the unintended effect of contributing to the government reliance on an expanding criminal justice system (Gottschalk, 2006; Walker, 1998).

❖ CHANGES IN CRIMINAL JUSTICE

How did the day-to-day operations of criminal justice change in the era of mass incarceration? It is a complicated story. On the one hand, plenty of evidence indicates shifts toward tougher crime control. On the other hand, the criminal justice system utilized a wide variety of mechanisms for controlling crime. While some relied on arrest, incarceration, and an embrace of retribution, others included innovative attempts at crime prevention and community development. In this text, we consider three distinct areas of change: juvenile justice, the death penalty, and policing.

Juvenile Crime and Juvenile Justice

In the last three decades of the twentieth century, juvenile crime and violence received increased public attention. Two major headlines dominated the period. First, the news media picked up on occasional examples of teenagers who committed acts of outrageous and unexpected violence. Stories of school shootings, gang conflict, and casual homicide all blended together to suggest that a portion of America's youth was becoming increasingly dangerous. Second, the media also highlighted the story of how political leaders responded to juvenile violence by changing state laws so that these most extreme young offenders would be tried under adult criminal laws and punished in adult institutions. Reading deeper, however, the full story also includes efforts by the juvenile justice system to find flexible ways to deal with a large and varied population.

The rate of arrests of individuals ages 10 to 17 increased steadily between 1970 and 1998. This does not necessarily mean that the amount of crime committed by this age group increased, however. Arrest rates are an indirect measure of crime that may indicate as much about police decisions, policies, and practices as about actual offending. Arrest rates nonetheless remain the most common measure of crimes by juveniles because arrest data provides reliable information about perpetrators' ages. Even with the apparent increase in juvenile crime, offenses by juveniles remained a limited portion of total crime. In 1998, arrests of people ages 10 to 17 accounted for less than 18% of arrests for the eight serious index crimes tracked by the FBI. The reality of juvenile crime is that violent attention-grabbing cases are least common. In 1998, about 4% of juvenile arrests were for violent index crimes, whereas about 23% were for property index crimes and about 73% were for nonindex crimes. That said, all measures—arrest data as well as victim surveys and self-reporting surveys—indicate that violent crimes by people ages 10 to 17 increased markedly in the late 1980s and early 1990s before decreasing just as sharply in the middle and late 1990s. This peak for juvenile violence was particularly evident in arrests for homicide and aggravated assault, and it was particularly concentrated among African American males, whose homicide rate was three times higher than that of white males. It was also geographically concentrated in large urban areas. One-third of homicides committed by juveniles in 1995 took place in just 10 urban counties containing cities such as Los Angeles, Chicago, Houston, Detroit, New York City, Dallas, St. Louis, and Philadelphia (Cook and Laub 1998; National Research Council 2001; Sickmund, Snyder, & Poe-Yamagata, 1997).

The overall juvenile justice system had to deal with the complicated totality of juvenile offenses. A tremendous amount of research went into the factors contributing to juvenile crime, and resulted in the development of detailed prevention plans. In 1993, for example, the federal government's Office of Juvenile Justice and Delinquency Prevention released a *Comprehensive Strategy for Serious Violent and Chronic Juvenile Offenders*. This proposal emphasized not so much policing, courts, and corrections but the ways that other social institutions could prevent crime. As examples, families could be given resources to support children, high schools could adopt mediation programs, communities could build prevention efforts, and schools and law enforcement could intervene at the first signs of trouble such as truancy or shoplifting. Although programs like these were only erratically implemented and received only limited federal funding, they nonetheless represented approaches to reducing juvenile crime that extended beyond simply enforcing the law (Donziger, 1996; Gest, 2001).

Even when police and law enforcement did become involved, formal adjudication was rarely the first option. One study from the 1990s found that only about 13% of encounters between police and juveniles ended with an arrest. If police did arrest a juvenile, however, they appeared to be more likely to handle them through a formal disposition process than in earlier decades. About 69% of juveniles taken into custody in 1998 were adjudicated in juvenile courts, and another 7% were tried in adult criminal courts. Of the young people adjudicated delinquent in juvenile courts nationwide in the 1990s, about half were put on probation, as were about one-fifth of those nonadjudicated, or found not guilty. About 18% of juvenile cases resulted in some form of institutionalization. While these figures were quite similar to those for boys processed through the Cook County Juvenile Court between 1899 and 1909 (see Chapter 3), what changed over the twentieth century was the proliferation of services and graduated institutions for young offenders. Probation in the late twentieth century involved much more intensive support and supervision than earlier; institutions became differentiated not only by the security level but by the types of educational, mental health, and drug treatment services they provided (National Research Council, 2001).

The operations of the juvenile justice system produced striking racial disparities. African American youth represented 15% of the U.S. population ages 10 to 17 in 1997, but they represented 26% of arrests of that age group, 30% of delinquency cases in juvenile court, and 40% of juveniles in long-term public institutions. The question arises whether African American youth were responsible for more delinquency or whether they were disproportionately targeted by the juvenile justice system. The answer is probably some of each. On the one hand, detailed analysis of all relevant data suggests that African American youth were more likely than white youth to commit certain offenses such as aggravated assault and robbery. On the other hand, studies of criminal justice operations show that, although race played a minimal role in decisions whether to make arrests, police departments tended to concentrate patrols in lower-income and minority neighborhoods, leading to more encounters with minority youth. Also some studies suggest that race may have played some role in juvenile court outcomes (National Research Council, 2001). In this context, William Ayers' (1997) first-person account of the Cook County (Chicago) Juvenile Court paints a typical picture in which inner city African American youth have committed crimes and have been funneled into a large impersonal judicial system that offers relatively little hope for change.

Juvenile crime also gained renewed public and political attention in the 1990s. In the wake of the youth violence in the late 1980s and early 1990s, at least 47 states and the District of Columbia modified their laws, either making it easier to transfer juveniles into criminal courts or modifying sentencing provisions (National Research Council, 2001). Prosecutors and politicians claimed that juvenile courts were not built to handle the kinds of crime juveniles had come to commit. Carolea Goldfarb of the Brooklyn District Attorney's office, for example, argued in 1994 that "These [juvenile] laws were drafted at a time when kids were throwing spitballs. . . . Now they're committing murders" (quoted in Tanenhaus & Drizen, 2002, p. 641). In response, states modified their laws to deal with the perceived threat. Newly elected Pennsylvania Governor Tom Ridge declared in 1995, "if you commit an adult crime in Pennsylvania, you will do adult time" (quoted in Leete, 1996, p. 493). Prior to the 1990s, states had most typically used a process called judicial waiver—in which judges had the option to transfer juvenile offenders into criminal courts—to change venues if circumstances warranted. In response to high-profile juvenile violence cases, however, states created a second set of mechanisms called automatic transfer or legislative waiver laws, in which young people accused of certain crimes would automatically have their cases heard in criminal courts. New York passed the first of these laws in 1978 following a double homicide by a 15-year-old named Willie Bosket. At Ridge's direction, Pennsylvania also passed a rigid automatic transfer law in 1995, requiring that anyone age 14 or older accused of one of eight serious offenses have their case tried in criminal courts. Other states—led by Florida, which passed one of the first such laws in 1981—gave prosecutors rather than judges the option to file cases against juveniles in criminal court. Still other states such as Texas created blended sentencing laws, in which juveniles could be subjected to determinate sentences that began in juvenile institutions and then continued in adult facilities after the youths turned 18 (National Research Council, 2001; Tanenhaus & Drizen, 2002).

The consequences of increased transfer of juveniles to adult courts—and from there to adult prisons and jails—are still being studied. The absolute numbers of juveniles involved remain relatively modest. That said, the number of juveniles committed to adult prisons and jails increased sharply from roughly 5,000 in 1985 to roughly 17,000 in 1997 before decreasing again in the 2000s. Moreover, minorities were dramatically overrepresented; of the approximately 7,400 juveniles committed to state prisons in 1997, 58% were African American (Austin, Johnson, & Gregoriou, 2000; Redding, 2008). Although the majority of juveniles who fell under transfer laws were 16 and 17, the laws often applied to children as young as 10 and 12. In many cases, the new transfer laws left few options for judges and juries. For example, in Florida in 1999, after a 6-year-old girl died while roughhousing with 12-year-old Lionel Tate, prosecutors transferred him to criminal court. Tate's family rejected a plea bargain, and he was convicted of first-degree murder. Under the law, the court had no choice except to sentence the 12-year-old to life in prison (Tanenhaus & Drizen, 2002). The research to date suggests that juvenile transfer laws have not been an especially significant factor in the decline of juvenile crime. Most studies have seen little general deterrence effect, in which the new laws prevented potential offenders from committing crimes. Juveniles convicted under the transfer laws also had higher rates of recidivism than young people adjudicated in the juvenile system and greater likelihoods of re-arrest (Bishop & Frazier, 2000; Redding, 2008).

Case Studies in Criminal Justice: Willie Bosket, Criminal Offender

Prison authorities considered Willie Bosket (born 1962) the most violent criminal in New York State history. At age 15, he shot and killed two men on the New York City subway. At this point, he already had a long criminal history. He had been institutionalized in a state reform school for the first time at age nine and spent the next several years in and out of various institutions. At the time he committed the subway killings, he was assigned to a New York Division of Youth halfway house but one that was only two blocks from his home in Harlem. Able to roam freely, he spent the summer of 1978 riding the subways and looking for drunks to rob. He admitted to committing over 200 robberies and stabbing at least 25 victims prior to the two killings. Convicted of the crimes, he was sentenced to the maximum possible sentence, but under New York law at the time, that was only five years in a state training school. Public outrage over his relatively light sentence led New York Governor Hugh Carey to push the state legislature to pass a new automatic transfer law, allowing juveniles as young as 13 to be tried for murder in criminal court. Upon his release, Bosket initially tried to stay out of trouble but was repeatedly arrested for minor neighborhood disputes. Back in prison in his twenties and facing increasingly long sentences, Bosket consciously decided to become the most dangerous prisoner he could be. He repeatedly set fires to his cells and attacked guards, nearly killing at least one, and eventually earned a series of consecutive life sentences under New York's habitual offender law (Butterfield, 1995).

Bosket is exceptional in many ways. His story is extremely well documented, having been studied in depth by *New York Times* reporter Fox Butterfield in his 1995 book *All God's Children*. In addition to his extraordinary violence, Bosket is also—according to reports—extremely intelligent, able to act effectively as his own attorney in later criminal trials. At least as he presents himself, Bosket is very thoughtful about his violence; he proclaims somewhat facetiously, "I am only a monster created by the system" (Butterfield, 1995, p. xv).

At the same time, Bosket also exemplified many trends that surrounded violence in late twentieth century. An African American, he grew up poor and in a single-parent home in New York City's Harlem neighborhood in the 1970s. As a child, he never knew his father, who was himself in prison for a double murder. Bosket also inherited a tradition of violence. His great grandfather had been a notorious brawler and criminal in Edgefield County, South Carolina in the early twentieth century, emerging from a tradition in which both white and African American men used violence to defend their reputations. With the Great Migration of whites and African Americans to the North in the middle of the twentieth century, this tradition seems to have migrated as well; accounts of modern urban violence emphasize conflicts over status in the eyes of others. As a boy, Willie Bosket also was a victim of sexual abuse by his grandfather and, by age eight, became a victimizer, taking purses from women on the streets, stealing cars, and setting fires. In addition, Bosket believed himself to be a victim of New York's juvenile justice system, which failed to provide either consistent supervision or services for him. His few male role models tended to be older men loosely involved with violent and criminal subcultures; these included his idealized image of his father. Of course none of this excuses Bosket's crimes, but it does highlight the ways in which multiple risk factors came together to contribute to his violence. Finally, the understandable outcry over the killings Bosket committed helps explain why New York and so many other states changed their laws so that they could treat juvenile offenders more like adult criminals.

The Return of the Death Penalty

Given the tone of the times, it is not surprising that the death penalty made a comeback in the final three decades of the twentieth century. Yet the way that it did so was very much a result of particular historical circumstances. As discussed in Chapter 7, the use of the death penalty had been in long-term decline since the Second World War, and had been effectively banned in the Supreme Court's 1972 decision *Furman v. Georgia* (see Figure 9.2). The symbolism of this decision, however, provoked a furious reaction among both the public and politicians. Within a day of the announcement, legislators in five states proposed new bills to reestablish the death penalty, and President Richard Nixon asked the FBI to find evidence that the death penalty was necessary. The specifics of the Supreme Court's decision in *Furman* almost provided a roadmap for states to reestablish it. The Court had not found the death penalty unconstitutional on principle; instead it had found the application of the death penalty unconstitutional because it was so grounded in discretion and local variation as to be almost random. In response, state legislatures crafted laws designed to eliminate that randomness. Some states simply declared that death would be mandated for all first-degree murder convictions. More typically, states borrowed a page from the Model Penal Code, a set of suggestions drafted by leading lawyers in the 1960s and separated the sentencing phase of a murder trial from the trial itself. The sentencing would consider both aggravating and mitigating circumstances, and the jury could select an appropriate penalty. On this basis, 35 states and the federal government passed new death penalty laws between 1972 and 1976, and courts immediately began handing down more death sentences than they had in decades (Banner, 2002; Oshinsky, 2010).

Actual executions, however, required the Supreme Court's blessing. In 1976, the Court took up a set of five death penalty cases under the collective title of *Gregg v. Georgia*. In these cases, opponents of the death penalty found that their earlier focus on the randomness of executions and on evolving community standards had boxed them into a legal corner. Death penalty proponents focused on the more directed guidelines of the new laws (undercutting the randomness argument) and the fact that public opinion favored the death penalty (contradicting the notion that community standards had rejected it). The Supreme Court ruled that using aggravating circumstances to guide the sentencing decisions of juries was constitutional (although mandatory death sentences were not) and allowed executions to resume (Banner, 2002; Gottschalk, 2006; Oshinsky, 2010). At the postmoratorium peak, 38

Figure 9.2 Executions under civil authority in the United States, 1930-2010

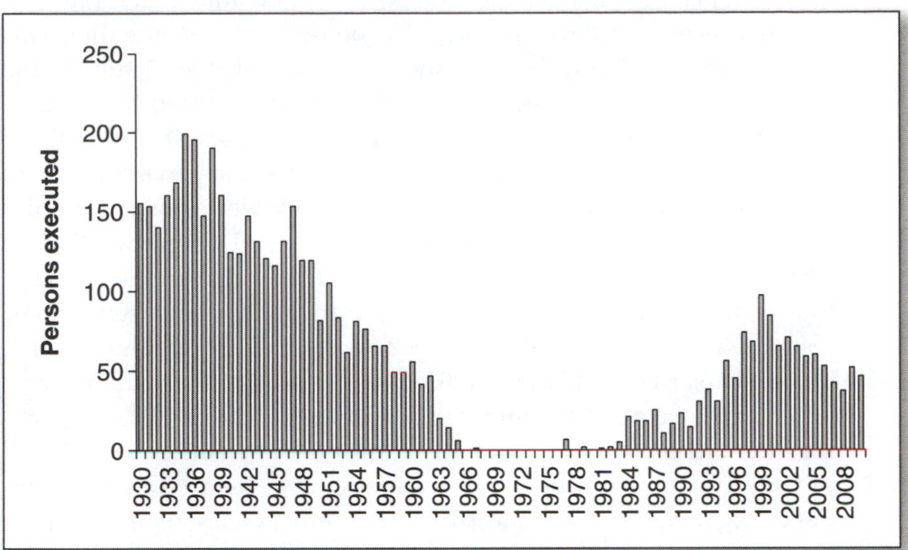

states and the federal government had a death penalty; they carried out a high of 98 executions in 1999 and had nearly 3,600 people under sentence of death in 2000 (Snell, 2001).

After the 1976 end of the moratorium on executions, the death penalty increasingly served a symbolic role of enacting retribution. Why the death penalty enjoyed widespread popular support is somewhat tricky to explain. On the one hand, polls showed that between 1977 and 1998, at least two-thirds of Americans typically favored the death penalty in cases of murder. On the other hand, the death penalty actually applied to only a tiny percentage of criminal cases and affected only a very few people directly. In addition, research in the 1970s and 1980s demonstrated fairly conclusively that one of the traditional justifications for having a death penalty—deterrence, or preventing other people from committing the same offense as people being executed—had very little basis in fact. Researchers found almost no causal relationship between the death penalty and crime (Banner, 2002; Walker, 1994). Moreover, since the death penalty was increasingly carried out by lethal injection behind prison walls before very small audiences, it further lost the deterrent function that might have been achieved by the public executions of the eighteenth century (Banner, 2002).

All this being the case, the increasingly important symbolic function of retribution helps explain the enduring American support for the death penalty. With the introduction of aggravating and mitigating circumstances into death penalty decisions, increased attention was focused on both the defendant and, in particular, the victim. In the 1991 case *Payne v. Tennessee*, the Supreme Court opened the door to considering the impacts of crime on victims. As a result, a number of states introduced victim impact statements into the penalty phase of cases. This focus on the victim made sentencing decisions much more about exacting retribution. In addition, the federal government in the 1990s dramatically expanded the number of federal offenses subject to the death penalty, allowing political leaders to demonstrate their responsiveness to crime (Banner, 2002; Gottschalk, 2006). The criminal justice scholar David Garland (2007) suggested that the death penalty functions like a negative mirror image of the earlier practice of lynching. Modern capital punishment is almost the opposite of lynching in its thorough bureaucratic regulation, fastidious attention to the defendant's legal rights, and concern to carry out executions in the most humane ways possible. Yet capital punishment still has many characteristics in common with lynching in that it is shaped by politics, is determined by ordinary people on juries, gives special considerations to victims, and reflects popular passions that extraordinary punishments should be the response to crimes considered particularly egregious.

Since the late 1990s, support for and the use of capital punishment dropped somewhat. This was less due to changing moral standards or concerns about uneven application than due to increased worries about mistakenly executing innocent people. Between 1987 and 1999, 61 people on death row were discovered to have been wrongly convicted, and in the 2000s the expansion of DNA testing helped exonerate even more (Banner, 2002; Mauer, 2006). In this context, states slowed the pace of carrying out the death penalty; the total number of actual executions dropped from 98 in 1999 to a low of 37 in 2008 (Maguire, 2012, table 6.79.2011). In addition, while the Supreme Court did not question capital punishment in principle, it increasingly narrowed the populations to whom it could be applied. In 2005, for example, the Supreme Court ruled in *Roper v. Simmons* that imposing the death penalty on persons under the age of 18 at the time of their crimes constituted cruel and unusual punishment, effectively banning executions of juveniles (Snell, 2006). Still, while capital punishment became an even more limited element of criminal justice, it remained symbolically important.

Changes in Policing

In the last three decades of the twentieth century, police developed new approaches to their jobs derived from both greater professionalism and greater demands to aggressively fight crime. Police departments took advantage of the availability of funding for professional training of officers. They also took advantage of the growth of criminal justice as a scholarly discipline to hire more officers with some college education. In addition, initially as a result of external pressure, police departments became more diverse, hiring more African Americans and women. The urban crisis of the 1960s focused public attention on the disparity between largely white police forces and African American urban populations. A series of lawsuits in the early 1970s broke down some of the barriers in police hiring processes that had tended to discriminate against African Americans. These changes helped lead to a gradual increase in the number of African American police, and police forces came closer to representing the diversity of the population. In Atlanta for example, African Americans increased from roughly 30% of the police force in 1975 to 47% in 1985. In addition, the 1972 amendment of the Civil Rights Act of 1964 extended legal protections to public employees and banned job discrimination on the basis of sex. As a result, more women were able to work as police. Equally importantly, they broke out of the traditional female roles of doing clerical work and dealing with juveniles and became full-fledged patrol officers (Dulaney, 1996; Fogelson, 1977; Wadman & Allison, 2004).

Despite these changes, many departments faced growing challenges in the 1970s as Americans lost some degree of confidence in their police. In 1970, NYPD officer Frank Serpico took allegations of widespread corruption to the *New York Times*, claiming that many of his fellow officers accepted bribes or protection money. A subsequent investigation by a citizens' commission chaired by attorney William Knapp largely substantiated these charges, finding that more than half of the city's officers took gratuities from citizens or, in fewer cases, overtly looked for financial gain. Large-scale resignations from the NYPD and a 1973 motion picture *Serpico* further brought these police corruption scandals to public attention. In the 1970s, crime victimization surveys also revealed that fewer than half of all offenses were actually reported to the police. While victims offered many reasons for this reluctance, one prominent one was that they had little confidence that reporting crimes would do much good. Finally in the 1970s the cost of policing increased dramatically. Not only did police departments hire more officers to cope with the increase in crime, they also invested in new equipment and raised salaries and benefits in an effort to attract more qualified officers. In the context of more crime and less public faith in law enforcement, however, urban police departments seemed to be costing more and delivering less (Fogelson, 1977; Roth, 2005).

In the 1980s, urban police began to engage in two major initiatives to help address their challenges. First, community policing involved integrating officers in neighborhoods and seeking to develop positive relationships between police and community members. Second, aggressive policing of offenses that affected the quality of life—sometimes called a zero tolerance approach—involved vigorous enforcement of ordinances affecting everyday behavior. Although often assessed in common, the two initiatives are better viewed as being distinct, or as two sides of the same coin. Both can be linked back to ideas popularized in a 1982 article in *The Atlantic Monthly* by George L. Kelling and James Q. Wilson called "Broken Windows" (see also Kelling & Coles, 1997). In the article, Kelling and Wilson argue that perceptions of public safety and orderliness matter tremendously in determining whether a neighborhood really will be safe and orderly. Public perceptions of safety increase when police visibly walk beats and enforce informal neighborhood rules, even if these rules have little to do with crime control. By contrast, Kelling and Wilson (1982) also argue that if the public perceives an area as unsafe or disorderly, it is likely to see an increase in crime. "Social psychologists and police officers tend to agree," they assert, "that if a window in a building is broken and left unrepaired, all the rest of the windows will soon be broken. . . . [O]ne unrepaired broken window is a signal that no one cares, and so breaking more windows costs nothing" (p. 31). Likewise untended misbehavior also leads to the breakdown of community controls that restrain crime. As solutions, Kelling and Wilson propose having more beat cops walk the streets and coordinating police efforts with citizen patrols and communities engaged in crime prevention.

Community-oriented policing had some success in reducing crime. As early as the 1970s, the Santa Ana, California, police worked closely with neighborhood groups and used affirmative action programs to recruit a more diverse workforce. In the process, they improved community relations and restrained increases in crime. In the 1980s, the Detroit police responded to rampant crime and the nation's highest murder rate by coordinating community-based "self-defense" programs. While maintaining traditional reactive policing, they also opened ministations across the city that citizens could walk into and report crime. In addition, they assigned roving officers to coordinate neighborhood crime prevention efforts. Although crime rates continued to increase in Detroit, the program nonetheless helped people feel safer in their neighborhoods (Wadman & Allison, 2004). Elsewhere community-oriented policing had more concrete results. San Diego police chief Jerry Sanders credited a 68% drop in burglary between 1980 and 1996 to community policing efforts such as volunteer neighborhood patrols (Roth, 2005, p. 318–319).

The zero tolerance model of "broken windows policing" was most directly implemented by the NYPD in the 1990s under Mayor Rudolph Giuliani and police commissioner William Bratton. The NYPD aggressively arrested people for offenses such as public drinking and urination, panhandling, street peddling, and subway turnstile jumping. Making arrests on these charges improved the quality of urban life and sent a message that the streets were safer. It also had the added benefit of allowing the police to apprehend some offenders carrying weapons or drugs or already wanted on outstanding warrants. In addition, the NYPD used computer tracking to map crime statistics down to particular city blocks and to identify targets for mobile plainclothes officers to make sweeps. Giuliani and the NYPD credited this new approach with not only making New York City more livable for middle- and upper-class residents but also with contributing significantly to the sharp drop in the city's homicide rate in the 1990s (Johnson, 2003; Mauer, 2006).

Critics, however, question how much credit broken windows policing should be given. Inquiries into the effectiveness of increased patrol activity in reducing crime date back at least to the Kansas City Preventive Patrol Experiment in 1972 and 1973, which compared beats receiving more police patrols than usual against those receiving no regular patrols. The conclusion was that patrol activity had no measurable impact on either the amount of crime or public perceptions of safety (Walker, 1994). In addition, the drop in New York City's homicide rate in the 1990s paralleled what was happening in other cities that did not implement broken windows policing and can also be explained by other factors such as an increased number of police, a decrease in the number of young males, positive economic conditions, and changes in markets for illegal drugs. Broken windows policing might be understood as a milder alternative to the mass incarceration pervasive in the late twentieth century. To the extent broken windows policing succeeded, a key element in its success was in establishing a justification for stopping and frisking potential criminal suspects and a criteria for removing those deemed disorderly from the streets (Harcourt, 2001; Mauer, 2006).

Police administrators in New York City and elsewhere also struggled with the persistent problem of police violence. On the one hand, beginning in the 1970s, the NYPD worked to restrict the use of deadly force. It created an internal review board to investigate each instance where police officers fired their weapons, enforcing a rule that restricted use of deadly force to defense of life or apprehension of violent felons. The number of civilian deaths from police shootings dropped precipitously in the 1970s and 1980s, as did the number of shootings of police officers. Police departments across the country gradually developed a consensus that deadly force was only appropriate to defend life. When the U.S. Supreme Court declared shooting fleeing felons unconstitutional in its 1985 ruling *Tennessee v. Garner*, the decision did little more than codify existing practice. That said, controversies over police use of violence—both shootings and other more routine forms of brutality—persisted in the 1970s and 1980s. Critics further argued that, in the 1990s, police used zero tolerance tactics to target poor and minority populations, making them more likely to become victims of police abuse (Johnson, 2003; Walker, 1998).

While police violence was probably far less common in the 1990s than it had been decades earlier, the instances of it received far more attention and highlighted enduring problems within policing. In March 1991, officers from the Los Angeles Police Department (LAPD) severely beat Rodney King, an African American, after pulling him over in his automobile following a high-speed chase. Unbeknownst to the police officers, an eyewitness recorded the beating on videotape. The subsequent scandal generated nationwide attention on the issue of police violence, and the eventual acquittal of the four police officers most responsible for the beating—all of whom were white—led to five days of rioting in May 1992 protesting the verdict. The King beating, investigations revealed, was not an isolated incident. Instead, in spite of the increased professionalization of police forces, brutality persisted, often implicitly sanctioned by the larger police culture. The Christopher Commission looking into the King beating—named for its chair, attorney Warren Christopher—found that a quarter of LAPD officers believed that brutality was common and that racial prejudice was a contributing factor. Testimony before the Christopher Commission suggested that this mentality emerged from the hardnosed proactive policing introduced in the 1950s, in which police aggressively sought to stop crime regardless of the constraints imposed by the law. Another investigation conducted by the National Association for the Advancement of Colored People (NAACP) found comparable practices and mindsets in cities across the country. The King incident also illustrates the cost of violence and brutality to police departments. In addition to literally paying the expenses involved with officers' defenses and settlements against them, police departments also paid in terms of lost support within their communities. Repeated investigations found African Americans disproportionately to be victims of police abuse; at the same time, when polled, African Americans were far more likely than whites to indicate their distrust of the police (Donziger, 1996; Skolnick & Fyfe, 1993).

❖ CONCLUSION

When future historians look back on the late twentieth century, they will likely regard the massive expansion of the criminal justice system in general and of incarceration in particular as among the most important developments of the era. It is not likely, however, that they will regard this change as one that caused a reduction of crime. Roughly speaking, rates of offending remained steady or increased between 1970 and 1994, and then decreased. The timing of the drop does not suggest that prisons caused it, coming 20 years after the rise of mass incarceration. In addition, most studies have found that the expansion of prisons and of criminal justice had very little effect on the incidence of offending. Instead historians may focus on the high social costs of mass incarceration: disproportionate minority confinement, greater instability and inequality in communities where large shares of young adults have been removed, and increased difficulties in individuals' lives (Gottschalk, 2006; Mauer, 2006; Pratt, 2009; Thompson, 2010).

Rather than thinking about late twentieth century criminal justice in terms of impacts, it is more easily understood in terms of continuities and changes. Many of the continuities are so obvious that they are hard to see. Communities continued to rely on police responding to crimes, courts prosecuting them, and prisons housing convicts. Poorer people and racial minorities remained disproportionately perpetrators of crimes, victims of offenses, and targets of the criminal justice system. Changes, by contrast, stand out. The long-term trend toward an increasingly national criminal justice system led by the federal government accelerated. The political and intellectual discourse shifted sharply toward an increasingly shared consensus that aggressive law enforcement, prosecution, and punishment were the best means to manage crime. New mechanisms were developed, ranging from mandatory sentencing to legislative waiver of juveniles to criminal courts, to more effectively punish offenders. The institutions of the criminal justice system in 2000 were fundamentally the same as those in 1900, but the scale and the scope of the modern criminal justice system would likely astonish an observer from a century earlier.

❖ REFERENCES

Alexander, M. (2010). *The new Jim Crow: Mass incarceration in the age of colorblindness.* New York, NY: New Press.

Austin, J., Johnson, K. D., & Gregoriou, M. (2000). *Juveniles in adult prisons and jails: A national assessment.* Washington, DC: The Bureau of Justice Assistance.

Ayers, W. (1997). *A kind and just parent: The children of juvenile court.* Boston, MA: Beacon Press.

Banner, S. (2002). *The death penalty: An American history.* Cambridge, MA: Harvard University Press.

Bishop, D. M., & Frazier, C. E. (2000). Consequences of transfer. In J. Fagan & F. E. Zimring (Eds.), *The changing borders of juvenile justice: Transfers of adolescents to the criminal court* (pp. 227–276). Chicago, IL: University of Chicago Press.

Butterfield, F. (1995). *All God's children: The Bosket family and the American tradition of violence.* New York, NY: Knopf.

Bureau of Justice Statistics. (2010). *Homicide Rate 1900–2006.* Retrieved from http://bjs.ojp.usdoj.gov/content/glance/hmrt.cfm

Christianson, S. (1998). *With liberty for some: 500 years of imprisonment in America.* Boston, MA: Northeastern University Press.

Cook, P. J., & Laub, J. H. (1998). The unprecedented epidemic in youth violence. In M. Tonry & M. H. Moore (Eds.), *Crime and justice: An annual review of research* (Vol. 24, pp. 27–64). Chicago, IL: University of Chicago Press.

Donziger, S. A. (1996). *The real war on crime: The report of the National Criminal Justice Commission* (1st ed.). New York, NY: HarperPerennial.

Dulaney, W. M. (1996). *Black police in America.* Bloomington: Indiana University Press.

Eckberg, D. L. (1995). Estimates of early twentieth-century U.S. homicide rates: An econometric forecasting approach. *Demography, 32*, 1–16.

Flamm, M. W. (2005). *Law and order: Street crime, civil unrest, and the crisis of liberalism in the 1960s.* New York, NY: Columbia University Press.

Fogelson, R. M. (1977). *Big-city police.* Cambridge, MA: Harvard University Press.

Garland, D. (2007). The peculiar forms of American capital punishment. *Social Research, 74(2)*, 435–464.

Gest, T. (2001). *Crime & politics: Big government's erratic campaign for law and order.* New York, NY: Oxford University Press.

Goldberg, P. (1980). The federal government's response to illicit drugs, 1969–1978. In Drug Abuse Council (Ed.), *The facts about "drug abuse"*. New York, NY: Free Press.

Gottschalk, M. (2006). *The prison and the gallows: The politics of mass incarceration in America.* New York, NY: Cambridge University Press.

Guerino, P., Harrison, P. M., & Sabol, W. J. (2011). *Prisoners in 2010* (No. NCJ 236096). Bureau of Justice Statistics Bulletin. Washington, DC: Bureau of Justice Statistics.

Harcourt, B. E. (2001). *Illusion of order: The false promise of broken windows policing*. Cambridge, MA: Harvard University Press.

Hughes, K. A. (2006). *Justice expenditure and employment in the United States, 2003* (No. NCJ 212260). Bureau of Justice Statistics Bulletin. Washington, DC: Bureau of Justice Statistics.

Kelling, G. L., & Coles, C. M. (1997). *Fixing broken windows: Restoring order and reducing crime in our communities*. New York, NY: Simon & Schuster.

Kelling, G. L., & Wilson, J. Q. (1982, March). Broken windows: The police and neighborhood safety. *The Atlantic Monthly*, 29–38.

Kohler-Hausmann, J. (2010). "The Attila the Hun law": New York's Rockefeller drug laws and the making of a punitive state. *Journal of Social History, 44(1)*, 71–96.

Johnson, M. S. (2003). *Street justice: A history of police violence in New York City*. Boston, MA: Beacon Press.

Jonnes, J. (1999). *Hep-cats, narcs, and pipe dreams: A history of America's romance with illegal drugs*. Baltimore, MD: Johns Hopkins University Press.

Lane, R. (1997). *Murder in America: A history*. Columbus: Ohio State University Press.

Leete, J. B. (1996). Treatment and rehabilitation or hard time: Is the focus of juvenile justice changing? *Akron Law Review, 29*, 491–508.

Mauer, M. (2006). *Race to Incarcerate* (2nd ed.). New York, NY: New Press.

Maguire, Kathleen, ed. (2012). *Sourcebook of criminal justice statistics* Retrieved from http://www.albany.edu/sourcebook/

National Research Council and Institute of Medicine (2001). *Juvenile crime, juvenile justice. Panel on juvenile crime: Prevention, treatment, and control*. J. McCord, C. Spatz Widom, & Crowell, (eds.). Committee on Law and Justice and Board on Children. Washington, DC: National Academy Press.

Oshinsky, D. M. (2010). *Capital punishment on trial: Furman v. Georgia and the death penalty in modern America*. Lawrence: University Press of Kansas.

Pratt, T. C. (2009). *Addicted to incarceration: Corrections policy and the politics of misinformation in the United States*. Thousand Oaks, CA: SAGE.

Redding, R. E. (2008). *Juvenile transfer laws: An effective deterrent to delinquency?* Washington, DC: Juvenile Justice Bulletin, U.S. Department of Justice Programs, Office of Justice Programs, Office of Juvenile Justice and Delinquency Prevention.

Reinarman, C., & Levine, H. G. (Eds.). (1997). *Crack in America: Demon drugs and social justice*. Berkeley: University of California Press.

Roth, M. P. (2005). *Crime and punishment: A history of the criminal justice system*. Belmont, CA: Thomson Wadsworth.

Schlosser, E. (1998, December). The prison-industrial complex. *The Atlantic Monthly, 282*, 51–78.

Sickmund, M., Snyder, H. N., & Poe-Yamagata, E. (1997). *Juvenile offenders and victims: 1997 update on violence*. Washington, DC: Office of Juvenile Justice and Delinquency Prevention.

Skolnick, J. H., & Fyfe, J. J. (1993). *Above the law: Police and the excessive use of force*. New York, NY: Free Press.

Snell, T. L. (2001). Capital punishment 2000 (No. NCJ 190598). *Bureau of Justice Statistics Bulletin*. Washington, DC: Bureau of Justice Statistics.

Snell, T. L. (2006). Capital punishment 2005 (No. NCJ 215083). *Bureau of Justice Statistics Bulletin*. Washington, DC: Bureau of Justice Statistics.

Sugrue, T. J. (1996). *The origins of the urban crisis: Race and inequality in postwar Detroit*. Princeton, NJ: Princeton University Press.

Tanenhaus, D. S., & Drizen, S. A. (2002). "Owing to the extreme youth of the accused": The changing legal response to juvenile homicide. *Journal of Criminal Law and Criminology, 92*, 641–705.

Thompson, H. A. (2010). Why mass incarceration matters: Rethinking crisis, decline, and transformation in postwar American History. *Journal of American History, 97(3)*, 703–734.

Wadman, R. C., & Allison, W. T. (2004). *To protect and serve: A history of police in America*. Upper Saddle River, NJ: Pearson/Prentice Hall.

Walker, S. (1994). *Sense and nonsense about crime and drugs: A policy guide* (3rd ed.). Belmont, CA: Wadsworth Publishing.

Walker, S. (1998). *Popular justice: A history of American criminal justice* (2nd ed.). New York, NY: Oxford University Press.

West, H. C., & Sabol, W. J. (2008). Prisoners in 2007 (No. NCJ 224280). *Bureau of Justice Statistics Bulletin*. Washington, DC: Bureau of Justice Statistics.

Wilson, J. Q. (1975). *Thinking about crime*. New York, NY: Basic Books.

Wolfgang, M. E., Figlio, R. M., & Sellin, J. T. (1972). *Delinquency in a birth cohort*. Chicago, IL: University of Chicago Press.

Zimring, F. E., & Hawkins, G. (1997). *Crime is not the problem: Lethal violence in America*. New York, NY: Oxford University Press.

10

American Criminal Justice in Global Context, 1800s–2000s

Readers of this chapter, because it is the final chapter, might well assume that the global and transnational dimensions of criminal justice became relevant only at the end of the twentieth century and only after most of the other developments chronicled in this text. Certainly a great deal of attention has been paid to the impacts of globalization on crime and justice in the last quarter-century, so much so that it would appear to be the most contemporary of all criminal justice issues. But, as this chapter makes clear, students and scholars should not overlook the long history of global criminal justice as well.

What do we mean when we study criminal justice in global terms? We suggest that it means approaching criminal justice across national borders in both *comparative* and *relational* terms. The comparative dimension is the more traditional of the two approaches, examining the variations among the criminal justice systems of the world. Comparative research offers an important reminder that criminal justice systems have developed from very different intellectual and cultural traditions in criminal law and procedure and within highly variable social and political systems. These differences produce significant variations in practice. A well-developed comparative literature on policing, for example, demonstrates significant cross-national differences in police organization and function (Bayley, 1985).

The more significant of the two approaches for this chapter is the study of criminal justice in relational terms—in other words, studying transnational connections and relationships in criminal justice. Peter Andreas and Ethan Nadelmann (2006) offer a helpful elaboration on this theme in their work *Policing the Globe,* in which they distinguish two important relational processes that reach across borders: *homogenization* and *regularization*. The first of these two processes, homogenization, refers to the global development of common criminal justice norms and practices. It isn't hard to see this process at work: consider the extent to which the major contemporary institutions of criminal justice, such as the prison, police forces, probation and parole, and juvenile justice all spread globally over the course of the twentieth century. Many scholars see homogenization as an inevitable by-product of a modernizing and globalizing world. Franklin Zimring (2001) predicts that, in an increasingly interconnected age, "common normative standards and technology transfer will push toward convergence in criminal justice practices and standards" (p. 216). Other scholars have called this the "McDonaldization" of criminal justice, by which they mean that global criminal justice systems—just as with the fast food industry—increasingly look to universal operational standards to promote efficiency, predictability, and control (Robinson, 2002; Shichor, 1997).

The second of these two processes, regularization, refers to the development of working criminal justice relationships across borders. Regularization is a different concept than homogenization, since it only involves the development of interdependent relationships between criminal justice systems—systems that could still retain differences between each other. Here, too, it is not hard to see a growing process of regularization: contemporary criminal justice systems include highly elaborate transnational working relationships that feature cooperative policing and surveillance, data sharing, regular fugitive extradition processes, and so forth (Joyce, 1999; Turner, 2007). Andreas and Nadelmann (2006) believe that this "transnational law enforcement community," represents an "increasingly important—though often overlooked and poorly understood—dimension of global governance and transgovernmental relations" (p. 9). Just as with homogenization, the process of regularization is often understood in terms of improving the predictability and efficiency of the criminal justice process.

These transnational processes are a real and important part of modern criminal justice history, but there are two important qualifications to the story. First, we must be cautious about assuming that global processes overwhelm everything in their path. Instead, it is helpful to remember that global developments are never perfectly or completely imposed on local places. Local places (by which we mean both nations and subnational areas) react to global developments with their own processes of adjustments, adaptations, and resistance. Put another way, the global always has to interact with the local (Nelken, 2011; Savelsberg, 2011). Sociologist Roland Robertson promoted the term "glocalization" to refer to this interactive process, a term which reminds us that the transfers of criminal justice institutions and practices are still influenced by local and national settings (Giulianotti & Robertson, 2006).

A second point of caution when thinking about these global processes is to remember to consider issues of power. It is all too easy to assume that the processes of homogenization and regularization are simply logical by-products of an evolving global system. In fact, not all nations are created equal in these global processes—changes sometimes flow from more powerful nations to the less powerful and reflect some national interests to the exclusion of others. A number of scholars have pointed out the uneven power dynamics at work in global criminal justice (Andreas & Nadelmann, 2006; Drake, Muncie, & Westmarland, 2009). Indeed, a healthy scholarly debate has taken place over whether global developments are working to reduce the power of traditional national boundaries and sovereign control over criminal justice matters or are actually a device by which the traditional nation state can reinforce its power and authority (McDonald, 2005; Wood & Kempa, 2006).

❖ EARLY TRANSNATIONAL SYSTEMS

Efforts to promote transnational criminal justice extend well back in time. Cooperative efforts aimed at solving particular criminal justice problems emerged in the nineteenth century. The policing of the Atlantic slave trade was one of the first and most important of these. When Britain abolished the slave trade in 1807, and banned the trade throughout its empire in 1833, the British government assumed the lead role in attempting to suppress continued traffic in slaves. One study of Britain's efforts observes that the slave trade was "suppressed by the twin weapons of diplomatic pressure and the exercise of naval power" (Lloyd, 1968, p. x)—in other words, through a focus on the homogenization of national rules on slavery through diplomatic negotiation and a focus on the use of the British Navy to support the regularization of policing activity. A series of bilateral agreements between Britain and other nations helped to spread formal legal prohibitions on slavery. At multilateral meetings in London (1817–1818), the British government pressed for a universal abolition of the slave trade. At the same time, these agreements helped regularize the policing of the slave trade by giving the British government authority to police slave traders in other national jurisdictions and by allowing for economic sanctions against governments who refused to cooperate in the reduction of slave-trading activity. At the London meetings, the British proposed the creation of an international naval police force on the coast of Africa, equipped with a right of visit and search based on a convention to be concluded among all maritime states. This police force would have been empowered to detain ships trading in slaves contrary to their national legislation and to hand them over to their own courts for adjudication (Kern, 2004). Although this proposal did not come to pass, the Royal Navy emerged as a kind of international criminal police force against the slave trade (Andreas & Nadelmann, 2006).

Other early areas of European cooperation show national governments acting in concert to respond to common concerns. The policing of political violence and terrorism led to the development of systems for international law enforcement cooperation. These developments date back at least to the European revolutionary movements of 1848 that prompted anxious governments to develop mechanisms for exchanging information about revolutionaries and political agitators. These efforts tended not to be very systematic or long lasting. But the 1898 assassination of Empress Elizabeth of Austria by an Italian anarchist resulted in the convening of an international conference in Rome (attracting delegates from 21 countries) to discuss strategies for suppressing anarchist violence (Andreas & Nadelmann, 2006; McDonald, 2005). Although the meeting resulted in relatively few formal diplomatic agreements, it further cultivated informal networks between national police forces. In fact, the Rome conference was perhaps most notable for the manner in which it allowed for police-to-police working relationships to bypass formal diplomatic channels, a feature of transnational policing that would become prevalent in the twentieth century.

The Rome meeting was the first in a series of international meetings intended to regularize criminal justice practices. The following year (1899), London hosted an international meeting to discuss the control of "white slavery"—a term which generally referred to the trafficking in women for the purposes of prostitution. As with the slave trade and political violence, national governments regarded white slavery as having a fundamentally transnational quality. As one private organization put it at the time: "the white-slave traffickers are in close contact in all parts of the world, in great cities as in small villages . . . in order to benefit fully from the techniques of the traffic and the advantages of combination" (Williams, 1999, p. 145).

As historian Mara Keire (2010, p. 69–88) points out, the emphasis on the commercial and organized nature of prostitution helped to justify new ways of organizing policing and control as well. A 1910 essayist made the connection clear:

> "Unless we make energetic and successful war upon the red-light district . . . we shall have Oriental brothel slavery thrust upon us . . . with all its unnatural and abnormal practices, established among us by French traders. Jew traders, too, will people our "levees" with Polish Jewesses and others who will make money for them. Shall we defend our American civilization, or lower our flag to the most despicable foreigners—French, Irish, Jews and Mongolians? . . . On both coasts and throughout all our cities, only an awakening of the whole Christian conscience and intelligence can save us from the importation of Parisian and Polish pollution, which is already corrupting the manhood and youth of every large city in the nation" (Block, 1999, p. 226).

This illustration, taken from Clifford G. Rowe's *The Great War on White Slavery; Or, Fighting the Traffic in Young Girls* (1910), shows the manner in which Progressive Era reformers framed the problem in terms of transnational migration. Here, two "white slave traders" meet young women arriving at a New York City dock.

The traffic in narcotics prompted some of the most extensive early efforts at coordinating criminal justice across borders. Although the international opium trade had been fiercely criticized since the nineteenth century, transnational control efforts did not begin to take shape until the United States-organized Shanghai Opium Commission in 1909. The Commission brought together representatives of Asian and European governments to discuss opium control; it led directly to a second conference at The Hague in 1911. The Hague Conference produced an agreement in early 1912 to establish an international regulatory and reporting system for opium, morphine, heroin, and cocaine. In fact, the international agreement actually *preceded* many national antinarcotic laws—including the Harrison Act in the United States (1914) and the Dangerous Drugs Act in Britain (1920).

The global drug control regime was placed under the authority of the League of Nations when that body came into being in 1920. The League subsequently held three major international conferences on trafficking, in 1925, 1931, and 1936, targeting the trafficking of narcotics across national borders. As with white slavery, the transnational dimensions of drug trafficking seemed clear enough to national governments. One typical League case from the 1920s began with the arrest of a single seaman in Hong Kong, involved a British citizen arranging for the smuggling of morphine manufactured in Britain and Western Europe, through Switzerland to Japan and Japanese-controlled colonies. These latter locations served as staging points for Japanese smugglers to bring the morphine into China (Meyer & Parssinen, 1998).

Defending national borders from the illicit movement of people and goods has long been an object of concern for law enforcement, and few borders areas have seen such sustained and conflict-ridden policing as that between the United States and Mexico. Here, federal agents in El Paso examine a freight car for illegal immigrants, in this 1944 photograph by Dorothea Lange.

Source: Courtesy of the Library of Congress, Prints & Photographs Division, FSA/OWI Collection, LC-USF34- 018222-E.

The League of Nations, without question, succeeded in globalizing antinarcotics efforts in the 1920s and 1930s. National governments signed on to international agreements and national police forces entered into informal (sometimes even secret) agreements to track the movements and activities of alleged drug traffickers (McWilliams, 1989). What the League was *not* able to do, of course, was to actually suppress the global trade in narcotic drugs. Ironically, these early antidrug efforts made the drug trade *more* global in nature, as traffickers adapted to control efforts by moving their operations to other locations. In a pattern that would repeat itself many times, transnational policing provoked transnational responses from illicit networks. Still, there is no question that the League's antidrug efforts were emblematic of a pre-World War Two embrace of criminal justice internationalization. Other League conventions from this period targeted slavery, pornography, terrorism, and sex trafficking, reflecting what Andreas and Nadelmann (2006) called "a broadly optimistic faith . . . in the power of international legal documents to transform international society" (p. 95).

Case Studies in Criminal Justice: "Billy Gard," Federal Agent

"Billy Gard" was an agent for the Bureau of Investigation (the precursor to the Federal Bureau of Investigation), who appeared in William Atherton Dupuy's 1916 book for younger readers titled *Uncle Sam, Detective*. Billy Gard was not a real Bureau agent but rather a lightly fictionalized composite of several agents who had told their stories to Dupuy. *Uncle Sam, Detective* summarizes 12 actual Bureau investigations, placing Billy in the role of investigator in each case.

The title of the book intentionally places "Uncle Sam" and "detective" together in a way that suggests the curiosity of their connection. In the very first sentence of the Introduction, Dupuy (1916) asked the reader: "May I ask you to close your eyes for a moment and conjure up the picture that is filed away in your mind under the heading 'detective'?" (p. ix). Dupuy imagined his young readers might be conjuring up images of a stout "graduate policeman" who "perspires freely, breathes heavily, moves with deliberation," and spent his time investigating minor local crimes. Or, Dupuy speculated, perhaps readers might be imagining the private detective of mystery stories—"the man of science and deductions"—who, in real life, "does not exist in all the world." Billy Gard, on the other hand, was a *new* type of detective, working for the nation and "performing as important work as ever came to the lot of men of his kind."

What makes *Uncle Sam, Detective* interesting reading is the extent to which this new type of detective was an international operator. In three of the 12 stories, Billy Gard is working overseas to break up various kinds of transnational criminal enterprise. In the first of these cases, "A Fiasco in Firearms," Billy uncovers a plot to illegally smuggle U.S.-manufactured arms

(Continued)

(Continued)

from New York to the Mexican government (the United States had imposed an arms embargo). Talking his way onto the ship itself, Billy traveled with the weapons shipment to Odessa, then to Hamburg, and finally on to Vera Cruz. Billy sends messages to U.S. Navy ships while on board, so that the American government will be prepared to act, which they did—invading the port of Vera Cruz before the shipment of arms arrives. The U.S. invasion and occupation of Vera Cruz lasted roughly six months; few today remember the critical role played by U.S. law enforcement in facilitating the collection of the intelligence or justifying foreign military intervention.

Billy's second international case, "'Roping' the Smugglers of Jamaica," presents "a huge conspiracy for the smuggling of opium and Chinamen into the United States." Involving Fun Ken, a wealthy Chinese merchant specializing in smuggling migrants, and Sing Foo who specialized in opium, they were "the richest Chinamen in the Caribbean"; the government had suspected that the Caribbean was an important base for the smuggling of both, and that Port Antonio, Jamaica, in particular was a critical departure point. Billy spies on smugglers discussing packing 10 men into a banana boat headed for Mobile, Alabama; he observes hundreds of Chinese loitering around, and surmises that "these superfluous Mongolians were waiting for an opportunity to be shuttled into the United States." He establishes a relationship with one smuggler, who tells him that "five dollars" worth of opium can be sold for "twenty seven fifty" in Philadelphia, and that by packing one ship with opium, good money could be made by making just one trip every two weeks. Billy traveled with the next shipment, selling opium to dealers in Philadelphia, New York, and Boston.

In the third case, "The Elusive Fugitive," Billy pursues a fugitive across national boundaries. His target is a corrupt customs broker, chased from Montreal to Chicago to London to Paris. In Paris, Billy works with the city police force to help set the trap that eventually results in the fugitive being caught—the police department provides a woman to be introduced into the fugitive's household as a maid. Billy then uses the undercover French detective to plant a listening device into the home, to uncover critical information about the fugitive's presence. The Paris police helped Billy make the arrest the next day.

A book like *Uncle Sam, Detective*, is just one example of a large collection of memoirs and other accounts of the criminal justice system in action. Few books of this vintage are widely read today, but they contain fascinating insights into the practical experience of criminal justice work. Happily, books like *Uncle Sam, Detective* are widely available to students of history and criminal justice. In fact, like most books now in the public domain, digital copies exist for students to access directly on their computers. Students of history are able to read stories like Billy's thanks to digitization projects that have made many thousands of books accessible online in their entirety. These projects include Google Books, Internet Archive, HathiTrust Digital Library, and others.

❖ MODERNIZATION, COLONIALISM AND THE HOMOGENIZATION OF CRIMINAL JUSTICE

Early international conferences, such as the 1898 Rome meeting on anarchist violence and the 1899 London meeting on white slavery, were notable for the extent to which they were attended as much by police officials as by formal diplomatic representatives. These meetings generated a whole series of more general gatherings of representatives from national police forces including, Buenos Aires in 1905, Madrid in 1909, São Paulo in 1912, and Washington in 1913. These meetings focused less on policy responses to particular issues than on what might be called "best practices" in policing—exchanging ideas and comparing procedures—an early trend toward the homogenization of criminal justice systems.

When police officials met in Rome, one of the agreements they reached was to develop a standardized practice for recording personal data on anarchist suspects. In particular, they agreed to a common set of criminal identification techniques that would use the system developed by Alphonse Bertillon. The Bertillon system, or *bertillonage*, employed a series of anthropometric measurements. Using calipers, police would record the specific features of a suspect's body—foot size, head length, cheek width, and the like—along with more conventional features such as eye color, hair color, and other physical characteristics. Even before the Rome meeting, police departments across Europe had been embracing the new system; in the United States, the Chicago Police Department was the first to adopt the Bertillon system, in 1890, and many other American police departments did likewise following the appearance of an English translation of Bertillon's work in 1896. The exchanges between agencies ultimately led to the creation (in 1915) of the International Association for Criminal Identification, later the International Association for Identification (Cole, 2001).

This photo, taken sometime between 1910 and 1915, shows a class studying the Bertillon method of criminal identification. Note the French term "portrait parle"—which refers to a front and side image of a suspect, not unlike the idea of a police mug shot.

Source: Courtesy of the Library of Congress, LC-B2- 2266-12.

The adoption of these new techniques served as a powerful symbol of progress and modernization in criminal justice. Not long after Bertillon's system had been widely adopted, and a newer system of fingerprinting also widely discussed, the 1905 World's Fair in St. Louis featured both in displays and literature for visitors. The International Association of Chiefs of Police sponsored an exhibit of the various criminal identification systems, while the New York State exhibit included fingerprinting in its tribute to modern "processes, as well as products." For ambitious American police officials and reformers, the study of European systems became nearly standard practice—a good example of what Daniel Rodgers (1998) refers to as the "Atlantic crossings" of Progressive Era policy innovations. Raymond Fosdick (1915), for example, made a grand tour of police departments—21 cities in all—in preparing his book, *European Police Systems* a study he concluded in admiring terms: "the European police department is, on the whole, an excellent piece of machinery. To its construction a high order of creative intelligence has been devoted; in its operation an equally high order of intelligence is constantly deployed" (p. 384).

The diffusion of criminal identification techniques reveals one aspect of the homogenization process—the embrace of new technologies and methods by criminal justice systems looking to embrace the latest in modern innovation. Importing criminal justice institutions served as one mechanism for local and national interests to promote a vision of modern governance. The global spread of the prison as a site of punishment illustrates the power of this modernizing impulse. Although historians continue to debate the exact timing and origins, the modern prison made its first appearance in the United States and Europe early in the nineteenth century, replacing older systems that tended to emphasize noncustodial forms of punishment. From that moment, the prison gradually spread across the globe over the course of the nineteenth and twentieth centuries, to the point where it became very close to a universal feature of world criminal justice systems.

Frank Dikötter (2002) has described the process by which China rapidly modernized its legal codes and criminal justice process at the start of the twentieth century, including the adoption of the prison. Although Western powers were certainly attempting to influence China in this direction, Dikötter makes clear that Chinese nationalists and modernizers played a critical role in the embrace of the prison as a symbol of modernity. Rapidly moving away from an older system that emphasized early modern modes of punishment—corporal punishment, capital punishment, exile—China adopted a prison-based system featuring, by 1918, 39 "model" prisons, with the Beijing No.1 prison being "the model of all models." Dikötter (2002) concludes that prison reform "was pronounced an essential political task in achieving equal status with foreign powers and in resuming full sovereignty over the concessions" (p. 66). Chinese penologists were well versed in international legal and correctional practice, participating in international conferences and publishing their findings from surveys of foreign prison systems (Dikötter, 2002). Mary Gibson (2011) suggests that the new Chinese prisons were even more "progressive and humane" by the 1930s than their European counterparts. On the other hand, Chinese reformers chose just one particular dimension of foreign reform—the notion of reformation and its idea of moral malleability—from a range of Western alternatives.

Similar impulses were at work in Latin America, though at varying times and to varying degrees. In postcolonial Peru, the construction of a modern penitentiary in the capital city of Lima marked the modern progress of an independent nation. Built in 1862, and modeled upon New York's Auburn Prison, Lima's new prison was its first modern building and an architectural symbol of civilization. Chile's first prison (built between 1844 and 1849) borrowed its design from the solitary system of the Eastern State Penitentiary in Philadelphia. American designs also influenced the pioneering penitentiaries of Ecuador (1874) and Argentina (1877) (Salvatore & Aguirre, 1996; Salvatore, Aguirre, & Joseph, 2001). In each instance, as historian Mary Gibson (2011) has observed, "the building of penitentiaries formed part of a larger wave of liberal reform. . . . Crucially linked to the overhaul of the justice system as part of state-building, the new penitentiaries in theory introduced a democracy of punishment for all citizens" (p. 1057).

Nationalist embrace of modernization was one factor in the diffusion of criminal justice institutions; the other was the imposition of those institutions on colonial subjects by imperial powers. In the case of colonialism, the transfer of policy had a distinct quality because it served two very distinct—and sometimes competing or contradictory—goals. The first goal was modernization, not unlike that championed by nationalists elsewhere. In other words, European colonial powers established criminal justice systems in the image of their own and justified the imposition as part of the necessary spread of civilization and modern practices to the colonies. The second goal was to establish and then sustain political control over colonized subjects. Colonial authorities knew that prisons and policing could be critical elements in defending themselves against anticolonial resistance, and the criminal justice system was frequently put to work suppressing political opposition.

Although both impulses are important, and co-existed throughout the colonial era, historians have tended to see the demands of political control as more influential. Sociologist Mathieu Deflem (1994), for example, points out that the British had two models of policing to choose from when they created colonial police forces across much of Africa and Asia. The first was their own Metropolitan Police, first established in London in 1829 and the model for domestic policing in Britain thereafter. Uniformed, unarmed, and bound by central authority to respect procedural rules, the Metropolitan Police were designed for a democratizing society suspicious of mixing politics and policing. The second model was the Royal Irish Constabulary, a far more militarized, armed force intended more for the purpose of upholding political authority than enforcing the criminal law. Deflem observes that it was the model of the RIC, not the Metropolitan Police, which had the greater influence on colonial policing in British colonies.

A very influential study of imprisonment in Vietnam under French colonial rule (Zinoman, 2001) shows modernization and political control at work, side by side, with the latter ultimately proving more dominant. Prior to French control, punishment practices in Vietnam had a distinctly early modern character to them, relying on corporal and capital punishment (often carried out in public), banishment and exile, and indentured servitude. As in much of the early modern West, Vietnamese authorities employed imprisonment far less often and mostly for those awaiting trial. French colonial rule in the latter part of the nineteenth century brought with it the rise of imprisonment as a "modern" tool for punishing criminal offenders. However, Vietnam's prisons hardly looked, on the inside, much like their counterparts in metropolitan France. Inmates were often housed not in individual cells, but in large communal rooms. Few efforts at rehabilitation or moral uplift could be found; instead, prisoners spent their days in chaotic, dangerous, and corrupt institutions in which "disciplinary practices were overshadowed by a host of ill-disciplined and exclusively repressive methods of coercion and control" (Zinoman, 2001, p. 17).

These methods of repression, historians argue, reflected the demands of colonial governance, in which prisoners were not simply antisocial, but antistate. For colonial administrators around the globe, the prison became one device by which political dissent could be suppressed. In this sense, the colonial prison departed—at least in theory—from Western prisons, which were based on notions of democratic punishment and social reform. In place of rehabilitation or justice, the colonial prison operated in defense of white authority over their colonial subjects. As bad as conditions in American and European prisons could be, the colonial version of the prison often exceeded their western models in disorder, disease, and violence (Gibson, 2011).

The legacy of colonialism for global criminal justice practice is just as mixed as the purposes behind colonial governance itself. On the one hand, colonial powers unquestionably succeeded in homogenizing criminal justice practice across the globe, even if that process *was* always modified by local practice. The French in West Africa, for example, extended their criminal justice system, in modified form, throughout the colonial sphere of West Africa; by the mid-twentieth century, they administered a complex system with multiple appeals courts, 12 criminal courts, 50 correctional courts for minor offenses, 56 police courts for summary derelictions, and 154 customary courts (Agozino, 2006). In general, these structures lasted into the postcolonial period; when the British Gold Coast colony became independent Ghana in 1957, for example, the Gold Coast Constabulary established by the British became the Ghana Police Service and retained much of its colonial-era organization.

But if the homogenizing of criminal justice had a postcolonial legacy, so, too, did the political orientation of criminal justice. As one study of postcolonial French West Africa suggests, the political orientation of criminal justice "remained after formal de-colonization, as the neo-colonial regimes continued with the forceful methods of domination they inherited from colonialism" (Agozino, 2006, p. 125). In postcolonial Ghana, for example, policing retained many aspects of its colonial-era character; rather than shifting to a model of bureaucratic autonomy, professionalism, and rights-based procedural rules, Ghanian police reforms emphasized the Africanization of the police structures, but retained their highly political and, at times, repressive orientation (Tankebe, 2008).

❖ GLOBAL CRIMINAL JUSTICE IN THE COLD WAR ERA

The emergence of the United States as a global superpower in the aftermath of World War Two transformed the nation's capacity to exert control and influence over global forms of governance—including criminal justice practices—and the rise of Cold War conflict with the Soviet Union provided an urgent rationale for doing so. This global role was new on several levels. First, the directionality of influence began to change. Before the war, transfers of criminal justice institutions and technologies were just as often coming into the United States as they were directed outward. Even into the 1930s, European models of criminal justice were still regarded by many American reformers and administrators as the quintessentially modern standard to emulate. After the war, the direction of policy transfer increasingly shifted to one in which the United States exported its own criminal justice processes (Findlay, 1999). Second, the United States assumed a new leadership role in organizing transnational criminal justice activities. Before the war, the American role in cooperative efforts between nations had been uneven at best. Moments of active engagement, such as the development of the Shanghai Commission and the Hague Convention against the narcotic drug traffic, were balanced by longer periods of disengagement, exemplified by the general unwillingness to participate in the League of Nations antidrug trafficking efforts. Third, the scale of American transnational activity increased dramatically during the Cold War era. The stories of the fictional agent, Billy Gard, are interesting as examples of early transnational activity, but the fact remains that there were never all that many "Billy Gards" before World War Two. During the Cold War, however, the United States began cultivating a massive international criminal justice presence, one that reached every corner of the globe.

The Cold War role for the United States built upon an earlier tradition of colonial and quasicolonial interventions that can be dated at least back to the Spanish-American War of 1898. One result of that conflict was the opportunity for the United States to assume effective control over Cuban governmental affairs and to impose colonial authority over the Philippines. As with European colonialism, the assertion of American power was justified as an effort to extend the wholesome benefits of order and modernity into the world beyond American borders. As Senator Albert Beveridge declared in 1900: "[God] has made us the master organizers of the world to establish system where chaos reigns. . . . Were it not for such a force as this the world would relapse into barbarism and night" (Jacobson, 2000, p. 227). For the United States, the need to "establish system" in a chaotic world included the mission of reshaping foreign criminal justice institutions.

In Cuba, American officials disbanded the existing police forces and re-established a new national police force over which the United States exercised ultimate direction and authority. In the Philippines, American authorities suspended the older Spanish criminal justice system and rebuilt it into a new hybrid of Spanish and American influences. This new system rapidly embraced aspects of modern criminal justice practice. Criminal justice officials began collecting systematic data on crime, prison officials set up classification systems for inmates, and police forces were re-organized and given more authority. Manila's Bilibid Prison became a site for intensive criminological study—a "great anthropological laboratory," according to one researcher whose work was eventually featured in the Philippine Commission's exhibit at the St. Louis World's Fair in 1904 (Kramer, 2006).

The modernizing project in Cuba and the Philippines, as it did in the European colonial experience, developed side by side with the use of the criminal justice system as a tool for maintaining political authority. In the Philippines, the Philippine Commission employed the criminal law, along with criminal justice, as a primary tool in suppressing resistance to American authority. The 1902 Brigandage Act, for example, defined Filipino resistance as "banditry" or "ladronism" (a Spanish term which implied organized resistance to legal authority) rather than as military insurrection. At the same time, the Philippine Commission established the Philippine Constabulary, a modernized police bureaucracy which, as one historian observes, "would in many ways function as a colonial army in police uniform, waging war in areas otherwise designated as 'pacified'" (Kramer, 2006, p. 155). As American soldiers returned home, the Constabulary kept up the work of fighting insurrection.

Historian Martha K. Huggins observed that the United States experience in Cuba and the Philippines was the precursor to growing number of interventions of Latin America between the 1910s and the 1930s. Here, too, criminal justice systems became the focus of American attention. Military interventions in Haiti (1915), the Dominican Republic (1916), and Panama (1918) all included efforts to reshape national police forces. Elements of American policing now became standard—a uniformed police corps, modern criminal identification techniques, rehabilitative prison programs, and more. At the same time, however, U.S.-aided police forces became the primary tool of political control, and actual police and correctional practice demonstrated terrible corruption and brutality (Butler, 2003; Kuzmarov, 2009; Huggins, 1987).

As the United States emerged as a global superpower in the wake of World War Two, domestic policing remained at the core of Cold War-era strategies for projecting American influence. Providing aid to foreign criminal justice systems became a favored indirect extension of American power; "even in the absence of an explicit territorial occupation of recipient countries, the United States wielded considerable influence over foreign internal security administration" (McLeod, 2008, p. 51). In South Korea before the start of the Korean War in 1950, the United States constructed a National Academy for police training, while American-funded police helped carry out anticommunist and political repression on behalf of President Syngman Rhee (Kuzmarov, 2009; Matray, 1985).

In a similar vein, the Thai National Police Department (TNDP) began receiving aid from the United States in 1951. With American support, the TNDP rapidly acquired modern equipment and organizational structures; at one point, over 200 American advisors were in country, assisting in training for counterinsurgency and domestic intelligence gathering (Weimer 2011, p. 88). The training of police in Vietnam began in 1955, as United States advisors replaced the departed French colonial authorities. The State Department contracted with one of the leading schools of police administration, Michigan State University (MSU), to develop the Vietnamese police forces into an efficient force for maintaining law and order. The Michigan State advisors helped establish an FBI-like national force, with a strong emphasis on weaponry and surveillance; MSU advisors helped create a national identity card system to help monitor political activity (Kuzmarov, 2009).

Much of this aid was delivered through the U.S. Civil Police Administration (CPA), guided by the belief that police units were the best mechanism for defeating local insurgencies (rather than employing military force more directly). In 1962, the Kennedy Administration established a successor agency to the CPA, the Office of Public Safety (OPS). During its 12 year existence, the OPS provided aid to police agencies in approximately 50 Third World nations, spending more than $300 million on training, weaponry, and telecommunications and other equipment. Hundreds of active and retired American police officers were sent to these countries, where they trained tens of thousands of police officials in administration, riot and traffic control, interrogation, surveillance, intelligence, and assorted other tasks. Thousands of mid- and high-level police officials from those countries came to Washington to study at the OPS-run International Police Academy (Nadelmann, 1993).

A tension existed within the OPS, caught between two missions—one, to help develop civil police forces subject to the rule of law and, two, to help friendly governments employ police and criminal justice resources in the task of fighting insurgent movements. In the end, the balance often shifted in the direction of counterinsurgency. Between 1962 and 1973, the OPS provided aid to more than 50 foreign governments, training and modernizing police forces throughout much of Southeast Asia and Latin America, but the controversy over its mission ultimately ended the program. Following extensive hearings, the U.S. Congress shuttered the OPS in 1974 and restricted aid to foreign law-enforcement organizations (McLeod, 2008).

The end of the OPS was hardly the end of the story, however, for U.S. interventions in foreign criminal justice. In practice, many of the resources and much of the mission behind the old OPS were simply shifted into different bureaucratic channels. The most important of these were concerned with advancing American interests in drug control (Weimer, 2011). The State Department's International Narcotics Control Program, the Drug Enforcement Administration, and the Foreign Assistance Acts, "filled much of the void" left by the end of the OPS (Weimer, 2011, p. 204). The shift to a drug focus was a precursor to major U.S. interventions through the 1970s and 1980s in Southeast Asia, Mexico, and Central America.

In fact, the fastest growing area of international policing was drug enforcement. The Federal Bureau of Narcotics and Dangerous Drugs (BNDD) had been consistently sending small numbers of its agents abroad since the end of World War Two. Their agents worked closely, and often informally, with their peers in other countries, who were often far more receptive to cooperative working relationships than the governments for whom they served (Nadelmann, 1993). In the process, they helped develop a strong transnational police culture; as Ethan Nadelmann (1993) has observed, "the sense of comradery among police of different nations often has succeeded in inducing cooperation between governments with severe political differences" (p. 134).

Narcotics enforcement abroad had always been a fairly small-scale affair, but this changed quickly at the start of the 1970s. In 1967, the last full year of the FBN's existence, the budget of the Treasury Department's drug agency was approximately $3 million. Roughly a dozen of its 300 agents were stationed in eight locations outside the United States. Six years and two bureaucratic reorganizations later, in the last full year of BNDD operations, the drug agency boasted a budget of $74 million and 1,446 total agents, of whom 124 were abroad in 47 offices in 33 countries. By 1976, just before a minor contraction in its size, the DEA's budget was just short of $200 million. Some 228 of its 2,117 agents were stationed overseas, in 68 offices in 43 countries. As Nadelmann concludes, "In less than a decade, a small overseas complement of American narcotics agents had grown into the first global law enforcement agency with operational capabilities" (Nadelmann, 1993, p. 141).

❖ CONTROLLING ILLICIT ENTERPRISE IN A POST-COLD WAR WORLD

The end of the Cold War era brought with it an intensified concern over the scope and influence of transnational criminal networks. The growth of global criminal enterprises was linked to the effects of globalization, which were said to facilitate the illicit movement of people and goods. One typical account of these developments, Moises Naim's 2005 book *Illicit: How Smugglers, Traffickers, and Copycats Are Hijacking the Global Economy*, warned readers to resist the temptation to conclude that "there is nothing new" about the illicit trades. Instead, Naim (2005) suggested, globalization had elevated the "age old" problems of illicit enterprise from a nuisance to a global threat: "incredible power [was] now residing in the hands of an entirely new kind of international entity, inherently stateless and deeply elusive . . . this story is no longer just about crime. It is about a new form of politics in the twenty-first century . . . a whole new set of political actors whose values may collide with yours and mine, and whose intentions threaten us all" (p. 7, 9).

During the 1990s, global crime was rapidly elevated to one of the leading threats to global security and governance. In a 1995 address to the United Nations, President Bill Clinton warned that transnational drug trafficking, money laundering, smuggling, and terrorism had become critical security challenges for the world, a theme picked up by U.S. Senator John Kerry in his 1997 book, *The New War: The Web of Crime That Threatens America's Security*. A large conference, hosted in 1994 by the Center for Strategic and International Studies, was provocatively entitled "Global Organized Crime: The New Empire of Evil," and defined this novel security threat as: "Worldwide alliances . . . forged in every criminal field from money laundering and currency counterfeiting to trafficking in drugs and nuclear materials that present a greater international security challenge than anything Western democracies had to cope with during the Cold War" (Edwards, 2006, p. 212). As it had during the Cold War, the language of crime—albeit now focused on illicit enterprise—melded with the language of foreign policy (McLeod, 2008).

Did a genuinely new global crime problem emerge in the 1990s? Some evidence supports the idea. The end of the Cold War brought with it a generally greater freedom of human movement around the world, a development hastened by advances in transportation and technology. This freedom of movement was coupled with a widespread trend toward the lowering of trade and finance barriers. The ratification of the North American Free Trade Agreement (NAFTA) and the creation of the European Union, both in 1993, were signal accomplishments for the advocates of freer international commerce. Even by the time NAFTA went into effect, the volume of U.S. merchandise trade had grown 1300% since 1970 (Farer, 1999, p. 14). By the 1990s, the cross-border flows of people and commerce created a circumstance highly advantageous for illicit networks. Like licit enterprise, traders in illegal goods have learned to utilize global networks, establishing international affiliate organizations and alliances, and effectively finding safe havens by corrupting weaker regimes around the world (Farer, 1999, p. 15).

Not everyone is wholly persuaded that global crime is a problem of novel scope and danger. In the wake of the Cold War, with the rationale of anticommunism and the Soviet threat fading, the focus on organized criminal activity served as a new and useful point of focus for international criminal justice and national security interests. Some studies have suggested that the threat of global crime has been distorted or manipulated by national governments as a way of advancing political interests (Edwards, 2006). Whether the global crime threat was genuine or overblown, there is no question that international criminal justice moved rapidly to expand its capacity to respond. Two case studies—money laundering and human trafficking—illustrate the important changes in criminal justice practice since the 1990s.

Money laundering is a critical process for illicit enterprise, allowing the source and flow of money to be disguised. Typically, money laundering schemes are designed to accomplish three things: to conceal the source of funds, to obscure the movement of those funds and, finally, to convert those funds into various legitimate forms. There is nothing particularly new about money laundering; organized criminals have always sought ways to convert illegally generated cash into legitimate forms. As far back as Prohibition, failure to successfully obscure the financial foundations of crime caused the downfall of gangsters like Al Capone, sentenced to prison on federal tax evasion charges.

Nor is transnational money laundering itself wholly new. The American gangster Meyer Lansky was a pioneer in using foreign banking systems to disguise his finances and keep out of reach of the Internal

Figure 10.1 The arrow has become one of the signature descriptors of modern, transnational crime. This government-produced image, from 1989, attempts to show global patterns in the trafficking of opium. As America entered into a post–Cold War moment, the menacing arrows pointed at the nation's borders served as a powerful representation of the threat of illicit enterprise. More recently, scholars (van Schendel, 2005) have criticized such maps for obscuring more than they show, but they remain a popular device for illustrating the flows of transnational crime.

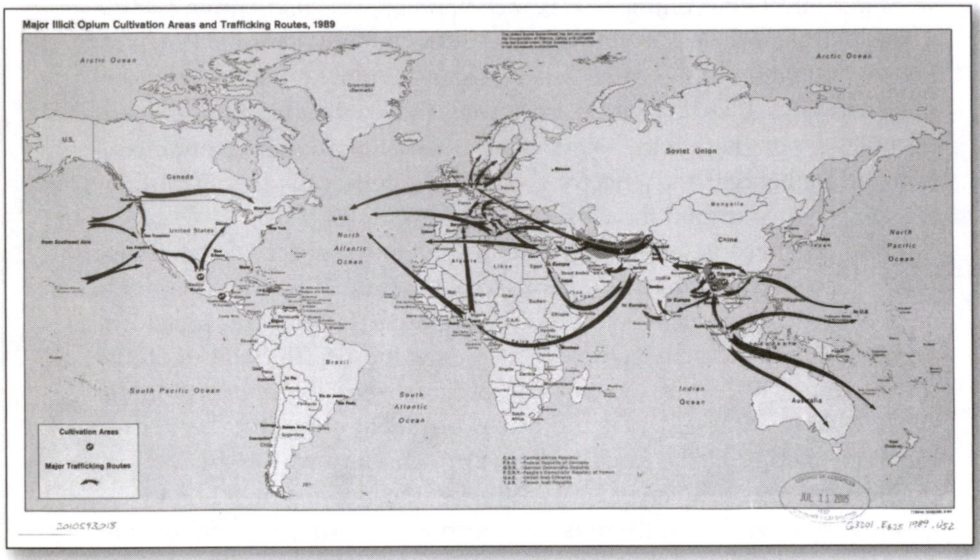

Source: United States Central Intelligence Agency. Major illicit opium cultivation areas and trafficking routes, 1989 : [world map]. http://hdl.loc.gov/loc.gmd/g3201e.ct003162

Revenue Service. After World War Two, Lansky and associates began aggressively shifting illegal profits to banks in Switzerland, whose exceptional bank secrecy rules effectively shielded the funds from United States scrutiny. Lansky also invested heavily in Cuban casinos, which provided a helpful set of legitimate business through which organized crime cash could be laundered. Cuban casinos with bank accounts in Miami would take cash and checks there for deposit and then transfer those funds out of the United States—that cash reportedly included profits from numerous illegal ventures (Lacey, 1992; Blum, 1999).

The scale and complexity of money laundering in the post–Cold War era was aided by two important developments. The integration of global financial systems aided both legitimate and illegitimate flows of currency. In addition, the emergence of a networked information economy allowed for money to be moved electronically. A few computer keystrokes now replaced the cumbersome and risky process of physically moving cash and other forms of wealth across national borders (Blum, 1999). To be sure, older and simpler systems of money laundering remained; large quantities of cash were still physically smuggled from one country to another (from the United States into Mexico, for example), and launderers could also rely on underground banking and money brokerage systems prevalent in India, China, and the Middle East, whose informality facilitated illicit flows of money. Still, as Naim (2005) noted, "money launderers were probably among the quickest to adapt to financial liberalization and integration in the 1990s" (p. 137).

Anti-money laundering activity on the transnational level is of comparatively recent origin. Indeed, even the domestic money laundering laws in the United States date back only to the Bank Secrecy Act of 1970 (which instituted reporting requirements for large movements of funds) and the Money Laundering Control Act of 1986 (which made money laundering a specific federal crime). Money laundering control policy has primarily been developed by, and diffused from, the United States. In 1974, the Basel Committee (composed of the central banks of large economies) established common rules for financial reporting, and systems for cooperative effort against money laundering. United Nations conventions require signatory nations to establish their own domestic laws and allow for sanctions against nations that actively circumvent international standards. Finally, the development of Mutual Legal Assistance Treaties (MLATs) between the United States and many other nations regularize cooperation and information sharing between national law enforcement agencies (Nadelmann, 1993).

Human trafficking is another signature crime of the global age. Referring generally (see "What's the Evidence?" on p. 304) to the illicit movement of people across national boundaries, human trafficking has become a standard point of reference for those who argue that globalization has created problems new in both scale and character. Of course, like money laundering, the traffic in people is not wholly new. As early as 1949, the United Nations ratified a Convention for the Suppression of Traffic in Persons and the Exploitation of the Prostitution of Others. The latter reference, to prostitution, reminds us that as far back as the nineteenth century, police and reformers worried about the international "white slave" trade.

In fact, the slavery metaphor has taken root once again, more than a century after the first white slave crusade (Block, 1999). Today, these concerns have given rise to new legislation, such as the 2000 Victims of Trafficking and Violence Protection Act, which targeted "forced prostitution, domestic servitude, debt bondage, or other slavery-like practices" (Clawson, Small, Go, & Myles, 2005). As in the past, these practices are typically linked to transnational criminal organizations, taking advantage of low local risk of prosecution, minimal local laws, or local corruption, to exploit economically vulnerable men and women. One study of the Eastern European traffic in prostitution makes what has become a fairly typical claim, that "Selling women into sexual slavery has become one of the fastest growing criminal enterprises on the international black market today" (Stone, 1998, p. 1).

What's the Evidence?: Estimates of Crime

The study of crime, past or present, means assessing various quantitative measures of criminal activity. As seen earlier in this text, developing more accurate measures of criminal activity and criminal justice performance were among the most important goals of professionalizing criminal justice in the twentieth century. Measurement matters a great deal. Numbers can give criminal justice agencies as sense of how well, or poorly, they are doing their jobs. Numbers can also serve as a way of defining problems, focusing public attention, or giving decision makers some sense of change and trends over time.

But numbers, after all, have to be generated before they can be disseminated, and students of criminal justice should be attentive to the process by which numbers are created. Estimates of criminal behavior may not always be as reliable as the seemingly concrete numbers suggest. In approaching quantitative reporting of crime and criminal activity, students of history and crime should be alert to several issues. Are the numbers reported based on empirical evidence, or are they simply estimates (and, if they are estimates, is the process for estimating clear)? Are numbers being generated for political or other purposes, or are they subject to manipulation for political purposes?

An early, and troubling, case of misleading numbers originated with the United States Treasury Department in 1919. That year, the Treasury Department published a report stating that there were "one million" narcotic addicts in the United States. The estimate was based on the flimsiest of formulas—but it was repeated extensively in the popular press and continued to be cited well into the 1930s. Subsequent government studies showed the number to be a gross overestimate, and historians have reached the same conclusion, but even today the original 1919 Treasury report is available for anyone to read and cite.

Quantitative reporting of crime activity should never be accepted uncritically, and this seems particularly true in the case of global or transnational crime. Consider a recent report intended to work through the problems of generating accurate numbers. The report began with the optimistic observation that, since "the phenomenon of transnational organized crime is real," it must therefore "be susceptible to measurement." On the other hand, the working group that produced the report also acknowledged that "formidable conceptual and institutional barriers" remain to actually provide accurate measurements (Reuter & Petrie, 1999, p. 22–27). One of the greatest barriers to accuracy is the problem of definition—once we create a category of criminal behavior, exactly what sorts of things "count" for purposes of data collection?

No contemporary example of transnational crime better exemplifies the problem of developing a consistent operational definition than the question of human trafficking. Between 1998 and 2000, national representatives debated the proposed United Nations Protocol to Suppress, Prevent and Punish Trafficking in Persons, Especially Women and Children. The Trafficking Protocol was eventually written and has been signed by over 110 countries, but before it had been the subject of intense debate. Two broad positions became apparent in the negotiations. One side wanted any international recruitment and transportation of women for the purposes of prostitution to be defined as trafficking, while others argued that there would have to be an element of fraud or force to meet the definition (and, indeed, argued against distinguishing sex trafficking from other kinds of human trafficking accomplished by force and fraud). Much of the debate centered upon the question of consent—to what extent can women consent to their employment in international sex work networks? As Jo Doezema (2002) and others have shown, this is a fundamental debate that goes back a century, to international discussions of what was then termed the "white slave" trade. In the end, the Trafficking Convention embraced the latter view, that there had to be an element of force or fraud involved. The text of the protocol read, in part:

> The recruitment, transportation, transfer, harboring or receipt of persons, by means of the threat or use of force or other forms of coercion, of abduction, of fraud, of deception, of the abuse of power or of a position of vulnerability or of giving or receiving payments or benefits to achieve the consent of a person having control over

(Continued)

(Continued)

another person, for the purpose of exploitation. Exploitation shall include, at a minimum, the exploitation of the prostitution of others or other forms of sexual exploitation, forced labor or services, slavery or practices similar to slavery, servitude or the removal of organs.

Of course, simply assenting to a definition on paper hardly solves the measurement problem. In the case of sex trafficking, how is one to draw the line between forced prostitution and sex work as a choice? Between sex trafficking and prostitution-related migration? The definition of trafficking hardly settles the question, and estimates of global sex trafficking would necessarily have to be based upon a subjective view of what the term means (Davidson, 2006). Does indebtedness, for example, constitute a form of force and fraud?

So many different estimates of the problem have been generated in recent years, that UNESCO (United Nations Educational, Scientific and Cultural Organization) is developing a database to compile and compare the various published numbers, noting: "When it comes to statistics, trafficking of girls and women is one of several highly emotive issues which seem to overwhelm critical faculties. Numbers take on a life of their own, gaining acceptance through repetition, often with little inquiry into their derivations. Journalists, bowing to the pressure of editors, demand numbers, any number. Organizations feel compelled to supply them, lending false precisions and spurious authority to many reports" (http://www.unescobkk.org/index.php?id=1022).

The capacity of the United States to influence foreign criminal justice practices, through a regularization of relationships and continued homogenization projects, grew substantially in the post–Cold War decade of the 1990s. The most notable developments included the growth of the Office of Overseas Prosecutorial Development Assistance and Training (OPDAT), begun in 1991, the International Law Enforcement Academy (ILEA), begun in 1995, and the International Criminal Investigative Training Assistance Program (ICITAP), all designed to bring foreign justice systems into a closer working relationship with U.S.-based institutions (McLeod, 2008). Predictably, these initiatives focused on transnational crimes of particular interest to the United States and on promoting international actions against illicit enterprise. The most substantial study of developments in this decade concluded that the United States had "advanced a distinct vision of what counts as transnational crime, one that excludes common categories of domestic interpersonal violence and is concerned primarily with international violations of financial regulation, intellectual property protections, migration controls, drug laws, and more recently, terrorism" (McLeod, 2008, p. 74). Ethan Nadelmann refers to OPDAT as "hegemony on the cheap"—meaning that the program serves as a useful device by which national interests can readily be projected out on a global scale.

The events of September 11, 2001, dramatically intensified these developments, in ways that could not have been predicted before that date. In fact, Gregory Treverton, a national security expert writing in 1999, attempted to summarize the extent to which global crime and terrorism represented security threats to America on the order of those faced during the Cold War. His answer? Probably not. Crime, Treverton felt, "will be a nuisance, one that will put pressure on U.S. institutions and practices, but it is not a serious threat" (Treverton, 1999, p. 39). Interestingly, he also discounted the ability of terrorism to serve as a policy-defining common threat: "It almost goes without saying that the Soviet threat, symbolized by nuclear terror, had a stun value that is not true of today's concerns. Terrorism may have a comparable effect, when a World Trade Center [the 1993 bombing] or Oklahoma City [the bombing of the Alfred P. Murrah federal building in 1995] occurs, but the stun is isolated. It does not provide a comparable catalyst for politics or policy" (p. 40).

Just two years later, the September 11, 2001, attacks on the World Trade Center (along with the Pentagon and United Flight 93, which crashed in rural Pennsylvania), upended this notion that terrorism could not serve as a catalyst for politics or policy. Rather than move global crime and criminal justice off the front pages, the 9/11 attacks brought the counterterrorism project into closer relationship with the global war on crime. These horrific attacks become the signal crime of the global age, the basis for one of the most sweeping re-organizations of federal law enforcement in U.S. history, and the spur to further international criminal justice.

Subsequent legislation in the United States, including the PATRIOT Act and the National Intelligence Reform and Terrorism Prevention Act of 2004, have broken down traditional barriers between national security, intelligence gathering, and domestic criminal justice operations. The global war on terror provided an opportunity for a simultaneous expansion of global criminal justice authority. Borderland regions across the globe, weakly governed by national states and often linked to illicit enterprise, now became security concerns as well. An American general, James Hill, gave voice to the new linkage in discussing areas like the Darien Gap between Panama and Colombia, and the tri-border region between Argentina, Paraguay, and Brazil:

> Today, the threat to the counties of the region is not the military force of the adjacent neighbor or some invading foreign power. Today's foe is the terrorist, the narco-trafficker, the international crime boss, and the money launderer. This threat is a weed that is planted, grown and nurtured in the fertile ground of ungoverned spaces such as coastlines, rivers and unpopulated border areas. This threat is watered and fertilized with money from drugs, illegal arms sales, and human trafficking. This threat respects neither geographical nor moral boundaries (quoted in Andreas and Nadelmann, 2006, p. 198).

General Hill's vision has become the global vision of the twenty-first century, a world in which the threat of terror and the threat of crime have become inseparable. And yet, none of these concerns are wholly new; the experiences of the past may well hold lessons for the global future. Although forces like technological change and globalization may appear to produce inevitable changes in international criminal justice, history suggests that there are still choices to be made and multiple possibilities for development.

❖ REFERENCES

Agozino, B. (2006). Crime, criminology and post-colonial theory: Criminological reflections on West Africa. In J. Sheptycki and A. Wardak, eds. *Transnational & comparative criminology*. London, UK: GlassHouse Press.

Andreas, P., & Nadelmann, E. (2006). *Policing the globe: Criminalization and crime control in international relations*. New York, NY: Oxford University Press.

Bayley, D. H. (1985). *Patterns of policing: A comparative international analysis*. New Brunswick, NJ: Rutgers University Press.

Block, A. A. (1999). Bad business: A commentary on the criminology of organized crime in the United States. In T. Farer, ed. *Transnational crime in the Americas*. London, UK: Routledge.

Blum, J. A. (1999). Offshore money. In T. Farer, ed. *Transnational crime in the Americas*. London, UK: Routledge.

Butler, S. (2003). *War is a racket: The antiwar classic by America's most decorated general*. New York, NY: Feral House.

Clawson, H. J., Small, K., Go, E. S., & Myles, B. W. (2005). Human trafficking in the United States: Uncovering the needs of victims and the service providers who work with them. In J. Albanese, ed. *Transnational crime.* Whitby, Ontario: deSitter.

Cole, S. (2001). *Suspect identities: A history of fingerprinting and criminal identification.* Cambridge, MA: Harvard University Press.

Davidson, J. O. (2006). Will the real sex slave please stand up? *Feminist Review* 83: 4–22.

Deflem, M. (1994). Law enforcement in British Colonial Africa: A comparative analysis of imperial policing in Nyasaland, the Gold Coast, and Kenya. *Police Studies 17*: 45–68.

Dikötter, F. (2002). *Crime, punishment and the prison in modern China.* New York, NY: Columbia University Press.

Doezema, J. (2002). Who gets to choose? Coercion, consent, and the UN trafficking protocol. *Gender and Development 10:* 20–27.

Drake, D., Muncie, J., & Westmarland, L. (2009). *Criminal justice, local and global.* Milton Keynes, UK: Willan/Open University Press.

Dupuy, W. A. (1916). *Uncle Sam, detective.* New York, NY: McKinlay, Stone & Mackenzie.

Edwards, A. (2006). Transnational organised crime. In J. Sheptycki & A. Wardak, eds. *Transnational & comparative criminology.* London, UK: GlassHouse Press.

Farer, T. (1999). *Transnational crime in the Americas.* New York, NY: Routledge.

Findlay, M. (1999). *The globalisation of crime: Understanding transitional relationships in context.* Cambridge, MA: Cambridge University Press.

Fosdick, R. B. (1915). *European police systems.* New York, NY: The Century Co.

Gibson, M. (2011). Global perspectives on the birth of the prison. *American Historical Review 116:* 1040–1063.

Giulianotti, R., & Robertson, R. (2006). Glocalization, globalization and migration: The case of Scottish football supporters in North America. *International Sociology 21:* 171–198.

Huggins, M. K. (1987). U.S.-supported state terror: A history of police training in Latin America. *Crime and Social Justice 27/28:* 47–56.

Jacobson, M. F. (2000). *Barbarian virtues: The United States encounters foreign peoples at home and abroad.* New York, NY: Hill and Wang.

Joyce, E. (1999). Transnational criminal enterprise: The European perspective. In T. Farer, ed. *Transnational crime in the Americas.* London, UK: Routledge.

Keire, M. L. (2010). *For business & pleasure: Red-light districts and the regulation of vice in the United States, 1890–1933.* Baltimore, MD: The Johns Hopkins University Press.

Kern, H. L. (2004). Strategies of legal change: Great Britain, international law, and the abolition of the transatlantic slave trade. *Journal of the History of International Law 6:* 233–258.

Kerry, J. (1997). *The new war: The web of crime that threatens America's security.* New York, NY: Simon & Schuster.

Kramer, P. A. (2006). *The blood of government: Race, empire, the United States, and the Philippines.* Chapel Hill: University of North Carolina Press.

Kuzmarov, J. (2009). Modernizing repression: Police training, political violence, and nation-building in the 'American Century.' *Diplomatic History* 33: 191–221.

Lacey, R. (1992). *Little man: Meyer Lansky and the gangster life*. New York, NY: Little, Brown and Company.

Lloyd, C. (1968). *The navy and the slave trade: The suppression of the African slave trade in the nineteenth century*. London, UK: Psychology Press.

Matray, J. I. (1985). *The reluctant crusade: American foreign policy in Korea, 1941–1950*. Honolulu: University of Hawaii Press.

McDonald, W. F. (2005). American and European paths to international law enforcement cooperation: McDonaldization, implosion, and terrorism. In J. Albanese, ed. *Transnational crime*. Whitby, Ontario: deSitter.

McLeod, A. M. (2008). *Exporting U.S. criminal justice: Crime, development, and empire after the Cold War.* (Doctoral dissertation) Stanford University.

McWilliams, J. C. (1989). On the origins of American counterintelligence: Building a clandestine network. *Journal of Policy History 1*: 353–372.

Meyer, K., & Parssinen, T. (1998). *Webs of smoke: Smugglers, warlords, spies, and the history of the international drug trade*. Lanham, MD: Rowman & Littlefield.

Nadelmann, E. A. (1993). *Cops across borders: The internationalization of U.S. criminal law enforcement*. University Park: Penn State University Press.

Naim, M. (2005). *Illicit: How smugglers, traffickers, and copycats are hijacking the global economy*. New York, NY: Random House.

Nelken, D. (2011). *Comparative criminal justice and globalization*. Burlington, VT: Ashgate Publishing Company.

Reuter, P., & Petrie, C. (1999). *Transnational organized crime: Summary of a workshop*. Washington DC: National Academy Press.

Robinson, M. B. (2002). McDonaldization of American police, courts, and corrections. In G. Ritzer, ed. *The McDonaldization reader*. Thousand Oaks, CA: Pine Forge Press.

Rodgers, D. T. (1998). *Atlantic crossings: Social politics in a progressive age*. Cambridge, MA: Harvard University Press.

Salvatore, R. D., Aguirre, C., eds. (1996). *The birth of the penitentiary in Latin America: Essays on criminology, prison reform, and social control, 1830–1940*. Austin: University of Texas Press.

Salvatore, R. D., Aguirre, C., & Joseph, G. M., eds. (2001). *Crime and punishment in Latin America: Law and society since colonial times*. Durham, NC: Duke University Press.

Savelsberg, J. J. (2011). Globalization and states of punishment. In D. Nelken, ed. *Comparative criminal justice and globalization*. Burlington, VT: Ashgate Publishing.

Shichor, D. 1997. Three strikes as a public policy: The convergence of the new penology and the McDonaldization of punishment. *Crime & Delinquency 43*:470–492.

Stone, T. (1998). Slavic women in demand in sex slave markets throughout world. *Crime & Justice International* 14: 7.

Tankebe, J. (2008). Colonialism, legitimation, and policing in Ghana. *International Journal of Law, Crime and Justice 36:* 67–84.

Treverton, G. F. (1999). International organized crime, national security, and the "market state." In T. Farer, ed. *Transnational crime in the Americas.* New York, NY: Routledge.

Turner, J. I. (2007). Transnational networks and international criminal justice. *Michigan Law Review 105*: 985–1032.

van Schendel, W. (2005). Spaces of engagement: How borderlands, illegal flows, and territorial states interlock. In W. van Schendel and I. Abraham, eds., *Illicit flows and criminal things: States, borders, and the other side of globalization*. Bloomington: Indiana University Press.

Weimer, D. (2011). *Seeing drugs: Modernization, counterinsurgency, and U.S. narcotics control in the Third World, 1969–1976*. Kent, OH: The Kent State University Press.

Williams, P. (1999). Trafficking in women and children: A market perspective. In P. Williams, ed. *Illegal immigration and commercial sex: The new slave trade*. London, UK: Frank Cass.

Wood, J., & Kempa, M. (2006). Understanding global trends in policing: Explanatory and normative dimensions. In J. Sheptycki & A. Wardak, eds. *Transnational & comparative criminology*. London, UK: GlassHouse Press.

Zinoman, P. (2001). *The colonial bastille: A history of imprisonment in Vietnam, 1862-1940*. Berkeley: University of California Press.

Zimring, F. E. (2001). Crime, criminal justice, and criminology for a smaller planet: Some notes on the 21st century. *Australian & New Zealand Journal of Criminology 34:* 213–220.

Index

Note: In page references, f indicates figures, and p indicates photos.

About the Authors

Joseph F. Spillane is Associate Professor of History and Criminology at the University of Florida. He received his Ph.D. in History from Carnegie Mellon University in 1994. He has published *Cocaine: From Medical Marvel to Modern Menace in the United States* (Johns Hopkins University Press, 2000) and co-edited *Federal Drug Control: The Evolution of Policy and Practice* (Haworth Press, 2004) and *Prison Work: A Tale of Thirty Years in the California Department of Corrections* (Ohio State University Press, 2005). Recent articles include "Keeping the Lid On: A Century of Drug Regulation and Control" in *Drug and Alcohol Dependence*. He has taught many courses related to criminal justice history, including: History of Criminal Justice; History of Corrections; Drugs in American History; and Law and Society.

David B. Wolcott is Assessment Director with Educational Testing Service in Princeton, N.J. He earned his Ph.D. in History at Carnegie Mellon University in Pittsburgh, Pennsylvania, and has been Visiting Assistant Professor both at Carnegie Mellon and at Miami University in Oxford, Ohio. He has taught many courses related to criminal justice history, including: Crime and Punishment in American History; Violence in American History; and Delinquency, Violence, and Juvenile Justice. He is the author of *Cops and Kids: Policing Juvenile Delinquency in Urban America, 1890-1940* (2005) and co-author of a reference volume, *Crime and Punishment in America* (2010). Any opinions expressed in this book are those of the authors and not necessarily of Educational Testing Service.